SUPERPOWER ON CRUSADE

The Bush Doctrine in US Foreign Policy

MEL GURTOV

LYNNE
RIENNER
PUBLISHERS

BOULDER
LONDON

Published in the United States of America in 2006 by
Lynne Rienner Publishers, Inc.
1800 30th Street, Boulder, Colorado 80301
www.rienner.com

and in the United Kingdom by
Lynne Rienner Publishers, Inc.
3 Henrietta Street, Covent Garden, London WC2E 8LU

Library of Congress Cataloging-in-Publication Data
Gurtov, Melvin.
    Superpower on crusade: the Bush doctrine in US foreign policy/
Mel Gurtov.
    Includes bibliographical references and index.
    ISBN 1-58826-431-9 (hardcover: alk. paper)
    ISBN 1-58826-407-6 (pbk.: alk. paper)
    1. United States—Foreign relations—2001–   2. Bush, George W. (George Walker),
1946–   —Political and social views. I. Title.
E902.G87   2006
327.73009'0511—dc22   2005029705

British Cataloguing in Publication Data
A Cataloguing in Publication record for this book
is available from the British Library.

Printed and bound in the United States of America

The paper used in this publication meets the requirements
∞ of the American National Standard for Permanence of
Paper for Printed Library Materials Z39.48-1992.

    5 4 3 2 1

To magnificent teachers
who made a difference in my life:

Doak Barnett, Harriet Mills, and Jim Shenton

Contents

Preface   ix

I   From the War on Communism to the War on Terror   1

Hegemony and Nationalism, 2
Cold War Legacies: Vietnam and Beyond, 8
National Security Consensus, 12
Crusades, 14

2   The Bush Doctrine   27

The Return of the Radical Right, 28
Reinventing Reagan, 30
George W. Bush and the Neocons, 33
September 11 and Endless War, 36
The Bush Doctrine at Its Core, 39

3   False Pretenses: The War on Iraq   57

Prelude: Pursuing bin Laden, 57
Eyes on the Prize, 61
Preparing for Iraq, 63
"Blind and Improvident," 66
Selling the War and Massaging the Evidence, 69
The Intelligence Game Revealed, 80
What Might Have Been, 85

4   Fallout: The Perils and Profits of Empire   99

The Strategic Agenda, 99
The Other Side of Victory, 105

The Days After: Bringing Order to Iraq and Afghanistan, 112
In Conclusion: Another Vietnam? 125

5 Rogues and Clients: The Long Arm of Unilateralism   137
The "Axis of Evil," 138
Friendly Rogues and Difficult Partners, 150
Regime Change in the Hemisphere, 165
Conclusion, 169

6 The United States as Global Citizen   181
Human Rights, 182
Poverty and Globalization, 185
Environmental Protection, 189
International Law and Organizations, 190
Weapons Proliferation, 197
Conclusion, 200

7 Crusading: Costs and Alternatives   209
Risky Business, 210
Failures of Leadership, 213
A Human Development and Common Security Agenda, 215
Toward Real Homeland Security, 221
Finding a Way Out, 226
The Second Bush Administration, 228

Bibliography   239
Index   251
About the Book   265

Preface

THIS BOOK IS a highly critical, heavily documented account of the foreign and national security policies of the George W. Bush administration. It covers policy thinking and practice from 2001 to the middle of 2005, tracing in particular the influence of the neoconservatives in the Bush administration. These were people on a mission—which the events of September 11, 2001, were indispensable to advancing—to remake the map of the Middle East and, still more ambitiously, take full advantage of the solitary superpower status of the United States. The Bush Doctrine that encompasses that mission is dangerous business—not without precedent in US foreign policy, yet also unprecedented in important ways that this book identifies.

As the line from that old Cat Stevens song "Peace Train" says, there is hope at "the edge of darkness." That line, and the song, speak to the outlook in this book—and, parenthetically, the outlook that I bring to my teaching: pessimism in the short run, optimism in the long run. The George W. Bush era marks a low point for the United States in world affairs, as numerous opinion polls abroad attest. But that circumstance can change. People everywhere are creating good news in their countries and communities, often without fanfare. National and international nongovernmental organizations are multiplying, working effectively to minimize violence, protect environments, and promote social justice. There is a peace train coming.

* * *

I wish to thank friends and colleagues who reviewed portions of the manuscript: Marty Hart-Landsberg, John Damis, and especially Pete

Van Ness and Jerel Rosati, who dissected the entire manuscript and made numerous suggestions for clarification. I am also grateful to Reg Audibert and Nour Crisu for research assistance, and to Tim Stoddard for help in putting the book into final form. Finally, I enormously appreciate the love and support of my bride-to-be, Jodi McDonald.

—Mel Gurtov

SUPERPOWER ON CRUSADE

1

From the War on Communism to the War on Terror

US FOREIGN POLICY, it is often said, moves in cycles: between isolationism and internationalism, bilateralism and multilateralism, generosity and stinginess, involvement in and disengagement from global issues. Viewed this way, foreign policy appears to be episodic, inconsistent, and therefore unpredictable. This book offers an alternative assessment: Continuity is the leitmotif of US foreign policy, and the unilateral pursuit of national interests, the hallmark of policy in the George W. Bush administration, has strong precedent. What makes today's unilateralism different from that of the past is the international and domestic context in which it is being carried out: a diffuse enemy, the absence of a counterweight to US power, the paucity of domestic opposition, and the single mindedness and moral certainty with which the Bush administration is managing US primacy.

The Bush administration's unilateralism is of a particularly muscular sort, arising out of the apparent conviction in official Washington that the war on terrorism has provided the opportunity not taken in the 1990s to seize the "unipolar moment." The contention here is that US unilateralism is not only entirely inappropriate to an increasingly interdependent (and unequal) world; it endangers world peace and further reduces opportunities to promote social justice, abroad and at home. The alternative I propose is that the United States focus its enormous international advantages and capacity to do good on policies, especially within multilateral settings, that strengthen human security[1] and common security.[2] Those interests, which have in common an emphasis on preventive action and international cooperation centered in new global institutions,[3] will promote real national security more effectively and decisively than will continued pursuit of unilateral advantage.

Unilateralism and the practices that, almost inevitably for a great power, seem to accompany it—unwarranted interferences in some countries' affairs, distasteful associations with others—need to be understood against the background of events since World War II. That background, explored in this chapter, takes us along two axes—hegemony and nationalism—that converge in an ideological consensus about the paramount role of the United States in world affairs. Chapter 2 discusses the more immediate origins of the Bush Doctrine—in the Ronald Reagan era and the rise of neoconservative thinking—and analyzes the doctrine's main elements: unilateralism, preemptive attack, and regime change. Chapters 3 and 4 are a critical assessment of the wars in Iraq and Afghanistan. The themes of "false pretenses" and a political more than an intelligence failure in Iraq policymaking are central to Chapter 3, whereas Chapter 4 examines other failures and misconceptions in Iraq and Afghanistan during the occupation period. Chapter 5 takes us beyond those conflicts to assessing the Bush Doctrine's application in other parts of the world and a variety of circumstances. I start with North Korea and Iran, the so-called rogue states, and go on to Central Asia, Russia and China, East Asia, and Latin America. Next, I examine how the Bush Doctrine measures up to the challenges of global issues, including human rights, poverty, environmental protection, and international law. A concluding assessment of Bush, as of the first year of his second term, occupies Chapter 7, where I make the case for basing national security thinking and foreign policy on a humane internationalism.

Hegemony and Nationalism

> Wars then must sometimes be our lot; and all the wise can do, will be to avoid that half of them which would be produced by our own follies, and our own acts of injustice; and to make for the other half the best preparations we can.
>
> —Thomas Jefferson, in Fawn M. Brodie,
> *Jefferson: An Intimate History* (1974), 29.

Well before the United States entered World War II, Henry Luce, founder of the *Time-Life* magazine empire, proclaimed that the postwar era was destined to be the "American Century," a time in which US economic superiority and universal values made it the world's "powerhouse."[4] Josef Stalin's Soviet Union also had pretensions to empire; but it had limited resources to achieve it, and needed first of all to ensure security along its western borders. Only the United States then had the capabilities, symbolized by the dollar and the atomic bomb, and the political will to conduct a truly global foreign policy—that is, to reconstruct the world in conformity with its own interests. The establishment on a world scale of military alliances and an open-door ("liberal") economic order after the 1944 Bretton Woods conference reflected the goal of primacy, not a commitment to multilateral partnership, self-determination for all peoples, or social and economic equity. The audacity and justifiability of such an undertaking was well understood by its architects—people like Dean Acheson, President Harry S Truman's secretary of state, who entitled his memoir *Present at the Creation* because that is where he believed he was.

In the name of collective security, both liberal and conservative leaderships from the Korean War to the present have authorized US interventions in the internal affairs of other countries, friend and foe alike.[5] The containment strategy was directed not only at the Soviet Union but also at Germany and Japan. Their recovery from defeat was deemed essential to postwar US economic predominance and alliance cohesion; but preventing them from acting independently of the United States was equally vital to preserving US political and military dominance.[6] Presidential "doctrines" from Truman to George W. Bush have brought whole regions (Europe, the Middle East, the Mediterranean, Latin America) and global issues (terrorism, nuclear nonproliferation, an open-door trading system) within the scope of vital US interests. The deployment, threats to use, and actual use of weapons of mass destruction (chemical as well as nuclear) put US diplomacy in a class by itself, as does the extensiveness of US force deployments and basing rights beyond its shores. The practice of selective adherence to international law, and occasional blatant violations of it—as in the Central America conflicts of the 1980s—has long been part and parcel of US foreign policy.

These actions, usually justified in order to contain a global menace, were prompted by great ambitions, a missionary impulse. Nationalism in the United States has always run strong, and belief in the superiority of the "American way of life" has shaped the foreign policy of all presidents.[7] Woodrow Wilson led the effort to "make the world safe for democracy" in World War I; Franklin D. Roosevelt saw the United States as "the arsenal of democracy" in World War II; and John F. Kennedy depicted the United States as the "keystone in the arch of freedom" at the height of the Cold War. Believing that the United States was rightful heir to Great Britain as custodian of freedom everywhere, US leaders decided long ago that only the United States could safeguard a politically and economically open world, and that to do so would require projecting and not merely protecting its values and the assets (such as corporate investments and military bases) that have come to represent those values.

Thus did US leaders come to see themselves as custodians of civilization itself. From Wilson to George W. Bush, the posture has been that when the United States fights, it is to protect the civilized world and not merely, as with all other governments, national security.[8] Such a rationalization makes the fight invariably defensive: Tyrants compel the United States to use force in defense of liberty everywhere. Wilson when announcing US entry into World War I, Roosevelt after Pearl Harbor, Truman when confronting the Soviet peril,[9] George W. Bush when declaring a war on terror—all put before the country the vision of civilization under attack by fanatics and imperialists: Kaiser Wilhelm, Emperor Hirohito, Mao Zedong, Ho Chi Minh, Josef Stalin, Fidel Castro, Osama bin Laden, Saddam Hussein. It was not enough to show that specific US interests were being threatened; the threat had to be painted with the broadest possible brush. Yet even if references to (Western) civilization under threat were sometimes exaggerated to mobilize public opinion and convert the war into a crusade, they seem to have been deeply believed by those who made them.

With the attacks of September 11, 2001, the conceptual origins of the Bush Doctrine—its emphasis on unilateralism, which in turn justifies preemptive (or, as I will argue later, preventive) attack and regime change—become plain. If the United States can only be secure when its (democratic-capitalist) values are universalized, threats to those values are likely also to be seen as worldwide. National security thus becomes synonymous with global security, which is why George W. Bush, like previous presidents, told West Point cadets in June 2002: "Our nation's cause has always been larger than our nation's defense."[10] Moreover, if only the United States stands in the way of the forces of evil—fascism, communism, terrorism, and other totalitarianisms—the United States must be free to act alone if necessary to thwart them. For US leaders, one long-accepted lesson of two world wars is that appeasement (accommodation) of aggression does not pay, and watchful waiting courts disaster. Something must be done, and it is the better part of wisdom to do it sooner, before the threat fully materializes. The history of preemptive unilateral actions by the United States thus goes back not merely to the early days of the Cold War—Truman's dispatch of military advisers to Greece in 1947, and his deployment of troops to Korea in 1950—but even further, for instance to the many US interventions in Latin America that started with the Spanish-American war over Cuba, when the name of the game was restoring order to preserve US economic interests and the United States retaliated over an incident that may never have occurred.[11] Until George W. Bush, however, preventive war had never been an accepted part of national security doctrine.

The fact that the past is still present has evoked the criticism that the United States today seeks not merely hegemony but empire, not merely primacy in international politics but imperium. But the distinction between hegemonic rule and empire, while academically much debated these days,[12] may not be the best way to understand the objectives of US policymaking today. Practice counts more than theory. In policymaking circles, leaders employ a different language: the necessity of US "leadership," "challenges" to it, and "options" to deter or neutralize opponents. Hegemony and empire are taken for granted; power, and only power, counts. As a global power since World War I, the United States has exerted hegemony through both indirect and direct forms of control, by relying on "soft" (financial, informational) as well as "hard" (military) assets, and by determining what is on and off the global agenda. Empire finds expression in the arbitrariness with which the United States follows the rule of law; in the frequent use of coercion and sanctions, military and commercial; in the consistent recourse to violence to restore order in far-flung parts of the globe; and in the employment of missionary language that justifies violence to achieve supposedly moral goals.

US leaders rarely refer to "hegemony" or "empire" except when accusing others of seeking it. They are content to speak matter-of-factly about why the United States must be the most powerful country in the world, with a military "second to none," and why no country should be allowed to disturb the balance of power—which, no matter in which region one looks, is really an imbalance in favor of the United States. In the context of the Bush presidency, however, there is a new ingredient in public discourse: Supporters of a US empire unabashedly endorse it, though always with the caveat that empire is necessary for global order and that the US empire, unlike any that preceded it, is benign.[13] They thus sustain the myth of the United States as the "reluctant superpower."[14] In fact, the United States has been anything but reluctant to exercise world leadership.

The crucible for empire, or hegemony—I will use both terms interchangeably—was the planning that went into National Security Council paper 68 (NSC-68), a top-secret strategic assessment of the Soviet threat that President Truman requested of the State and Defense Departments in April 1950.[15] NSC-68's dire language depicted the Soviet Union as leading an all-out assault on the "free world" and as being capable of "delivering a surprise atomic attack" on the United States within four years. The assessment set the stage not only for a major increase in the US military budget—from $13.2 billion in 1950 to $48.2 billion the next year—but also for fighting a "limited war" in Korea from 1950 to 1953.[16] But NSC-68 addressed much more than the US-Soviet confrontation. The document states in three separate places that containing the Soviet Union is only part of the US mission. Following are two of those statements:

> In a shrinking world, which now faces the threat of atomic warfare, it is not an adequate objective merely to seek to check the Kremlin design, for the absence of order among nations is becoming less and less tolerable. This fact imposes on us, in our own interests, the responsibility of world leadership. It demands that we make the attempt, accept the risks inherent in it, to bring about order and justice by means consistent with the principles of freedom and democracy. . . .
> Even if there were no Soviet Union we would face the great problem of the free society, accentuated many fold in this industrial age, of reconciling order, security, the need for participation, with the requirements of freedom. We would face the fact that in a shrinking world the absence of order among nations is becoming less and less tolerable.[17]

Anticommunism thus was not the be-all and end-all of US national security, any more than antiterrorism is today. (Substituting "terrorism" for "Soviet Union" in the second paragraph would bring NSC-68 up to date.) It was a subset of a larger agenda—imposing order on the world—an agenda that necessitated a much more lasting and deeper commitment than anticommunist containment alone.

Putting together a grand strategy to deal with the USSR by no means involved "groupthink" among decisionmakers, however: There were important differences of view between NSC-68's director, Paul Nitze, who was quite willing to exaggerate the Soviet danger in order to gain the president's and the public's attention to fighting it, and some senior State Department (George Kennan) and Defense Department (Louis Johnson) officials. Their objections ranged from opposition to making a grand design the basis of policy planning to concern over the eventual costs of taking the ideological offensive against Moscow. Interagency competition for resources also played into the debate over NSC-68. In the end, Kennan's concerns, which he would hold to for many years afterward, were born out. These were that wide-ranging policy declarations like NSC-68 undermined the formulation of policy in particular cases, and that bold but open-ended commitments risked leading to crusades that would thwart the real interests of the United States. The Korean War became just that, for while Truman resisted General Douglas

A. MacArthur's call for carrying the war into China—which in one reading of NSC-68 might have seemed required—the president and his successors, as Robert Tucker has written, "globalized containment." The US intervention in Korea brought the United States deeply into East Asia, with new commitments to the defense of Japan, South Korea, and Taiwan, financial support of French colonialism in Indochina, and of course a new level of enmity with the People's Republic of China. War in Korea also greatly intensified the Cold War with the Soviet Union and, coming so soon after the communist coup in Czechoslovakia, deepened the division of Europe.

The main lesson of NSC-68 is not that national security doctrines cause wars, but that because they invoke ideological arguments, militant doctrine tends to take precedence over reflective, calculated policymaking and diplomacy. NSC-68's insistence that negotiations with Moscow should only occur from a position of strength, albeit strength backed by alliances, informed US diplomacy for many years. Once war broke out in Korea, Truman, who until then had not formally approved NSC-68,[18] bought into both its logic and its cost. So did all the other agencies, military and civilian, that were concerned with national security: NSC-68, with its emphasis on rearmament, promised something for everyone. With Korea, Paul Y. Hammond wrote, "NSC-68 now represented the continuity which was so apparently lacking in defense policy, and the evidence that the turn of events had not been unanticipated."[19] If NSC-68 was not a blueprint for the Korean War, it was a blueprint—or better still, a manifesto—for the rest of the Cold War.

But it was not only NSC-68 that set the stage for empire building. That paper was the product of a major overhaul of the entire national security system, the 1947 National Security Act (NSA). The NSA established the NSC as well as the Central Intelligence Agency, created the new cabinet position of secretary of defense (and eventually the Department of Defense), and established the air force as a separate service. The real import of the NSA, however, lay in the displacement of the State Department at the top of the policymaking system. From then on, as one scholar has argued, "national security" became more important than the national interest, with the result that "policymakers were predisposed toward worst case scenarios and tended to favor military instruments of power and influence."[20] Diplomacy would suffer accordingly, whereas the likelihood increased that force would be used in pursuit of foreign policy objectives.

This expansive notion of national security lent itself to a self-interested understanding of the just war. The traditional US view, as documented by Robert Tucker, is that war can only be justified when "waged in self or collective defense against armed aggression," at which point it becomes "an instrument of international policy, even though such a war may also serve to advance distinctly national interests."[21] Thus, war is always forced upon the country, but in the end superior moral and material attainments will bring about inevitable victory. Such ideas may be seen as ultimately self-serving, Tucker wrote, given the hegemonic position of the United States since the end of World War II. US leaders have never believed they needed to use war to advance US interests; and preemptive intervention (as distinct from preventive war) has rarely been acknowledged as being an element of US strategy. Since all wars thus end up being imposed, needlessly, by America's enemies, responding with force necessarily is just and in keeping with international law and the United Nations Charter.

As we shall see, both the idea of grand strategy represented by NSC-68 and the traditional doctrine of just war have gained new life in the administration of George W. Bush.

Cold War Legacies: Vietnam and Beyond

The notion that the Cold War is over, and—according to Bush's first secretary of state, Colin Powell—that the *post*-post–Cold War era is upon us, are at best only partial truths. To be sure, world politics has produced new (though very possibly transitory) realignments of states, and the distance in power between the United States and others is greater than ever. But in other key respects, namely, US leaders' framework of beliefs, core values, and patterns of behavior, the Cold War remains very much alive. A brief look back at the Vietnam era may be a useful reminder of that other reality.

Two powerful forces affected US decisionmaking in the Vietnam War. Neither was a matter of simple anticommunism. One was the intellectual inability to comprehend the way in which prolonged underdevelopment in a colonized Third World country provided fertile ground for a popular antigovernment movement. The Vietnamese communist guerrillas, or Viet Cong, were dismissed as terrorists, "scavengers of the modernization process."[22] It seemed that despite an abundance of evidence early on of the Viet Cong's nationalist credentials and of its ability to recruit mainly on that basis, US officials were mystified by its staying power.[23] At the same time, the Saigon government's ineptitude, unpopularity, and corruption were privately and frequently acknowledged within US councils.[24] But the chagrin of US leaders over having to work with such an illegitimate partner against a popular foe never translated into a decision to withdraw from Vietnam. In the final analysis, the perceived global and domestic political stakes were judged too high to warrant disengagement—globally, the US reputation if it were humiliated; domestically, Johnson's fear of impeachment stemming mainly from a right-wing backlash. So high, in fact, that the US ambassador to South Vietnam felt justified in arguing that the United States had "the right and duty to do certain things with or without the [Saigon] government's approval."[25]

Ignoring Vietnamese nationalism and pushing aside state sovereignty were essential to the US takeover of the war in Vietnam. But that process did not originate there; it had several antecedents. One of the most striking was the Dominican Republic. When the dictator Rafael Trujillo was assassinated in 1961, President Kennedy developed a rule to guide US policy: "There are three possibilities, in descending order of preference: a decent democratic regime, a continuation of the Trujillo regime, or a Castro regime. We ought to aim at the first, but we really can't renounce the second until we are sure that we can avoid the third."[26] Since the United States rarely if ever had a democratic alternative, the next best choice was to find another friendly dictator to replace the one who had been eliminated. Political "stability" and "order" counted for more than a government committed to social justice and political independence. Just as would happen in Vietnam, the United States faced consistently unpalatable choices—and invariably aligned with anyone willing to serve its interests. In the end, it was Lyndon Johnson who sent the marines to the Dominican Republic rather than accept an elected, supposedly left-leaning Juan Bosch as its president. And it was Johnson who also followed up on Kennedy's early commitment of US advisers in Vietnam by deploying ground combat troops on a large scale, all the while (as we have since learned) wondering privately whether victory was really possible at any level of commitment.

Behind this intolerance of others' nationalism lay a second force: simple and disastrous hubris—the conviction that, come what may, the United States would have to press ahead with the war effort, and take increasing casualties, in order to restore world order. Vietnam was thus addressed as another test of the United States, like the crises over Berlin and Soviet missiles in Cuba. To Walt Rostow, the outcome in Vietnam therefore hinged on "the simple fact that at this stage of history we are the greatest power in the world—if we behave like it."[27] Johnson, despite growing private doubts about winning, concluded that "national security" required hanging on.[28] Publicly, he would often say that to "turn tail and run" would amount to another Munich. The prospect of a humiliating defeat and damaged credibility became the argument for "national security."[29] Efforts by doves such as Ambassador John Kenneth Galbraith and Undersecretary of State George Ball to warn (in Ball's words) of impending "national humiliation . . . *even after we have paid terrible costs,*" far from prompting consideration of ways to cut losses in Vietnam, were instead met with renewed commitment to fighting on.[30]

Vietnam is often considered the great divide between the era of the imperial presidency and the era of limitations brought on by a more activist US Congress. Though Congress did reassert its authority in the foreign policy process during most of the 1970s, with passage of the War Powers Resolution in 1973 the high point, the erosion of that authority was well underway by the end of that decade. Some of the same Vietnam-era doves led the charge back to the future, driven by events in Iran and Afghanistan but also by the recurrent belief in the necessity to "restore" US primacy. As the next chapter will discuss further, Ronald Reagan's presidency was a natural evolution to roll back the clock as much as to roll back "international communism." But at the same time he laid the groundwork for the Bush Doctrine's unilateralism and its war on terror.

Between 1991—the Gulf War and the collapse of the USSR—and the September 11, 2001, attacks, there was considerable debate in the United States over policy choices and grand strategy. Conflicts in Somalia, Bosnia, and Kosovo, US participation in the Earth Summit, the North American Free Trade Agreement (NAFTA), partnership with China, and North Korea's nuclear weapons program were among the issues that fueled the debate. The absence of an overriding external threat to the United States led some critical voices to call for withdrawal of US forces from abroad, an end to interventionism, and a refocusing of foreign policy on human security interests such as job creation, energy conservation, and dramatic arms reductions.[31] Other critics, however, such as Senators Robert Dole of Kansas and Jesse Helms of North Carolina, took a different tack. These formerly ardent anticommunists now became leaders of an influential group of nationalists who argued on the basis of preserving US sovereignty. They urged disengaging from UN peacekeeping operations, the International Monetary Fund (IMF), and other international bodies that were believed to be undermining US freedom of action. Such thinking was hardly isolationist, however; it favored unilateral action in certain instances, such as supplying arms to the Bosnians, defending Israel as always, and containing Iraq.

These views fell outside the mainstream of foreign policy discussion, which, as Christopher Layne has put it, still rested on US preponderance and thus the same ideas that had guided policy in 1945: "ambitions, interests, and alliances."[32] President Bill Clinton's "engagement and enlargement" doctrine, for instance, was distinctive in its reliance on global economic instruments and multilateral groups to project US values and power. But contrary to his critics, Clinton was a realist too: When it came to defending perceived US interests, he neither shied away from the use of force nor allowed allies or the UN to dictate US actions, as he demonstrated in Serbia and the Taiwan Strait. Whether in Clinton's time or in George H. W. Bush's, the political mainstream was dominated by those who believed the United States must protect Israel and the oil-rich states, must maintain and enlarge its alliances, must prevent the proliferation of weapons of mass destruction (WMD), must promote world trade, must bail out financially troubled Mexico and the East Asian countries to protect foreign investors, must watch out for China, and must maintain large, flexible, high-tech, and dispersed military forces. The great challenge mainstream analysts saw for the post–Cold War United States was how to avoid isolationism. All the signposts—an inward-looking US public, congressional budget-watching, suspicions about globalization, wariness of "another Vietnam," nasty communal wars in fragile states, and the lack of a major new enemy ("we have run out of enemies," in General Colin Powell's oft-quoted words)—pointed to difficulty for the US political leadership in trying to arouse support for staying globally engaged.[33] The conventional wisdom was that US foreign policy would have to be much more discriminating than before about when to commit US power and prestige.

"Selective engagement" was the new prescription, but it still amounted to containment of enemies and deterrence of a host of old and new threats. As a major Pentagon strategic planning document put it in 1997,

> Despite our best efforts to shape the international security environment, the US military will, at times, be called upon to respond to crises in order to protect our interests, demonstrate our resolve, and reaffirm our role as global leader. Therefore, US forces must also be able to execute the full spectrum of military operations, from deterring an adversary's aggression or coercion in crisis and conducting concurrent smaller-scale contingency operations, to fighting and winning major theater wars.[34]

Under Clinton, this document lent legitimacy to the idea of coalition building in response to international crises, to focusing resources on rapid deployment to small-scale conflicts, and to preparedness to deal simultaneously with wars in two distant theaters. It introduced the idée fixe that the United States faced a greater diversity of threats than during the Cold War, as well as regional powers with "both the desire and the means to challenge US interests militarily." All of these "challenges" were said to require very high military budgets, emphasis on high-technology weapons, and across-the-board preparedness in new security arenas such as information warfare, terrorism, and environmental sabotage. As in the past, "national security" translated into global "responsibilities" and huge expenditures.

National Security Consensus

The underlying consistency of US purposes in foreign policy raises serious doubts about whether or not the term "national interest" has real meaning. For at bottom all these presidential doctrines and strategic debates are less serious examinations of national interest than they are threat analyses. National interests are assumed and declared but rarely enumerated. Threats, meanwhile, are endless and constantly reforming, such that there is always the need to overinvest in weapons and deploy troops all over the world. From time to time presidents and their foreign policy advisers have announced that they would take a hard look at national commitments and interests with the intention of paring them down to realistic proportions. Richard M. Nixon promised this when he took office, and Condoleezza Rice said so before being appointed Bush's special assistant for national security. But in those and all other cases, threats (from the Soviet Union, from terrorists, from "rogue states") came to define and thus overwhelm interests. This reality helps explain why the Pentagon's role in national security has magnified over the years since NSC-68, and why concepts such as "selective engagement" are anything but selective in their application.

In place of careful analysis of what US national interests truly are is consensus about America's role in the world. Whether liberal or conservative, realist or globalist, members of the foreign policy elite subscribe to certain fundamental axioms of national security, which are:

- Great powers make history; others are condemned to follow it.[35] Frances Fukuyama's famous "end of history" thesis was merely a logical extension of that view.
- History is not determined by national experiences but by diplomacy backed by power. The underlying causes of social, economic, and political change (such as revolutions) are not as important as the decision to enforce one's will on others.
- As the world's greatest power, the United States has a responsibility—even a right—to impose and maintain order in an anarchic

world. Isolationism and withdrawal from world affairs are un-thinkable. The aim of national security policy must be control. The United States must pay attention to all sources of global in-stability, since any significant disorder is a potential threat to US interests.

- The United States will work with national leaders who support US objectives. Those who get in the way of those objectives will be sidetracked or physically removed.[36] Regime change, as it is now known, is always an option. Strategic usefulness, not demo-cratic practices or past loyalty, determines friends and enemies.

- The "free world" depends on the United States for leadership. It is indispensable, the hub of the wheel; there is no one else. The United States is "the sheriff of the posse,"[37] but sometimes it must act even if there is no posse. No country can be allowed to take America's place, pose as a third force, or be in a position to de-fine US goals and strategies.[38] Hence, the US reputation is a crit-ical resource that cannot be allowed to suffer, even in distant and seemingly marginal conflicts.

- "National security" really means global security. Market expan-sion and access to resources are essential to the US economy and the well-being of its citizens. Threats to US interests are numer-ous and come in many forms. To contain if not eliminate them requires maintaining a vast array of capabilities and very high spending levels for national security, including a far-flung net-work of military bases, partnerships, and access points.

- Domestic support to pursue national security objectives can be counted on if the threat is appropriately magnified, kept con-stantly before the public, and proclaimed to bear a close relation-ship to security at home.

What lies behind these axioms? Structural factors are certainly an important piece of the explanation. Robert Lieber has proposed that these are "the absence of a plausible challenger" to US leadership, the indis-pensability of an American role in responding to all urgent international issues, and an external threat sufficient to galvanize public and congres-sional support.[39] But beyond those factors may lie deeper impulses. Some critical writers, such as William Appleman Williams, have pointed to a history of "open-door" expansionism—a quest for access to markets that traces its roots to the westward expansion of the United States.[40] Other critics, such as Richard A. Barnet, have identified the "national security state" as representing the institutionalization of US global ambitions. Still others, myself included, see ideology as the fundamental problem:

a philosophical belief system ingrained in the US foreign policy elite that emphasizes global responsibilities and the moral and political mission of the United States to lead.[41] Commentators who go back to the beginning of the United States underscore the shared belief of US elites in exceptionalism—the self-styled vision of the United States as the "City upon a hill," that peculiar (and peculiarly successful) experiment to create "a new nation, conceived in liberty" and henceforth a model for others.

From whichever angle one critically assesses America's rise to global power, two factors seem to be constant: the moral certainty that American leaders have traditionally carried abroad, and the fusion of ideals and self-interest in the pursuit of global primacy.

Crusades

As Jerel Rosati has written, the notion persists among the public and US leaders alike that the United States stands above all other nations in its unique (one might say, God-given) historical advantages and consequently selfless international behavior. Rosati identifies three attributes of that self-image: innocence (the desire merely to be the "City upon a hill" from which American leaders despair of the world's chaos); benevolence (the desire to do good for the world and not merely for oneself); and exceptionalism (a confidence and optimism about the superiority—not merely the distinctiveness—of the American experiment).[42] These beliefs could have led to a turning inward, a determination to perfect the experiment and rely on its successes to inspire the world. Instead, they have translated into a justification of America's destiny to lead—to globalize US ideals and, when faced with resistance, to project US power to enforce those ideals and the practical economic and other interests behind them.[43]

Such a powerful sense of destiny seems born of the conviction that God is on the side of the United States. No other country's leaders so frequently invoke the Lord's name to bless its international enterprises. For the United States represents not only material progress but moral purity—civilization itself, as George W. Bush and many who preceded him in office have said. And just as "moral clarity was essential to our victory in the Cold War," Bush told West Point cadets in June 2002, it would be essential against terrorism. Fortunately, there is no need to debate issues of right and wrong: "Moral truth is the same in every culture, in every time, and in every place. . . . We are in a conflict between good and evil, and America will call evil by its name."[44] What perhaps so outraged Americans about 9/11, Mark Slouka has dared to suggest, is that

> it had happened *here*. To *us*. And, lest we forget, we Americans had been commissioned by God himself to be the light of liberty and religion throughout all the earth. Rwanda? Bosnia? Couldn't help but feel sorry for those folks, but let's face it: Rwanda did not have a covenant with God. And Jesus was not a Sarajevan.[45]

Bestowing the blessings of liberty on others thus comes naturally. But it can lead to destructive decisions. Contrary to US expectations, oppressed people abroad may reject such blessings. Faced with angry anti-American demonstrations in the Middle East, Dwight Eisenhower wondered why it was so hard for "people in these down-trodden countries to like us instead of hating us." But that did not stop him from authorizing a CIA operation to overthrow the Iranian leadership.[46] Lyndon Johnson worried that unless the Vietnamese communists were put in their place, revolutionaries everywhere would "sweep over the US and take what we have."[47] The same fear seems to have colored George W. Bush's interpretation of Al-Qaida's motives for attacking the United States. They hate us, said Bush in his September 20, 2001, address to the US Congress and in numerous speeches around the country, because of our freedoms, which they are determined to destroy. Like Johnson, Bush substituted cultural arrogance for fact: Most likely, Al-Qaida sought to force Islamic governments and peoples—starting in Saudi Arabia, where rich sheiks were accused of having corrupted Islam and sold the country out to the United States and its Israeli partner—to choose between its extremism and "the idol-worshiping enemies of God."[48] Past humiliations and the restoration of self-respect in the face of US-led globalization also seem to have motivated Al-Qaida.[49] Just as the Vietnamese communists fought to win over patriots who detested the Saigon regime and its US patron, Al-Qaida sought to keep the United States out of "its" domain. Neither group cared a whit about taking away Americans' freedoms.

Defenders of US foreign policy crusading sometimes depict it as a break from a traditional isolationism. Henry Kissinger, for example, has described a United States that has always "oscillated between isolationism and commitment."[50] At other times these defenders, often foreign-policy leaders at one time, have insisted that US policy acts on principle and not merely on interests.[51] Neither view stands reasonable scrutiny. Isolationism? The United States has certainly gone through periods of reduced international commitments (such as before 9/11), and serious efforts by the Congress to constrain presidential power (as in the 1970s). But US leaders, most often with legislative support, have never wavered either in their missionary zeal to make the world hospitable to US values or in their preparedness to project US power to protect or acquire what they wanted. An arrogant disregard for the sovereignty or rights of others has long been a hallmark of US foreign policy. As one secretary of defense said in conveying the US preparedness to take over Saudi and other Middle East oil fields in 1973, Washington would not tolerate an oil embargo by "underdeveloped, underpopulated" and unreasonable countries.[52]

Acting on principle? Espousing noble ideals such as the self-determination of peoples and respect for democratic processes has never been in short supply in official Washington's pronouncements. But too often ideals have yielded to concrete US interests, to the point of "saving" those who cannot save (or refuse to save) themselves. At that point "saving" democracy means intervening abroad and contributing to official repression. Those who believe the United States consistently aspires to build and work with democratic governments have to answer a simple question: Why is the historical record, to which the George W. Bush administration has significantly added (see Chapter 5), replete with instances of close US cooperation with authoritarian regimes?

Two examples, one past and one present, illuminate the priority of interests over principles. Faced with the election of a socialist president of Chile in 1970, President Nixon and Secretary of State Kissinger determined that the United States could not accept the result. It was "irresponsible," Kissinger reasoned, since Allende had been elected with only 36 percent of the vote in a three-way race.[53] Nixon's decisions to make the Chilean economy "scream" and in the end back a military coup by General Augusto Pinochet, who proceeded to round up and kill thousands of Chileans without a word of criticism from Washington, are well known. Recent documentation embellishes this sordid picture: Kissinger's disdain for democracy and human rights—his assurances to General Pinochet that US "support" of human rights did not apply to Chile, and his dismissal of the concerns of State Department subordinates who protested the conflict between US principles and Pinochet's repression.[54] Nor was Chile an isolated case: Under Operation Condor, Latin American dictators banded together to carry out political assassinations and torture of leftist and other opponents with the knowledge and approval of US leaders. Kissinger personally condoned official crackdowns as necessary to maintain order, for example in Argentina following a military coup in 1976.[55]

A second example comes from the war on terror. It shows how readily US intelligence services, given the green light at the highest levels in Washington, will dispense with respect for human rights and principles of law in the name of national security.[56] After the 9/11 attacks on the United States, US government lawyers from the Justice Department and other agencies set to work redefining legal responsibilities toward soldiers captured in Afghanistan and, later, Iraq. Law was construed in ways that served official policy, which aimed at enlarging the basis for holding soldiers and civilians without charge or time limit, and using any and all means to extract information from them. The clear objective of various internal memoranda prepared for the secretary of defense and other high officials by the president's chief counsel (in January 2002) and the Justice Department's top legal counsel (in August 2002) was to narrow US obligations under US and international law, including the federal War Crimes Act of 1996, the Geneva Conventions, and the United Nations Convention on Torture.[57] More specifically, the legal advice sought to immunize the president, other officials, and US soldiers from potential war crimes charges, and to widen the latitude for intelligence gathering using very harsh and normally illegal methods of interrogation. The consequences of such advice were surely known in advance: to rationalize use of torture and maximize presidential authority to act outside the law, as happened in Afghanistan and Iraq. This suspension of presumably sacred legal principles was hardly new. It was practiced by the United States in other wars as well, such as Vietnam, and it was condoned when practiced by US allies such as the secret services of Chile, South Korea under military rule, Pakistan, and Iran under Shah Reza Pahlevi.

Such blatant inconsistencies between preaching and practice lead us to examine the two principal philosophies that guide US foreign policy: realism and globalism. Realism urges the pursuit of national interest by acquiring strategic advantages and political influence in the world—in a word, geopolitics. Globalism speaks for the virtues of the market (geoeconomics) and the spread of US ideals, such as democracy, that free markets will encourage. Though often depicted as being contradictory and therefore mutually constraining impulses, realism and globalism are really two sides of the same coin.[58] Their convergence in doctrines that seek to define world order is what US foreign policy is all about. Certainly globalist ideals and realist self-interest sometimes clash in particular instances; but far more often they are mutually reinforcing, in what has sometimes been called the liberal-conservative consensus, liberal internationalism, or simply the mainstream belief system.[59] Different schools of thought in the study of US foreign policy have attributed both very narrow motivations to particular US policies—to promote the military-industrial complex or the profits of multinational corporations, for example—and very grand ones—such as to protect a capitalist world order or democracy. But the thrust behind US foreign policy typically transcends (even if it may in specific cases include) the interests of specific groups and is broader still than either globalist or realist interests alone. For is not the bottom line, in official Washington's view, to promote and protect "the American way of life"? That way of life is simultaneously more than capitalism, democratization, or military preponderance alone; it is the sum total of all those professed ideals, material interests, strategic preferences, and acquisitive values that together make us what "we" are—number one, and determined forever to remain so.[60]

The notion that US policymakers are somehow divided in their worldview was put to rest by Condoleezza Rice. Writing before her appointment as the Special Assistant for National Security, she said:

> In fact, there are those who would draw a sharp line between power politics and a principled foreign policy based on values. This polarized view—you are either a realist or devoted to norms and values—may be just fine in academic debate, but it is a disaster for American foreign policy. American values are universal. . . . the triumph of these values is most assuredly easier when the international balance of power favors those who believe in them.[61]

What Rice was really saying is that in Washington's world, political will counts. There is no grand contradiction between realism and globalism in US attitudes or behavior because as policymakers see things, "great powers do not just mind their own business."[62] If the United States is, as Madeleine Albright famously put it, "the indispensable nation," that is not just a fact of international life but a role US leaders have consciously chosen. (And lest we forget, one of the occasions on which she used that expression was during debate about attacking Iraq.[63]) In theory, the US government could choose to pursue an entirely different course, such as isolationism or multilateral cooperation; but in practice, the will of US leaders has been to make the world safe for *their* values and interests, just as Rice, now secretary of state, plainly said.

Unilateralism comes naturally to a country that has been at the top for many years. From Theodore Roosevelt and Woodrow Wilson to Dwight Eisenhower and John F. Kennedy, US leaders historically have been internationalist in their commitment to world order through some form of security cooperation, but nationalist in their determination that no multilateral group would ever have binding authority over US actions.[64] Hence, whether in alliances, in wars (from Korea[65] to the war on terrorism), or in international policies (such as on trade, environment, and immigration), the common and pivotal factor for the United States has been control.[66] This objective has spawned a long-held principle of US policy: The United States should act multilaterally (i.e., in concert with others) where its interests would be well served, but otherwise unilaterally. Prior to George W. Bush, for example, both George H. W. Bush[67] and Bill Clinton[68] endorsed this principle, notwithstanding their diverse rhetoric about a "new world order" and "engagement and enlargement."[69] Under George W. Bush, however, unilateral action has become etched in stone.

Notes

1. Human security, though an imperfect concept, continues to be refined and quantified in national terms by the United Nations Development Program (UNDP) in its *Human Development Report* (published periodically by Oxford University Press). The concept owes much to the work of the Indian economist Amartya Sen and his notion of human capabilities. A working definition of human security is that it entails enhancing opportunities for people to lead a fulfilling, dignified life, meaning freedom from violence and degradation, and freedom to work and be at peace in a socially just society. Human security is thus intertwined with human development and human rights. See the discussion and fuller definitions in Commission on Human Security, *Human Security Now,* pp. 4–10.

2. Common (or cooperative) security was initially proposed with the threat of weapons of mass destruction in mind. In contrast with collective security, common security seeks to move the global security agenda "from preparing to counter threats to preventing such threats from arising—from deterring aggression to making preparation for it more difficult." Prevention requires cooperation among states, hence in broader application today, common security may refer to preventive measures for dealing with many different kinds of threats (not just military, and not just outright aggression) that face humanity. Ashton B. Carter, William J. Perry, and John D. Steinbruner, *A New Concept of Cooperative Security,* pp. 5–6.

3. "Thus," say Carter, Perry, and Steinbruner, "the development of a regime for cooperative engagement is the new strategic imperative." Ibid., p. 6.

4. Writing in 1941, Luce called on the United States to use its enormous resources to feed the world and be the greatest trading country. But spreading US ideals was just as important, for "we are the inheritors of all the great principles of Western civilization . . . For the moment it may be enough to be the sanctuary of these ideals. But not for long. It now becomes our time to be the powerhouse from which the ideals spread throughout the world." Walter LaFeber, ed., *Origins of the Cold War, 1941–1947,* p. 30.

5. The best recent work on US interventions is by Michael J. Sullivan III, *American Adventurism Abroad.*

6. Christopher Layne and Benjamin Schwarz, "American Hegemony—Without an Enemy."

7. Minxin Pei, "The Paradoxes of American Nationalism," *Foreign Policy,* pp. 31–37.

8. See Andrew J. Bacevich, *American Empire: The Realities and Consequences of US Diplomacy.*

9. For example, Truman, in farewell remarks of November 21, 1952, spoke of America's free world leadership—"We are at the top"—and said: "We have to assume it now, because it has again been thrust upon us. It is our duty, under Heaven, to continue that leadership in the manner that will prevent a third world war—which would mean the end of civilization." In Michael H. Hunt, ed., *Crises in US Foreign Policy: An International History Reader,* p. 169.

10. "Bush's United States Military Academy Graduation Speech," *Washington Post,* June 2, 2002, online at www.washingtonpost.com/ac2/up_dyn/A47940-2002June2? Cited hereafter as West Point speech.

11. "Remember the *Maine*" may have been a false cry, since Spain may not have been responsible for the sinking of the US battleship. See Charles Glass, "The First Lies Club."

12. The difference between seeking hegemony and seeking empire would seem to rest on three issues: control, national assets, and leadership. Does the United States exert direct or indirect control in the system? Are its assets—the means of control—mainly military and economic or also political and cultural? Does it seek to lead by example, and with the concurrence of other powerful states—in order to promote "hegemonic stability" in the international system— or does it seek to make the rules and punish transgressors? A concise summation of these issues is by Niall Ferguson, "Hegemony or Empire?" For a review of the recent literature on empire, see Tony Judt, "Dreams of Empire."

13. I am indebted for this idea to Amitav Acharya. Examples of the pro-empire view include Joshua Muravchik, "The Bush Manifesto," pp. 29–30; Niall Ferguson, *Colossus;* and, as explained in Chapter 2, issues of the *Weekly Standard* and papers of the Project for the New American Century. Favoring "empire" does not, it should be emphasized, mean agreement among users of the term about the details of how, when, and where. Ferguson, for example, argues that unilateralism "is seldom a realistic option for an empire." *Colossus,* p. 297.

14. Bacevich, *American Empire,* p. 8.

15. The full text of NSC-68 was not released until 1977. See S. Gleason, ed., *Foreign Relations of the United States 1950,* pp. 235–292.

16. The principal source for the origins of NSC-68 is Paul Y. Hammond, "NSC-68: Prologue to Rearmament," in Warner R. Schilling, Paul Y. Hammond, and Glenn H. Snyder, *Strategy, Politics and Defense Budgets*, pp. 271–378. See also Cabell Phillips, "Secret Paper Set Korea War Policy," *New York Times* (hereafter, *NYT*), April 13, 1964, p. 1.

17. Gleason, ed., *Foreign Relations of the United States 1950,* pp. 241, 263.

18. In referring the report to the National Security Council, Truman remarked on the need for "a clearer indication of the programs which are envisaged in the Report, including estimates of the probable cost of such programs." He was "concerned that action on existing programs should not be postponed or

delayed." Truman to James S. Lay Jr., April 12, 1950, in Gleason, ed., *Foreign Relations of the United States*, p. 235.

19. Hammond, "NSC-68," pp. 346–350; quotation at p. 349.

20. Douglas T. Stuart, "Ministry of Fear: The 1947 National Security Act in Historical and Institutional Context," p. 303.

21. Tucker, *The Just War*, p. 14.

22. Walt W. Rostow, speech at the US Army Special Warfare School, June 28, 1961; in Hunt, ed., *Crises*, p. 331.

23. "The ability of the Viet Cong continuously to rebuild their units and to make good their losses is one of the mysteries of this guerrilla war," Ambassador Maxwell Taylor told top US officials in November 1964. Neither forced recruitment nor infiltration of soldiers from North Vietnam provided "plausible explanation of the continued strength of the Viet Cong . . . Not only do the Viet Cong units have the recuperative powers of the phoenix, but they have an amazing ability to maintain morale." Neil Sheehan et al., eds., *The Pentagon Papers*, p. 372. Hereafter cited simply as *Pentagon Papers*.

24. See, for example, the documents in Hunt, ed., *Crises*, pp. 340–341 (a memorandum from Secretary of Defense Robert S. McNamara to President Lyndon Johnson in 1963) and p. 352 (a meeting with Johnson in which the US ambassador to South Vietnam, Henry Cabot Lodge, declares: "I don't think we ought to take this government seriously"); and in *Pentagon Papers*, pp. 208–209 and 217–218 (two 1963 cables from Lodge).

25. Lodge's comments in meeting with President Johnson and top advisers, July 21–22, 1965, in Hunt, ed., *Crises*, p. 353.

26. Arthur M. Schlesinger Jr., *A Thousand Days*, p. 769.

27. Memorandum from Rostow to Secretary of State Dean Rusk, November 23, 1964; in *Pentagon Papers*, p. 422.

28. See the record of his meeting with advisers in July 1965, in Hunt, ed., *Crises*, pp. 351–358. Only George Ball, the undersecretary of state, among Johnson's closest advisers understood the hopelessness of the situation: "Like giving cobalt treatment to a terminal cancer case," he said of the idea of increasing US aid to the Saigon regime. Ibid., p. 353.

29. As one of McNamara's top aides, John McNaughton, put it, "70%" of the US war effort by early 1965 had come down to "avoiding a humiliating defeat" and only "10%" to "permit the people of SVN [South Vietnam] to enjoy a better, freer way of life." Memorandum of March 24, 1965, in *Pentagon Papers*, p. 432.

30. Ball's comments (italics in original) were made in a memorandum to Johnson of July 1, 1965; in Hunt, ed., *Crises*, p. 348. Galbraith, then ambassador to India, called for a neutral South Vietnam and reduction of the US commitment to its government in a memorandum to President Kennedy of April 4, 1962; ibid., pp. 335–336.

31. See, for example, Eugene Gholz, Daryl G. Press, and Harvey M. Sapolsky, "Come Home, America: The Strategy of Restraint in the Face of Temptation," in Michael Brown et al., eds., *America's Strategic Choices*, pp. 200–243; and Chalmers Johnson, *Blowback: The Costs and Consequences of American Empire*.

32. Layne, "From Preponderance to Offshore Balancing," in Brown et al., eds., *America's Strategic Choices*, pp. 244–282.

33. Brown et al., eds., *America's Strategic Choices,* is an excellent collection of these views.

34. William S. Cohen, *Report of the Quadrennial Defense Review* (May, 1997), at www.dtic.mil/defenselink/pubs/qdr/sec2.html.

35. Thus, the United States is always on "the right side of history." See quotations from liberal and conservative leaders alike in Clyde Prestowitz, *Rogue Nation: American Unilateralism and the Failure of Good Intentions,* p. 34.

36. The manner of regime change has taken many forms. Sometimes it has occurred by supporting a coup or by subversion, other times by assassination of a leader, or by covert actions to influence elections. Sometimes the aim has been to displace an enemy and at other times to replace a one-time friend. Thus, the United States in past years has played a central role in seeking the overthrow of radical nationalist and leftist leaders such as Patrice Lumumba in Congo, Fidel Castro in Cuba, Salvador Allende in Chile, Arbenz in Guatemala, Sukarno in Indonesia, Mossadegh in Iran, and Muammar Qaddafi in Libya; in replacing leaders judged unacceptably "soft" on communism such as Archbishop Makarios in Cyprus, João Goulart in Brazil, and Norodom Sihanouk in Cambodia; and in removing friendly but no longer useful leaders such as Ferdinand Marcos in the Philippines, Rafael Trujillo in the Dominican Republic, François Duvalier in Haiti, Mobutu Sese Seko in Zaire, Manuel Noriega in Panama, Anastacio Somoza in Nicaragua, and South Vietnam's trio of presidents in the 1950s and 1960s: Ngo Dinh Diem, Nguyen Khanh, and Nguyen Van Thieu. Of interest is the comment made by General Paul Harkins, who opposed US support of a coup to oust Diem in 1963: "Leaders of other underdeveloped countries will take a dim view of our assistance if they too were led to believe the same fate lies in store for them." *Pentagon Papers,* p. 221.

37. See Richard N. Haass, "Beyond Containment: Competing American Foreign Policy Doctrines for the New Era," in Eugene R. Wittkopf and Christopher M. Jones, eds., *The Future of American Foreign Policy,* pp. 22–38. Haass, who became the State Department's director of policy planning in the G.W. Bush administration, concluded: "For now and for the immediate future, the real question hanging over the promise of posses is not so much their utility as it is the willingness and ability of the United States to saddle up and to lead."

38. Layne and Schwarz, "American Hegemony—Without an Enemy."

39. Lieber, "Foreign Policy and American Primacy," in Lieber, ed., *Eagle Rules? Foreign Policy and American Primacy in the Twenty-First Century,* pp. 1–15.

40. Williams, "Empire as a Way of Life."

41. Melvin Gurtov, *The United States Against the Third World: Antinationalism and Intervention.*

42. Rosati, *The Politics of United States Foreign Policy,* p. 408.

43. As two writers have said, belief in exceptionalism "can exist without moral arrogance, and pride and patriotism can exist without paternalism." A foreign policy built on expansionism is not preordained. See Tami R. Davis and Seam M. Lyn-Jones, "City Upon a Hill," in Jerel A. Rosati, ed., *Readings in the Politics of United States Foreign Policy,* pp. 376–386.

44. Bush, West Point speech.

45. Slouka, "A Year Later: Notes on America's Intimations of Mortality," p. 39.

46. Eisenhower was speaking in 1953 after his special assistant had told him it would be nice if, for a change, mobs in the Middle East were waving American flags instead of rioting against the United States. See the memorandum of conversation in Hunt, ed., *Crises in US Foreign Policy,* p. 390.

47. Johnson said in 1966: "There are three billion people in the world and we have only 200 million of them. We are outnumbered 15 to 1. If might did make right, they would sweep over the US and take what we have. We have what they want." Quoted in Richard J. Barnet, *Intervention and Revolution: The United States in the Third World,* p. 25.

48. For this reading of Al-Qaida and Osama bin Laden, see Michael Scott Doran, "Somebody Else's Civil War," pp. 22–42.

49. Jessica Stern, "Holy Avengers," *Financial Times,* June 11, 2004, online ed.

50. Kissinger, "The New World Order," in Chester A. Crocker and Fen Osler Hampson, eds., *Managing Global Chaos: Sources of and Responses to International Conflict,* p. 173.

51. Colin Powell is merely the latest secretary of state to insist that principles such as promoting "human dignity and democracy" actually *are* US interests. Powell, "A Strategy of Partnerships," pp. 22–34.

52. Previously secret British documents revealed this US threat, which was conveyed to the UK ambassador to Washington by Secretary of Defense James R. Schlesinger. See Lizette Alvarez, "Britain Says US Planned to Seize Oil in '73 Crisis," *NYT,* January 2, 2004, p. A4.

53. Kissinger's statement, made just before the election of Salvador Allende, was: "I don't see why we need to stand by and watch a country go Communist due to the irresponsibility of its own people." Quoted in James Petras and Morris Morley, *The United States and Chile: Imperialism and the Overthrow of the Allende Government,* p. vii.

54. Publicly, Kissinger upheld the importance of human rights in Latin America, as in a speech to the Organization of American States in June 1976. Privately, however, he told Pinochet: "The speech is not aimed at Chile. I wanted to tell you about this. My evaluation is that you are a victim of all left-wing groups around the world, and that your greatest sin was that you overthrew a government which was going communist." Lucy Komisar, "Big-Time Embarrassment."

55. In a meeting in Santiago, Chile, Kissinger told the Argentine junta that had just seized power: "If there are things that have to be done, you should do them quickly." Argentina's "dirty war" followed. National Security Archive Update, August 27, 2004, online at www.nsarchive.org, and Peter Kornbluh, "Chile Declassified," pp. 21–24. Condor was founded by the Chilean government in 1974 and eventually included six other Latin governments. Kornbluh shows that Washington was well aware of Condor and regarded it as a "counterterrorism organization."

56. The main sources for this paragraph are Dana Priest and Barton Gellman, "US Decries Abuse But Defends Interrogations," *Washington Post,* December 26, 2002; *NYT,* June 9, 2004, p. A10; and *Washington Post,* June 24, 2004. The latter two articles carry summaries of the pertinent legal memoranda. See also Neil A. Lewis and Eric Schmitt, "Lawyers Decided Bans on Torture Didn't Bind Bush," *NYT,* June 8, 2004, p. A1; Karen J. Greenberg, Joshua L.

Dratel, eds., and Anthony Lewis, *The Torture Papers: The Road to Abu Ghraib;* Michael Isikoff, "Memos Reveal War Crimes Warnings," *Newsweek,* May 18, 2004, online at www.msnbc.msn.com/id/4999734/site/newsweek; and John Barry et al., "The Roots of Torture," *Newsweek,* May 24, 2004, online at www .msnbc.msn.com/id/4989422/site/newsweek.

57. Not until the end of 2004 did the Justice Department rescind its ruling. The State Department disputed the original ruling; Secretary Powell pointed to the "high cost" to US foreign policy of ignoring the Geneva Conventions' requirements. The chief counsel who favored widening the range of acceptable interrogation techniques, Alberto R. Gonzales, later was confirmed as attorney general in the second Bush administration and vowed to uphold all laws governing torture. But he continued to maintain that the Geneva Conventions and other laws did not apply to Al-Qaida fighters or to non-Iraqis fighting with the insurgency. *NYT,* January 8, 2005, p. 1.

58. John G. Ruggie ("The Past as Prologue?" pp. 166–182) seeks to show that historically, US presidents, whether inclined more toward realism or toward globalism-idealism, had to cloak national interest arguments in world-order garb in order to sell the American public on international engagement. My argument is not about selling internationalism but about the convergence of realist and globalist interests in the actual practice of US foreign policy.

59. The continuity of this dominant belief system has been well established by Ole R. Holsti and James N. Rosenau, "A Leadership Divided: The Foreign Policy Beliefs of American Leaders, 1976–1984," in Charles W. Kegley Jr. and Eugene R. Wittkopf, eds., *The Domestic Sources of American Foreign Policy: Insights and Evidence,* pp. 30–44.

60. Benjamin Schwarz, "Why America Thinks It Has to Run the World," pp. 92–102.

61. Rice, "Promoting the National Interest," p. 49.

62. Ibid.

63. "If we have to use force [against Iraq]," Albright said on February 25, 1998, "it is because we are America. We are the indispensable nation. We stand tall. We see further into the future."

64. Ruggie, "The Past as Prologue?" pp. 167–182. Here (ibid., p. 182, n. 74) and in other writings, Ruggie makes the useful distinction between US commitments to a multilateral world order and its resistance to the independent authority of multilateral organizations.

65. During the Korean War, the British government became worried that Washington was misinterpreting China's behavior and thus possibly missing an opportunity to negotiate, wanting to extend the war into China instead. London proposed the formation of a joint US-UK committee to run the war. Truman disagreed. A memorandum noted that Truman "said again that his attitude was that we stay in Korea and fight. If we have support from others, fine; but if not, he said we would stay on anyway." Hunt, ed., *Crises in US Foreign Policy,* p. 222.

66. "Simply put, the US foreign policy establishment does not want international responsibilities to be reallocated because it fears diminished American leadership and a greater—perhaps even equal—German and Japanese voice in international affairs. Better, they say, to bear disproportionate costs than to yield American control." Layne and Schwarz, "American Hegemony—Without an Enemy," p. 6.

67. As Bush once said, "We are the leaders and we must continue to lead." (*New York Times,* March 11, 1992, p. 1.) Bush's statement was in response to questions raised about a leaked Pentagon draft document on defense planning, discussed in Chapter 2, that called for the United States to maintain the capacity to act unilaterally inasmuch as action through a UN-based coalition was not reliable.

68. "We will act with others when we can, but alone when we must," reads the White House document, *A National Security Strategy of Engagement and Enlargement.* For documentation of Clinton's unilateral actions, see the essays in Lieber, ed., *Eagle Rules?*

69. Bacevich's *American Empire* offers an extensive discussion of the agreement on foreign policy essentials between the first Bush and the Clinton administrations.

2

The Bush Doctrine

WITH VICTORY IN the Gulf War, public opinion turned away from foreign affairs, a trend most evident in the virtual absence of foreign policy issues from all of the presidential campaigns between 1992 and 2000. As noted in the previous chapter, liberal and some conservative internationalists watched with alarm what they saw as the rise of anti-internationalist and isolationist thinking. Samuel Huntington bemoaned the inability of presidents to articulate a new vision commensurate with the great strategic transformation of the decade: the demise of the Soviet Union. To him, the absence of a new doctrine meant that foreign policy was taken over by two kinds of "particularistic" interests: ethnic politics and commercialism.[1] But neoconservative (or neocon) internationalists lamented a lost opportunity for the United States to take matters in its own hands. Charles Krauthammer, a leading neocon voice, wrote that the United States's "unipolar moment" was squandered not merely by the failure to drive Saddam Hussein from power in Iraq. The United States should have been "unashamedly laying down the rules of world order and being prepared to enforce them."[2] With regimes such as North Korea's and Iraq's able (or so the neocons claimed) to threaten the United States with nuclear weapons, this was no time for depending on multilateral cooperation.

Here was a radical version of an emerging new realism—radical in its belief that the time was ripe for the United States to impose its power and its values in world affairs. Whereas the realism of Dole and Helms suggested paring down US overseas commitments to those it would lead, and Clinton's realism relied on soft power and a high threshold for the unilateral use of force, Krauthammer explicitly endorsed foreign policy crusading. All these viewpoints were firmly rooted in US nationalism,

27

but Krauthammer's meant carrying the flag around the world. And, he wrote, the country could easily afford to do so. The cost of "ensuring a safe world for American commerce—5.4 percent of GNP [in military spending] and falling—is hardly exorbitant."[3] To more traditional realists, the neocons were overcompensating for the past, hell bent on involving the United States everywhere, seeking to control everything, and engaging in a kind of dangerous utopianism about the virtues of the United States.[4] But to Krauthammer, those realists were deluding themselves into believing that the end of the Soviet Union allowed the United States to return to normalcy.

The Return of the Radical Right

Krauthammer's brand of unilateralism—or "offensive realism," as some observers called it[5]—found a home in the Project for the New American Century (PNAC).[6] The group was formed in 1997 to advance the neocons' cause, which they explicitly defined as "hard-headed internationalism." The group's choice of name could hardly have been accidental, for its arguments echoed those of Henry Luce's "American Century" speech over fifty years earlier: US power and ideals needed to assume center stage in world affairs. Ronald Reagan was its hero; Jimmy Carter and Bill Clinton were cast as appeasers and opponents of US hegemony.[7] The PNAC advocated substantial increases in US military spending, aggressive pursuit of US interests, and "moral clarity" about the US right to be the global leader. Reagan "championed American exceptionalism when it was deeply unfashionable," wrote the two founding members of the PNAC, who also argued that the United States, rather than curry favor with authoritarian regimes, should seek to overturn them.[8] By contrast, the PNAC had little patience with George H. W. Bush, whose "pseudo-realism," the group argued, had done little to advance US interests. "Republicans have spent the past few years attacking Clinton for his handling of Iraq, the Balkans, Haiti and Somalia," Robert Kagan said. "Yet every one of these was an unexploded Bush bomblet." Bush's failure to eliminate Saddam Hussein was easily his greatest error.[9]

The twenty-five signers of the PNAC's initial statement of principles, as well as others involved in the PNAC, represented a cross section of neocons.[10] Most were hardliners on defense policy who had held national security positions in previous administrations, usually Reagan's or George H. W. Bush's. This group included two former defense secretaries, Dick Cheney (under the elder Bush) and Donald Rumsfeld (under Gerald Ford); two former undersecretaries of defense for policy, Paul

Wolfowitz and Fred Iklé, as well as four other former top Pentagon officials—Frank Gaffney, Richard Perle, Zalmay Khalilzad, and Henry S. Rowen; and former State Department officials such as Elliott Abrams, Peter W. Rodman, and Francis Fukuyama. Other signers or project leaders were prominent conservative voices such as Robert Kagan and William Kristol, the PNAC's co-founders and the principal editors of *The Weekly Standard;* Norman Podhoretz of *Commentary* magazine; Steve Forbes of *Forbes* magazine; two leading figures in the Christian right, Gary Bauer and William J. Bennett, Reagan's one-time secretary of education; former vice president Dan Quayle; Jeanne Kirkpatrick, the former US representative to the UN; and Governor Jeb Bush of Florida, brother of the president.

George W. Bush's victory in 2000 assured that the PNAC's nationalist-realist agenda would be highly influential in shaping US national security strategy. Besides Vice President Cheney, many PNAC adherents were appointed to key positions, most prominently Rumsfeld as secretary of defense, Wolfowitz as his deputy secretary, Abrams and Khalilzad in the NSC, and Perle as chair of the Defense Policy Board. No less important is that other PNAC signers held important positions in influential national security think tanks and research organizations, such as Gaffney as head of the Center for Security Policy, Iklé at the Center for Strategic and International Studies, and Vin Weber as board chairman of the National Endowment for Democracy.

At the top of the PNAC's policy agenda was firm support of Israel, ballistic missile defense, Taiwan independence, high levels of military spending, and toppling of rogue regimes. Thus, the PNAC called for "removing Saddam Hussein and his regime from power" in a letter to President Clinton in January 1998.[11] Clinton evidently agreed with that objective, or at least felt politically compelled to do something about it. He authorized Operation Desert Fox, the periodic US and British air attacks on Iraqi air defense installations that challenged patrols over the no-fly zones in northern and southern Iraq. Subsequently, Clinton signed into law the Iraq Liberation Act, which the PNAC and the Republicans in Congress had strongly promoted, putting a bipartisan stamp of approval on the objective of overthrowing Saddam. The act set aside modest funds to support anti-Saddam groups inside and outside of the country, though it is by no means clear that Clinton regarded such support as likely to do the job. In any event, during the 2000 presidential campaign, George W. Bush took the same position as Clinton on how best to handle Iraq: He argued for containing him, relying mainly on the UN inspections and sanctions.[12]

This position, among others taken by Bush and his foreign policy advisers during the campaign (such as on US involvement in peace-keeping operations), set the neocons' teeth on edge; it smacked of retreat from their agenda of US "global leadership."[13] With specific respect to Iraq, the PNAC's view was that regardless of whether or not Saddam's regime could be overthrown, the United States needed to strive for "a substantial American force presence in the [Persian] Gulf," a goal it realized would not be adopted "absent some catastrophic and catalyzing event—like a new Pearl Harbor."[14] Nevertheless, Bush's election, and not just the events of September 11, 2001, clearly represented an opportunity for the neocons to pursue their agenda; he was simply the best thing that had happened since Reagan.

Bush's personality and managerial style suited them too, as it turned out, for like Reagan, Bush (at least until 9/11) delegated authority. With limited overseas experience or intellectual interest, Bush was inclined to let others shape policy and avoid delving into details.[15] After 9/11, Bush, whether delegating or not, apparently closed the circle of advisers tightly around him. This limitation on viewpoints meshed with his faith-based "instincts," which likewise shut out diversity of opinion. He was certain about what to do; further discussion was unnecessary.[16]

Reinventing Reagan

To appreciate fully the conceptual bridge between the Reagan years and the George W. Bush administration, we have to step back briefly to the 1980s. One interpretation of Reagan's emergence is that his "conserva-tive internationalism" replaced "liberal internationalism" as a conse-quence of the Vietnam-induced breakdown of the great bipartisan con-sensus that had guided foreign policy. But this "return to the Cold War" really was less of a dramatic restoration of containment than is com-monly thought. Jimmy Carter's promise of a new foreign policy based on priority to human rights and a more nuanced approach to the com-munist threat was ephemeral, a two-year phenomenon. Carter ended it himself when he chose to interpret the Soviet intervention in Afghanis-tan as the opening move in a bid for control of the entire Middle East. From that moment until his last day in office, when US hostages were finally released by Iran, the hardliners around Carter—men who (as "Team B") had unsuccessfully sought to upgrade the Soviet threat and later formed the Committee on the Present Danger to lobby that view—were in charge. Military spending rebounded, arms control moved off the table, and a get-tough policy toward Moscow was back in vogue.

Liberals in Congress contributed to Reagan's victory in 1980 by insisting on a more muscular foreign policy—and voting the money for it. The "congressional comeback" in foreign affairs that had marked the Vietnam War years was dead.

Reagan's appeal to national pride and for renewed toughness in dealing with foreign threats found ready acceptance among believers in US primacy. After years of being on the defensive, conservatives and many liberals seemed hungry for a strong response to the Soviet threat and equally to domestic critics of an imperial presidency. Reagan turned the tables on his critics: He called the Vietnam War a "noble cause," persuaded the US public that the USSR was an "evil empire" whereas the United States had never been imperialistic, and restored exceptionalism to pride of place in popular mythology. What is most relevant to the Bush Doctrine is how much it owes to Reagan's policies. Reagan's apocalyptic worldview had a fundamentalist streak: He was convinced that the United States was ordained to oppose the Soviet Union, "the focus of evil in the modern world."[17] That view, pitched to the Christian right, informed his strong backing of Israel and his appointment of pro-Israel neocons (and Cold Warriors and former one-time Democrats) such as Jeanne Kirkpatrick at the UN and Richard Perle in the Defense Department.[18]

Reagan reinvigorated the containment strategy in two ways—first, by determining to roll back radical and Marxist regimes in Grenada, Cambodia, Nicaragua, Afghanistan, and Angola; and by abandoning corrupt old allies such as François Duvalier in Haiti and Ferdinand Marcos in the Philippines and supporting their replacement. Reagan thus gave renewed impetus to "regime change." His endorsement of unilateral US action and preemptive attack on terrorist states likewise was a preview of the Bush Doctrine.[19] Continuing a long US tradition of ignoring the undemocratic practices of friendly regimes and endorsing violations of international and domestic law, as in the Iran-Contra affair and the mining of Nicaragua's harbors, Reagan showed (as would Bush) that using terrorist tactics was acceptable in the name of "national security." These views were widely shared by the policymaking team Reagan brought on board. Like Reagan himself, many appointees (over twenty, in fact) were graduates of the Committee on the Present Danger—Cold War hardliners who had an ideological commitment to confronting Moscow, dramatically pushing the pace of military spending and weapons procurement, and putting national security considerations ahead of human rights when it came to supporting allies.[20]

The identification of terrorism as a US foreign policy priority in the Reagan years may be, in retrospect, his most enduring legacy to George

W. Bush. Only days after Reagan's inauguration, Secretary of State Alexander M. Haig Jr. accused the Soviet Union of "training, funding and equipping" international terrorists, and said that "international terrorism will take the place of human rights in our concern."[21] By 1985, Reagan referred to "a confederation of terrorist states" and cited Iran, Libya, North Korea, Cuba, and Nicaragua as its chief members. Iraq was never mentioned, a deliberate omission that we will return to in the next chapter. Nor was it ever mentioned that US support of "freedom fighters" such as the contras and Al-Qaida to overthrow "terrorist" governments amounted to support of terrorists just the same. To the chagrin, reportedly, of some in his administration, who questioned the loose terminology and unproven accusations of terrorism, Reagan insisted "we must act together, or unilaterally if necessary, to insure that terrorists have no sanctuary—anywhere."[22] "Terrorism" became a scattergun charge throughout the 1980s: when the Soviets downed a Korean Airlines commercial flight in 1983; when the US Marine barracks in Beirut was attacked in 1983, resulting in 241 deaths; when US forces intervened in Grenada the same year, on the argument that the island "was a Soviet-Cuban colony" loaded with weapons "to supply thousands of terrorists";[23] and when Libya was said to have engaged in assassination plots and airline bombings, which the United States answered with the shooting down of Libyan jets, the imposition of economic sanctions, a disinformation campaign to undermine Qaddafi's rule, and the bombing of Libya in an attempt to kill him. Reagan's antiterrorism effort also had its domestic side, which included administration efforts to weaken wiretapping laws, protect CIA agents abroad, and exempt intelligence agencies from disclosure requirements under the Freedom of Information Act.[24]

In sum, the Reagan presidency contributed in three specific ways to the national security policies of George W. Bush. It brought into government service some of the same neoconservatives who would populate Bush's national security staff. Reagan also activated the cardinal elements of the Bush Doctrine—unilateralism, preemptive attack, and regime change. And the Reagan administration planted the seeds for a global crusade against an amorphous transnational threat, terrorism.

During the administration of Reagan's successor, George H. W. Bush, the Pentagon leadership sought to give added weight to those elements when the team of Cheney and Wolfowitz circulated a draft "Defense Planning Guidance" paper.[25] The paper argued that the traditional US notion of maintaining a favorable balance of power in the new post-Soviet world order required a particular kind of US leadership—the kind that ensured no competition for regional or global supremacy. This rule applied to rivals and allies alike: They should all be convinced that there was no point in "challenging our leadership" or "even aspiring to a larger regional or global role." While achieving that objective did not require becoming the world's policeman, said the document, "by assuming responsibility for righting every wrong, we will retain the preeminent responsibility for addressing selectively those wrongs which threaten not only our interests, but those of our allies or friends." Among the interests cited were access to Persian Gulf oil, proliferation of weapons of mass destruction (WMD), and terrorist threats. In the one-superpower world of Cheney and Wolfowitz, unilateral US military actions was presumed, dual containment of Germany and Japan was still required, and the need for a huge military budget, a wide variety of ready military forces, and large US nuclear forces to deter potential nuclear weapon states were all needed. The draft evoked the possibility of fighting Iraq and North Korea simultaneously, and it seemed to favor a preemptive as well as a retaliatory attack on a country that was developing or possessed WMD. Russia and China were still regarded as strategic rivals. Nothing was said about collective security through the UN; coalitions were not held in high regard because they were always fragile and might not be able to form quickly enough.

The Pentagon draft drew heavy fire once word of it leaked out. The reasons were clear enough: Leaders of the countries mentioned in the document as having malevolent intentions were not pleased, and diplomatic officials everywhere, including the State Department and allied capitals, objected to the apparent neglect of alliances and the UN.[26] Pentagon spokesmen sought cover by contending the document had not circulated at high levels when in fact Cheney's and the Joint Chiefs of Staff's approval were apparent. By May collective action was back in the document and dual containment was out, reportedly due in part to concerns expressed by General Colin Powell, then head of the Joint Chiefs of Staff.[27] But were they? The revised document, following President Bush's lead,[28] accepted cooperating with allies, but pointed out that "we must maintain the capabilities for addressing selectively those security problems that threaten our own interests."[29] In short, Cheney and Wolfowitz had had to soften the language; but the principles of unilateral action and preemptive attack, not to mention the wide range of US security interests and resource "needs," had by no means been discarded.[30]

George W. Bush and the Neocons

Had the 9/11 attacks not occurred, the draft Pentagon study would be far less significant than it is today. For in key respects it foreshadowed the neocon national security agenda that George W. Bush adopted. Even before 9/11, Reaganite thinking had already insinuated itself into the Bush camp. During Bush's 2000 presidential campaign, his eight primary foreign policy advisers, nicknamed the Vulcans, included two neocons, Paul Wolfowitz and Richard Perle. All of them had reputations as defense hardliners,[31] and all but one went on to serve in Bush's first administration, including his chief mentor on foreign affairs, Condoleezza Rice. Bush's other top-level appointments in the Defense and State Departments were likewise veterans of the two previous Republican administrations—and again, all but Powell were well-known hardliners. Dick Cheney and Paul Wolfowitz were back; they, along with Cheney's chief of staff, Lewis "Scooter" Libby, were all PNAC signatories. But the key player then and afterwards was Rumsfeld, Cheney's mentor for over a quarter century. More than any other individual, it was Rumsfeld who, as defense secretary, would position the Pentagon as the most influential player on national security matters. And Rumsfeld had plenty of help: His advisory panel, the Defense Policy Board, was chaired by Perle and included three other influential neocons—Kenneth Adelman, James Woolsey (former director of Central Intelligence), and Eliot Cohen.

What about Bush's own thinking? Ivo Daalder and James Lindsay make the case for Bush being his own man in foreign affairs rather than a captive of the neocons. His "logic" is that of a realist "hegemonist," they contend.[32] The fact that Bush looked both to his father's and Reagan's foreign policy teams when it came to selecting his own would suggest that George W. was indeed his own man. On closer examination, however, the differences between a neocon and a hegemonist are slim, and the argument that Bush entered office with a clear conception of the world slimmer still. Neocons such as Cheney and realists such as Rice are all hegemonists, and after 9/11 that common ground was solidified. They believe in leading with power, especially military power—rolling back the enemy (regime change) and punishing opponents unilaterally if necessary. Thus, they want more military spending, regard China and Russia as strategic competitors, and consider "rogue states" major threats to US security interests. By contrast, the security import of global issues such as environmental degradation, energy and resource competition, and growing poverty receive virtually no consideration. Both groups reject giving much weight to international law, norms, and institutions ("Wilsonianism," they derisively call it), except when they serve US interests. Instead, they intend to safeguard sovereignty and the prerogatives of leadership—to be "sheriff of the posse"—rather than yield control to multilateral groups. Neocons and realists alike believe that national security achieved through the exercise of US power will promote the spread of US values, which are "universal."[33] Both groups take as an article of faith that the United States is the exceptional country and has purity of purpose in world affairs. And last, in the specific context of a post–Cold War world, realists and neocons alike believe in the "American century," that moment when US power has no competition and US purposes are fully realizable.[34]

When Daalder and Lindsay describe Bush's foreign policy goals as "thoroughly conventional," however, they are on the mark. Between the time he took office and 9/11, Bush had nothing original to say about foreign affairs; but what he did say was well within the mainstream of US ideals and self-interest.[35] An internationalist, he viewed the US role in the world as "an essential part of America's national greatness."[36] He committed his administration to an open world economy, gave great weight to the interests of energy and other global corporations, and primed the pump of the defense industry giants. In fact, Bush before 9/11 had much in common with Bill Clinton on the historical destiny of the United States, on the centrality of both US values and US interests in foreign policy, and on US selflessness in avoiding empire.[37] Like Clinton, Bush assumed and wanted to continue US leadership in "free trade," eastward expansion of the North Atlantic Treaty Organization (NATO), high military spending, reliance on high-tech precision weapons, control of Middle East diplomacy, and of course global "democratization." As one writer concluded in describing the context of Iraq, the greatest danger in the foreign policy of George W. Bush was "imperial overreach: a 'one size fits all' approach to democracy promotion fomented under Clinton."[38]

Most of these views fit with the PNAC's agenda. Once Bush took office, moreover, it found still more of his positions to laud: Bush's view of China as a strategic competitor rather than partner; his rejection of arms control treaties such as the Comprehensive Test Ban Treaty in favor of missile defense and toughness when dealing with nuclear weapons proliferation; his distaste for Clinton's "Wilsonian faith in international conventions" and multilateralism; and his support of Israel, which (like Reagan's) also drew on the religious right and its strong coterie of representatives in Congress.[39] In a word, the second George Bush took his main political cues from Reagan's presidency and not his father's.[40]

If George W. Bush's ideas about foreign policy echo those of the people around him, the same cannot be said for his religious views. Bush's political fortunes rose when he became a born-again Christian and discovered that devotion to the evangelical agenda was a key to national political prominence.[41] He wears his moral convictions on his sleeve—as the oft-told story goes, when asked about his father's administration, Bush said he relied on the Father upstairs. Two foreign policy implications flow from Bush's moralism. One is a faith-based certainty in the rightness of his actions and a strong tendency to ignore facts that get in the way of decisions already made. Another is his belief in the oneness of God's and US purposes. Some accounts suggest he is convinced he is designated to serve God's purpose. Even if such accounts are exaggerated, many of the country's evangelicals, believed to number from 30 to 40 percent of the population, see Bush as God's chosen instrument.[42] Their support proved crucial to Bush's successful run for reelection in 2004. After the 9/11 attacks, Bush fed their perception with constant references to the country's "higher calling" to save civilization from the terrorists. "This will be a monumental struggle between good and evil," he told reporters.[43]

Moral certainty and religiously informed devotion to the national interest are a dangerous combination. They create a sense of destiny that mirrors the vision of fundamentalist regimes and movements. In the hands of a leader with awesome military and economic power at his disposal, they have the potential to convert US exceptionalism into US adventurism.

September 11 and Endless War

> The great struggles of the twentieth century between liberty and totalitarianism ended with a decisive victory for the forces of freedom— and a single sustainable model for national success: freedom, democracy, and free enterprise.
> — *The National Security Strategy of the United States*

In the new Bush administration, money, energy ties, and (born-again) conservative credentials counted most. An unusual number of cabinet and other high-level posts were awarded to corporate leaders and lobbyists; those connected with the major energy corporations dominated the list.[44] Some key policymaking positions went to individuals who were indicted for their actions during the Reagan administration's illegal support and subsequent coverup of aid to the Nicaraguan contras.[45] Equally indicative of Bush's policy bent were some early moves: the elimination of "strategic ambiguity" from US policy toward Taiwan following the April 2001 spy plane incident with China; the upgrading of military and diplomatic ties with Taiwan; the rejection of engagement

The Bush Doctrine   37

options for dealing with North Korea and Cuba; and the renewed emphasis on military spending, arms sales, and domestic intelligence gathering in the name of national security. This is not to say that neo-conservatism won out on every policy question. Powell's cautious realism at the State Department clearly won the day in the spy plane incident with China,[46] and probably helps account for Bush's later willingness to seek UN support for the war with Iraq and his avoidance of an immediate military showdown with North Korea over its nuclear weapons program.[47] But 9/11 decisively tilted the balance of influence away from traditional diplomacy and toward the Pentagon, where the disciples of neo-Reaganism were firmly ensconced and, reportedly, where the belief ran strong that the State Department was simply not up to the job of carrying out the president's tough policies in the war on terror.[48]

Specifically, 9/11 had three transforming effects. First, it elevated neocon thinking—a vigorous US nationalism—to the intellectual center. What had been a peripheral policy thrust became the dominant school of thought. Where once the limits of US power were the chief topic of public discussion, now there was to be no apologizing for US imperial ambitions.[49] Second, 9/11 downgraded the particularities of traditional realism and globalism in favor of a new crusade akin to the Cold War crusade that fused anticommunism with an open-door world economy.[50] The crusade was evangelical in more ways than one, since it combined an "end-of-history" rationale (Bush's "single sustainable model") with religious devotion. Third, 9/11 crystallized two simple but very expansive strategic objectives: winning the war on terror and undermining rogue states that possessed, or might possess, weapons of mass destruction.

In a word, the 9/11 terrorist attacks were a gift to the unilateralists—a once-in-a-lifetime chance to reshape the substance and objectives of US foreign policy. "As Rumsfeld was quick to discern, September 11 created 'the kind of opportunities that World War II offered, to refashion the world.'"[51] Here was the "new Pearl Harbor" that the PNAC believed in 2000 was prerequisite to redefining the US national security agenda. Without 9/11, the neocons would have had a very difficult time persuading a sufficient number of Congress members that national security required a dramatic refocusing of policy priorities and budget allocations. After all, this was an administration without a popular mandate; Bush had lost the popular vote for president. Nor, clearly, would it have been possible to twist the domestic agenda to serve foreign policy ends—a task that was welcomed after 9/11 by Attorney General John Ashcroft, whose millenarian views made him well suited to a moral crusade.[52] It was just as Samuel Huntington had written four years earlier:

Only some new international crisis could snap Washington out of its ideological lethargy and infuse the notion of national interest with new meaning.[53]

With 9/11 many of the constraints on US policy disappeared, including opposition from leading Democrats. (It should be remembered that some members of the Democratic Party elite, such as Senator Joseph Lieberman, the vice presidential candidate in 2000, already supported parts of the neocon agenda, such as overthrowing Saddam Hussein.) Bush bought into the essential elements of the neocon agenda. Overnight, it seems, he changed from a realist in the mold of his father—the man who, as candidate in 2000, had urged that the United States be "a humble nation" to gain worldwide respect[54]—to a crusader in the mold of the neocons. His speech to the nation on September 20, 2001, set the direction, not only by drawing a line in the sand—"Either you are with us, or you are with the terrorists"—but also by globalizing the new conflict. It will be "civilization's fight," he said then and on later occasions.[55] Realist objectives—defeating Al-Qaida and ousting the Taliban, demonstrating US power and will, controlling the conduct of the war, preventing the spread of weapons of mass destruction, establishing bases and creating alliances against terrorism wherever possible and regardless of the ally's domestic politics—were only part of the justification for going to war. Globalist objectives were equally strong: crusading "for a just peace—a peace that favors human liberty,"[56] rebuilding Afghanistan, and securing access to oil. As Vice President Cheney put it, using language that also harked back to the Cold War, winning the war on terrorism was uniquely a US "responsibility," equally for idealistic and power-political reasons.[57]

One is tempted to conclude from the words and actions of the Bush administration that post-9/11 foreign policy was an attempt to create the "new world order" that the Reagan revolution only partly brought about, and that Bush's father failed to achieve. Condoleezza Rice would later say that neither Reagan's targeting of Libya and his grand struggle with Moscow, nor the end of the Cold War under George H. W. Bush, nor certainly Clinton's "engagement" policy, had kept terrorists at bay. In her view, presented at a time when the real reasons for initiating war on Iraq were being critically scrutinized, George W. Bush was the first president to carry out a "sustained, systematic and global response" to terrorist attacks on US interests.[58] Her assertion runs up against two problems, however. The first was her notion of international terrorism, which she made out to be as monolithic as international communism once was considered. To Rice's mind, every terrorist act, starting with the 1983 attack on the US Marine barracks in Lebanon, was part of the same "sustained, systematic campaign to spread devastation and chaos." Such blurred vision separated her from the realist tradition she once embraced, a tradition that called for responding to specific threats to specific interests.[59] Her second error was to pretend that Bush really put terrorism at the top of his list. His war on Iraq not only exposed the pretense; it dramatically increased the number of young people who were attracted to Al-Qaida's brand of terrorism.

Nevertheless, terrorism provided the national security niche that had evaded both Reagan and the elder Bush. The first Bush administration was thwarted by economic troubles at home and the traditional tendency of the US public and the Congress to turn attention away from a distant conflict once victory was in hand. Reagan undermined his appeal to fight state terrorism by authorizing various illegalities: an abortive arms-for-hostages exchange with Iran and support of the Nicaraguan contras in spite of congressional restrictions. But George W. Bush could credibly claim, and exploit, the fact that the terrorist threat represented a new kind of war, one with no end game and no clear targets. Such a war lent itself to an open-ended strategy: "Our war on terror begins with Al Qaeda, but it does not end there. It will not end until every terrorist group of global reach has been found, stopped, and defeated."[60]

Early in 2002 Bush warned that the war had entered a "second stage," "a sustained campaign to deny sanctuary to terrorists who would threaten our citizens from anywhere in the world."[61] By mid-year it was clear that Afghanistan would be just the beginning, and that the United States reserved the right, in the name of self-defense, to carry the war on terrorism wherever it saw fit.[62]

The Bush Doctrine at Its Core

Preemption

The Bush Doctrine rejected deterrence and containment as useful strategies. Preemptive attack now *was* deterrence, said Bush. His speech at West Point was crystal clear on this point: "Yet the war on terror will not be won on the defensive. We must take the battle to the enemy, disrupt his plans, and confront the worst threats before they emerge. In the world we have entered, the only path to safety is the path of action." Shortly after, press reports indicated that Bush had directed top officials to formalize the idea, with specific attention going to leaders of the three states—Iraq, North Korea, and Iran—that Bush had already dubbed an "axis of evil."[63] The formal statement appeared as *The National Security Strategy of the United States* in September 2002.[64] It sanctified preemption as being "compelling . . . even if uncertainty remains as to the time and place of the enemy's attack." And it backed the case for preemptive attack by arguing that it would be exercised on behalf of all states and persons. All the United States was now seeking, said the document, was to "create a balance of power that favors human freedom."[65]

Colin Powell was correct to say that "preemption has always been available as a tool of foreign policy or military doctrine." What had changed, he added, was that preemptive attack had risen in importance on Bush's list of options.[66] These remarks glossed over three important points, however. Preemption had never before been used to initiate a full-scale war. Since 1945, the numerous previous uses of force by the United States either were in support of one side in an ongoing civil war (Korea, Vietnam), or were punitive raids carried out against other countries (such as Libya in the Reagan years and Afghanistan and Sudan in Clinton's), or were time-limited interventions (Eisenhower in Lebanon, Johnson in the Dominican Republic, Reagan in Grenada, the elder Bush in Panama). The notion of Bush advisers such as Condoleezza Rice as well as Bush himself that President Kennedy's quarantine of Cuba in the 1962 missile crisis was a precedent for preemptive attack was entirely misguided with respect both to the perceived threat and the management of the outcome.[67] The chief point about the missile crisis is precisely that both Kennedy and Soviet Chairman Nikita Khrushchev rejected preemptive attack. Despite great uncertainty in the Kennedy administration about Soviet motives in deploying nuclear-armed missiles in Cuba, it did not attack and ask questions later. Instead, it resorted to private as well as public diplomacy. Both Washington and Moscow sought to stop the drift toward war, recognizing the dangers of miscalculation in a crisis environment.

The better analogy relevant to Cuba would have been Kennedy's authorization of the Bay of Pigs invasion in 1961, with its intention of regime change, its obliviousness to the nationalism of the Cuban people, and the Kennedy administration's obsession to remove a dictator it disliked.[68] Yet even there the analogy falls short, for we now know that Kennedy, shortly before his assassination, expressed a willingness to explore a back-channel dialogue with Castro in recognition that the use of force and threat had failed to dislodge him.[69]

Then again, preemptive attack is the wrong term, used by the Bush administration—one suspects—for political reasons. A preemptive strike is defensive, undertaken first in reasonable expectation of being attacked almost immediately. What the Bush administration was really touting was preventive war, which is waged offensively to destroy an enemy's war-making assets and its government so as (presumably) to render it unable to become strong enough to attack.[70] That the administration knew the difference between preventive and preemptive attacks is clear from the Department of Defense's own publication, which properly defines preventive war as "a war initiated in the belief that military conflict, while not imminent, is inevitable, and that to delay would involve greater risk."[71] That is precisely what the administration did in attacking Iraq.

Preemption strongly implies, moreover, that the sovereignty of unfriendly states is limited. Should those states fail to conduct themselves in accordance with US rules and preferences, they can expect to come under US pressure and the threat of military intervention. During the Cold War this outlook was known as liberal interventionism—the idea that overthrowing undemocratic, oppressive regimes was a perfectly legitimate exercise of US power. The idea stood as a companion to strategic interventionism—the use of force against a communist threat in order, as in Vietnam, to stem the tide of Sino-Soviet expansionism. The many efforts to get rid of Fidel Castro, starting with the Bay of Pigs incident, exemplified liberal interventionism. In the Bush era, the equivalent of Castro's Cuba is the three "axis of evil" states—states believed to be sponsoring terrorism, seeking to acquire weapons of mass destruction, and having deplorable human rights records. But whereas previous administrations were willing for some purposes to talk to "evil" leaders, from Castro to Kim Il Sung in North Korea, the Bush administration rejects direct dialogue in the belief that such leaders lack legitimacy and have forfeited their state's sovereignty.

The limited-sovereignty thesis as a basis for projecting US power apparently has deep roots in the Bush administration, according to a senior State Department official during Bush's first term. In an interview, Richard Haass said the prevailing view was that:

Sovereignty entails obligations. One is not to massacre your own people. Another is not to support terrorism in any way. If a government fails to meet these obligations, then it forfeits some of the normal advantages of sovereignty, including the right to be left alone in your own territory. Other governments, including the United States, gain the right to intervene. In the case of terrorism, this can even lead to a right of preventive, or peremptory, self-defense. You essentially can act in anticipation if you have grounds to think it's a question of when, and not if, you're going to be attacked.[72]

Haass himself, echoing his boss Colin Powell, drew a distinction in the interview between US leadership and US unilateralism, arguing that foreign policy "has to be multilateral. We can't win the war against terror alone. We can't send forces everywhere." Unfortunately, that was very much a minority view; the dominant view was broadly interventionist and expansionist.

The Bush administration's argument was not merely that state sovereignty might be limited by the genocidal behavior of a leader; that much was argued by Kofi Annan at the UN as well. "Support of terrorism" also was deemed by Bush to limit a country's sovereignty. But that view exposed two dangerous possibilities: that the United States might take matters into its own hands on the claim of limited sovereignty, and that the United States would not have to wait to be threatened, but may attack at a time of its choosing, that is, preventively. Governments as different as Israel, Russia, and China, all facing what they regarded as terrorist threats, appreciated such logic.

Unilateralism and Regime Change

"We don't do empire," Donald Rumsfeld declared after 9/11. "We do not seek an empire," said George W. Bush.[73] Yet more than one analyst has labeled the Bush Doctrine "neoimperial" and the United States "a revisionist state." Among them is John Ikenberry who, like many European critics, pointed out that the doctrine is "ultimately unconstrained by the rules and norms of the international community," and that it invites a careless use of force based on "hunch or inference."[74] Where once it was US policy to "get" Libya's Qaddafi, North Korea's Kim Il Sung, Iran's Ayatollah Khomeini, Cuba's Fidel Castro, and the Congo's Patrice Lumumba, all of whom were considered illegitimate rulers, the Bush Doctrine now legitimized "getting" Iraq's Saddam Hussein, North Korea's Kim Jong Il, and Iran's clerical leadership. Nor are governments friendly to the United States immune from the Bush Doctrine. Indonesia, for example, with its troubled history of popular unrest in East Timor, Aceh, and other outlying regions, might one day be a target if Australia, for example, becomes disenchanted with the destabilizing consequences of the Indonesian military's human rights abuses.

The attack on Iraq demonstrated that unilateralism can mean, in Theodore Sorensen's elegant turn of phrase, "a preference for invasion over persuasion." But a neoimperial foreign policy does not require the direct use of force. Colin Powell often insisted that unilateral, preemptive attack would not be the norm in US relations with distasteful regimes.[75]

As a practical matter, the United States cannot police the world, as became clear in dealing with North Korea following the overthrow of Saddam Hussein, when the US military was stretched thin while occupying Iraq. The more salient point, however, is that the United States has not often needed preemptive attack to achieve control. Thus, the Bush administration has usually relied on traditional hegemonic tactics to achieve its objectives. China policy is the clearest example of use of the twin prongs of realism and globalism—containment and deterrence on one hand, markets on the other—to keep Beijing's presumed ambitions in check. Maintaining forward-deployed military forces, keeping Taiwan well armed, bringing Japan into regional defense, and erecting a theater missile defense system in which Japan and possibly Taiwan participate are among the military ingredients—and the ones favored by the neocons. Tying China to the global economic system through the World Trade Organization (WTO), technology trade, and foreign investment is the globalist side of containment—though some in the Bush camp chose to dignify the strategy by calling it "integration."[76] Thus George W. Bush the realist was just as firm as Bill Clinton the globalist in arguing that an open trading system would eventually transform China's political system.[77]

Expanding Capabilities

The US armed forces, like those of other countries, are deeply committed to a "revolution in military affairs" (RMA). Prominent features of RMA are the acquisition of vast new response capabilities—for defense against attacks by terrorists, missile attacks, and attacks on space and information assets, for example—and, as Secretary Rumsfeld wrote, the capacity to prevent enemies "from building dangerous new [weapons] in the first place."[78] He defined his job as one of transforming the Pentagon from a threat-based to "a new 'capabilities-based' approach—one that focuses less on who might threaten us, or where, and more on how we might be threatened and what is needed to deter and defend against such threats."[79]

Actually, it was Powell and Wolfowitz who had initiated the new approach before the Gulf War when they sought to preserve a full-scope military in the face of pressure to cut costs.[80] Both men were convinced that the 9/11 attacks had eroded deterrence as a military strategy. Wolfowitz would say in a 2003 interview that diplomacy only works "with people who . . . share your values and your interests." The trick is to rely on "the ultimate threat of force," but only when prepared actually to use it, a throwback to John Foster Dulles's much-ballyhooed idea of brinkmanship in the 1950s.[81] In keeping with the Bush Doctrine, Rumsfeld gave deterrence a new twist. He said it now meant "that we take the war to the enemy," which required high-tech firepower and power-projection capabilities in space, undersea, and everywhere else. Michael Klare did not exaggerate when he argued that Rumsfeld's real intention was to "acquire a capacity to defeat *any* conceivable type of attack mounted by *any* imaginable adversary at *any* point in time."[82]

Rumsfeld's explanations of the new US military left several points unsaid. One was the acceleration of a trend already under way in the Clinton years to give senior military officers foreign policy making authority. Regional commanders in particular would be expected to promote nation building and civil society as well as internal security—activities normally reserved for civilians and an important piece of the militarization of foreign policy that the Bush Doctrine cemented.[83] Second, Rumsfeld never let on that nuclear weapons would once again be considered a usable strategic option. That crucial determination did not come to light until a Nuclear Posture Review (NPR) was submitted to the Congress on the last day of 2001.[84] Reflecting Rumsfeld's promise of a capabilities-based approach to strategic planning, the NPR said nuclear weapons will "provide credible military options to deter a wide range of threats, including WMD and large-scale conventional military force." But again, the strategy was to go beyond deterrence. The document specified that five "rogue states" (North Korea, Iraq, Iran, Libya, and Syria) as well as China and Russia would be potential nuclear targets. Contingencies for using nuclear weapons might include "an Iraqi attack on Israel or its neighbors, or a North Korean attack on South Korea or a military confrontation over the status of Taiwan." But nuclear weapons could also be used in other ways—to "dissuade adversaries from undertaking military programs or operations that could threaten US interests," for instance, and to reach an enemy's underground bunkers. The clear implication of the NPR was that new kinds of nuclear weapons, and therefore new nuclear tests, would have to be designed, and that international treaties signed by the United States or in negotiation that might impede the new nuclear strategy would be downgraded or abandoned. All these prospects became realities under Bush (see Chapter 6).

Just as happened with NSC-68, September 11, 2001, was an opportunity to give all the players in the national security state—the military services, the members of Congress with military bases in their states or districts, the arms makers, the intelligence community, and the State Department—most of what they wanted. Talk of cost cutting and restructuring gave way to a spending spree such as had not been seen since the Reagan years. Not that Clinton had scrimped on the military: For example, from 1995 to 2000 the US share of world military expenditures was 37 percent, greater than the combined military spending of the next nine countries.[85] But the claim of wartime conditions gave the Bush administration a virtual blank check on military spending. "We're at war, and when the president asks for additional resources for national defense, he generally gets it," said a Democratic senator.[86] By 2003 official US military spending was $417 billion, or 47 percent of military spending worldwide and higher than the next fourteen countries' spending.[87] Military spending in that year rose 16 percent, the largest percentage increase in twenty years, compared with a 7 percent increase for nonmilitary spending.[88] By 2007, Bush planned to increase military spending to over $450 billion,[89] though if spending on war in the Middle East is counted, actual military spending was already close to $500 billion in 2004.[90]

US contracts for arms sales, amounting to over $18 billion in 2000, accounted for about one-half the world total.[91] As we shall see, arms sales and other forms of military assistance expanded after 9/11 as the United States rewarded governments that cooperated with it, regardless of their internal political circumstances. Rumsfeld's RMA was a boon to US arms manufacturers before 9/11. After 9/11, Lockheed Martin, Boeing, and Northrop Grumman enjoyed a windfall of Pentagon contracts.[92]

The real margin of difference between the first George W. Bush military budget and the one inherited from Clinton had mostly to do with cost and force deployments. Bush's budget in 2003 was about $115 billion more than Clinton's, but only a tiny fraction of that difference was accounted for by the war on terrorism.[93] The difference is therefore better explained by the Bush administration's extraordinary ambitiousness to remake the world by assigning new importance to weapons of every kind, and by retaining a redesigned global network of overseas deployments. The Bush military budget called not just for increased financing of ballistic missile defense and nuclear submarines reconfigured to fire cruise missiles; it also revived weapons programs once considered defunct, such as the V-22 *Osprey* tilt-rotor transport aircraft and the Army's *Comanche* reconnaissance helicopter.

Meantime, the administration in 2004 announced a long-term plan to redeploy about 70,000 troops, mostly from Germany and South Korea, of a total of around 260,000 troops stationed overseas.[94] This meant downsizing bases and forces in western Europe (Germany especially; the Pentagon in 2004 planned to reduce forces there by as much as 70,000) but introducing them in Poland and in general nearer to the Caucasus, the Middle East, and Central Asia; moving forces in South Korea away from the demilitarized zone (the 38th parallel) and Okinawa, but increasing the number of facilities for air and naval use elsewhere in East Asia; and removing forces from Saudi Arabia but deploying them around the Horn of Africa. Unlike the Cold War years, these "lily-pads" and their rapidly deployable soldiers are intended as jumping-off points for fulfilling the Bush Doctrine's objectives of regime change and pre-emptive attack where believed necessary.[95] The essence of the so-called revolution in military affairs after 9/11 really seems to be matching capabilities with the Bush Doctrine of global policing.

But these major changes are terribly shortsighted. First, as became apparent in Kazakhstan and Uzbekistan (see Chapter 5), basing US forces in countries with authoritarian governments and repressive politics risks identification with state terrorism. Arming such governments directly supports terrorism. Second, the new model, as postwar Iraq and Afghanistan show, gives only secondary attention to rebuilding defeated, devastated countries. The administration's abhorrence of nation building has come back to haunt it, just as its love affair with high-tech warfare has been unfulfilling.[96] Third, the victories over Iraq in 1991 and 2003 provided a false sense of optimism, mainly among the neocons, that they could be easily replicated.[97] Forgotten, or buried, was Iraq's weakness in those wars—weakness caused by years of sanctions, war with Iran, and the failure of its WMD programs.

A fourth planning oversight concerns soldiers. This has two aspects. One is that if the United States gets bogged down in conflict, as happened in Iraq, the slimmed-down military is inadequate. By 2004 around 40 percent of US forces in Iraq came from National Guard and reserve units. Tours of duty for all soldiers had to be stretched and doubled, causing considerable consternation in the ranks and among families. The overstretched army also led to a second problem: the administration's greatly expanded reliance on private contractors to replace regular soldiers in performing every function except combat.[98] Use of private companies' services was not new: "During the Persian Gulf war in 1991, one of every 50 people on the battlefield was an American civilian under contract," for example.[99] Private soldiers were active in several subsequent conflicts, including Bosnia and Colombia. Something like 20,000 contract personnel are serving in Iraq alone during the occupation, making the ratio to regular US soldiers roughly one to seven. Contractors provide security for Iraqi and US officials and companies, interrogate prisoners, train security forces, and provide logistical support.

Private contracting suddenly is indispensable, and big business. But it raises serious problems of legal, moral, and military responsibility. The Abu Ghraib prisoner abuse scandal underscored the fact that contractor personnel fall outside the law. They also fall outside the purview of Congress, the media, and public opinion; being essentially mercenaries, contractors are a perfect fit with a national security strategy that emphasizes unilateralism and limited accountability.

Secrecy

Accurate or not, the George W. Bush administration has earned the reputation of being the most secretive in US history. Following again in the footsteps of the Reagan administration, which elevated the art of news control and exploitation of secrecy to new heights,[100] Bush

> not only rehired several of the Iran-contra intriguers, but he has also reproduced elements of the climate in which the plot was hatched— obsessive secrecy, a premium on loyalty, a taste for working through foreign proxies, an impatience with Congressional oversight.[101]

Journalists complain loudly and often about the paucity of press conferences and briefings, which may be a function of the president's well-known aversion to leaks and insistence on loyalty to the official line. In his first four years, Bush placed controls to limit the public release of information, such as under the Freedom of Information Act, reversing a trend of declassification of documents. The right to claim executive privilege and thus bar the release of records was dramatically extended to previous power holders, as was the power of government bureaucrats to stamp official documents as "classified."[102] In a celebrated case involving Cheney, records of meetings with corporate leaders on energy policy as the administration took office were kept private, forcing a court battle over the right of public access. The available record indicates that Cheney put energy policy in the hands of the largest corporations, in exchange for their contributions to the Republican Party and assurances that they would not lobby to make changes in the administration's legislation.[103] This chumminess extended beyond energy policy. The country's most powerful conservatives in business, religion, and politics were organized as a secret group, the Council for National Policy, to push their agenda. Leading figures in the Bush administration, including Bush himself, attended the council's meetings to brief its members on national policy.[104]

Controlling the policy agenda has always been the administration's chief ambition. During the war on Iraq the US military came up with the idea of "embedding" reporters with military units. Clearly, the Bush administration learned from the Gulf War that too many reporters let loose in the desert, snooping around for independent sources of information, could be hazardous to official policy. Embedding journalists in Iraq often transformed them into instruments of the military, citizen soldiers in their own right. In campaign financing, a report of the Center for Public Integrity noted that executives of companies that received the great majority of US government contracts for work in Afghanistan and Iraq were big-time contributors to the Bush 2000 race, with over $500,000 donated.[105] Whistle blowers on priority national defense matters such as missile defense were ignored and moved out of their jobs. The same arguments used by administrations throughout the Cold War in defense of greater secrecy reemerged—protecting the executive branch's prerogatives, "national security," and officials' right to privacy.

To summarize, the expansionist tendencies inherent in the Bush Doctrine are what made it both radically different from past US strategic perspectives and in company with them. Erasing the line between national defense and national security, and insisting on the right to take unilateral action against threats, were not new to US foreign policy. But stretching the boundaries of preemptive action to embrace preventive war, rejecting deterrence, demoting alliances, putting the United States on a permanent war footing, and firmly believing in the efficacy, necessity, and morality of absolute military preponderance *were* new.[106] In a nutshell, the Bush Doctrine represented an elaboration of traditional doctrine; but in a one-superpower world, such an elaboration amounted to an unprecedented assertion of a US right to global domination. To rephrase the metaphor used by globalist intellectuals in the Clinton years, the United States under Bush was ready to be not just the sheriff of the posse, but the sheriff without one.

Notes

1. Samuel P. Huntington, "The Erosion of American National Interests," in Eugene R. Wittkopf and James M. McCormick, eds., *The Domestic Sources of American Foreign Policy: Insights and Evidence,* 4th ed., pp. 55–65.

2. Krauthammer, "The Unipolar Moment," p. 33. In that article (p. 23) Krauthammer also wrote: "American preeminence [is] based on the fact that it is the only country with the military, diplomatic, political and economic assets to be a decisive player in any conflict in whatever part of the world it chooses to involve itself."

3. Ibid., p. 29.

4. One such critique is by a distinguished Australian diplomat and commentator; see Owen Harries, *Benign or Imperial? Reflections on American Hegemony,* especially pp. 96–102, on Robert Kagan's writings.

5. See Christopher Layne, "From Preponderance to Offshore Balancing: America's Future Grand Strategy," in Brown et al., eds., *America's Strategic Choices,* pp. 249–250.

6. References to this group are based on documents that appear at its Internet site: www.newamericancentury.org.

7. See, for instance, the essay by William Kristol and Robert Kagan, "Reject the Global Buddy System."

8. William Kristol and Robert Kagan, "Toward a Neo-Reaganite Foreign Policy," pp. 18–32.

9. Kagan, "Ticking 'Legacies,'" *Washington Post,* November 5, 2000; online at www.newamericancentury.org/def_natl_sec_018.htm. Even Dick Cheney, a signer of the PNAC principles, came under fire in this article for insisting that leaving Saddam in power in 1991 was the right thing to do.

10. The list of signers and other PNAC principals is in John Feffer, ed., *Power Trip: US Unilateralism and Global Strategy After September 11,* pp. 205–209.

11. www.newamericancentury.org/iraqclintonletter.htm.

12. James Mann, "This Election Has Foreign Affairs Written All Over It," *Washington Post,* October 26, 2003.

13. See William Kristol's *Washington Post* editorial, "For the Defense," August 31, 2000, online at www.newamericancentury.org/def_natl_sec_020.htm.

14. PNAC, "Rebuilding America's Defenses" (September, 2000), cited by Craig Unger, *House of Bush, House of Saud: The Secret Relationship Between the World's Two Most Powerful Dynasties,* p. 211.

15. Fred I. Greenstein, "The Changing Leadership of George W. Bush: A Pre- and Post-9/11 Comparison," in Wittkopf and McCormick, eds., *Domestic Sources,* pp. 353–362.

16. See Ron Suskind, "Without a Doubt," p. 49.

17. Reagan shared his belief in an eventual nuclear Armageddon in the Middle East with a leading California legislator in the 1970s. See James Mills, "The Serious Implications of a 1971 Conversation with Ronald Reagan," pp. 140–141, 258.

18. Alison Mitchell, "Israel Winning Broad Support from US Right," *NYT,* April 21, 2002, online ed.

19. Secretary of State George P. Shultz was the leading proponent of preemptive attack. See his "New Realities and New Ways of Thinking," p. 717.

20. Robert Scheer, "Détente Yields to Nuclear Superiority," *Los Angeles Times,* September 28, 1981, p. 1.

21. Philip Taubman, "US Tries to Back Up Haig on Terrorism," *NYT,* May 3, 1981, p. 1.

22. Bernard Weinraub, "President Accuses 5 'Outlaw States' of World Terror," *NYT,* July 9, 1985, p. 1.

23. Reagan's speech of October 27, 1983, in *NYT,* October 28, 1983, p. 10.

24. See Tom Wicker, "A New Security Mania," *NYT,* October 9, 1981, p. 31.

25. The 46-page classified draft document was officially entitled "Defense Planning Guidance for the Fiscal Years 1994–1999." Excerpts were published in the *NYT*, March 8, 1992, p. 14. Supplementing the excerpts were articles by Patrick E. Tyler on which the following paragraphs are based: "Pentagon Imagines New Enemies to Fight in Post–Cold War Era," *NYT*, February 17, 1992, p. 1, and "US Strategy Plan Calls for Insuring No Rivals Develop," *NYT*, March 8, 1992, p. 1.

26. Patrick E. Tyler, "Senior US Officials Assail Lone Superpower Policy," *NYT*, March 11, 1992, p. 6.

27. Patrick E. Tyler, "Pentagon Drops Goal of Blocking New Superpowers," *NYT*, May 24, 1992, p. 1.

28. At a press conference on March 1, 1992, Bush, saying he had not read the earlier Pentagon draft, proposed that "We are the leaders and we must continue to lead. We must continue to stay engaged. Now that does not preclude working closely with multilateral organizations. For people that challenge our leadership around the world, they simply do not understand how the world looks to us for leadership." *NYT*, March 2, 1992, p. 8.

29. Tyler, "Pentagon Drops Goal."

30. So-called bipartisan statements of national security policy at the time also lent themselves to US unilateralism and preemptive strikes. See, for example, the Commission on Integrated Long-Term Strategy, "Discriminate Deterrence" (January, 1988). The commission was chaired by neoconservatives Fred C. Iklé and Albert Wohlstetter, and included former secretaries of state Henry Kissinger and Zbigniew Brzezinski.

31. See Ivo H. Daalder and James M. Lindsay, *America Unbound: The Bush Revolution in Foreign Policy*, pp. 22–31.

32. Ibid., pp. 36–46. They argue (pp. 46–47) that the neocons are "democratic imperialists" while Bush's "Vulcan" advisers are "assertive nationalists."

33. As Rice said in "Promoting the National Interest" (p. 47), "doing something that benefits all humanity" is a "second-order effect. America's pursuit of the national interest will create conditions that promote freedom, markets, and peace." Her list of five "top priorities" in foreign policy did not contain any reference to promoting US values or institutions; but she did write that "American values are universal . . . the triumph of these values is most assuredly easier when the international balance of power favors those who believe in them."

34. As in the following statement by PNAC writer Gary J. Schmitt: "Rarely, if ever, has any state in modern times held such a commanding position [as the United States does today] and enjoyed a world order as conducive to its own principles. Grand strategy should preserve and, when possible, extend such a secure situation as far as possible into the future. . . . Global preeminence requires a relatively constant exercise of US leadership." ("American Primacy and the Defense Spending Crisis.")

35. Bush's language on this point is almost identical with Rice's in her *Foreign Affairs* article ("Promoting the National Interest," p. 36) cited previously, namely, that the "choice between American ideals and American interests . . . is false."

36. See, for example, the *Weekly Standard* editorial by Kristol and Kagan, "'A Distinctly American Internationalism,'" November 29, 1999, online at www.newamericancentury.org.

37. See Bacevich, *American Empire,* pp. 200–204, for examples of symmetry in Clinton's and Bush's thinking.

38. Dimitri K. Simes, "America's Imperial Dilemma," p. 102.

39. Within the Congress, evangelical Christians and other conservative Republicans formed a group known as the Christian Zionist movement. It is headed by the House Republican majority leader, Tom DeLay of Texas. DeLay's position on the Palestinian-Israeli conflict was to the right of Ariel Sharon, as evidenced in DeLay's opposition to Bush's "roadmap" peace plan of 2003.

40. Bill Keller, "Reagan's Son," pp. 26–31, 42.

41. See the PBS *Frontline* production, "The Jesus Factor," an excellent study of the role of religion in Bush's political rise. Aired April 28, 2004, in Portland, Oregon. See also Daalder and Lindsay, *America Unbound,* pp. 88–89.

42. Suskind, "Without a Doubt," p. 64.

43. Quoted in Bob Woodward, *Bush at War,* p. 45.

44. Aside from Bush himself (CEO of Spectrum 7 and a director of Harken Energy), other senior figures that headed energy companies include Richard Cheney (Halliburton), Secretary of the Treasury Paul O'Neill (Alcoa), and Secretary of Commerce Don Evans (Tom Brown). Others who were closely connected with energy companies include National Security Special Assistant and now Secretary of State Condeleezza Rice (board member of Chevron Oil), Secretary of the Army Thomas White (vice-chairman of Enron Energy Services, the largest single contributor to the Bush campaign), and White House chief counsel Alberto Gonzales (an attorney for Enron). Several Bush appointees had been lobbyists for energy industries, such as White House Chief of Staff Andrew Card (American Automobile Manufacturers Association). A useful listing is provided in "The Big Book of Bush," *Sierra,* pp. 39, 41.

45. These are Otto J. Reich, assistant secretary of state (and later special envoy for Western Hemisphere affairs) and John D. Negroponte, ambassador to the UN, the first US ambassador to post-Saddam Iraq (in 2004), and the first director of national intelligence (in 2005). Late in 2002, two other indicted former officials joined the administration: John M. Poindexter as director of Total (later, Terrorist) Information Awareness in the Pentagon, and Elliott Abrams as senior director for Near East and North African affairs in the National Security Council. In addition, Lino Gutierrez, like Reich, was deeply involved with the Cuban exiles before his State Department appointment in Latin American affairs. (Poindexter was forced to resign in August 2003 after a uniquely harebrained scheme that developed under him was revealed, and withdrawn by the Pentagon leadership: to promote Internet-based funds that terrorism "experts" would purchase in order to speculate about the probability of violent events occurring, such as an assassination.)

46. See, for instance, Michael Swaine, "Reverse Course? The Fragile Turnaround in US-China Relations," pp. 1–7; John Keefe, "A Tale of 'Two Very Sorries' Redux," *Far Eastern Economic Review,* March 21, 2002, pp. 30–33; and Powell's own thoughts on the virtues of diplomacy in that episode in the *Far Eastern Economic Review,* October 28, 2004, p. 16. For the neocons' angry critique of US diplomacy, see Robert Kagan and William Kristol, "A National Humiliation," *The Weekly Standard,* April 15–23, 2001, online ed. at www.new americancentury.org.

47. Powell did say in 1992, in testimony before a House committee: "I want to be the bully on the block" so that the United States would not be challenged militarily. (See Prestowitz, *Rogue Nation,* p. 23.) But that statement suggested use of military power to deter and not to preempt.

48. Knight Ridder Washington Bureau report, "Rumsfeld, Powell at War for Control of US Foreign Policy," May 4, 2003.

49. For example, see Max Boot, *The Savage Wars of Peace: Small Wars and the Rise of American Power;* and Michael Hardt and Antonio Negri, *Empire.*

50. See, for example, Condoleezza Rice's remarks in Nicholas Lemann, "The Next World Order," p. 44, as well as Bush's remark to business executives after 9/11, "We will defeat them [the terrorists] by expanding and encouraging world trade." Quoted by Bacevich, p. 233.

51. Interview with the *New York Times,* October 12, 2001; quoted by Bacevich, *American Empire,* p. 227.

52. See Lewis H. Lapham, "Notebook: Deus Lo Volt," pp. 7–9.

53. Huntington, "The Erosion of American National Interests," p. 65.

54. "If we are an arrogant nation," said Bush, "they'll view us that way. But if we're a humble nation, they'll respect us." Quoted in Prestowitz, *Rogue Nation,* p. 35.

55. Text of the speech in *NYT,* September 21, 2001, p. B4. In November, speaking to US soldiers stationed at Fort Campbell, Kentucky, Bush elaborated: "America has a message for the nations of the world. If you harbor terrorists, you are terrorists. If you train or arm a terrorist, you are a terrorist. If you feed a terrorist or fund a terrorist, you're a terrorist, and you will be held accountable by the United States and our friends." *NYT,* November 22, 2001, p. B2.

56. "Our nation's cause has always been larger than our nation's defense," he said. West Point speech.

57. Speech on February 15, 2002, to the Council on Foreign Relations, excerpted in *NYT,* February 16, 2002, p. A6. Cheney said that terrorism had answered the post–Cold War question of where the supreme threat to the United States lay and what role the United States should play. "Only we can rally the world in a task of this complexity against an enemy so elusive and so resourceful," he said. "The United States and only the United States can see this effort through to victory. This responsibility did not come to us by chance. We are in a unique position because of our unique assets, because of the character of our people, the strength of our ideals, the might of our military and the enormous economy that supports it."

58. David E. Sanger, "Rice Faults Past Administrations on Terror," *NYT,* October 31, 2003, p. A6.

59. See Nicholas Lemann, "The War on What?"

60. Speech to Congress of September 20, 2001; *NYT,* September 21, 2001, p. B4.

61. Speech of March 10, 2002; text in *NYT,* March 11, 2002, online ed.

62. See Donald H. Rumsfeld's comments in *NYT,* June 7, 2002, p. A8, and June 10, 2002, p. A8.

63. David E. Sanger, "Bush to Formalize a Defense Policy of Hitting First," *NYT,* June 17, 2002, p. 1. The "axis of evil" phrase appeared in Bush's State of the Union address in January 2002.

64. Text in *NYT*, September 20, 2002, online ed.

65. *The National Security Strategy of the United States,* p. 1.

66. James Dao, "Powell Defends a First Strike as Iraq Option," *NYT,* September 8, 2002, p. 1.

67. As reported by Elisabeth Bumiller and David E. Sanger ("Threat of Terrorism Is Shaping the Focus of Bush Presidency," *NYT,* September 11, 2002, online ed.), an unnamed Bush adviser said "it's old-fashioned self-protection—and it comes from the president's gut. The example he refers to from time to time is the Cuban Missile Crisis. In his mind, it's got that urgency." Rice was more specific: "Preemption is not a new concept. There has never been a moral or legal requirement that a country wait to be attacked before it can address existential threats. . . . The United States has long affirmed the right to anticipatory self-defense—from the Cuban Missile Crisis in 1962 to the crisis on the Korean Peninsula in 1994." "Condoleezza Rice Discusses President's National Security Strategy," Waldorf Astoria Hotel, New York, October 1, 2002, online at www.whitehouse.gov/news/releases/2002/10/20021001-6.html.

68. See James G. Blight and Peter Kornbluh, *Politics of Illusion: The Bay of Pigs Invasion Reexamined,* and Peter Kornbluh, *Bay of Pigs Declassified: The Secret CIA Report on the Invasion of Cuba.*

69. "Kennedy Sought Dialogue with Cuba," National Security Archive Update, November 24, 2003, online at www.nsarchive.org/NSAEBB/NSAEBB103/index.htm.

70. See Charles W. Kegley Jr. and Gregory A. Raymond, "Preventive War and Permissive Normative Order," pp. 385–394.

71. *DOD Dictionary of Military and Associated Terms* (Department of Defense, April 12, 2002), cited by Jeffrey Record, *Bounding the Global War on Terrorism,* p. 49, n. 51.

72. Interviewed by Lemann, "The Next World Order," pp. 45–46.

73. Quoted in Roger Cohen, "Strange Bedfellows: 'Imperial America' Retreats from Iraq," *NYT,* July 4, 2004 (Week in Review section), online ed.

74. G. John Ikenberry, "America's Imperial Ambition," pp. 44–60.

75. Powell, "A Strategy of Partnerships."

76. Richard Haass said: "The goal of US foreign policy should be to persuade the other major powers to sign on to certain key ideas as to how the world should operate: opposition to terrorism and weapons of mass destruction, support for free trade, democracy, markets. Integration is about locking them into these policies and then building institutions that lock them in even more." Lemann, "The Next World Order," p. 46.

77. Bush said in May 2001: "When we promote open trade, we are promoting political freedom. . . . Look at our friends in Mexico and the political reforms there. Look at Taiwan. Look at South Korea. And someday soon I hope that an American president will end that list by adding, 'Look at China.'" *NYT,* May 8, 2001, online ed.

78. Rumsfeld, "Transforming the Military," p. 27.

79. Ibid., p. 24.

80. David Armstrong, "Dick Cheney's Song of America," pp. 77–78.

81. Interview in *Vanity Fair,* May 9, 2003, at www.defenselink.mil/transcripts/2003/tr20030509-deosecdef0223.html.

82. Klare, "Endless Military Superiority."

83. This often overlooked trend, which Clinton's Kosovo operation made plain, is discussed at length in Bacevich, *American Empire,* Chapter 7.

84. Excerpts from the Nuclear Posture Review Report are at www.global security.org/wmd/library/policy/dod/npr/htm (hereafter, NPR Report). See also Michael Gordon, "US Nuclear Plan Sees New Weapons and New Targets," *NYT,* March 10, 2002, online ed.

85. Based on Stockholm International Peace Research Institute (SIPRI) figures; http://projects.sipri.se/milex/mex_major_spenders.html.

86. Senator Kent Conrad of North Dakota, chairman of the Senate Budget Committee; *NYT,* February 2, 2002, p. A7.

87. SIPRI, "The Major Spenders in 2003," online at www.sipri.se.

88. *NYT,* October 11, 2003, p. A10.

89. See "Vital Statistics: The US Military," in *The Defense Monitor* (Center for Defense Information, Washington, D.C.), vol. 32, No. 5 (November–December, 2003), pp. 1–7.

90. *NYT,* October 1, 2004, p. C2.

91. Thom Shanker, "Global Arms Sales Rise Again, and the US Leads the Pack," *NYT,* August 20, 2001, online ed.

92. *NYT,* October 1, 2004, p. C1.

93. Michael E. O'Hanlon, "A Flawed Masterpiece," p. 61; SIPRI figures on US military expenditures in constant dollars, online at http://first.sipri.org/non_first/result_milex.php?send.

94. Elisabeth Bumiller, "Bush Tells Veterans of Plan to Redeploy G.I.'s Worldwide," *NYT,* August 17, 2004, p. A6. At the time of Bush's announcement, the United States had about 71,500 troops stationed in Germany and nearly 40,000 in South Korea. Final negotiations with an unhappy Korean government led to the announcement late in 2004 that 12,500 US troops would not be withdrawn until 2008.

95. Kurt M. Campbell and Celeste Johnson Ward, "New Battle Stations?"

96. Wesley K. Clark, *Winning Modern Wars: Iraq, Terrorism, and the American Empire.*

97. See, for example, Max Boot, "The New American Way of War," pp. 41–58.

98. The best study of the issue is P. W. Singer, *Corporate Warriors: The Rise of the Privatized Military Industry.*

99. Leslie Wayne, "America's For-Profit Secret Army," *NYT,* October 13, 2002, online ed.

100. Under Reagan the following occurred: approval of a strategy of "disinformation" to disrupt the rule of Qaddafi in Libya; an embargo on news concerning the US invasion of Grenada; limits on reporters' questioning at official functions; use of the US Information Agency to prevent the export or import of films the administration disapproved of by refusing to certify them; establishment of an official government news organization; efforts to stop the broadcasting of unfavorable television programs; and continuation of the practice of CIA-financed "black" news activities to destabilize disliked governments.

101. Keller, "Reagan's Son," p. 30.

102. A good overview of the Bush record is by Adam Clymer, "Government Openness at Issue as Bush Holds on to Records," *NYT,* January 3, 2003, p. A1.

103. See Robert F. Kennedy Jr., *Crimes Against Nature: How George W. Bush and His Corporate Pals Are Plundering the Country and Hijacking Our Democracy,* pp. 97–107. Legal efforts to force disclosure of the records of those meetings ended when a suit was quashed by a US appeals court in May 2005.

104. David D. Kirkpatrick, "Club of the Most Powerful Gathers in Strictest Privacy," *NYT,* August 28, 2004, p. A10.

105. Among the companies were Dell Computer, General Electric, and Halliburton Inc. Edmund L. Andrews and Elizabeth Becker, "Bush Got $500,000 from Companies That Got Contracts, Study Finds," *NYT,* October 31, 2003, p. A8.

106. See David C. Hendrickson, "Toward Universal Empire: The Dangerous Quest for Absolute Security," pp. 1–10; James Chace, "Imperial America and the Common Interest," pp. 1–9.

3

False Pretenses:
The War on Iraq

CONSISTENT WITH THE history of US interventions and alliances in Third World countries, Bush's Iraq policy rested on ideology, self-interest, and opportunism. As this chapter will show, replacing Saddam, a leader once ardently courted by Washington, with a pro-US regime was the name of the game. It was an objective far more important than capturing Osama bin Laden, liberating Iraq's people, or even destroying weapons of mass destruction. In fact, the WMD issue seems clearly to have been a false front, knowingly erected by an administration determined to implement its dogma and display its power. The Bush team rode roughshod over international law and the United Nations, ignoring opportunities for avoiding war in Iraq. When one looks in the mirror of the war on terrorism, consequently, one sees the outline of the war on communism.

Prelude: Pursuing bin Laden

The terrorist attacks on the twin towers of the World Trade Center in New York and on the Pentagon are widely considered to have transformed world politics. Suddenly, the new number-one enemy of the United States became international terrorism, and any country that directly or indirectly supported terrorism was ipso facto a terrorist state subject to US military action. As one historian (and PNAC signatory) put the new "9/11 rules": "we help our friends, punish those who impede us, and annihilate those who attack us."[1] Such hubris was picked up by the conservative press. Only power counts now, the *Wall Street Journal* editorialized. When the United States chooses to display it, everyone else will follow, like it or not.[2] The simplicity of the formula betrayed bad judgment and the tendency to imperial overreach.

Osama bin Laden had been tracked for roughly a decade before the attacks as he made his way from his home country, Saudi Arabia, to Sudan and Afghanistan in search of recruits. It became increasingly clear to US intelligence that his main objective was to rid the Middle East, and Saudi Arabia first of all, of the US presence and the ruling groups that supported it.[3] In August 1996 he publicly declared war on the United States, though the evidence for Al-Qaida's direct involvement in a number of terrorist attacks on US and Saudi interests up to that time—such as the 1993 World Trade Center bombing and the June 1996 truck bombing at the Khobar Towers residential complex in Saudi Arabia—remains murky and circumstantial.[4] From 1996 on, the CIA worked with the so-called Northern Alliance of anti-Taliban fighters in Afghanistan, trying to buy its cooperation in tracking bin Laden down.[5] In August 1998 President Clinton ordered a cruise missile attack on a bin Laden stronghold that was believed to be the scene of a major meeting of Al-Qaida. The attack failed to get him and the tracking continued.

From then on the Clinton administration was in contact with the Taliban leaders in Afghanistan on more than thirty occasions as it sought to get bin Laden deported. The Taliban consistently denied that bin Laden was engaged in terrorist activities or even that they knew where he was. Prior to 9/11, the Bush administration also had contacts with the Taliban, for the same reason and with the same outcome.[6] But neither president made pursuit of Al-Qaida a top-priority US objective, although Clinton in his memoirs says otherwise.[7]

Considering that both administrations saw Al-Qaida behind all of the terrorist attacks just mentioned, and believed that a major Al-Qaida attack on the United States was a distinct possibility, why did it not become the number-one US priority? The question will probably be debated for many years; as hearings before the 9/11 Commission in 2004 brought out, there is more than enough blame to go around.[8] Bush administration officials sought to pin the blame on "structural problems" between the FBI and the CIA that prevented intelligence coordination. But other sources in a position to know argued, and documentation produced by the 9/11 Commission showed, that the administration, up to and including the president, had plenty of advance warning of Al-Qaida's intentions and its capabilities within the United States.[9] The point here, however, is not that the Bush administration was more remiss than previous administrations in failing to move international terrorism to the top of the list of national security concerns. Only if every element of the national security establishment had been riveted on what the intelligence people were saying about Al-Qaida, and only if coordination within the intelligence community had been far superior to what it actually was, might the 9/11 attacks have been prevented.

Rather, I make two contentions here. First is that after 9/11 Al-Qaida and its leader became a legitimate target of international action. Bin Laden later admitted, in tape recordings, his organization's responsibility for the attacks. His plot to commit mass murder against civilians made him guilty of crimes against humanity, prosecutable within the newly established International Criminal Court (which the United States under Bush refused to join). By the end of September 2001 the United States had in hand two strong international endorsements of action against a terrorist group: the UN Security Council, whose Resolution 1368 unanimously called upon all member states to cooperate in denying financing, arms, and safe haven to terrorist groups; and NATO, which agreed to support US action in Afghanistan on the basis, for the first time, that a terrorist attack on the United States constituted an "attack against all" its members.[10] Had the Bush administration responded by leading an international mission, with the Security Council's authorization, to break up Al-Qaida and bring bin Laden to justice, it would have enjoyed nearly universal support. That support would have been all the more forthcoming if the collective response had comprised not only military forces but, even more essentially, intelligence agencies.[11] Arab countries, and all others, would have been hard put to reject a UN and US appeal to act together in the name of international law. Al-Qaida, for all its audacity and success on 9/11, was an isolated organization. Its only possible source of official support may have been Saudi Arabia, though the bipartisan 9/11 Commission concluded that before 9/11 Al-Qaida did not receive support from any government—not Iraq (see below) and not Saudi Arabia. (There is, however, extensive evidence of private financing of Al-Qaida for its extremist teachings in the mosques by Saudi charities and wealthy Saudis who "could both establish their bona fides as good Muslims and even buy 'protection' from militants."[12])

In sum, a coordinated international response was within reach, with the potential to deal Al-Qaida a crushing blow in its mountainous hide-outs in Afghanistan. But the administration made two fatal detours from the objective of eliminating Al-Qaida that undermined the legitimacy of its retaliatory policy. First, the retaliation was unilateral; the Bush administration rejected UN Secretary-General Kofi Annan's proposal for Security Council authorization, arguing that it would not adopt the coalition formula used during the Gulf War.[13] The US aim, clearly, was to avoid "entangling alliances" and ensure that no body interfered with the larger agenda, which was to eliminate not just Al-Qaida but also the Taliban. Anticipating the argument in the *National Security Strategy* paper for preemptive attack, Bush demanded a tough ultimatum to the Taliban, backed by the willingness to use overwhelming force. He not only wanted to intimidate the Taliban; he also wanted to "signal this is a change from the past. We want to cause other countries like Syria and Iran to change their views."[14]

Beyond these purposes lay domestic political considerations: the old need to "show resolve. I had to show the American people the resolve of a commander in chief that was going to do whatever it took to win. No yielding. No equivocation. No, you know, lawyering this thing to death, that we're after 'em."[15] The exercise was not going to be a negotiated outcome in the manner of Clinton's 1994 Agreed Framework with North Korea, which was despised by conservatives because of the bargain it struck with a "rogue state."[16]

We will never know whether or not talking to the Taliban leaders— "lawyering"—would have led to the capture of bin Laden. Various conflict-resolution formats might have been tried for such talks, such as Track II diplomacy and mediation by a third country.[17] Even though Taliban leaders had previously stonewalled the United States on numerous occasions, it is possible that under persistent international pressure they would have made a simple cost-benefit calculation: that bin Laden had become a liability, and that the survival of the regime was not worth the price of continuing to harbor him. Possibly, the international community could have provided incentives to the Taliban to "sweeten the pot." To be sure, the Taliban regime was among the world's most oppressive and least interested in upholding international law. But liberating the Afghani people was not US policy, any more than liberating Iraqis from Saddam would be US policy in 2003. To the contrary, during the Reagan years, US support via Pakistan of the Taliban, which included bin Laden's loyalists, was a matter of record. By including the overthrow of the Taliban in the US intervention's goals, the administration got rid of a brutal regime and responded to domestic outrage in the United States; but in the process it killed perhaps thousands of civilians, reduced an already impoverished, war-torn country to rubble, became committed to democratic nation building (an objective candidate Bush had once disavowed, and which is nowhere in sight today—see the following chapter), and never did succeed at finding bin Laden or decimating Al-Qaida. Al-Qaida's leadership was disrupted and its forces dispersed by the US invasion; but Al-Qaida lived on as a decentralized organization, its anti-Western message reinforced by the US occupation of Iraq.

The further problem with the US reliance on military force to exact revenge for 9/11 is that it convinced many people, and governments, abroad that US priorities in the world were badly skewed. For people concerned about their own government's corruption, ineptitude, unfairness, and oppressiveness, the US invasion of Afghanistan, followed by Iraq, appeared selfish, overzealous, and unbalanced. Here was the United States suddenly asking for worldwide approval of invasions while suffering of far greater proportions than 9/11 was taking place on a daily basis throughout the Third World. Some time after 9/11 Kofi Annan put the matter this way:

> All of us know there are new threats that must be faced or, perhaps, old threats in new and dangerous combinations, new forms of terrorism and the proliferation of weapons of mass destruction. But while some consider these threats as self-evidently the main challenge to world peace and security, others feel more immediately menaced by small arms employed in civil conflict or by so-called soft threats such as the persistence of extreme poverty, the disparity of income between and within societies, and the spread of infectious diseases, or climate change and environmental degradation.[18]

Eyes on the Prize

The other half of the argument here is that Bush slighted the intelligence on Al-Qaida before 9/11 and abandoned an all-out effort to nab bin Laden in Afghanistan in order to go after bigger game, namely the overthrow of Saddam Hussein. Once the goal became regime change in Iraq, many of the key resources that might have flowed into Afghanistan were shifted to Iraq. Then, when the occupation of Iraq began, Al-Qaida was given a new lease on life. Was this because the Bush administration misread the intelligence on Iraq's ties to Al-Qaida? Was it so overwhelmed by the notion of a global terrorist menace that it mistakenly conflated several different kinds of threats into one?[19] Or was the shift to Iraq predetermined by the ideological framework within which the administration operated?

Under George W. Bush, Al-Qaida never really was the main US concern. As none other than L. Paul Bremer III, the later head of the Coalition Governing Authority in Iraq, said several months *before* 9/11: "The new administration seems to be paying no attention to the problem of terrorism. What they will do is stagger along until there's a major incident and then suddenly say, 'Oh, my God, shouldn't we be organized to deal with this?'"[20] In his memoirs, Richard A. Clarke, Bush's (and Clinton's) one-time head of counterterrorism, wrote scathingly about the administration's real agenda. Recalling how the president and his inner circle reacted to the 9/11 attacks, Clarke said he was

> incredulous that we were talking about something other than getting Al Qaeda. Then I realized with almost a sharp physical pain that Rumsfeld and Wolfowitz were going to try to take advantage of this national tragedy to promote their agenda about Iraq. Since the beginning of the administration, indeed well before, they had been pressing for a war with Iraq. My friends in the Pentagon had been telling me that the word was we would be invading Iraq sometime in 2002.[21]

Clarke subsequently testified before the 9/11 Commission that his and other intelligence officials' warnings before September 11, 2001, of a catastrophic terrorist attack in the United States were ignored by Bush administration officials. Just as L. Paul Bremer had said, there was no sense of urgency, and no particular plan to meet the threat.[22] If terrorism had been the true focus of US efforts, Clarke's testimony suggested, the United States would have gone all-out in Afghanistan against Al-Qaida. Among top officials, it appears that only Colin Powell, who warned that the United States would lose its coalition of supporting countries if it expanded the war, argued for putting Al-Qaida first and letting Iraq sit.[23] Consequently, writes Clarke, "When the Taliban and Al-Qaida leaders escaped, [Bush] dispatched fewer US troops for all of Afghanistan than the number of NYPD [New York Police Department] assigned to Manhattan."[24]

Bush himself appeared to be in no hurry to attack Iraq. Woodward's account portrays him as focused on Al-Qaida and getting bin Laden, "dead or alive." At the same time, though, Bush reportedly was on the same page as Rumsfeld, Wolfowitz, and the rest of the national security team in believing that (in Woodward's words) "full-scale war against terrorism would have to make Iraq a target—eventually."[25] Just as Clarke said, the Pentagon had war plans for Iraq, and well before 9/11. The former secretary of the treasury and Alcoa chairman, Paul O'Neill, would later confirm that "From the very beginning, there was the conviction that Saddam Hussein was a bad person and that he needed to go. . . . It was all about finding a way to do it." Planning for Saddam's removal and postwar issues such as control of oil contracts took place during the first months of 2001.[26] Holding off on Iraq thus had nothing to do with indecision within the administration; it was simply a matter of first things first.

Immediately after the 9/11 attacks, the president was insistent that his intelligence staff keep looking for a tie between Iraq and Al-Qaida.

Richard Clarke informed him that "we have looked several times" and come up empty. "'Look into Iraq, Saddam,'" the president said testily and left us."[27] Indeed, all branches of the intelligence community were virtually certain that no ties existed.[28] Yet Wolfowitz and other Pentagon hardliners kept pushing the opposite view.[29] One explanation, a terrorism specialist has suggested, may be "a reluctance to abandon the idea that terrorism had to be state based."[30] Cheney, Rice, and Wolfowitz all reportedly thought that only a state sponsor could have pulled off such a sophisticated attack as 9/11.[31] What we may have here is a classic case of groupthink, a shared consensus among Bush's advisers that terrorism was part of a "sustained, systematic campaign to spread devastation and chaos" (in Rice's words), and that the best way to attack terrorism was to attack the state that was presumed to be "exporting" it (as Cheney reportedly said).[32] Such groupthink mirrored the Cold War pattern for interpreting revolutions and civil wars—seeing terrorism as single minded, schematic, and therefore state centered. Terrorism thus lent itself to a "crusade," Bush reportedly said.[33]

The truth of the matter took a long time to see the light of day. Not until mid-2004 did the 9/11 Commission offer the devastating conclusion that

> to date we have seen no evidence that these or the earlier contacts [between Iraq and Al-Qaida] ever developed into a collaborative operational relationship. Nor have we seen evidence indicating that Iraq cooperated with al Qaeda in developing or carrying out attacks against the United States.[34]

This finding came just days after Vice President Cheney had repeated the canard that Saddam Hussein "had long established ties" with Al-Qaida. What the commission found was a substantial difference between the reception Osama bin Laden received from the Taliban and the one he received from Saddam Hussein. Iraqi officials did meet with bin Laden in Sudan; but Saddam apparently rejected his request to provide training camps and weapons inside Iraq. So it seems did everyone else. But those facts were immaterial for, as Richard Clarke discovered, attacking Iraq "was an idée fixe, a rigid belief, received wisdom, a decision already made and one that no fact or event could derail."[35]

Preparing for Iraq

The Bush *National Security Strategy* paper cautioned that force would not be used "in all cases to preempt emerging threats," and promised that the United States would rely on other governments and regional organizations "whenever possible." But the paper also was emphatic that the United States "will not hesitate to act alone, if necessary." Neocons such as Richard Perle, a former assistant secretary of defense under Reagan before becoming director of Bush's Defense Policy Board, put their weight behind unilateral action.[36] Having previously helped prepare a report to the right-wing Israeli prime minister, Benjamin Netanyahu, that advocated a preemptive strategy for dealing with Israel's neighbors, including Iraq,[37] Perle now pushed hard for preemption as the only way to end Saddam Hussein's rule.[38] In a November 2001 speech, Perle argued that Saddam "has motive and he has means"; he would not be deterred by threat of retaliation; and he was working on nuclear weapons in hundreds of impossible-to-find locations. Reagan, Perle reported, thought Israel's 1981 surprise attack on the Iraqi nuclear reactor at Osirak was "a terrific piece of bombing," and thus was a workable precedent. The real choice is between waiting for Saddam to act and "tak[ing] some preemptive action," Perle said. And Iraq should only be the beginning. Once having made clear that other terrorist states will come to the same end—Perle's message would be, "You're next unless you stop the practice of supporting terrorism"—"there's a reasonable prospect . . . they will decide to get out of the terrorist business. It seems to me a reasonable gamble in any event."

Kenneth M. Pollack represented a second influential opinion on behalf of the neocon cause.[39] Pollack, who had served as director for Gulf affairs on the National Security Council from 1999 to 2002, argued that "a nuclear-armed Saddam" was reason enough for a US invasion of Iraq; his links to terrorism were not. The threat Saddam posed was a future one—that he "might wreak havoc in his region and beyond, together with the certainty that he will acquire such weapons eventually if left unchecked." Containing Saddam through inspections and sanctions was no longer working, according to Pollack. Nor was there any prospect of strengthening either of those tools through the UN system. Deterring Iraq from again attacking its neighbors likewise was unworkable because of Saddam Hussein's "pathologies" as a decisionmaker. Nor, finally, was military support of the Iraqi opposition a practical alternative to directly carrying out regime change. Though, in Pollack's opinion, pursuing Al-Qaida should have had priority over invading Iraq, the United States needed to take care of business in Iraq sooner rather than later. Pollack would later recant some of these views, but by then the damage had been done.[40]

The Bush administration was convinced that unilateral attack required only a presidential decision; the United Nations, international law, allies,

Congress, and the US public could and should be bypassed. Yet the UN Security Council's resolution (under Chapter 7 of the UN Charter) on cooperating in fighting terrorism, passed unanimously at US initiative in late September 2001, neither defined "terrorism" nor endorsed unilateral action by a state against it. The United States rejected Kofi Annan's proposal to seek explicit Security Council endorsement, on the grounds that Washington already had it under the resolution.[41] Such a view went well beyond a reasonable understanding of what international law allows when it comes to the use of force.[42] As for allied opinion, the argument was that since the United States is the chief target of international terrorism, it could not allow other countries to get in the way of its single-minded pursuit of the culprits.[43] The president and other officials were effusive in expressing their gratitude to the seventeen or so countries that deployed military forces in the war in Afghanistan. As Rumsfeld wrote, however, and as preemption implies, surprise is a key element in fighting terrorists. This was no time for making war "by committee."[44]

NATO allies that understood the US commitment to multilateralism to mean genuine collaboration on the basis of equality and in the search for peace were sorely disappointed.[45] They had apparently forgotten that in Washington's view, the United States was indispensable but they were not. And if they did forget, officials such as Cheney reminded them:

> America has friends and allies in this cause, but only we can lead it. Only we can rally the world in a task of this complexity against an enemy so elusive and so resourceful. The United States and only the United States can see this effort through to victory.[46]

US allies were already at odds with Washington over Bush's tendency to take its own road on international issues, such as the Kyoto Protocol on global warming, capital punishment, and nuclear weapons testing. But Iraq pushed tensions over the top. The European Union's (EU) fifteen members officially threw their full weight behind working through the UN to disarm Iraq. Their statement reminded the United States that "force should be used only as a last resort. It is for the Iraqi regime to end this crisis by complying with the demands of the Security Council."[47] The French foreign minister was moved to say that Europe was "threatened by a new simplistic approach that reduces all the problems in the world to the struggle against terrorism."[48] Such criticisms could be heard around the Middle East as well, even by strong supporters of the United States such as Crown Prince Abdullah of Saudi Arabia. He argued that the emerging war on terror was overshadowing Israel's repression of the Palestinians, making it hard for Arab states to support a war on Iraq.[49] Abdullah proposed a peace plan: Israel would be given full diplomatic recognition and security guarantees by all the Arab states in return for restoration of the pre-June 1967 war borders. The proposal apparently was never seriously pursued.

The problem posed for other countries came down to this: How could a superpower that believed it was unconstrained to act alone be stopped?

"Blind and Improvident"

The Logic of War and the Politics of Threat

> If we know Saddam Hussein has dangerous weapons today—and we do—does it make any sense for the world to wait to confront him as he grows even stronger and develops even more dangerous weapons?
> —*President Bush,* October 7, 2002

Deceit and cover-ups are part and parcel of the "business" of a superpower's foreign policy. Their origins can be traced to the 1950s, when the US government decided that any and all means to combat international communism were legitimate. Instances of playing fast and loose with the truth and the law were therefore commonplace. Truman lied about Soviet involvement in the Greek civil war when he announced the containment policy. Eisenhower lied about outside intervention in Lebanon when he dispatched marines there in 1958. To justify CIA intervention, he also lied about a communist threat to Iran in 1953 and to Guatemala in 1954. Kennedy lied about Castro's threat to the United States and Latin America in the early 1960s, and covered up Operation Mongoose, which involved numerous attempts to assassinate Castro. Johnson lied about a second North Vietnamese attack in the Gulf of Tonkin in 1964 in order to clear the way for a US bombing campaign. He never revealed provocative US aerial surveillance operations over North Vietnam at that time. Nixon covered up the secret bombing of Cambodia for which, had he not resigned, he probably would have been impeached. Carter lied about human rights conditions in Iran under his one-time friend, the shah, and lied again when he said in 1979 that the United States would not repeat the error of Vietnam by interfering in Iran's internal affairs. Reagan lied about Soviet nuclear weapons superiority and Nicaragua's threat in Central America. Faced with congressional restrictions, he covered up a global network of secret programs to finance the contras. The George H. W. Bush administration lied about giving sanctions a chance to work in Iraq. And Clinton lied about the Rwanda genocide by refusing to call it that.

The evidence concerning policymaking on Iraq under George W. Bush strongly suggests outright efforts to deceive the US public, Congress, and the world community. Bush's policy team did not merely misread the intelligence on Iraq's military capabilities and intentions. Nor was it misled by the intelligence. Just as had happened so often during the Vietnam War, top policymakers under Bush substituted their own, politically motivated judgments for the findings and uncertainties of the professionals who were charged with providing and assessing intelligence. The administration's purpose was to eliminate Saddam; that end justified twisting the "war on terror" to serve a wholly different objective. Just as Richard Perle argued soon after 9/11, the difficulties of removing Saddam were nothing in comparison with the opportunities: "look at what could be created, what could be organized, what could be made cohesive with the power and authority of the United States fresh from a successful campaign to destroy the Taliban in Afghanistan." America, sheriff of the posse; mount up! There were constraining factors, of course: the 2002 elections, which would favor the Democrats by focusing on the poor performance of the economy; Enron and other corporate scandals; the faltering nation-building effort in Afghanistan; the gradual weakening of support in Congress for further military adventures in the absence of new terrorist attacks; and the buildup of opposition to a war on Iraq in foreign capitals.[50] The key problem was therefore how to sell the war on Iraq to Congress and the people of the United States.

Lost in all the post-9/11 anxieties and the rush to retribution was dispassionate analysis of US interests in the Middle East and the nature of the presumed Iraq threat. Only the most critical voices noted that Iraq had been treated as anything but a threat in the 1980s, when Saddam's war with Iran served US purposes.

The United States and Iraq in the 1980s

The documentary record concerning policy in the Reagan years provides damning evidence of the extent to which Washington went to find favor with Saddam's regime, much in the manner of Nixon's and Kissinger's support of General Pinochet after the 1970 coup in Chile.[51] Reagan's "tilt" toward Iraq during its terribly costly war with Iran that would ultimately claim about one million lives was motivated by both power-political and economic reasons: Saddam's hostility toward Iran, the main US enemy in the Persian Gulf; his usefulness in keeping oil prices low; Iraq's market for US goods; and the opportunity through engagement to deflect his hatred of Israel and his rivalry with Saudi Arabia. During the 1980s, the administration, supported by members of Congress, rejected imposing sanctions on Iraq, arguing that Saddam could be worked with and seeing trade opportunities as a useful vehicle for engaging his interest. In removing Iraq in 1982 from the list of countries believed to be supporting terrorism, and then resuming full diplomatic relations in 1984, the Reagan administration accepted Iraq's assurances that it would end support of terrorists they were harboring. Thus, as mentioned earlier, Reagan did not include Iraq in the "confederation of terrorist states." The State Department overrode lower-level bureaucrats in the Export-Import Bank and elsewhere who questioned (though not on moral grounds) official policy.

Under Reagan, every opportunity to send Saddam a tough message was bypassed. Instead, the administration provided his regime with substantial agricultural credits, loan guarantees for purchasing US exports, satellite intelligence on Iranian troop deployments and bombing targets, and equipment and technologies with military value. So open was the aid spigot that a US government agency unwittingly sent Iraq biological samples that found their way into Iraq's germ-warfare program. US economic aid easily transferred to Iraq's military budget.[52] The administration brushed aside the complaints of those few members of Congress who urged sanctions in response to Iraq's notorious human rights record and use of poison gas against Iran. Secretary of State Shultz did condemn Iraq for using poison gas against its Kurdish minority in 1988. But when it came to Iraq's use of chemical weapons against Iran, which they knew of in advance, he and his colleagues had nothing to say, so desperate were they to block an Iranian victory.[53]

The Reagan administration's coddling of Saddam was just fine with Bechtel Corporation and other US businesses that had plans for energy and other major projects, though an oil pipeline scheme ultimately failed. Bechtel, Shultz's former firm, decided to use "non-US suppliers of [chemical] technology and continue to do business in Iraq," according to a confidential cable from the US ambassador.[54] Just as Kissinger had assured Iraq's foreign minister in 1975 that there was no "basic clash of national interests" between the two countries,[55] various Reagan administration officials—including Vice President Bush and Donald Rumsfeld, who visited Saddam as a special US envoy in December 1983 and March 1984—assured Saddam of the US desire to improve relations.

He was urged not to regard public US criticism of chemical weapons as an anti-Iraq act.[56]

In short, the United States once again "waltzed" with a dictator. If Saddam was not exactly a creature of the United States, he was certainly considered a friendly asset—so long as he could be bought off. It can hardly be coincidental that some of the same US officials who carried out the policy of nurturing Saddam in the 1980s later led the way to eliminating him in 2003. Saddam, like other US-supported dictators before him, had moved from the friendly to the enemy side of the ledger. His interest in weapons of mass destruction, once of little concern in Washington, suddenly was presented as worth going to war over.

Selling the War and Massaging the Evidence

By the time congressional hearings on Iraq got under way in August 2002, the US military was widely reported as being actively engaged in war planning. The reason? By then if not before, Bush had made the decision for war. A secret memorandum of July 23, 2002, that was leaked to the British press—now known as the Downing Street Memo—makes crystal clear that Bush decided on war eight months prior to the invasion and three months prior to a congressional vote on going to war. Classified as "Secret and Strictly Personal—UK Eyes Only," and further marked "extremely sensitive," the memorandum of a meeting of Prime Minister Tony Blair and his top aides states:

> C [the head of British intelligence, Sir Richard Wilson] reported on his recent talks in Washington. There was a perceptible shift in attitude. Military action was now seen as inevitable. Bush wanted to remove Saddam, through military action, justified by the conjunction of terrorism and WMD. But the intelligence and facts were being fixed around the policy. The NSC had no patience with the UN route, and no enthusiasm for publishing material on the Iraqi regime's record. There was little discussion in Washington of the aftermath after military action.[57]

Not only does the memorandum show that all the top US leaders (whom Wilson met while in Washington) were committed to war early on. It also undermines the notion that the failure to find WMD was exclusively an intelligence failure; Bush's policy determined "the intelligence and facts." Nothing was going to be allowed to get in the way of that policy, even though—as the document goes on to state—"the [US] desire for regime change was not a legal base for military action" and "the case was thin. Saddam was not threatening his neighbours, and his WMD capability was less than that of Libya, North Korea or Iran." The document also validates the accounts of Clarke and O'Neill, which give mid-2002 as the actual time of the decision for war.

The official case for war was indeed thin on evidence. Regarding Iraq's supposed connections to terrorism and to Al-Qaida in particular, the administration offered a number of unproven (but suitably alarming) assertions—not at the hearings, significantly, but in public speeches. Rumsfeld offered as "bulletproof" evidence, for example, that "some" Al-Qaida members had been in Baghdad at one time and had received "possible chemical- and biological-agent training" by Iraq.[58] Bush said that Al-Qaida members had been trained in Iraq "in bomb-making and poisons and deadly gases," and that "alliances with terrorists could allow the Iraqi regime to attack America without leaving any finger-prints."[59] The administration's case concerning Iraq's WMD capabilities was equally weak. Bush's most memorable accusation, made in his 2002 State of the Union address, became known as the sixteen-word fiasco. He said that "the British government has learned that Saddam Hussein recently sought significant quantities of uranium from Africa." This was a reference to an alleged sale in Niger of so-called yellow cake ore that never took place. In later speeches, Bush argued that Iraq posed a direct threat to the United States, and that Iraq's possession of WMD would enable it to dominate its neighbors.[60]

Everyone in Bush's inner circle contributed to dramatizing, and overstating, the Iraq threat. Secretary Powell, in a much-ballyhooed pre-sentation before the UN Security Council on February 5, 2003, con-tended that Iraq possessed hundreds of tons of chemical and biological agents, an ongoing nuclear weapon program, and the means to deliver these weapons. (Powell would later say how much he regretted these exaggerations of the evidence.) Cheney portrayed Iraq as "reconstitut-ing its nuclear weapons program" (August 7, 2002) and seeking to be in a position to "subject the United States or any other nation to nuclear blackmail" (August 26, 2002). His sources were mainly Iraqi exiles on the Pentagon payroll, people with no inside or current knowledge of Iraq's WMD programs but with political ambitions and every reason to tell their benefactors exactly what they wanted to hear.[61] At the very time in fall 2002 that the government's nuclear experts, notably in the Depart-ment of Energy, as well as British intelligence, were dismissing a central piece of evidence in the administration's case—aluminum tubes Iraq had imported, not for use in uranium centrifuges (as some CIA analysts contended) but in rockets—Cheney was insisting the administration had "irrefutable evidence" that Iraq was "actively and aggressively seeking to acquire nuclear weapons" and Rice was telling CNN that the tubes were "only really suited for nuclear weapons programs."[62]

A key source for these mistaken views, though far from the only one, was a National Intelligence Estimate (NIE) that the administration's top intelligence officers completed in October 2002. Their overall conclusion: "Since [UN] inspections ended in 1998, Iraq has maintained its chemical weapons effort, energized its missile program, and invested heavily in biological weapons; in the view of most [US] agencies, Baghdad is reconstituting its nuclear weapons program."[63] Nearly two years later a US Senate committee on intelligence would lambaste the intelligence community for overstating Iraq's WMD capabilities in the NIE, for using dated information that led to misinforming top US leaders, for ignoring contrary evidence, and for failing to challenge the NIE's assumptions. The NIE's authors were guilty of "groupthink," the bipartisan Senate committee concluded.[64] Yet for all its exaggerations, the NIE did contain several important qualifications. For example, the document noted a "lack [of] specific information on many key aspects of Iraq's WMD programs," and Iraq's need of "sufficient weapons-grade fissile material" to make a nuclear bomb, without which it could probably not make one until 2007 at the earliest. (The State Department's Intelligence and Research Unit, in a crucial footnote, maintained that while it believed Iraq was making "at least a limited effort" to acquire nuclear weapons, there was no "compelling case [for] an integrated and comprehensive approach" by Iraq to doing so. State joined with the Department of Energy's experts in arguing that Iraq's acquisition of aluminum tubes, which the administration's hawks were then insisting was a clear sign of an active nuclear weapons program via uranium enrichment, were not intended for that purpose.) And although the intelligence estimate erred in stating that Iraq possessed chemical and biological stockpiles and expertise, and therefore had a significant capability to produce weapons, Iraq was not said to have yet weaponized these materials. Especially noteworthy was the intelligence community's judgment that Saddam Hussein would most probably not use WMD except in various circumstances of self-defense, such as "after an initial [US] advance into Iraqi territory"; nor was he judged likely to provide terrorists with WMD unless an attack on Iraq threatened the survival of his regime.

What the Senate investigators failed to do was take account of how US policymakers treated the NIE and related intelligence assessments of Iraq. By limiting their conclusion to the view that the "Intelligence Community did not accurately or adequately explain to policymakers the uncertainties behind" the NIE,[65] the Senate committee let Bush and his team off the hook. In reality, they cherry-picked from some evidence and "massaged" the rest in order to buttress decisions on war already made. Top US decisionmakers surely knew, for instance, that one of its main sources in support of Iraq's supposed WMD threat, General Hussein Kamel, who was in overall charge of WMD programs until he defected, had told senior figures in the UN Special Commission on Iraq (UNSCOM) in 1995: "I ordered destruction of all chemical weapons. All weapons—biological, chemical, missile, nuclear were destroyed." Only a few missile launchers and some chemical weapons components were kept, Kamel said.[66] Bush's Defense Intelligence Agency concluded in September 2002: "There is no reliable information on whether Iraq is producing and stockpiling chemical weapons."[67]

By 1998, when UNSCOM was kicked out of Iraq amidst accusations by Baghdad (which proved correct) that CIA operatives were part of the inspection teams, UNSCOM's chief inspector, a US Navy intelligence officer, was convinced that "the vast majority" of Iraq's unconventional weapons capability had been destroyed. "What was left, if anything, represented nothing more than documents and scraps of material," not enough to reconstitute a WMD program.[68] A nuclear threat from Iraq was not even mentioned in the CIA director's January 2002 review of worldwide nuclear proliferation problems; the review referred only to probable "low-level theoretical R&D [research and development] associated with its nuclear program." The Bush team surely knew—and did not have to wait for the final verdict that the president's own Iraq Survey Group (ISG) under Charles A. Duelfer would deliver in October 2004—that during 1991 and 1992 Saddam Hussein had decided to abandon his WMD program in hopes of ending the sanctions.[69] In short, as two specialists later concluded, "it now appears that intelligence agencies and policymakers disregarded considerable evidence of the destruction and deterioration of Iraq's weapons programs, the result of a successful strategy of containment in place for a dozen years."[70]

Intelligence or Public Relations?

Deliberate distortion and selective use of information were only part of the story of the administration's deceptions. The real game in Washington was the hardliners' persistent pressure on the intelligence community to produce findings that would support their two-edged charges concerning Iraq's WMD and its ties to Al-Qaida.[71] Their problem was that even the evidence partial to their cause did not justify portraying Iraq as an imminent threat. With opinion polls a year after 9/11 showing no taste for war with Iraq, the administration had to exaggerate the intelligence so as to bring around both public and congressional opinion. As the account of Judis and Ackerman states:

> Had the administration accurately depicted the consensus within the intelligence community in 2002—that Iraq's ties with Al Qaeda were inconsequential; that its nuclear weapons program was minimal at best; and that its chemical and biological weapons programs, which had yielded significant stocks of dangerous weapons in the past, may or may not have been ongoing—it would have had a very difficult time convincing Congress and the American public to support a war to disarm Saddam.

It took several months, but the administration won the battle by attacking on two fronts. First, Rumsfeld and Wolfowitz, unhappy with what the CIA and Defense Intelligence Agency (DIA) were turning out, relied on their own intelligence team to evaluate the Iraq threat. The Office of Special Plans (OSP) had been established in the Pentagon within a month of the 9/11 attacks. Douglas J. Feith, an undersecretary of defense and another longtime neocon warrior, was put in charge of the secret office.[72] It was to Feith and his colleagues that the Iraqi exiles loyal to Ahmad Chalabi and his Iraqi National Congress fed their exaggerations. The CIA, which had ended its relationship with the Iraqi National Congress (INC) in 1995, was sidelined.[73] Feith, apparently without the knowledge of the director of central intelligence, George J. Tenet, briefed senior aides to Cheney and Bush about the supposed Al-Qaida–Iraq connection, disparaging the CIA's uncertain views on the subject and substituting his (Feith's) own.[74]

On a second front, the neocons directly and indirectly pressured the intelligence community to toe the official line. Cheney paid several visits to CIA headquarters. Perle was outspoken in his criticism of the agency's work on Iraq. Feith's office ignored CIA efforts to correct or delete disputed statements, and apparently used different evidence when presenting its case on an Al-Qaida–Iraq connection to senior Pentagon and White House officials than when dealing with CIA colleagues.[75] Leaks to the press, such as about the aluminum tubes, added to the war hawks' hemming-in operation. Senior officials such as Rice appeared on news programs to parade information that was not simply one-sided but also dishonest, since it was presented as though beyond dispute.[76]

Publication of the declassified version of the NIE, which omitted most of the qualifications of the official line, and Bush's Cincinnati speech, with its horrendous exaggerations of Iraq's WMD and the threat posed to the United States, had the desired effect on public opinion. Polls in November showed a huge shift in favor of invading Iraq and in support of the administration's contentions regarding Iraq. While public support faded again during ensuing months, the administration had established a strategy for capturing it that it would use successfully up to the time of the invasion: keep overstating the dimensions of the Iraqi threat, keep the intelligence community under wraps, and don't allow the UN or allies to get in the way of US purposes.[77] The public only got a hint of the debate that was going on within the administration before the war. One such came when Tenet, true to the NIE cited above, contradicted the official insistence that Iraq might strike the United States first—contending that the far greater probability was that Saddam Hussein would use WMD only in response to an attack.[78] But otherwise, Tenet played the good soldier, as when he reportedly assured the president that finding Iraq's WMD was "a slam-dunk case!"[79] Only many months later would he tell a Senate committee that he had personally spoken with Cheney (and by implication others) on several occasions in order to correct the "misconstruing [of] intelligence," but to no avail.[80] Tenet therefore must share responsibility for politicizing intelligence reports; but in the main he was the fall guy for an intelligence failure that really began in the White House.

The issue is not that Saddam Hussein had no intention of one day acquiring WMD capabilities. The International Atomic Energy Agency (IAEA), the principal arm of the UN for reporting on nuclear activities and conformity with the 1968 Nuclear Nonproliferation Treaty (NPT), had established the existence of an Iraqi nuclear weapons program in 1990, at the time of Iraq's invasion of Kuwait. A UN investigation in 2005 established that Saddam skimmed $1.8 billion from the oil-for-food program to acquire conventional weapons and hoped that an end to UN sanctions would provide the opportunity to try again to gain a WMD capability. Nor is there reason to doubt that Saddam's regime had once had contacts with Al-Qaida operatives, given their common hostility to the Saudi government, Israel, and the United States. But as became apparent after the invasion, Iraq had by 2003 either destroyed or never possessed the WMD attributed to it. Its ambitions with respect to WMD exceeded its capabilities; and its intentions never, so far as is known, were such as would have posed the "mortal threat" to the United States that Vice President Cheney ascribed to Iraq.

Nor had Iraq had operational dealings with Al-Qaida. Notwithstanding their shared belief in repression at home and violence against US interests abroad, Saddam's Iraq and Al-Qaida were fundamentally different political phenomena: the one, a dictatorship based on state power and nationalism; the other, an absolutist transnational religious movement. Osama bin Laden was on record as having a low regard for Saddam Hussein; one of his top lieutenants, captured by US forces, "told the C.I.A. that Mr. bin Laden rejected the idea of working with Mr. Hussein, a secular leader whom Mr. bin Laden considered corrupt and irredeemable."[81] Saddam, perhaps concerned that ties with Al-Qaida would make his regime even more of a target for a US attack, had reason to steer clear of Al-Qaida. Not until December 2003, however, was the canard of an Iraq–Al-Qaida connection finally put to rest when the administration's most important evidence for it—a supposed meeting in Prague between an Iraqi intelligence official and the presumed leader of the World Trade Center attack—collapsed.[82]

The UN inspectors who were able to return to Iraq after the Security Council in November 2002 passed Resolution 1441—in which Iraq was declared to be in "material breach" of its past promises—found nothing to indicate an imminent Iraqi WMD threat or emerging WMD capabilities. Mohamed ElBaradei, head of the IAEA, reported: "We have to date [late January 2003] found no evidence that Iraq has revived its nuclear weapon program since the elimination of the program in the 1990's."[83] Hans Blix, head of the UN Monitoring, Verification and Inspection Commission (UNMOVIC) in Iraq for chemical and biological weapons, reported on areas of uncooperativeness by Iraqi officials; but he disputed a number of specific allegations by the Bush administration concerning Iraq's violations as well as its links to Al-Qaida. There were any number of reasons that might explain why Iraq preferred to maintain the impression that it had some kind of WMD program ongoing when in fact it had none, Blix concluded.[84] He was emphatic that continuing inspections and diplomacy were preferable to war.[85] Some senior US military figures backed him up, doubtless reflecting reported resistance to going to war among some of the top brass.[86] Said one retired four-star US general: "It's a question of what's the sense of urgency here, and how soon would we need to act unilaterally? So far as any of the information has been presented, there is nothing that indicates that in the immediate, next hours, next days, that there's going to be nuclear-tipped missiles put on launch pads to go against our forces or our allies in the region."[87]

Dispensable Partners: Congress, the UN, and Allies

Opposition in Congress to attacking Iraq was carefully circumscribed by the 9/11 attacks. The legalities, not to mention the ethics, of going to war were hardly debated. Even if members of Congress had wanted to assert their constitutional prerogative and enforce the 1993 War Powers Resolution (WPR), their hands were tied by precedent. Well before 2001, the WPR had been treated as an unwanted orphan of the 1970s. Unable to repeal it, various administrations tried their best to ignore its key provisions, notably one that starts a 60-day "clock" when US forces become involved in "hostilities" that are "imminent." Presidents are required not merely to report such involvement; they must withdraw US forces within 60 days unless Congress specifically authorizes an extension.

Presidents found that by deploying the military but not sending it into battle, they could avoid starting the 60-day clock. They could thus put forces in the field to fight or threaten brief wars using overwhelming firepower without the need to refer to the WPR. This is what George H. W. Bush did in 1990, building up US forces in Saudi Arabia well before the first bombs fell on Baghdad, all the while maintaining that their purpose was to defend that country. George W. Bush did the same thing in 2002, quietly mobilizing the military and acquiring access points within striking distance of Iraq months before the first attack on March 20, 2003. Congress consistently authorized funds to support these moves. But both presidents Bush failed to seek authorization from Congress for making war—just as Truman had failed to do for Korea, Kennedy for Vietnam, and Clinton for Haiti, Bosnia, Somalia, and Kosovo.[88] For its part, Congress never started the 60-day clock to force the president's hand.

To be sure, the War Powers Resolution was mentioned in the congressional authorizing resolutions in 1991 and 2002. These required that the president report to the Congress on progress in the war; but the resolutions did not say that the 60-day clock would start. Nor did either Bush go to Congress in deference to the WPR. Both asked for congressional endorsement of their troop deployments while claiming that they actually had all the authority they needed to make war. Bush the elder felt compelled to go to Congress because he (rightly) feared a political rebellion if he didn't. Public opinion in 1990–1991 was divided on going to war, and hearings in Congress had established that opposition to war had spread to members of the foreign policy elite, civilian and military. As for George W. Bush, he probably sought congressional approval out of a political sense that obtaining it would be useful to generating greater public support for prosecuting the war. What differentiated George W. Bush from his father and all other predecessors is that whereas they at least drew on UN Security Council resolutions as part of their authority to act—for example, the authorization of the UN to use force if Saddam Hussein failed to withdraw from Kuwait by January 15, 1991—George W. Bush ignored the UN.

The House and Senate committed the same mistake after 9/11 that it had made early in the Vietnam War, and again in 1991 and 1992, when it approved resolutions on the use of force that were wide open to abuse. In September 2001 Senate and House resolutions gave President Bush a virtual blank check—first, by authorizing use of "all necessary and appropriate force" to combat terrorism, without any geographical or time limits; second, by asserting that the president "has authority under the Constitution to take action to deter and prevent acts of international terrorism against the United States"; and third, by tying the 9/11 attacks to Iraq and resolving that Iraq's refusal to allow full UN inspection of Iraq's weapons sites presented "a mounting threat to the United States, its friends and allies, and international peace and security."[89]

Some Republican leaders in Congress argued that Bush thus had all the authority he needed to wage war on Iraq.[90] Various Bush administration spokespersons went further, suggesting that even those resolutions were unnecessary, since UN Security Council resolutions during the Gulf War and congressional support at that time still applied in 2002. Congress was thus well on the way to being shut out, quite literally. Yet few members complained. One who did, Senator Robert C. Byrd, decried as "dangerous nonsense" the view that Congress had no right to question administration strategy. "To question is not to accuse or to condemn," he wrote. "To question is to seek the truth. The less forthcoming a president is, the more Congress will have to probe for answers."[91] In a later speech he decried the haste with which his colleagues were supporting a decision for war: "blind and improvident," he called it.[92] But the Bush administration felt no compulsion to be forthcoming. And Democrats, most of whom remained compliant in the face of war, had only themselves to blame.

Having reluctantly accepted the need for congressional approval of war making, Bush in late September 2002 submitted a resolution to Congress (Senate Joint Resolution 46) that authorized him to

> use all means that he determines to be appropriate, including force, in order to enforce the United Nations Security Council Resolutions [of 1990–1991], defend the national security interests of the United States

against the threat posed by Iraq and restore international peace and security in the region.[93]

The final version closely followed that language and, as in 2001, tied it to the WPR only with respect to reporting requirements.[94] This "Authorization for the Use of Military Force Against Iraq" followed by only four days Bush's October 2002 speech in Cincinnati in which he grossly exaggerated the threat posed by Iraq. After several days of "debate"—speechmaking, in fact—the House of Representatives voted 296–133 in favor and the Senate voted 77–23. (More Democrats favored than opposed the measure in the Senate; the opposite was true in the House.) The vote was considerably more lopsided than the one given Bush's father on January 12, 1991, that backed his decision for war against Iraq.[95] Once again, Congress allowed a president to define national security in the broadest possible sense, evade the intended restraints of the War Powers Resolution, and have free rein to use military power in the manner and to the extent the president wished. It was, as Senator Patrick J. Leahy of Vermont said, an extraordinary "surrender to the president [of] authority which the Constitution explicitly, explicitly reserves for the Congress."[96]

The United Nations and allied opinion were the only potential remaining barriers to US war policy. The fact that US diplomats, with assistance from US and British spying on foreign UN delegations,[97] lobbied hard to win Security Council endorsement spoke to the preference for acting with the UN's seal of approval. But Bush had warned a year after the 9/11 attacks that the United States would act if the UN did not disarm Iraq, and (in a speech before the General Assembly) if it did not, the UN would become "irrelevant." Secretary-General Annan pointedly criticized countries that chose to act multilaterally only when it was politically convenient to do so. "There is no substitute for the unique legitimacy provided by the United Nations," he said.[98] Resolution 1441 met most of the US demands, but it did not endorse war on Iraq, which is why Annan, in an interview with the BBC in September 2004, said the US decision to wage war was "illegal."

Iraq responded to Annan's entreaties by offering international inspection "without preconditions." In December 2002 Saddam Hussein told his top subordinates that they should "cooperate completely" with UN inspectors.[99] But Bush and his advisers were not merely skeptical; they pushed in the Security Council for a tight one-week deadline for Iraq's agreement to unfettered access. The draft resolution proposed by the United States virtually guaranteed Iraq's rejection and, as the French and others were well aware, made an invasion almost certain. The Bush administration seems to have deliberately withheld intelligence from the UN inspectors in order to support its case that only an invasion could uncover the truth about Iraq's WMD capabilities. Although US officials had assured Congress that the UN inspectors had been provided with a complete list of all the major suspected Iraqi WMD locations, it later emerged that the CIA in fact had omitted about twenty-one of 105 such sites. The CIA's response to this revelation—that it tried to provide information only on the most "fruitful" sites to search—rings hollow.[100] In the context of Bush administration efforts to discount the UN inspections and clear the way for an invasion, there is every reason to believe that it simply did not want the inspections to succeed.

Leaders of the EU countries and their publics distanced themselves from US policy. Germany's Prime Minister Gerhard Schröder firmly rejected participating in an attack on Iraq even if the UN Security Council approved it. His defense minister announced that if an attack occurred, Germany would withdraw its counter-WMD force from Afghanistan. French Prime Minister Jacques Chirac said US policy on Iraq was "extraordinarily dangerous" and warned that such unilateralism would, among other consequences, intensify anti-American feelings worldwide.[101] German, British, and other EU-member opinion polls indicated broad opposition to war with Iraq. Only Britain's Prime Minister Tony Blair was supportive, even as many in his party were not.

Among US Middle East allies, antiwar feelings were just as prominent. "Just open a map," a member of the Kuwaiti royal family described as being close to Washington decisionmakers said. "Afghanistan is in turmoil, the Middle East is in flames, and you want to open a third front in the region?"[102] If, as Prince Abdullah averred, Al-Qaida's purpose was to drive a wedge between the United States and Saudi Arabia, it was succeeding.[103] Responding to widely reported administration comments about using bases in friendly countries for the invasion, King Abdullah II of Jordan vowed that "Jordan will not be used as a launching pad."[104] Even Pakistan's president, Pervez Musharraf, whose government no more welcomed international inspection of its nuclear facilities than did Iraq, said on several occasions that an invasion of Iraq was unwise. In fact, he insisted that US military aid was foisted on his army against his wishes, and that the invasion was not supported in the Muslim world. He was being put in a difficult spot politically, he said, and therefore he would only send peacekeeping troops to Iraq under UN auspices.[105] Only the Turkish government, beset by economic problems and desperate for debt relief and membership in the European Union, was willing to consider allowing the United States to use air bases (but not deployment of ground forces) in the event of a war with Iraq.[106] Yet even Ankara's parliament, in an unexpected display of democratic decisionmaking, voted against allowing US forces to use Turkish territory for the invasion of Iraq. Once the UN Security Council voted to demand Iraq's compliance with its disarmament resolutions, however, every Middle East government except Turkey acquiesced to US pressure that its territory be available for war on Iraq. All those governments could do was voice their hope that the war would be brief and not result in Iraq's being carved up.

The Intelligence Game Revealed

Unwilling to make the case for regime change to the public on the basis of Saddam Hussein's actual behavior and capabilities, the Bush administration concocted a tale of imminent threat. In a word, it fit the facts to the thesis and discarded or ignored those that did not fit. The reality was that:

- Iraq once had programs or aspirations to develop weapons of mass destruction, not actual stockpiles. Prior UN inspections were among the factors that had convinced Saddam Hussein to abandon his WMD dream.
- Iraq did not present an imminent threat: It had no demonstrated plans to use WMD against its neighbors or anyone else.
- The intelligence community both carefully qualified and mistakenly exaggerated elements of Iraq WMD capabilities.
- The invasion of Iraq was principally the result of a deliberate administration effort to exaggerate Iraq's intentions as well as its capabilities—the same flaw, ideologically motivated, that has plagued US national security planning ever since NSC-68,[107] but until Iraq, without leading to preventive war.

The crumbling of the official case for war only became plain, however, after Saddam was overthrown. The administration's case started to unravel when some CIA, State Department, and other intelligence professionals complained that they had come under pressure to amass and dramatize only information that would "prove" Iraq's possession of WMD.[108] As two *Washington Post* reporters concluded after interviewing some key US officials and viewing previously undisclosed evidence:

The new information indicates a pattern in which President Bush, Vice President Cheney and their subordinates—in public and behind the scenes—made allegations depicting Iraq's nuclear weapons program as more active, more certain and more imminent in its threat than the data they had would support. On occasion administration advocates withheld evidence that did not conform to their views. The White House seldom corrected misstatements or acknowledged loss of confidence in information upon which it had previously relied.[109]

Allegations about aluminum tubes, yellow cake ore, new nuclear facilities, and the testimony of Iraqi scientist defectors greatly (and deliberately) overstated the known facts. Exactly how and why particular pieces of "intelligence" found their way into official speeches, while information that detracted from the official line did not, became the subject of much speculation after the war. The false story about Niger's sale of yellow cake, for instance, was revealed when a former US ambassador, Joseph Wilson, wrote a *New York Times* article and later a memoir about his February 2002 mission to Niger at the CIA's request.[110] In it he criticized that and other elements of the official rationale for war. Tenet accepted blame for the story's appearance in a Bush speech, even though the CIA had always discounted it.[111] But that did not stop some Bush officials from continuing to cite the yellow cake story as evidence for their case.[112] In apparent retaliation, someone in the Bush administration apparently leaked to a newspaper columnist that Wilson's wife worked undercover for the CIA in Washington. To leak the name of a covert operative violates US law. Wilson believed the intention was to silence him and other potential establishment critics.[113] The affair led to the appointment of a special counsel to determine the source of the leak (which, as of mid-2005, appears to have been Karl Rove, Bush's deputy chief of staff, and perhaps others).

The best US arms inspectors could come up with after the war were a few mobile trailers, previously unreported by Iraq, that the CIA concluded—and Bush and Powell pointed to as evidence in public remarks—were in fact laboratories to experiment with ways to produce biological weapons. Powell's own Bureau of Intelligence and Research disputed the CIA's conclusion.[114] Even so, the CIA's assessment acknowledged that its examination had failed to find any biological agents or signs of weapons development.[115] Later, the evidence concerning the mobile labs pointed precisely in the direction Iraqi officials had told US interrogators: Their purpose was to produce hydrogen for weather balloons.[116]

Much the same scenario of politically massaged intelligence was being played out in Britain at the same time. The BBC reported, on the basis of an interview with a top intelligence professional, that the intelligence community had felt compelled by the government to "sex up" a report in September 2002 on Iraq's WMD capabilities. The report was then used by Prime Minister Tony Blair to claim that Iraq could deploy chemical and biological weapons within forty-five minutes.[117] The British press dubbed the government's report the "dodgy dossier." Two subsequent parliamentary inquiries could not establish that the government deliberately hyped the evidence; but they did reveal that the government had ignored contrary evidence on Iraq and had exaggerated the Iraqi threat. Blair's decision to support the United States—a decision that his own foreign secretary later asserted was made only to satisfy the Americans and not out of genuine conviction about the evidence,[118] and which the so-called Downing Street Memo and other documents showed went against advice that raised questions about the war's legality[119]—had generated considerable internal dissension, just as Bush's decision had within the US intelligence community. But the British inquiries went further, finding that the government had tried to keep dissenting views from becoming available to the intelligence oversight committee of the House of Commons.[120]

Coming up short on evidence, Rumsfeld said (in an April 17, 2003, news conference) that he did not expect to find any WMD and that inspections were unlikely to yield any unless Iraqis told occupying forces where they were. In later months he would not repeat that view, instead falling back on what became an administration mantra, namely, that the Iraq Survey Group needed more time and "there's work yet to be done." Yet while that work went on, one of the war's great ironies occurred: With the IAEA no longer around, nearly 380 tons of dual-use equipment and material from Iraqi military sites—such as engines, metals, and missile parts, equipment tagged by the IAEA precisely because of its potential value in WMD programs—were carted off to other countries, such as Jordan. Satellite photos showed that some sites had basically been stripped bare.[121] A senior Marine Corps commander was more honest than Rumsfeld. He expressed "surprise" that Iraq did not use WMD against advancing US forces and that "we have not uncovered [mass destruction] weapons. . . . We were simply wrong [about Iraq's intentions]."[122] Indeed, in the months before the war, a central part of the vigorous debate within the administration about how to deal with Iraq centered on when and how Iraq might use its chemical and biological weapons.[123] Those who thought Saddam might order missiles launched against Israel, or biological weapons against invading troops, now had to answer the question why, since he had the capability and was faced with the destruction of his regime, he did not issue such orders. Why, moreover, if Saddam was the "homicidal dictator who is addicted to weapons of mass destruction" that Bush described in Cincinnati, did he not follow the script? Could it be that the administration's hawks had misled Bush about the weapons at Saddam's disposal and fed Bush's notions about Saddam's psychological makeup?

As for the alleged Baghdad–Al-Qaida link, it now appears that the administration suppressed information from interrogation of captured high-level Al-Qaida leaders that disputed any such link.[124] As mentioned, these leaders, in separate interrogations by the CIA, said Osama bin Laden had considered and rejected working with Iraq. The Bush administration had this information a year before the invasion and evidently chose not to include it in public statements. Nor did it clarify that when the president had spoken in October 2002 of "high-level contacts [between Baghdad and Al-Qaida] that go back a decade," those "occurred in the early 1990s, when Osama bin Laden . . . was living in Sudan and his organization was in its infancy." Instead, Bush and others ignored the cautious language of the NIE concerning the Al-Qaida connection and apparently relied on those Iraqi defectors and captured Al-Qaida fighters who told their captors what they wanted to hear, that such a connection existed.[125] Justifying the war meant keeping the fictitious link alive, as when Bush in September 2003 told the nation: "We are rolling back the terrorist threat to civilization, not on the fringes of its influence, but at the heart of its power."[126] Not until January 2004 did Colin Powell admit he had "not seen smoking gun, concrete evidence about the [Al-Qaida–Iraq] connection." This from the man who, in his February 2003 speech to the UN Security Council, had insisted that a "sinister nexus" existed that "combines classic terrorist organizations and modern methods of murder."[127] Other indications of sharp differences between Al-Qaida and pro-Saddam Iraqis emerged in the postwar period.[128]

On the ground, the search for thousands of supposed WMD sites proceeded remarkably slowly, considering how important finding them was originally said to have been. The main US inspection team departed empty handed after less than two months of searching.[129] UN inspectors, whose services surely ought to have been needed, were not invited back; instead, a second and much larger US team was dispatched. It consisted of about 1,400 inspectors and was headed by David Kay, who had previously been a leader of UN weapons inspections in Iraq. But Kay's Iraq Survey Group had to report to Congress in October that it had failed to turn up anything of consequence after four months in the field, despite having had access to many Iraqis who had direct knowledge of WMD projects.[130] Once he left government service, Kay was more explicit: Iraq did not have chemical or biological weapon stock-piles at the time of the war because of UN inspections and Iraq's decision to get rid of them.[131] This was precisely what Charles Duelfer would later report after an even more extensive survey with the ISG in Iraq. None of these reports ever stopped administration spokesmen from insisting that WMD arsenals eventually would be discovered in Iraq. But the last weapons inspectors were pulled from Iraq at the start of 2005, a quiet admission of failure.

Hans Blix and his successor, Demetrius Perricos, derided the official US and British "culture of spin, the culture of hyping" surrounding Iraq's WMD. Blix compared the search to a medieval witch hunt: "when people were convinced there were witches, they certainly found them." Perricos agreed, adding that it was becoming "more and more difficult to believe stocks [of WMD] were there."[132] Clearly, there was an element of personal pique here—Kay and Blix had parted company years earlier in apparent disagreement over Kay's overly tight relationship with the CIA[133]—but that could not obscure the truth of the matter: The administration's case for an imminent Iraqi threat was fatally flawed.

"We were all wrong, probably," David Kay testified before Congress in February 2004. "We do not yet know if any reconstitution efforts [on nuclear weapons] had begun," acknowledged CIA director Tenet, contradicting the finding in the 2002 NIE, "but we may have overestimated the progress Saddam was making." As for chemical and biological weapons, "we have not yet found the [chemical] weapons we expected," and "we do not know if production [of biological weapons] took place."[134] In any case, Tenet insisted, the CIA never presented Iraq as an imminent threat. Yet he and Kay still agreed that the administration was right to act on the basis of Saddam's presumed intentions. This was also the bottom line with Secretary Powell, who admitted, in answer to the question of whether or not he would have recommended invading Iraq if he knew that Iraq did not have stockpiles of WMD:

> I don't know. I don't know, because it was the stockpile that presented the final little piece that made [Iraq] more of a real and present danger and threat to the region and to the world. . . . The absence of a stock-pile changes the political calculus. It changes the answer you get, the formula I laid out.[135]

Powell got sandbagged, and he knew it: He campaigned for months to get an explanation from the CIA about the sources it used when he prepared his UN speech on Iraq's WMD.[136] And Tenet paid a price too: He resigned in June 2004 after seven years of service.

When all was said and done, Iraq's WMD was a false issue. Nothing short of regime change in Iraq would have satisfied the Bush administration. As in past administrations, Bush and his most hawkish advisers twisted intelligence findings, lied to the American people about their true motives, and used the WMD issue—and, as the decision for war drew closer, the theme of "liberating" Iraq from dictatorship—to manipulate public opinion. US leaders assumed the worst about Iraq's intentions because the worst-case scenario suited their larger ambitions in the Middle East and beyond.[137] Paul Wolfowitz came close to admitting how little specific issues on Iraq really mattered, telling an interviewer that "bureaucratic reasons" accounted for the emphasis on Iraq's WMD before the war "because it was the one reason everyone could agree on."[138] But that fallback position wasn't quite right either, since not "everyone" did agree on what Iraq possessed. The false story about Iraq's uranium purchase from Niger and the inflated estimates of Iraq's WMD, for instance, survived multiple questioning—mainly from analysts at the CIA and the State Department—because the vice president, the Pentagon, Condoleezza Rice, and eventually the president were determined to build a case for war. Those who challenged the official line were dismissed by Bush as "revisionist historians," much in the manner of Reagan's dismissal of anyone who disagreed with his version of the Soviet peril.

Faced in an election year with having to acknowledge a monumental policy failure, the administration made a further step back in its official rationale, arguing that Iraq posed a potential threat regardless of its actual WMD capabilities. Bush said on January 27, 2004, that Saddam had posed "a grave and gathering threat to America and the world." Condoleezza Rice followed up by contending that Saddam "was a very dangerous man in a very dangerous part of the world. And the president of the United States had no choice but to deal with that gathering threat to American interests and to the interests of our friends abroad."[139] They and other officials, with an obvious glance at the calendar, insisted that there was no point to having an inquiry into an intelligence failure until the ISG submitted a final report. Unexpectedly, the Duelfer Report appeared before Election Day, and it was devastating. But it did not prevent Bush's reelection.

What Might Have Been

War can never be considered inevitable unless and until all paths to a peaceful, honorable agreement have been exhausted. In the Iraq case, the Bush administration's unabashedly confrontational approach to international politics, a mixture of evangelical spirit and flexing of military power, left very little room for compromise with Baghdad. But there *was* room for a negotiated outcome. Bush dissembled when he said in a televised interview on February 8, 2004, that the United States went to war only "because we had run the diplomatic string in Iraq" once the UN issued its ultimatum.[140] At least two alternatives were available to the administration.

Iraqi intelligence officials tried to open a back-channel line to Washington before the US invasion, reportedly with Saddam Hussein's approval. A deal was proposed in which the country would be open to US inspection for WMD, cooperation on terrorism, and even oil concessions to the United States. But Washington never pursued this line.[141] Another negotiating opportunity was provided by Canada, whose UN ambassador suggested "setting a series of tests of Iraqi co-operation, on a pass-or-fail basis, and a limited time frame within which to assess results." The ambassador would later write that the compromise had substantial support even among backers of the war option. US arguments about Iraq's WMD had few believers. Yet in the end, he wrote, even though the compromise "would have been in everyone's interests, especially Washington's, . . . in the end, the horses would not drink."[142]

What if those efforts had not succeeded, however? What might the United States, and other parties, have done to avert war while still meeting the UNSC's demands that Iraq disarm? From the standpoint of human and cooperative security, any alternative policies would have had to meet at least three conditions: reliance on multilateral rather than unilateral action; implementation within the UN framework; and minimization of violence matched by promotion of human well-being. There was every opportunity to meet those conditions. The international inspections were working; so long as they were being carried out, Iraq's leadership was on the defensive. And yes, the Bush administration's credible threats to use force unilaterally if necessary no doubt registered in Baghdad, helping force it to soften its stance on weapons inspections. If Iraq indeed possessed chemical and biological weapons, it would have to bury or dismantle them. In return for Iraq's full and verified compliance with the UN resolutions, sanctions on its oil production and restrictions on humanitarian assistance to Iraq would be lifted. Saddam Hussein would thus have faced a clear set of choices. If he chose the path of evasiveness and uncooperativeness such that the inspectors were prevented from doing their job, the UNSC, under Resolution 1441, could have authorized more intrusive measures, such as an international armed force strong enough to coerce inspections if necessary.[143] Saddam would have risked war if he resisted a UN force, a war that would have had the entire international community behind it.[144]

Alternatives such as these would not have eliminated the possibility that upon termination of the inspections, Saddam would have ordered a resumption of WMD programs. Nor, of course, would ending sanctions have alleviated the plight of Iraqis living under a dictatorship. But they held out the possibility of making Iraq's continued investment in unconventional weapons programs even more unwise than (as we now know) the Iraqis had already determined. A different policy would also have defused the issue of Iraq as an immediate threat to its neighbors or terrorist base and, however slightly, pried open Iraq's door to the world. In any case, until the international community is prepared to take collective action against regimes that meet some standard of brutality, it is ultimately up to the people concerned—backed by international sanctions and the power of imposed isolation—to get rid of a dictator. As long term a prospect as that might be, it still would have served the Iraqi people—as well as international law and the UN system—better than invasion and occupation by a foreign power following a highly destructive bombing campaign that caused far more violent deaths than prewar Iraq had experienced.

The Bush administration clearly had no patience with the workings of diplomacy. It was operating on a timetable geared to military requirements and the objective of "regime change." Much like his father during the Gulf War, George W. Bush was not about to let last-minute diplomatic efforts sidetrack his personal agenda, which this time included ridding Iraq of Saddam Hussein. During the Gulf War, the prospect that Saddam might withdraw his troops from Kuwait was a nightmare scenario for the Bush administration. Withdrawal would have responded to the principal US demand and forced the president to consider whether or not to use the half-million soldiers deployed in the Saudi desert. Likewise in 2002, what if Saddam had continued to be forthcoming on the UN inspectors' demands under Resolution 1441, filling in some of the important information gaps in Iraq's WMD record and allowing the most complete access to inspectors? In July, after all, Iraq extended invitations to the UN to resume discussion on inspections; in August it invited the Congress to send a delegation, with experts, to examine anyplace it wished for evidence of WMD; and by the end of the year, as noted, it opened the country to inspections "without preconditions," with Iraqi officials under orders to cooperate fully. What if, moreover, inspections failed to find solid evidence of nuclear, chemical, or biological weapons? The administration seemed urgent about starting military action. Could it be that Iraq's cooperativeness was the younger Bush's nightmare scenario? After all, Iraq did permit the inspectors access to places and people it had previously kept them away from.[145] And David Kay said, after stepping down as the administration's chief WMD inspector, that the Iraq government was probably "telling the truth" when it denied having stockpiles. They had WMD *programs,* he emphasized. But that much was already well known.

Notes

1. Eliot A. Cohen, "Iraq Can't Resist Us," *Wall Street Journal,* December 18, 2001, p. A16.

2. *Wall Street Journal,* December 19, 2001.

3. The following background information on Al-Qaida comes from the 9/11 Commission's Staff Statement No. 15, "Overview of the Enemy." Online at www.9-11commission.gov/hearings/hearing12/staff_statement_15.pdf.

4. The 9/11 Commission concluded that "it would be misleading to apply the label 'al Qaeda operations' too often" to attacks before February 1998, when bin Laden issued a public fatwa to strike at US targets. The post-fatwa attacks on US interests probably were directed by Al-Qaida. New York Times, *The 9/11 Report: The National Commission on Terrorist Attacks Upon the United States,* pp. 88–91. Hereafter, *The 9/11 Report.*

5. James Risen, "US Pursued Secret Efforts to Catch or Kill bin Laden," *NYT,* September 30, 2001, online ed.

6. "The Taliban File Part IV," *The National Security Archive,* September 11, 2004, online at www.gwu.edu/~nsarchiv/NSAEBB/NSAEBB134/index.htm.

7. Clinton wrote that when he talked with Bush during the transition to the new administration in January 2001, he put bin Laden at the top of his list of foreign policy priorities. Iraq ranked last of the six. Clinton, *My Life,* p. 935.

8. *The 9/11 Report.*

9. When Condoleezza Rice made an unprecedented appearance before the 9/11 Commission on April 8, 2004, she maintained that the administration was aware of and had done everything possible to avert an attack, though its eyes were on attacks outside rather than inside the country. But her account is vulnerable on at least two matters. One is a memorandum to her on January 25, 2001, from Richard A. Clarke, the counterterrorism director, "urgently" calling for a meeting of senior policymakers on Al-Qaida. Attached to the memorandum were two strategy papers from the Clinton years on the Al-Qaida threat. (These documents were declassified in 2004 and reproduced by the National Security Archive at www.gwu.edu/~nsarchiv/NSAEBB/NSAEBB147/index.htm [March 24, 2005].) Second is an August 6, 2001, intelligence briefing for the president at his Texas ranch, entitled "Bin Laden Determined to Attack Inside the United States." Rice insisted the briefing was "historical" and too vague to be the basis for heightened preparedness. In fact, the document was far more than "historical." It made crystal clear bin Laden's intention that Al-Qaida keep on attacking US targets both inside and outside the country. Some Al-Qaida

members were US citizens, the document says, and Al-Qaida had a cell in the United States. Bush said he could not recall being briefed on the August 6 report. In fact, he had been briefed on that report and on some forty previous reports concerning Al-Qaida. See Eric Lichtblau and David E. Sanger, "Bush Was Warned of Possible Attack in US, Official Says," *NYT,* April 10, 2004, p. A1, and Benjamin DeMott, "Whitewash As Public Service: How *The 9/11 Commission Report* Defrauds the Nation," pp. 35–45.

10. See Dilip Hiro, *Secrets and Lies: Operation "Iraqi Freedom" and After,* p. 2, and *NYT,* September 29, 2001, online ed.

11. As Jeffrey Record (in *Bounding the Global War on Terrorism,* p. 3) has put it: "If there is an analogy for the [war on terror], it is the international war on illicit narcotics."

12. Unger, *House of Bush, House of Saud,* p. 181. The 9/11 Commission found that while the House of Saud did not officially finance Al-Qaida, its sponsorship of Islamic charities of all kinds probably did result in diversion of funds to Al-Qaida. *The 9/11 Report,* pp. 531–532.

13. As one official put it, "the fewer people you have to rely on, the fewer permissions you have to get." The provision of refueling, staging, and rescue by nearby countries would be sufficient to conduct a war, he said. *NYT,* September 29, 2001, online ed.

14. Woodward, *Bush at War,* p. 98.

15. Ibid., p. 96. Richard A. Clarke's memoir, *Against All Enemies: Inside America's War on Terror* (New York: Free Press, 2004), p. 24, reports a similar remark by Bush: "I don't care what the international lawyers say, we are going to kick some ass."

16. Yet the Agreed Framework was one of Clinton's diplomatic triumphs in the face of pressure to use force. See Leon V. Segal, *Disarming Strangers: Nuclear Diplomacy with North Korea* (Princeton, N.J.: Princeton University Press, 1998).

17. The Reverend Jesse Jackson, who had successfully interceded with Syria, Iraq, and the Serbs to gain the release of imprisoned soldiers and hostages, in fact received a positive response from the Taliban leaders to mediate. But for reasons unknown, he never made the trip to Afghanistan. See Raymond Hernandez, "Jesse Jackson Says He Might Go to Taliban to Seek Turnaround," *NYT,* September 28, 2001, p. B3.

18. *NYT,* September 24, 2003, p. A11.

19. For that argument, see Record, *Bounding the Global War on Terrorism.*

20. Speech of February 26, 2001, reported in *NYT,* April 30, 2004, p. A19.

21. Clarke, *Against All Enemies,* p. 30. Woodward's unfootnoted account (*Bush at War,* pp. 48–85, 137) basically supports Clarke on the pro-war roles of Wolfowitz and Rumsfeld.

22. Philip Shenon and Richard W. Stevenson, "Ex-Bush Aide Says Threat of Qaeda Was Not Heeded," *NYT,* March 25, 2004, p. A1.

23. Woodward, *Bush at War,* pp. 49, 84, 87. According to Woodward, Powell's main arguments were that US public opinion was riveted on the Al-Qaida threat, not Iraq; that US allies would sign up for dealing strongly with the former, not the latter; and that Iraq could always be taken up later. Vice President Cheney is said to have joined Powell early on in opposing immediate action on Iraq. Ibid., p. 91.

24. Clarke, *Against All Enemies,* p. 245.

25. Woodward, *Bush at War,* p. 49. Bush's views are portrayed at pp. 48, 84, 87, 99, and 107.

26. CBS News, January 10, 2004, based on an interview of O'Neill for the program, *60 Minutes,* reported online at www.commondreams.org/headlines04/0110-03.htm. O'Neill lost his job because of his persistent questioning of the president's tax cuts.

27. Clarke, *Against All Enemies,* p. 32.

28. "The Central Intelligence Agency has no evidence that Iraq has engaged in terrorist operations against the United States in nearly a decade, and the agency is also convinced that President Saddam Hussein has not provided chemical or biological weapons to Al-Qaida or related terrorist groups, according to several American intelligence officials." (James Risen, "Terror Acts by Baghdad Have Waned, US Aides Say," *NYT,* February 6, 2002, p. A10.) At the Federal Bureau of Investigation, one unnamed official said: "We've been looking at this hard for more than a year and you know what, we just don't think it's [the Al-Qaida–Iraq connection] there." James Risen and David Johnston, "Split at C.I.A. and F.B.I. on Iraqi Ties to Al Qaeda," *NYT,* February 2, 2003, online ed.

29. Risen and Johnston, "Split at C.I.A. and F.B.I."

30. Peter R. Neumann, "Why Nobody Saw 9/11 Coming," *NYT,* March 27, 2004, p. A29.

31. Clarke, *Against All Enemies,* p. 30. Clarke told Wolfowitz, to no avail: "I am unaware of any Iraqi-sponsored terrorism directed at the United States, Paul, since 1993, and I think FBI and CIA concur in that judgment." Ibid., p. 231.

32. Rice's views were quoted by David E. Sanger, "Rice Faults Past Administrations on Terror," *NYT,* October 31, 2003, p. A6. For Cheney's views, see Woodward, *Bush at War,* p. 48.

33. Woodward, *Bush at War,* p. 94.

34. *The 9-11 Report,* p. 97.

35. Clarke, *Against All Enemies,* p. 265.

36. Perle's role as one of the key ideologues behind the Bush Doctrine is clear from his book, co-authored with David Frum, *An End to Evil: How to Win the War on Terror.*

37. Hiro, *Secrets and Lies,* p. 19.

38. Perle, "Next Stop, Iraq," speech to the Foreign Policy Research Institute, Philadelphia, November 30, 2001, online at www.fpri.org.

39. Pollack, "Next Stop Baghdad?" pp. 32–47.

40. In "Spies, Lies, and Weapons: What Went Wrong" (pp. 79–92), Pollack criticized the administration's untruthfulness about Iraq's military capabilities and wrote that Bush's "rush to war was reckless, even on the basis of what we thought we knew in March of 2003," not to mention later.

41. Elaine Sciolino and Steven Lee Myers, "Bush Says 'Time Is Running Out' as Forces Move into Place," *NYT,* October 7, 2001, online ed. It was just at the time of the resolution that the Bush administration hurried to pay the longstanding US debt to the UN and endorse two UN conventions on terrorism (related to funding and bombings) that the United States previously had ignored. See Serge Schmemann, "Annan Urges New Methods to Fight Terrorism," *NYT,* September 25, 2001, p. B3.

42. See Richard Falk, "The New Bush Doctrine," pp. 9–11.

43. Contrary to Secretary of State Colin Powell's contention that "as a result of 9/11 particularly, he [Bush] sees the value of coalitions and friends." (*International Herald Tribune,* May 23, 2002.) As Richard Perle said, whereas forming a coalition to deal with Saddam Hussein was necessary due to divided views in the United States about going to war, a coalition "today is really not essential . . . the price you end up paying for an alliance is collective judgment, collective decision-making. That was a disaster in Kosovo." Perle voiced the suspicion that the real purpose of those who were promoting a coalition was to restrain the United States. "I think we should reject that" (Perle, "Next Stop, Iraq"). Bush may have become more diplomatic after 9/11 when talking about the Russians or the Chinese, but policy toward partners clearly never changed.

44. Today's wars "should not be fought by committee," Rumsfeld has written. "The mission must determine the coalition, the coalition must not determine the mission, or else the mission will be dumbed down to the lowest common denominator." Rumsfeld, "Transforming the Military," p. 31.

45. See, for example, Patrick E. Tyler, "Europeans Split with US on Need for Iraq Attack," *NYT,* July 22, 2002, online ed. An adviser to the German prime minister is quoted as saying: "After Sept. 11, we had the feeling there would be a more multilateral approach" to international affairs by the Bush administration. But more recently, "We have been seeing a very assertive administration on the move in so many areas that people on this side of the Atlantic come to the question whether really there is a new approach." A French official said: "The important thing is to build a coalition for peace in the Middle East, not to build a coalition for war in Iraq."

46. Speech to the Council on Foreign Relations, quoted in David E. Sanger, "Allies Hear Sour Notes in 'Axis of Evil' Chorus," *NYT,* February 17, 2002, online ed.

47. Text in *NYT,* February 18, 2003, p. A11.

48. Suzanne Daley, "French Minister Calls US Policy 'Simplistic,'" *NYT,* February 7, 2002, p. A10.

49. On a visit to Washington, Crown Prince Abdullah was unusually blunt in saying, with reference to US policy toward the Palestinians: "In the current environment, we find it very difficult to defend America, and so we keep our silence." He made clear that the suicide bombings in the West Bank and elsewhere were the result of Israeli repression, and "America has a duty to follow its conscience to reject repression." Excerpts from an interview in *NYT,* January 29, 2002, p. A12.

50. In a study of Bush's chief political adviser, Karl Rove, the authors specifically charge that Rove favored invading Iraq to preempt these Democratic issues. James Moore and Wayne Slater, *Bush's Brain: How Karl Rove Made George W. Bush Presidential.*

51. This section relies, in addition to the sources indicated and other news accounts of the time, on Joe Conason, "The Iraq Lobby"; Mark Hosenball, "The Odd Couple: How George Bush Helped Create Saddam Hussein"; and Pamela Fessler, "Congress' Record on Saddam: Decade of Talk, Not Action." All are reproduced in Rosati, ed., *Readings in the Politics of United States Foreign Policy,* pp. 228–238, 267–278, and 417–421.

52. See Matt Kelley, "US Gave Germs to Iraq in '80s," Associated Press, at http://news.channel.aol.com, October 1, 2002.

53. Among numerous sources on secret US aid to Iraq, see Patrick E. Tyler, "Officers Say US Aided Iraq in War Despite Use of Gas," *NYT,* August 18, 2002, online ed., which is based on interviews with Defense Intelligence Agency officers who were involved in the aid program.

54. "The Saddam Hussein Sourcebook," National Security Archive, December 2003, online at www.nsarchive.org.

55. Ibid.

56. Unger, *House of Bush, House of Saud,* pp. 67–68.

57. The memorandum appears at www.downingstreetmemo.com.

58. Eric Schmitt, "Rumsfeld Says US Has 'Bulletproof' Evidence of Iraq's Links to Al Qaeda," *NYT,* September 28, 2002, p. A8.

59. Bush's speech in Cincinnati, October 7, 2002, in *NYT,* October 8, 2002, p. 8.

60. For example, in a speech by Bush to the UN General Assembly; text in *NYT,* September 13, 2002, p. A10.

61. Douglas Jehl, "Agency Belittles Information Given by Iraq Defectors," *NYT,* September 29, 2003, p. A1. After the war, the Department of Defense acknowledged that the great majority of information provided by these defectors—most of whom were selected by the department's favorite Iraqi exile, Ahmad Chalabi (discussed later)—was worthless. The exiles altogether were paid about $1 million. Reportedly, State Department and CIA intelligence analysts had long been skeptical of the credibility of these defectors' reports, just as they had been of Chalabi himself.

62. David Barstow, "How the White House Embraced Disputed Iraqi Arms Intelligence," *NYT,* October 3, 2004, online ed.

63. National Intelligence Estimate, "Iraq's Continuing Programs for Weapons of Mass Destruction," excerpted at www.washingtonpost.com/wp.srv/nation/nationalsecurity/documents/nie_iraq_wmd.pdf (posted July 24, 2003).

64. US Senate, Select Committee on Intelligence, *Report on the US Intelligence Community's Prewar Intelligence Assessments on Iraq.*

65. Ibid., p. 16.

66. The interview of Kamel by Rolf Ekeus, head of UNSCOM, an IAEA official, and others took place August 22, 1995, in Amman, Jordan. Kamel later returned to Iraq, only to be executed by the Saddam regime. See the UNSCOM record (marked "Note for the File,UNSCOM/IAEA Sensitive") at www.fair.org/press-releases/kamel.pdf, p. 13.

67. Spencer Ackerman and John B. Judis, "The First Casualty."

68. Scott Ritter, *Endgame: Solving the Iraq Problem—Once and For All,* pp. 127 and 219.

69. Among the report's key findings was that "As with other WMD areas, Saddam's ambitions in the nuclear area were secondary to his prime objective of ending UN sanctions." From the report's section on "Regime Strategic Intent: Key Findings." ("Nuclear," p. 1). US Central Intelligence Agency, "Regime Strategic Intent" (hereafter cited as Duelfer Report).

70. George A. Lopez and David Cortright, "Containing Iraq: Sanctions Worked," p. 91.

71. The following argument relies mainly on the lengthy analysis by Ackerman and Judis, "The First Casualty." They trace the evolution of intelligence assessments by CIA and the Defense Intelligence Agency (DIA) of Iraq's WMD

and its alleged Al-Qaida connections between January 2002 and October 2002, when the above-cited NIE was produced.

72. Eric Schmitt and Thom Shanker, "Pentagon Sets Up Intelligence Unit," *NYT,* October 24, 2002, p. 1; Hiro, *Secrets and Lies,* pp. 13–15.

73. Douglas Jehl, "Pentagon Pays Iraq Group, Supplier of Incorrect Spy Data," *NYT,* March 11, 2004, p. A8. The Defense Intelligence Agency continued to pay the Iraqi National Congress $340,000 a month well into the occupation despite the largely valueless intelligence provided by defectors.

74. The Feith briefing took place in August 2002. Tenet said he only learned about it in March 2004. *NYT,* March 10, 2004, p. A12.

75. Based on a report issued by Democratic members of the Senate Armed Services Committee; see Greg Miller, "Iraq Evidence 'Manipulated,' Inquiry Finds," *Los Angeles Times,* October 22, 2004.

76. Ackerman and Judis, "The First Casualty."

77. See ibid. for details.

78. In a letter of October 7, 2002, to Florida's Senator Bob Graham, Tenet offered the CIA's conclusion that the probability of Saddam Hussein's initiating use of WMD was "low," whereas the likelihood was "pretty high" that he would use WMD if the United States attacked Iraq, perhaps in a desperate last act of revenge. Text of the letter in *NYT,* October 9, 2002, p. A12.

79. James Risen, "C.I.A. Held Back Iraqi Arms Data, US Officials Say," *NYT,* July 6, 2004, p. A1.

80. Douglas Jehl, "C.I.A. Chief Says He's Corrected Cheney Privately," *NYT,* March 10, 2004, p. A1. Even so, Tenet clung publicly to the belief that policymakers had not deliberately exaggerated the evidence to justify the war, saying only that: "Policymakers take data. They interpret threat. They assess risk. They put urgency behind it, and sometimes it doesn't uniquely comport with every word of an intelligence estimate." Ibid., p. A12.

81. Based on a classified intelligence report of September 2002 obtained by the *New York Times.* The report cited the CIA's interview of the captured Al-Qaida leader Abu Zubaydah, who also said that the organization's leaders "viewed the Iraqis, particularly the military and security services, as corrupt, irreligious and hypocritical in that they succumb to Western vices while concurrently remaining at war with the United States." James Risen, "Iraqi Agent Denies He Met 9/11 Hijacker in Prague Before Attacks on the US," *NYT,* December 13, 2003, p. A8. See also Hiro, *Secrets and Lies,* p. 28, for the views of a Saudi intelligence chief, who said that bin Laden "thinks of Saddam Hussein as an apostate, an infidel."

82. The meeting, which was supposed to have taken place in April 2001 between Ahmad Khalil Ibrahim Samir al-Ani, the Iraqi official, and Mohamed Atta of Al-Qaida, never happened. The CIA and the FBI had come to suspect that was the case; and al-Ani, like other captured high-level Al-Qaida officials, said the meeting had not occurred and pointed to numerous criticisms by Al-Qaida of the Iraqi regime. See Risen, "Iraqi Agent Denies He Met 9/11 Hijacker," and Hiro, *Secrets and Lies,* p. 28.

83. *NYT,* January 28, 2003, p. A9.

84. In his *Disarming Iraq: The Search for Weapons of Mass Destruction* (New York: Pantheon Books, 2004), pp. 265–266, Blix lists the possible reasons, which included Saddam's belief that cooperating more fully with inspectors in

the past had not ended sanctions, the insult to Saddam's pride, and the deterrent effect of having other countries believe he still had prohibited weapons, "like someone who puts up a sign warning BEWARE OF DOG without having a dog."

85. "I think it would be terrible," he said, "if this comes to an end by armed force, and I wish for this process of disarmament through the peaceful avenue of inspections." Judith Miller and Julia Preston, "Blix Says He Saw Nothing to Prompt a War," *NYT,* January 31, 2003, p. A11.

86. See Thomas Ricks, "Military Trying to Head Off Iraq Strike," *International Herald Tribune,* May 25–26, 2002.

87. General Wesley K. Clark, former NATO commander and commander of the 1999 Kosovo operation, quoted in Eric Schmitt, "3 Retired Generals Warn of Peril in Attacking Iraq Without Backing of U.N.," *NYT,* September 24, 2002, online ed. In the same article, another retired general, the former chairman of the Joint Chiefs of Staff, John M. Shalikashvili, added: "We must continue to persuade the other members of the Security Council of the correctness of our position, and we must not be too quick to take no for an answer."

88. Louis Fisher, "Presidential Wars," in Eugene R. Wittkopf and James M. McCormick, eds., *The Domestic Sources of American Foreign Policy: Insights and Evidence,* 4th ed., pp. 155–169. In Clinton's case, he consistently proclaimed that he did not need prior approval from Congress to use force; but his actions in the four cases mentioned clearly were influenced by hostile sentiment in Congress. In Haiti, he was able to land US forces without a fight by virtue of a brokered agreement with the Haitian military leaders. In Bosnia, Congress only "resolved" to support US peacekeeping troops. In Somalia, Clinton moved up the timetable of US troop withdrawal, preempting a congressional vote. And in Kosovo, Clinton won support for air strikes by not committing ground forces; Congress never voted on limiting his war-making power. See Andrew Bennett, "Who Rules the Roost? Congressional-Executive Relations on Foreign Policy After the Cold War," in Lieber, ed., *Eagle Rules?* pp. 62–64.

89. Senate Joint Resolution 23 of September 14, 2001, "Authorization for Use of Military Force," authorizes the president "to use all necessary and appropriate force against those nations, organizations, or persons he determines planned, authorized, committed, or aided the terrorist attacks . . . in order to prevent any future acts of international terrorism against the United States. . . ." The resolution acknowledged the War Powers Resolution, but "Congress declares that this [authorization] is intended to constitute specific statutory authorization within the meaning of section 5(b) of the War Powers Resolution." The effect of the latter statement, which appeared in supporting congressional resolutions before the Gulf War, was to maintain reporting requirements for the president but eliminate the requirement that he withdraw US forces from the Middle East after sixty days in the absence of congressional authorization. House Joint Resolution 75 of December 20, 2001, provided the president with the quoted support for action against Iraq.

90. For instance, the Republican leader in the Senate, Trent Lott: see James Dao, "Experts Warn of High Risk for American Invasion of Iraq," *NYT,* August 1, 2002, online ed.

91. Byrd, "Why Congress Has to Ask Questions," *NYT,* March 12, 2002, p. A29.

92. Speech of October 3, 2002; in *NYT,* October 4, 2002, p. A13.

93. *NYT,* September 23, 2002, p. A10.

94. The joint House-Senate resolution authorizes use of force "as he [the president] determines to be necessary and appropriate in order to: (1) defend the national security of the United States against the continuing threat posed by Iraq; and (2) enforce all relevant United Nations Security Council resolutions regarding Iraq." Text in *NYT,* October 12, 2002, p. A10.

95. That vote was 250–183 in the House and 52–47 in the Senate.

96. *NYT,* October 12, 2002, p. A11.

97. Two spying operations became known after the war. The first was outlined in a US National Security Agency memorandum that was discovered and leaked by an employee of British intelligence, Katharine Gun, after the war. The operation was directed at the UN delegations of countries on the Security Council. Her efforts led to prosecution by the Blair government, which then dropped the case out of concern that the decision to support the war effort would itself be on trial. (See Bob Herbert, "A Single Conscience v. the State," *NYT,* January 19, 2004, online ed.) In the second spy incident, Clare Short, a member of Blair's cabinet who resigned in protest of the war, revealed that Britain had eavesdropped on conversations in the office of Secretary-General Kofi Annan before the war began. *NYT,* February 27, 2004, p. A1.

98. Excerpts from the speech are in *NYT,* September 12, 2002, online ed.

99. Duelfer Report. See also Douglas Jehl, "Inspector's Report Says Hussein Expected Guerrilla War," *NYT,* October 8, 2004, p. A6.

100. Douglas Jehl and David E. Sanger, "C.I.A. Admits It Didn't Give Weapon Data to the U.N.," *NYT,* February 21, 2004, p. A7. As this article indicates, specific assurances were made in a letter by Condoleezza Rice to Senator Carl Levin on March 6, 2003, and in testimony by CIA Director Tenet on February 12, 2003.

101. Elaine Sciolino, "French Leader Offers Formula to Tackle Iraq," *NYT,* September 9, 2002, online ed.

102. Quoted in Patrick Tyler and Richard W. Stevenson, "Profound Effect on US Economy Seen in War on Iraq," *NYT,* July 30, 2002, online ed. Jordan's King Abdullah II was even more scornful of US invasion plans. During a visit to Britain he gave an interview with the *London Times* in which he said: "In the light of the failure to move the Israeli-Palestinian process forward, military action against Iraq would really open Pandora's box." An invasion would "destabilize American strategic interests even more in the Middle East." Regarding the possibility discussed by US officials of using Jordan as one base for such an attack, Abdullah was clear: "Jordan will not be used as a launching pad." Warren Hoge, "Jordan Says US Attack on Iraq Would Roil Mideast," *NYT,* July 30, 2002, online ed.

103. A briefing by a RAND Corporation analyst on July 10, 2002, to the Defense Policy Board, a Pentagon advisory board headed by Richard Perle, drew considerable press attention. The briefing was so sharply anti-Saudi—accusing the Saudis of being fully supportive of terrorism and "the most dangerous opponent" in the Middle East—that the Department of Defense had to disavow it. Saudi leaders were incensed. Thomas E. Ricks, "Briefing Depicted Saudis as Enemies," *Washington Post,* August 6, 2002, p. A1.

104. Hoge, "Jordan Says US Attack on Iraq Would Roil Mideast."

105. Musharraf's interview with Peter Jennings on *ABC Evening News,* www.abcnews.com, September 22, 2003.

106. Turkey's support was surely also contingent on the United States promising not to support any form of Kurdish independence in exchange for their help in fighting Saddam. Turkey badly needs US support for EU membership inasmuch as France and several other EU members have strongly objected to Turkish entry on human rights grounds.

107. It was precisely the conflating of Soviet intentions and capabilities that bothered George Kennan when NSC-68 was being drafted. See Schilling, Hammond, and Snyder, *Strategy, Politics and Defense Budgets,* p. 310.

108. See Nicholas D. Kristof, "Save Our Spooks," *NYT,* May 30, 2003, p. A29.

109. Barton Gellman and Walter Pincus, "Depiction of Threat Outgrew Supporting Evidence," *Washington Post,* August 29, 2003, online ed.

110. Joseph Wilson, *The Politics of Truth: Inside the Lies That Led to War and Betrayed My Wife's CIA Identity.*

111. See *NYT,* July 12, 2003, p. A5. A White House statement at the same time acknowledged that the uranium story was incorrect. David Sanger, "Bush Claim on Iraq Had Flawed Origin, White House Says," *NYT,* July 8, 2003, online ed.

112. See, for example, David E. Sanger and James Risen, "C.I.A. Chief Takes Blame in Assertion on Iraqi Uranium," *NYT,* July 12, 2003, p. A1; David E. Sanger, "A Shifting Spotlight on Uranium Sales," *NYT,* July 15, 2003, p. A12; and James Risen, "Bush Aides Now Say Claim on Uranium was Accurate," *NYT,* July 14, 2003, online ed.

113. Besides Wilson's memoir (*The Politics of Truth*) cited above, see Douglas Jehl, "Iraq Arms Critic Reacts to Report on Wife," *NYT,* August 8, 2003, p. A9.

114. Douglas Jehl, "Agency Disputes C.I.A. View of Trailers as Iraqi Weapons Labs," *NYT,* June 26, 2003, online ed.

115. William J. Broad, "US in Assessment, Terms Trailers Germ Laboratories," *NYT,* May 29, 2003, online ed. Dispute over the purpose of the trailers became public when some senior US and British scientists who had examined them contended the final analysis went beyond the facts in the rush to indict Iraq. See Judith Miller and William J. Broad, "Some Analysts of Iraq Trailers Reject Germ Use," *NYT,* June 7, 2003, online ed.

116. Engineers in the Defense Intelligence Agency came to that conclusion after the CIA and the Defense Department had first made their case in May 2003 (and reportedly without consulting the DIA) that the mobile labs were probably used to produce biological weapons. Douglas Jehl, "Iraqi Trailers Said to Make Hydrogen, Not Biological Arms," *NYT,* August 9, 2003, online ed.

117. Sarah Lyall, "Blair Denies Britain Distorted Reports on Iraqi Weapons," *NYT,* May 31, 2003, p. A6. The British government's report is in *NYT,* September 24, 2002, online ed. An earlier British intelligence report on Iraq, released in February 2003, also proved embarrassing when it turned out to be nothing more than a cut-and-paste job using secondary sources, mainly an undergraduate student's thesis. Nevertheless, a parliamentary foreign affairs committee investigation yielded only a polite slap on the wrist. The committee concluded in July 2003 that the Blair government had not deliberately manipulated

the facts of Iraq's WMD, though it had blundered in the way it compiled the facts. David Kelly, the British intelligence expert who was the source of the BBC report, committed suicide shortly after his testimony.

118. Robin Cook, who quit the cabinet in March 2003 to protest Blair's pro-war stance said, "I cannot defend a war with neither international agreement nor domestic support" (Hiro, *Secrets and Lies,* p. 174) and wrote in a memoir that in fact Blair conceded on two essential points about Iraq's WMD capabilities. According to Cook, Blair did not believe Iraq could quickly deploy them, nor did he believe that Iraq posed a "clear and present danger" to Britain. Why, then, did Blair say what he did about Saddam's ambitions? Cook was "certain the real reason he went to war was that he found it easier to resist the public opinion of Britain than the request of the President of the United States." (Warren Hoge, "Blair Doubted Iraq Had Arms, Ex-Aide Says," *NYT,* October 6, 2003, p. A5.) Cook gained a measure of vindication when, in July 2004, Blair admitted: "I have to accept we have not found [WMD in Iraq], that we may not find them," *NYT,* July 6, 2004, online ed.

119. Documents leaked at the time of Britain's general elections in May 2005, which Blair won, seemed to show that Blair secretly committed Britain to Bush's war. Blair did not share either his commitment or the legal arguments against the war with his cabinet or with military leaders when Parliament voted on the war in March 2003. Alan Cowell, "Iraq Backlash in Britain May Affect Future Military Moves," *NYT,* May 4, 2005, p. A3.

120. See Warren Hoge, "Inquiry Shows How Blair's Inner Circle Made Case for Iraq War," *NYT,* August 24, 2003, online ed.; Glenn Frankel, "Blair Aides Shaped Iraq Dossier," *Washington Post,* August 29, 2003, online ed.; Warren Hoge, "Parliamentary Panel Faults British Government on Iraq But Clears It of Falsifying Intelligence," *NYT,* September 12, 2003, p. A12. A later government-appointed committee in January 2004 cleared Blair and, amidst accusations of itself playing politics, blamed the BBC for overstepping the bounds of proper journalism. The BBC's top two executives thereupon resigned.

121. Warren Hoge, "Suspect Items from Iraq Shipped Abroad, U.N. Says," *NYT,* June 10, 2004, p. A12, and James Glanz et al., "Huge Cache of Explosives Vanished from Site in Iraq," *NYT,* October 25, 2004, p. A1.

122. Lt. Gen. James Conway, commander of the First Marine Expeditionary Force, quoted in *NYT,* May 31, 2003, p. A6.

123. See Seymour M. Hersh, "The Debate Within," March 11, 2002, pp. 34–39.

124. James Risen, "Captives Deny Qaeda Worked with Baghdad," *NYT,* June 9, 2003, p. 1.

125. See Walter Pincus, "Bush Overstated Iraq, al-Qaida Link," *Washington Post,* June 23, 2003.

126. *NYT,* September 8, 2003, p. A10.

127. Christopher Marquis, "Powell Admits No Hard Proof in Linking Iraq to Al Qaeda," *NYT,* January 9, 2004, online ed. The best reason Powell could offer for attacking Iraq was that Bush "believed that the region was in danger, America was in danger and he would act."

128. See, for example, Douglas Jehl, "Al Qaeda Rebuffs Iraqi Terror Group, US Officials Say," *NYT,* February 21, 2004, p. A1.

129. Barton Gellman, "Frustrated, US Arms Team to Leave Iraq," *Washington Post,* May 11, 2003.

130. Douglas Jehl and Judith Miller, "Draft Report Said to Cite No Success in Iraq Arms Hunt," *NYT*, September 25, 2003, p. A1; James Risen and Judith Miller, "No Illicit Arms Found in Iraq, US Inspector Tells Congress," *NYT*, October 3, 2003, p. A1. What Kay's team did find were materials that might have had application to research and production of chemical and biological weapons, as well as weapons. But most of these materials were previously known to UN inspectors.

131. Richard W. Stevenson, "Iraq Illicit Arms Gone Before War, Inspector Insists," *NYT*, January 24, 2004, p. A1.

132. "Blix Decries 'Spin and Hype' of Iraq Weapon Claims," Reuters (London), September 18, 2003, online via http://news.channel.aol.com, September 20, 2003.

133. Douglas Jehl, "For Leader of Arms Hunt, Report Is a Test of Faith," *NYT*, October 3, 2003, p. A12.

134. Speech at Georgetown University, February 5, 2004; text at www.cia.gov/cia/public_affairs/speeches/2004/tenet_georgetownspeech_02052004.html.

135. Interview in *Washington Post*, February 4, 2004, online ed.

136. Douglas Jehl and David E. Sanger, "Powell Presses C.I.A. on Faulty Intelligence on Iraq Arms," *NYT*, June 2, 2004, p. A12. Powell said the CIA's "sourcing was inaccurate and wrong and in some cases, deliberately misleading."

137. As Ron Huisken, an Australian specialist, has contended, the issues in US decisionmaking on Iraq extended beyond the misuse of intelligence. "Regime change in Iraq was also intended as a definitive statement of America's ability and determination to project its unique position as the most powerful state since the Roman Empire into the indefinite future, that the 'Bush doctrine' was not a lofty ambition but an objective fact." Huisken, "We Don't Want the Smoking Gun to be a Mushroom Cloud: Intelligence on Iraq's WMD," p. 28.

138. Quoted in Paul Krugman, "Waggy Dog Stories," *NYT*, May 30, 2003, p. A29.

139. *NYT*, January 30, 2004, p. A8.

140. *NYT*, February 9, 2004, p. A19.

141. James Risen, "Iraq Said to Have Tried to Reach Last-Minute Deal to Avert War," *NYT*, November 6, 2003, online ed. The intermediary in this attempt at negotiations was a Lebanese businessman, who was able to speak with Richard Perle. Perle is said to have talked with CIA officials, who rebuffed the idea.

142. Paul Heinbecker, "Canada Got It Right on Iraq," *The Globe and Mail* (Toronto), March 19, 2004.

143. See Joseph Cirincione and Jessica T. Mathews, *Iraq: A New Approach*, for suggestions of various nonviolent but coercive forms of intervention.

144. As James P. Rubin has written ("Stumbling into War," p. 50), "the Bush administration should have then shown a willingness to adjust its military timetable to diplomatic realities. . . . All of the key players in Europe now say that they would have been prepared to support or at least sanction force against Iraq if it had not fully disarmed by then."

145. Rubin (ibid., p. 52) mentions presidential palaces that had previously been off limits to inspectors, but also Iraq's destruction of "dozens of al Samoud missiles after the UN declared that they exceeded their allowed ranges."

4

Fallout:
The Perils and Profits of Empire

JUST AS THE Gulf War was a test case of a "new world order" for the elder Bush, the war in Iraq tested George W. Bush's doctrine—and the Pentagon's domination of the policymaking process in wartime. When Bush declared victory in Iraq in May 2003, it seemed that the administration had passed the test: US forces had overwhelmed the Iraqi army, imposed a friendly regime, and secured Iraq's oil. But as this chapter will show, the administration was unprepared for what followed: a nationalist uprising and prolonged insurgency in Iraq, and the resumption of warlordism and the resurfacing of the Taliban in a destitute, drug-ridden Afghanistan. The US public's support for the occupation began to fray as casualties mounted. Neither peace nor "freedom" broke out in the Middle East. A number of allied governments were no longer willing to pay the price of reconstructing Iraq. Nor was Iraq's oil revenue going to make up the difference anytime soon. While elections were held in Iraq and Afghanistan, the prospect of their becoming stable, democratic countries seemed remote and civil war more likely. The picture that was emerging was not a carbon copy of the Vietnam War. But like Vietnam, the war on terror was demonstrating that the arrogance of power, which has tended to center in the Pentagon, carries a high price tag.

The Strategic Agenda

Forcibly bringing about regime change in Iraq and disarming it was clearly intended to "send a message" to North Korea, Iran, Libya, and Syria, in essence warning these "rogues" that US power was deployable anywhere if they failed to comply with US demands. As one "senior administration official" was quoted as saying, "Iraq is not just about Iraq"; it was "a unique case," but so far as his boss was concerned, "It is of a type."[1] At the very least, hardliners in the administration believed that the North Koreans, the Iranians, the Libyans, and the Syrians would have to think twice about their next steps before crossing the US path. In their view, the threat worked with Libya and Iran when both countries agreed to international inspections of their nuclear programs during 2003.[2] But the celebration (see the following chapter) would be short lived in the case of Iran.

Iraq was also "of a type," Bush said, in that "the triumph of democracy and tolerance in Iraq, in Afghanistan and beyond would be a grave setback for international terrorism. The terrorists thrive on the support of tyrants and the resentments of oppressed peoples."[3] Victory in Iraq would therefore, in his mind, reverse the domino effect: The Middle East as a whole would be blessed with freedom, and terrorism would be defeated, by virtue of US accomplishments in Iraq and Afghanistan. "Now is the time and Iraq is the place in which the enemies of the civilized world are testing the will of the civilized world," Bush said at a news conference on April 13, 2004. "We must not waver." He was right about the reasons for terrorists' gains, but terribly wrong to imagine that a lengthy US occupation of an Arab country, pro-Israel policies, and continued close ties with authoritarian states such as Saudi Arabia and Pakistan would play well among restive young people in the Middle East.[4]

In all, Iraq became the centerpiece of a foreign policy agenda that had been shaped years earlier by neocon intellectuals and one-time officials. That agenda, it will be recalled, emphasized strong support of Israel, regime change in Iraq, and the deployment of military muscle wherever necessary to assert the US will. The US objective is invariably described as the democratization of the Middle East, but it is more accurately rendered as US hegemony. As a former US foreign service officer in Iraq, one who supported the earlier Gulf War, has written: "The underlying objective of this war is the imposition of a Pax Americana on the region and installation of vassal regimes that will control restive populations."[5]

Oil and Other Business

As in all wars, in Iraq there is money to be made and there are resources to secure and economic interests to promote. The ever-present oil factor in US Middle East policymaking is too big to hide. The war on Iraq was not all about oil; but no less than in the 1991 war,[6] oil was (and remains) a prominent factor. Iraq's oil production and reserves—the second-largest among OPEC states, 11 percent of the world total, and 5 percent of total US oil imports at the time of the war[7]—plus the prominence of oil men in the Bush administration and the contributions of the energy industry to the Bush campaign's war chest assured top billing for oil when it came to prioritizing US interests. If those factors were not enough, Cheney's closed-door meetings with energy industry leaders, to the exclusion of environmental groups, early on established the administration's willingness to cater to the industry's interests. The administration reaffirmed that direction in several other ways: in the statement of Secretary of Energy Spencer Abraham that "America faces a major energy supply crisis over the next two decades," in Cheney's commission of a report on energy strategy from the James A. Baker Institute and the Council on Foreign Relations,[8] and in Cheney's National Energy Policy report, released in May 2001, on diversifying US oil supplies, partly by increasing production at home (meaning Alaska's Arctic National Wildlife Refuge) but mainly by relying on increased imports.[9] In September 2002 senior administration officials set up an Energy Infrastructure Planning Group in anticipation of war with Iraq—only weeks after Cheney, in a speech of August 26, had warned (in shades of 1991) that Saddam Hussein, with weapons of mass destruction at his command, "could then be expected to seek domination of the entire Middle East, take control of a great portion of the world's energy supplies, [and] directly threaten America's friends throughout the region."[10]

Soon after the war officially ended (May 1, 2003) and the UN Security Council lifted sanctions on Iraq, it granted the US "Coalition Provisional Authority" (CPA) virtually complete control over Iraq's oil industry.[11] Not coincidentally, and noticeable to all Iraqis, US forces protected the oil ministry while other ministries were being looted.[12] The guiding idea, pushed by the neocons but opposed by both the major oil companies and the State Department, was to privatize Iraq's oil industry and thus remove it from the OPEC quota system.[13] Former US oil company executives were placed in overall charge of Iraq's oil, with Iraqi officials reporting to them—Philip Carroll, chief executive officer of Shell Oil in the 1990s, who was succeeded by Rob McKee, formerly with ConocoPhillips. With a friendly regime installed in Baghdad, and production restored to pre–Gulf War levels, the United States could expect access to cheap oil and increased influence over oil prices.

Oil field service companies, including Kellogg Brown & Root (KBR), a division of Cheney's former firm, Halliburton Corporation, were widely reported to be eager to get into Iraq. The US government, concerned about what Iraq's oil industry would look like in the aftermath of war, responded. KBR's first contract in Iraq was awarded in secret by a Pentagon energy task force under the direction of Douglas Feith in November 2002. (It was later discovered that senior Bush officials, including one in Cheney's office, knew in advance about the Halliburton contract, despite Cheney's repeated denials that he had always distanced himself from such business.[14]) This contingency planning contract was followed by another to Halliburton, to implement the plan. It was awarded by the Army Corps of Engineers without competition in March 2003, and although the bulk of the contracted work was supposed to be open to competitive bidding, at the start of 2004 only Halliburton had earned revenue from it—about $2.2 billion.[15] Only after the war was it announced that Halliburton would not only be responsible for assessing damage to the oil industry but would also operate oil fields, supply oil equipment, and market the oil. It took on the job with evident gusto: The company was accused of greatly overcharging the government for the oil it imported from Kuwait, and that was just the beginning of its well-earned troubles.[16]

Rebuilding Iraq's dilapidated facilities was expected to increase production by about one-third, experts said; and with Saddam Hussein out of the way, US firms would have a clear edge over rival European and other companies.[17] The edge was ensured by an administration announcement that only countries that had taken part in the war would be eligible for major construction contracts in Iraq. In fact, US control of Iraq's oil increased leverage over Russian oil companies, which would have to bargain with Washington to get back into Iraq, and over the Russian government, which was owed about $7.6 billion by Iraq at the time of the war.[18] These developments added to the Russians' and the Europeans', as well as the Canadians', hesitancy to respond to Washington's pleas for help in rebuilding Iraq—such as by reducing Iraq's external debt, estimated at around $116 to $120 billion. But the major oil companies found a way that made everybody a winner: By buying stakes in Russian oil companies that once owned concessions in Iraq, US and other oil companies—such as ConocoPhillips and France's Total—positioned themselves as well as the Russians to get back in business there.[19] Russia also hoped to leverage a major reduction of Iraq's debt for the right to resume its prewar oil development arrangements. Canada won Bush's approval to compete for contracts in return for its participation in reconstruction projects.

As world oil prices surpassed $45 in 2004 and reached $65 a barrel in 2005, the US search for sources of oil outside OPEC took on added urgency.[20] Global oil supplies tightened, and the major oil companies were forced to reveal that their estimates of reserves were way off the mark. The higher oil prices went, the more important Iraqi oil became. As will be seen in Chapter 5, oil politics also assumed importance for the Bush administration in other places, including Venezuela, the Caspian Sea region, and several African countries. But Saudi Arabia remained the key player. Plenty of people in the Pentagon and in both parties in Congress were annoyed with the Saudis over their presumed support of Al-Qaida cells and criticism of US policy on Israel. These critics openly spoke of withdrawing US forces from Saudi Arabia.[21] Cheney is said to have supported withdrawal prior to the start of the invasion of Iraq, on the basis that taking over Iraq would reduce US dependence on Saudi oil, which was then about 16 percent of US oil imports.[22] After the war, all but a token US force was removed from Saudi Arabia as the Pentagon prepared four bases in Iraq for long-term use.[23] Bases in Iraq gave the United States not only an alternative to those in Saudi Arabia, but also the means of close-up protection of Iraqi oil and aerial surveillance of Iran.

Surging oil consumption and the failure of Iraq's postwar oil production to match expectations eroded Washington's bargaining position, however. Despite bold official predictions about Iraq's oil production and revenues,[24] the administration knew from a lengthy Pentagon-based study that Iraq's oil industry had been so badly damaged by trade sanctions and the dilapidated state of equipment that production and revenues would fall well short of official predictions.[25] Far from reducing the administration's future aid bill for Iraq, its oil industry might require $20 billion to restore it.[26] The neocons, Cheney included, apparently acquiesced to the old, Saddam-era model of a state-owned oil company in Iraq, with operating control in the hands of the oil majors and production in accordance with OPEC rules.[27] Thus Saudi Arabia, with its excess capacity of roughly 2 to 3 million barrels a day, emerged still in the driver's seat.[28] Nor did the US troop withdrawal end military ties with the Saudis: Vinnell Corporation continued to train the Saudi National Guard, and Saudi Arabia was still among the top buyers of US arms. And the Saudis could rely as always on dispensing favors and employing a phalanx of lobbyists to influence favorable legislation in Washington.[29] As Arab nationalism intensified in reaction to the US occupation of Iraq, the Saudi leaders were more hesitant than in the past to listen to US appeals to increase production and bring down gas prices for US consumers—and for a president facing reelection. The kingdom did respond to Bush's appeal to increase production, but not enough to bring gasoline prices down, showing that the Bush-Saudi connection remains one of mutual dependence.[30]

Despite the unanticipated problems in Iraq's oil industry, by mid-2003 a plan for its rehabilitation was completed. It called for production of 2.8 million barrels of oil a day by the spring 2004. This was short of the prewar figure of around 3 million barrels a day, but it was still impressive—or at least optimistic. KBR, armed with a $1 billion contract from the US government, was the lead private US firm in the plan, development of which also involved the US Army Corps of Engineers and the chief US adviser to Iraq's oil ministry.[31] (The supreme irony here is that KBR, during Cheney's tenure as CEO of Halliburton, earned around $24 million in the late 1990s for rebuilding Iraq's oil fields.[32]) Iraq's oil production now seems likely to take far longer to recover than some US government and oil executives had predicted before the war. But its importance in prewar and postwar policy planning seems incontrovertible.

War profiteering was by no means limited to the oil industry. Iraq benefited multinational business interests of all kinds, notably private military contractors. Prior to the first Iraq war in 1991, an influential business group, the Iraq Business Forum, in which Henry Kissinger played a key role, helped insure that US corporations were committed to Saddam's Iraq. In the second war, a similar business lobby, the Committee for the Liberation of Iraq, headed by the former vice president of Lockheed Martin Corporation (another major defense contractor), pressed the case for putting Iraq back in the column of friendly countries.[33] Several of the Defense Department's principal military contractors did business in postwar Afghanistan and Iraq, including Vinnell Corporation (to train the Iraqi army) and DynCorp (to protect the Afghan president and advise on Iraq's new police and penal systems).[34] Some of these businesses had political ties to the Bush administration and were often awarded contracts without competitive bidding, as in the case of KBR. For instance, many contracts were awarded to Bush 2000 presidential campaign contributors such as General Electric ($72,000) and Halliburton ($28,000)—in all, about a half-million dollars in contributions from seventy companies.[35]

Iraq became a particularly attractive place in which to invest after the war thanks largely to the influence of the neocons. Iraq was the "honey pot," and L. Paul Bremer III was the queen bee.[36] During his tenure as occupation head, Bremer, who had served previously in the Reagan administration as head of counterterrorism and then as managing director of Kissinger & Associates, administered classic "shock therapy" to Iraq's economy. Bremer's CPA fired large numbers of state workers, removed all restrictions on imports, privatized state-owned enterprises, slashed corporate tax rates, and allowed 100 percent foreign ownership of Iraqi assets and 100 percent repatriation of profits—the essentials of the "structural adjustment" strategy long preached by the "Washington consensus" and put into effect by the IMF.

Thus it comes as no surprise that by one account, of the initial $1.5 billion in contracts awarded by the CPA, 74 percent went to US firms.[37] Once again, those with White House connections fared especially well. One news report, for instance, cited Crest Investment, a company based in Houston that was formed to advise businesses interested in investing in Iraq. Its chairman, Joe M. Allbaugh, was long active in Texas politics, was a Bush appointee to head FEMA, and managed the Bush-Cheney presidential campaign. Other executives in Crest Investment had also previously worked in the administration and/or had ties to his political campaigns.[38] Another contract, for consulting work with the Iraqi government, went to the husband of a deputy assistant secretary of defense.[39]

The ultimate insider was James Baker III, the secretary of state under the elder Bush, who in December 2003 was appointed by Bush to seek help in restructuring Iraq's debts from European and Arab countries. Baker, who also represented the Bush presidential campaign during the disputed 2000 Florida election, had all sorts of potential conflicts of interest when it came to doing business in Iraq. Besides being a partner in a Houston law firm (Baker Botts) whose clients included Halliburton and various Middle East businesses, Baker was senior counselor to the $16-billion-strong Carlyle Group. Carlyle's far-flung investments included supply contracts with the Saudi air force and other business with the Saudi royal family. It was Baker's institute at Rice University that presented Cheney with an early report on energy strategy. George W. Bush was once one of Carlyle's directors, and George H. W. Bush is a current director.[40]

The Other Side of Victory

The Dead "Road Map"

An essential piece in the administration's strategy was a "road map" for a Palestinian-Israeli settlement. Bush's credibility on a settlement was already tarnished, for even though he had publicly endorsed a Palestinian state, he had also dismissed Arafat as an acceptable negotiating partner and a suitable leader of the Palestinian Authority.[41] Bush repeatedly sided with Ariel Sharon's militant policies in the Gaza Strip and the West Bank for dealing with Palestinian suicide bombers. Initially the road map made headway as all sides seemed to agree to the formula of an end to terrorist attacks in exchange for a reopening of Israel's borders, release of Palestinian prisoners, and dismantling of certain settlements, all steps that would take place in sequence over a three-year period. But the violence resumed, and the Bush administration seemed incapable of either sustaining diplomatic momentum or reining in Sharon, who had bottled Arafat up in his Ramallah compound and talked openly about exiling or killing him. Once Sharon decided to impose his own solution—building a 23-mile barrier to wall in the Palestinians and ordering that some isolated settlements be abandoned—the road map was essentially dead.

During 2004 and 2005, Sharon succeeded at bringing Bush all the way over to Israel's side. Bush accepted Sharon's plan to retain the principal settlements built after the victory in the 1967 June War. He joined Sharon in rejecting the longstanding Palestinian claim of a "right of return" of refugees to what had once been their homeland in Israeli territory. And, following Arafat's death in late 2004, the president endorsed Sharon's unilateral decision to pull out of the Gaza Strip by August 2005—a politically difficult one for Sharon, but typical of his approach of taking action without negotiating with the new Palestinian leadership. In reality, Israel's withdrawal still leaves it in control of Gaza's borders and with a presumed right of reintervention. Israel retains control of the West Bank, where the settler population continues to expand with Bush's support. In these circumstances, Gaza, one of the world's poorest and most crowded areas, might become the setting for another *intifada*.[42] The administration thus lost an opportunity to broker a new round of peace talks that might have included other interested parties, such as the EU and the Arab states.

In truth, however, the road map was never adequate for a true resolution of the Palestinian-Israeli conflict. A just settlement rests on the willingness of both sides to transform their thinking and mutual perceptions as well as their policies—a process of reconciliation not provided for in the road map and completely at odds with Israel's unilateral decisionmaking and Bush's support of it. This failure to search for common ground has major implications for the war on terror, providing fuel for the fires of Al-Qaida, Hamas, and other fanatical groups seeking recruits for suicide missions.

A Compliant Public and Press

The real motives behind US policy received only the flimsiest of scrutiny. As in previous wars, low US casualty figures counted more with the general public than did the failure to find weapons of mass destruction, the cost of the war, or the results of efforts to democratize Iraq. In one opinion poll at the war's end, for instance, 57 percent of the public said that the war on Iraq was "worth it" even if no WMD were found.[43] That figure held up for some time, with roughly 40 percent of those polled expressing the opposite view. This difference represented quite a turnaround since, before the invasion, polls showed general support of the war but also a willingness to give the inspectors more time to do their job.[44] So seamlessly had the Pentagon shifted ground from talk of ridding Iraq of WMD to talk of liberating Iraq from dictatorial rule that few Democrats and none of the mainstream media outlets challenged the new line. And when Saddam was finally captured on December 13, 2003, the administration had further ambit for diverting the public's attention from the original reasons for going to war, to the point of brushing aside the question of Iraq's WMD as (in Bush's word) a "nonissue."[45]

Equally telling is that long after the president and some other senior officials acknowledged—and in the process went against Cheney's contention—that there was no connection between Saddam Hussein's regime and the 9/11 attacks, polls showed that a majority of the public still believed there was one. As 2004 began, Bush had an overall approval rating of around 60 percent and nearly as high a level of support for his Iraq policy. Not until US casualties topped 1,000 in late summer did the approval rating slip below 50 percent. It took until mid-2005, by which time Iraq was off most front pages, for a majority of the US public to express opposition to the initial decision to invade Iraq. Virtually all major polls showed that the public now believed the fight against the Iraqi insurgents was going badly, and disapproved of the way Bush was handling the war in particular and foreign policy in general.[46]

If truth is the first casualty of war, it takes considerable time to resuscitate. Mass media in the early days after 9/11 was a follower, and therefore a tool, of the administration. No institution was more pro-war, more inclined to follow official opinion more loyally, and more closed to alternative viewpoints than the US mass media in the days and weeks after the administration decided that "we" were at war.[47] In fact, the post-9/11 period produced something new: "the Fox effect," denoting the explicitly pro-war viewpoint that dominated Fox News, a component of the Australian archconservative Rupert Murdoch's media empire. As a result, not only was the news from Afghanistan and Iraq slanted in deference to patriotism. News reporters were cleverly "embedded" in military units, in many instances compromising their reporting. Media sometimes engaged in self-censorship: Antiwar documentaries such as Michael Moore's

Fahrenheit: 9/11 and David O. Russell's re-release of *Three Kings* were refused distribution by Walt Disney Company and Warner Brothers on the basis that they were too "political." At the same time, media conglomerates such as the Sinclair Broadcasting Group, whose executives contributed money to the Bush presidential campaign, took explicit prowar actions to influence opinion.[48] Most important in policy terms, the key ingredients of the administration's case for war—Iraq's WMD capabilities and its links to terrorist groups—were uncritically accepted by all the major news outlets as late as several months after victory was declared in Iraq. It is hardly surprising that public opinion mimicked the media's reporting and even outdid it, believing the administration's case well after the media itself had ceased to believe it.

But the media was victim as well as perpetrator. The media had no independent source for figures on civilian casualties in Iraq, for instance, and US authorities have always refused to provide them. Even when the first careful study of casualties was finally reported, it was a day's worth of news, despite the extraordinary figure: about 100,000 people killed between the US invasion and the fall of 2004.[49] Dealing with a highly secretive administration, the mainstream media also had limited access to the president and other high officials. Making the supposedly "historic" meeting of Bush and Cheney with the 9/11 Commission off limits to the media is just one example. For while the administration's eventual (and begrudging) agreement to have them testify (but not under oath) was unusual, the media was barred not just from viewing and reporting on the meeting but even from photographing it. (Only one person was allowed to take notes on what was said; no recording was allowed.) The media was also barred by the Pentagon from taking photos of the returned bodies of service people. One person who did—she was not a journalist but a contract worker—was fired, along with her husband, and it was only because of an enterprising web site that hundreds of such photos were displayed.

Eventually, as happened in Vietnam, a few publications, such as the *New York Times* and the *Washington Post,* turned against the administration. Editors of the *Times* went so far as to issue a statement in May 2004 that acknowledged a number of shortcomings in its coverage of the administration's case for war. They did not probe very deeply, however, and omitted numerous examples of slanted reporting that favored the Bush war policies.[50] But at least the acknowledgment showed how easily a great newspaper could be duped by political leaders who wrap themselves in the mantle of national security.[51] Few other media made similar admissions of error.[52] But it was all too little, too late, to repair the damage done to democratic processes.

Disruption in the Foreign Policy Process

Another casualty of the war on Iraq was deepening divisions in the Bush administration's foreign policy making ranks. Early signs of contention had appeared before the war, for example, over Powell's diplomatic handling of the air incident with China (as noted in Chapter 2), US assistance for UN-administered family planning programs, the choice between engaging or stonewalling North Korea, and, in general, the priority to attach to multilateral cooperation in US foreign policy. None of these sources of controversy was abnormal in the rough-and-tumble world of Washington. Every administration goes through times when interagency bickering and personal and philosophical differences become matters of public knowledge, and even an administration such as Bush's that prides itself on running a tight ship could not suppress all news of dissension.

What made seemingly ordinary sources of contention in the first George W. Bush administration noteworthy was the Pentagon's hijacking of US foreign policy. Despite the administration's best efforts to maintain a façade of unity, the reality was a sharp division between functional pragmatists and professionals such as Powell and Tenet, and true believers such as Rumsfeld, Cheney, Wolfowitz, Rice, and Perle.[53] Powell reportedly regarded the Cheney-Pentagon alliance as equivalent to a separate government.[54] The alignment of the Christian right with the neocons certainly did not help Powell's cause.

Powell's situation represented a classic bind in foreign policy making. When it comes to the use of force abroad, State Department leaders and country desk officers are often accused by hardliners of being liberal wimps—too soft-headed in their commitment to diplomatic solutions, too inclined to take account of the target country's history, culture, and security sensitivities, and thus too often willing to give that country the benefit of the doubt. Henry Kissinger, for example, wrote scathingly in his memoirs about the obstructionism of the State Department's Latin America Bureau when he and Nixon decided to run a coup against Chile.[55] James C. Thomson, in a seminal essay on the Vietnam War, recounted the "banishment of the experts" from policymaking circles as US bombing and troop commitments escalated.[56] Once the winds of war blow through official Washington, State and other country and issue experts invariably seem to be put on the defensive. On the other hand, it is often, and equally, the case that officials who are in the minority when it comes to the use of force must play to the hardliners' position in order (so they believe) to maintain credibility.

Powell's influence was most deeply felt in the "road map" for an Israeli-Palestinian settlement, a multilateral approach to addressing North Korea's nuclear weapons program, and Africa diplomacy, including putting US troops on the ground in Liberia. He parried with the Defense Department on all these issues.[57] China policy is a good example of the duel between State and the Pentagon for control of foreign policy. Powell followed the traditional course, promoting trade and investment, using diplomacy to resolve contentious issues (such as the spy plane incident and PRC military transfers), occasionally (and politely) chiding China on human rights, and relying on a multilateral approach with China to defuse the long-running nuclear crisis with North Korea. Rumsfeld and company clearly preferred more confrontational methods, for example by imposing trade sanctions on Chinese companies believed to be involved in exporting technology and equipment with potential use in weapons of mass destruction (mainly to Iran and Pakistan).[58]

On the central issue in US-China relations, Taiwan, whereas the State Department sought to halt what it regarded as a dangerous drift toward an outright declaration of independence by the Taiwan government, the Pentagon, reflecting the pro-Taiwan views of the neocons, sought to maintain a strong US commitment to Taiwan's defense. This difference came to a head when China's premier, Wen Jiabao, visited Washington in December 2003 at a time when Taiwan's President Chen Shui-bian was seeking (in the context of his campaign for reelection in March 2004) a popular referendum and constitutional revisions to clarify Taiwan's independent status.[59] Bush gave Wen what the premier came for—an explicit statement opposing any unilateral alteration of the status quo in China-Taiwan relations. Nor did the president say anything about China's missile buildup across the strait from Taiwan. This rather direct rebuke of Chen Shui-bian, and apparent victory for the State Department's position, was undercut almost immediately in response to protests quickly organized by key figures in the PNAC. They called Bush's statement a "mistake" and "appeasement of a dictatorship," and urged that the United States "stand with democratic Taiwan." The administration quickly issued a qualification of Bush's statement that the United States "would have to get involved if China tried to use coercion or force to unilaterally change the status of Taiwan"—a strong reaffirmation of Bush's 2001 pledge that the United States would do "whatever it took to help Taiwan defend herself."

One might conclude that US policy on Taiwan had simply come to rest where it had always been—ambiguously committed to defend Taiwan from attack, but above all seeking to keep Taiwan from getting in the way of positive movement in relations with China. Nevertheless, the State-Pentagon tug-of-war also had the effect of leaving Chen Shui-bian with room to continue his game of leveraging US support to make a formal break with China, an outcome that most observers believe would force the Chinese military into action against Taiwan.

When it came to Iraq policy, Powell and colleagues may not have been convinced that going to war was the only or best course of action in late 2002. Powell's vulnerable position amidst the neocons and their allies became evident as war talk heated up. His preference seemed to be to keep open avenues to a diplomatic resolution; but as he would later say, diplomacy never had a chance for the simple reason that Cheney and others weren't interested in it.[60] Powell's problem came down to this: how to demonstrate that diplomacy was worth pursuing in the face of Iraq's intransigence, the EU's resistance to the use of force, and, surely most important, determination by the administration's hawks to go into action with or without the UN. Iraq's efforts to delay the return of the UN inspectors, and then to leave many questions about their WMD programs unanswered once the inspectors arrived, seemingly hardened Powell's views.[61] Moving further to the right as war preparations intensified, Powell insisted that "There comes a time when soft power or talking with evil will not work—where, unfortunately, hard power is the only thing that works."[62] Powell's subsequent speech to the Security Council in which he presented the case for finding Iraq in material breach of UN resolutions fully embraced the hardliners' position, yet was rife with exaggeration and misstatements, if not outright falsehoods.[63] The speech may have been the low point in his State Department career, especially as Powell reportedly had misgivings about the evidence on Iraq's WMD that was coming out of the Pentagon, such as the testimony of Iraqi defectors.[64]

There is other evidence that Powell was sidelined when it came to the use of force. Powell reportedly became upset that Rumsfeld was openly talking about applying the supposed lessons of Iraq to Syria, Iran, and North Korea.[65] Later events showed that there were grounds for such concern. The White House issued public warnings to Syria for harboring Iraqi leaders. US forces crossed into Syrian territory, supposedly in pursuit of those leaders, and (in yet another sign of interagency disputation) only objections from the CIA and other agencies prevented John R. Bolton, a leading State Department hardliner, from presenting an ominous picture of Syria's WMD programs to a congressional committee.[66]

With Iran, Powell and other State Department officials discovered that their Pentagon counterparts had held unauthorized meetings with a one-time Iranian arms dealer who was involved in the Iran-Contra scandal, at a time when US policy on Iran—specifically, the choice between engagement and confrontation—was not settled.[67]

The Days After:
Bringing Order to Iraq and Afghanistan

> We ought to look in a mirror and get proud, and stick out our chests and suck in our bellies and say, "Damn, we're Americans!"
> —General Jay Garner, outgoing head of the postwar occupation of Iraq, *New York Times* (May 19, 2003), p. A10

> You are going to be the proud owner of 25 million people. You will own all their hopes, aspirations and problems. You'll own it all. You break it, you own it.
> —Colin Powell to President Bush,
> Quoted in Bob Woodward, *Plan of Attack* (2004), p. 150

Rumsfeld's domination of Iraq policy stemmed from Bush's decision, in National Security Directive 24 on January 20, 2003, that authorized the civilian leadership in the Pentagon not only to run the war but also to plan its follow-up.[68] The key planners under him and Wolfowitz were reportedly chosen for their political loyalty, not their area or technical expertise. In turn, the Pentagon handpicked Iraq's future leaders with the idea that the US occupation would be brief and leadership turned over to them. Their favorite was Ahmad Chalabi, head of the INC that the US government—and the sponsorship of Richard Perle and the American Enterprise Institute[69]—helped create in 1992 and, upon passage of the Iraq Liberation Act in 1998, largely financed. A wealthy, MIT-educated man who had fled Iraq in 1958, Chalabi had many enemies inside Iraq, and thus was by no means its natural leader. He was also suspected of fraudulent business practices in Jordan, and had worked with the CIA on a coup attempt in Iraq in 1995. Nevertheless, Chalabi's "Free Iraqi Forces," trained by the US military, were flown into Iraq by the Pentagon once the war started, probably in the mistaken belief Iraqis would rise up and help take power from the Iraqi military. Chalabi's INC was debunked by State and the CIA, however; they had their own favorites for future leadership.[70]

The Pentagon did not win out in its efforts to promote Chalabi to the head of the class. Nor did Bush's vesting of policy control in the Pentagon last long (see below). But Chalabi did become one of the most prominent figures in the Iraqi Governing Council under the US occupation, and when a transitional government took over, he was appointed interim oil minister. Rumsfeld was also responsible for decisions that demobilized the Iraqi army and eliminated all Baathist Party members from their posts in the civil service, academia, and elsewhere. (These steps proved disastrous for restoring order once the war ended.) None of this pleased the State Department, which starting as far back as October 2001 had been running a Future of Iraq Project that involved specialized working groups, other agencies, and numerous Iraqi professionals in exile.[71] The project's 2,000 pages of studies anticipated many of the problems the occupation forces faced, such as too-early disbandment of military units, widespread looting, and, most important, weak civil administration. But State's study seems to have been "mostly ignored," as one "senior defense official" said.[72]

The Pentagon evidently wanted to keep postwar reconstruction entirely under its wing, in the hands of Douglas Feith, Rumsfeld's man. It was a matter of ideology, not expertise. State's Future of Iraq Project leader was sidelined; General Garner "says he was instructed by Secretary of Defense Rumsfeld to ignore" the project; and (in the view of one of Garner's staff) the State Department's "Arabists weren't welcome because they didn't think Iraq could be democratic."[73] Nor was the CIA a key player in reconstruction planning: Like State, it had consistently warned (according to a "senior administration official") that "reconstruction rather than war would be the most problematic segment of overthrowing Saddam." In the end, it seems the Pentagon planned for the wrong war—for crises that never occurred, such as oil field fires and chemical weapons attacks, instead of for quickly restoring basic services, protecting against looting, and preparing for a turnover of political authority to a broad spectrum of Iraqis whom they themselves would select.[74]

How Iraq's reconstruction might have gone with State in control is anybody's guess; after all, State's Future of Iraq Project had its own disagreements and doubts, such as over how and whether democracy could be built in Iraq, and how to deal with the expected security issues and resistance to foreign occupation.[75] But under the Pentagon, in Wolfowitz's own estimation in mid-2003, serious errors were committed, and these amounted to political misjudgments that, with the involvement of other agencies, might have been avoided.[76] Certainly a fair part of the blame can be laid at Rumsfeld's door, for it was he who trumpeted the idea that Iraq was being liberated rather than occupied. It was also Rumsfeld who removed General Jay M. Garner and Margaret Tut-willer, ambassador to Morocco, from their leadership positions in the occupation and installed L. Paul Bremer. Bremer, who reported to Rumsfeld, issued the orders in June 2003 that discharged some 35,000 civil servants who were Baath Party members and dissolved the 400,000-man Iraqi army—decisions that greatly helped the recruitment efforts of the Iraqi resistance.

Thus did the occupation—including crucial decision areas such as the reconstitution of an Iraqi government and legal system, the allocation of major business contracts for Bechtel, Halliburton, and other US firms in the rebuilding of Iraq, and the securing of Iraq's oil fields under overall US authority—become a Pentagon show. And by becoming a Pentagon show, liberators indeed became occupiers[77] and corporate profits took on unseemly dimensions. Curiously, it was not only Colin Powell (as in the epigraph above) who understood all the problems that "ownership" of Iraq would bring. Dick Cheney also understood, or at least once did. Prophetically, in 1991 Cheney, as defense secretary, opposed carrying the war to Baghdad in order to depose Saddam—and did so for all the right reasons.[78] That he apparently did not repeat his opposition in 2003 suggests the extent to which hegemonic ideology and sheer opportunism dictated official thinking.

For Rumsfeld, overweening ambition did occasionally meet with obstacles. As the body count of US soldiers mounted, and the Taliban reemerged in Afghanistan, Bush in October 2003 appointed Rice to head an "Iraq Stabilization Group." This unexpected reorganization, whose effectiveness never was publicly measured, did not go over well with Rumsfeld. He responded testily to questions about it. But his hurt feelings had to give way to political realities: the unfavorable trend of events in Iraq and Afghanistan, the Abu Ghraib prisoner abuse scandal in Iraq, and Bush's reelection plans. With his popularity dipping in the polls, the president had to be seen as exerting more control over a situation that was spinning out of control.[79] Rumsfeld also was seared by the remarks of a Pentagon general, who before an evangelical audience characterized the war as a religious conflict between "their" and "our" God, with Islam's the equivalent of "Satan." Given the opportunity to rebuke his general, Rumsfeld chose to commend his competence. The president, on the other hand, did criticize the general's remarks, but did not replace him. Rumsfeld came under fire from some Republican members of Congress and neocon intellectuals who were reportedly upset with his arrogant behavior in general, and specifically with his failure to provide sufficient US forces to assure internal security in Iraq. Yet when the smoke had cleared, Rumsfeld remained the premier player, and whereas Powell resigned after Bush's reelection (it was widely reported that he had not been invited to stay), Rumsfeld carried on.

Nation Building in Iraq

The Bush administration forgot two of the most elemental rules of war fighting: plan for the peace and have an exit strategy. Rumsfeld's Pentagon devoted far more resources to managing the war in Iraq than to developing and transforming Iraqi society after the war.[80] Both phases required substantial resources, human as well as technical, for the key issue would surely be sensitivity to the physical and psychological needs of the people being planned for. Iraq, after all, was going to be an occupied country for many years. Rebuilding a society demanded different kinds of resources—troops and civilians trained in Arabic language and cultural traditions, mediation skills, sensitivity to nationalism and religious differences, administrative experience in governance—that were in short supply, and always have been.[81] Next, if the goal was to build democratic institutions in Iraq, not only would representative elections have to be held; demobilizing and integrating private armies, providing adequate security for ordinary people, and crafting a power-sharing arrangement acceptable to the main factions would be just as critical. Finally, the turnover of full authority to a new government and its assumption of internal security responsibilities would have to be accompanied by a timetable for the removal of occupying forces. These elements, too, were only belatedly, and inadequately, addressed.

Iraq would require a long period of economic rebuilding and governmental restructuring. To govern, the United States had to rely on its military presence, with nongovernmental organizations (NGOs) doing much of the behind-the-scenes economic and social rebuilding and multinational companies scrambling to get contracts. Iraqis, kept from quickly forming an interim government, inevitably became suspicious of US intentions and squabbled among themselves. Struggles for local control occurred among political factions, and opportunities developed for Islamic fundamentalist groups to gain a following. Guerrilla warfare and terrorist bombings became the order of the day. Washington officials began using Vietnam-era language to defend their cause, such as Bush's insistence that the United States would "stay the course" and "never run" (November 3, 2003), his criticism of those in the media who paid too much attention to bad news from Iraq, his emphasis on a liberating and democratizing mission for the United States, and his fatuous argument that defeating "the terrorists in Iraq" would mean "that we will not have to face them in our own country."[82]

Despite warnings even from within the US military of the enormous difficulties history taught lay ahead,[83] Bush officials persisted in drawing simplistic comparisons between Iraq and the democratization of Japan and Germany after World War II. The president referred on various occasions to making Iraq a showcase of democracy in the Middle East, apparently oblivious to the violent suppression of democracy that was taking place at that very time by governments near and far that Washington supported. After the war, during a stopover in the Philippines, Bush proposed that that country would also be a model for Iraq—notwithstanding its forty-eight years of American colonial rule, its lengthy period of cronyism and autocratic rule under Ferdinand Marcos, the frequent intrusions of the military into politics, and US doubts about security for Bush's visit, which in consequence lasted a mere eight hours.[84]

The US top-down approach to nation building—actually, state building and unrestrained private investments rather than civil society—was under suspicion in Iraq well before the invasion started. Many people in the Iraqi opposition were reportedly at odds with US officials because it seemed that US officials wanted to dictate the timing, structure, and membership of a post-Saddam government.[85] After the war, Bremer, perhaps to avoid adding to the Iraqis' fractiousness, sought to sideline the various faction heads by appointing them to a "political council" that he would "consult," in contrast with their common desire to form an interim government and convene their own assembly that would draw up a new constitution.[86] But pressure from the Iraqis forced Bremer, in July 2003, to appoint a twenty-five member "governing council," still subordinate to him but able to make government appointments and many other day-to-day decisions. Trouble is, the council lacked international legitimacy as well as the authority to make and implement important decisions. Iraq was being run by the CPA—a US protectorate, in short.

The US authorities seriously underestimated postwar resistance. Though some of its members initially were drawn from militant groups in neighboring countries, and from ordinary Iraqis angry over the occupation's failure to restore basic services and security, most of the resistance came from former Baathists and Sunni Iraqis, the latter a minority that under Saddam had been the dominant ruling group. The resistance consisted of men who had either fled the country and then returned, or went into hiding and, according to some US speculation, reemerged after the war based on a predetermined plan spawned by Saddam himself.

Contrary to administration efforts to focus on foreign fighters in Iraq, as part of their attempt to make the case for globalizing the war on terror, US commanders on the scene saw the ongoing war as an indigenous contest. They concluded that foreigners constituted only a small percentage of the insurgents—estimated in mid-2005 at about 1,000 of a total of 16,000[87]—who were opposing the occupation. "I want to underscore that most of the attacks on our forces are by former regime loyalists and other Iraqis, not foreign forces," said one senior US officer.[88]

With the occupation, US troops became the targets of daily assaults. Even the killing of Saddam's two sons and the capture of Saddam himself late in 2003 did nothing to deter these groups from carrying out suicide bombings and roadside hit-and-run attacks on US troops. As time went on, the impression of many observers was that the occupation was in disarray. The occupation timetable had to be revised; actual costs were nearly double the estimates (from a prewar Pentagon estimate of around $2.1 billion a month to over $4 billion a month in January 2003[89]); troop stays were extended; and (by the end of August 2003) the number of US soldiers killed during the occupation surpassed the number killed in combat. Even if Bremer and US officials in Washington were correct in their claim that anti-US violence was limited to a mere fraction of Iraq's territory, the psychological impact was far greater, as in any insurgency.

Increasing US casualties spelled political trouble for the administration as well as endangered the occupation itself. The administration faced two choices, both of which the Pentagon opposed: respond to members of Congress from both parties who were calling for a major increase in the US troop commitment so as to improve security, or make concessions at the UN so as to win its endorsement of the mission and open the door to deployment of more non-US troops. Some US commanders contended that the United States would need to commit 300,000 to 500,000 troops to restore order.[90] They were ignored. Yet L. Paul Bremer angered the administration when he expressed regret that he had not pushed for more troops when he took over in Iraq.[91] To the Bush administration, a huge troop commitment smacked of "another Vietnam"—a slippery slope to long-term counterinsurgency. US military commanders recognized the liability, moreover, of a prolonged foreign presence in Iraq.[92] US civilian and military leaders were therefore determined to keep the US troop level from edging upward—in mid-2005 it was still around 139,000—but at the same time none of them, and Bush least of all, was willing to set a firm timetable for withdrawal.

The administration's alternative was to create an Iraqi civil defense force as quickly as possible and enlist private US companies to train Iraqis for guard duty at oil pipelines and other facilities. To the extent that Iraqi soldiers and police could replace US troops on the front lines, the face of the occupation would literally be transformed, and other Muslim countries might be persuaded to join the occupation force. Meantime, it was hoped that other countries would maintain their troop contributions. But this plan achieved very limited success. While US officials in Washington insisted in 2004 that 120,000 Iraqi soldiers were battle ready, senior military officers in Iraq put the number at around 4,000. In fact, worsening security in Iraq forced Bush to shift over $3 billion appropriated by Congress for reconstruction into training Iraqis for military and police duties.[93]

As for other governments, just over thirty did send troops, but half of them withdrew their troops by early 2005, with other withdrawals scheduled for later in 2005 or early in 2006.[94] Of approximately 23,000 foreign (non-US) troops in Iraq, the largest contingent—other than Britain's approximately 8,200—is about 3,000 from Italy, where the war is very unpopular. Italian troops were scheduled to be pulled out in September 2005.[95] The governments of India, Pakistan, and Japan, also mindful of the views of their publics, balked at sending troops to Iraq without the UN's endorsement and some confidence about security. Spain initially dispatched 1,300 troops; but following a horrendous series of train bombings in Madrid on March 11, 2004, by terrorists linked to Al-Qaida, Spanish voters, about 80 percent of whom had opposed the government's support of the US invasion, elected a new socialist leadership that withdrew the troops.

In late September 2003, the commander of US forces in the Persian Gulf reported to Congress that the military, already stretched thin and forced to lengthen the stays of units in Iraq, would have to call up additional National Guard and reserve units. At year's end about one-third of US Army combat-ready troops were serving in Iraq. In answer to the US appeal, Japan (about 600) and South Korea (about 3,500 combat troops and 675 engineering troops) responded, though mainly with soldiers to aid in reconstruction. The Turkish government initially responded positively as well; its parliament defied public opinion and voted in favor of a deployment of 10,000 soldiers. Several members of the Iraqi Governing Council denounced the move, however, and in the end Ankara withdrew its pledge, saying it would not act without an invitation from the council.[96]

Not until mid-October 2003 was the United States able to obtain a face-saving resolution from the UN Security Council that qualifiedly endorsed the occupation.[97] Resolution 1511 tried to address France's and others' desire for a quick transfer of authority from the occupation to an elected, constitutionally supported Iraqi leadership. The Governing Council was granted interim status as representing Iraqi sovereignty, but was required to provide a timetable for a new constitution and elections. While accepting "the temporary nature of the exercise by the [occupation authority of] . . . obligations under applicable international law," the resolution asserted that such authority would cease once an authentic Iraqi government was installed.[98] Meanwhile, the UN was granted authority to form a multinational peacekeeping force to help maintain order in Iraq. Member states were urged to contribute to Iraq's reconstruction and public security, though the precise role of the UN itself in promoting "economic reconstruction," "sustainable development," and "representative government" was kept vague.

With Resolution 1511 in hand, the Bush administration had a stronger claim on UN members for aiding in Iraq's reconstruction. The UN had previously calculated that Iraq would need around $55 billion over the next five years. That figure assumed economic growth in Iraq, however, whereas the reality (in mid-2005) was a rising GDP matched by a large foreign debt. The greater part of the debt is owed to the oil-exporting countries of the Middle East (an estimated $45 billion) and to the Paris Club of industrialized countries (around $42 billion). At an international conference in Madrid in October 2003, the Bush administration received pledges for Iraq's recovery totaling over $13 billion. The sum was more than it expected, but a good deal less than was needed, which (even when account is taken of money authorized by the US Congress) was about $22 billion. About two-thirds of the pledged money was in loans, moreover, not grants. The richest Arab states—Saudi Arabia, Kuwait, and the United Arab Emirates—came up with around $2.2 billion, a paltry sum that was mainly in export credits and loans. (Iraq still owes Kuwait reparations for its attack in 1990.) France and Germany did not pledge anything. The main backers were the World Bank and the IMF, and their money was, as always, in loans too.

Despite persistent US pressure, only $2 billion of the $13 billion promised at Madrid has materialized. Debt forgiveness agreed to in 2004 by the Paris Club—an 80-percent reduction of its share of Iraq's debt over a four-year period—still leaves Iraq with a foreign debt of over $80 billion. Iraq's Arab neighbors continue to hold back on aid— they are not even returning ambassadors to Baghdad—because of concerns about Shiite domination of the Iraqi government and the unstable security situation.[99] Yet the Bush administration did not set them much of an example: About a third of the $18.4 billion allocated by Congress for rebuilding Iraq remained unspent as of spring 2005.[100]

During early November 2003, thirty-nine US soldiers were killed in four helicopter gunship incidents. Bush's occupation policy shifted accordingly. The turnover of authority to the Iraqis was put on a fast track, to June 30, 2004; self-government could now precede the writing of a constitution and elections. The new US policy was obviously keyed to the 2004 presidential election: Casualties needed to be reduced and simmering Iraqi resentment quelled.[101] Though the UN's Resolution 1511 requirement of a new constitution and elections by December could not be met, the longstanding demands of the Europeans and the Iraqi Governing Council for first creating a transitional government could be. These steps, even if smoothly taken, would not avoid serious potential problems—for example, the leadership of the transitional government, which was put in the hands of a one-time Baathist, Iyad Allawi, who headed a CIA-funded exile organization and was often pictured being guarded by a private US security force; the role of Islam in the constitution; the distribution of power among the religious and ethnic groups; and the exact timetable of complete US withdrawal—but at least it would put a façade of legitimacy over the occupation. The UN Secretary-General was called upon to assess the practicality of holding elections by June 30. By March 2004 the Iraqis agreed to an interim constitution that was supposed to make the government legitimate.

Nevertheless, the US refusal to step into the background and allow Iraqis to determine their own political and economic future provided fertile ground for an angry nationalism to manifest. Even the Pentagon's man in Iraq, Chalabi, became a spokesman for a quick restoration of Iraqi sovereignty, apparently sensing the shifting mood in Iraq and the opportunity to reposition himself as an ardent nationalist—and presidential aspirant.[102] Iraqi nationalism provided opportunities for anti-US terror groups to thrive on the ensuing chaos and fatalism among the general population. Here was Al-Qaida's chance to turn the tables on the United States, a terrorism expert wrote: to go from being on the run in Afghanistan to making Iraq the main battleground of Al-Qaida's jihad.[103] As had happened so often during the Cold War, US interference in the internal affairs of another country, far from liberating it, fueled what came to be described as an "insurgency." Even L. Paul Bremer was forced to admit in September 2003: "The reality of foreign troops on the streets is starting to chafe. Some Iraqis are beginning to regard us as occupiers and not as liberators."[104] The CIA's November report on Iraqi opinion cited above drew an even tighter conclusion: *Most* Iraqis held that view.

The quandary of occupation was reflected in official haziness about when US forces could begin to depart from Iraq. In December 2003 the commander of coalition forces in Iraq, Lieutenant General Ricardo Sanchez, said that US forces would have to remain in Iraq for "a couple more years," meaning until the end of 2005.[105] During the 2004 presidential election campaign, however, Bush and other officials became more realistic, saying that a substantial US presence would be required for around four more years. In 2005, while the Pentagon officially sought ways to begin drawing down US forces within two years, unofficially, US commanders were skeptical that they could be replaced anytime soon by Iraqi forces.[106] Cheney insisted the insurgency was in its "last throes," but Rumsfeld admitted that the insurgents' attacks were killing more people each time, and therefore that it might take "five, six, eight, ten, twelve years" to subdue them.[107]

Rumsfeld's projection was probably closest to the mark. Even as elections for a national assembly and provincial offices were carried out in Iraq at the start of 2005, leading to the formation of a Shiite-dominated government and the drawing up of a new constitution, the situation on the ground was deteriorating. It was not just that insurgents were gaining strength and were able to return to areas from which they had been ousted. Sunnis are dissatisfied with their representation in the new government and in the constitution-writing process, the future of Kurdish nationalism remains uncertain,[108] and corruption is rife in the oil industry and elsewhere. Personal security and quality of life have yet to improve for millions of Iraqis, particularly in the areas of crime and restoration of electricity.[109]

None of these adversities seems to have affected Bush, who told the nation in June 2005 that the United States was not going to set a timetable for withdrawal and would "stay the course." As US war dead moved toward the 2,000 mark, no date was in sight for the time when Iraqis might take over the main security functions.[110] Just as Vietnam became "Johnson's war," Iraq became Bush's: "You break it, you own it."

In Afghanistan

Many of the same misguided US notions about nation building in Iraq were also true for Afghanistan, which became an orphan of the war on terror once Iraq took center stage. With the quick removal of the Taliban from power and Al-Qaida from its cells, Afghanistan at first seemed to be an example of the virtues of a hard-hitting military response. But the Afghanistan story did not end there: Al-Qaida and Taliban troops remained at large; they regrouped to carry out guerrilla raids in the southern Pashtun part of the country and in the mountainous border region with Pakistan, causing tension between the Afghan and Pakistani governments. As one seasoned observer reported from the border area, the Taliban were everywhere:

> In Quetta, the capital of Pakistan's Baluchistan province [adjacent to southeastern Afghanistan], thousands of Taliban fighters reside in mosques and madrassas with the full support of a provincial ruling party and militant Pakistani groups. Taliban leaders wanted by the US and Kabul governments are living openly in nearby villages, and the families of Taliban have found safe haven in refugee camps inside Pakistan.[111]

Two years beyond 9/11, moreover, the country was still plagued by fighting between warlord factions and by terrorist bombings in the cities. Women's rights activists were living in fear, with a high rate of suicide among them. Drug-related crime was endemic, leading one UN envoy to say that Afghanistan could become "a narco-state." Though national elections were scheduled for 2004, the government's authority beyond Kabul was in doubt so far as foreign embassies and NGOs were concerned.[112] Promises of aid to Afghanistan were not being met. Not only had only about one-half the aid promised at a conference in Tokyo in January 2002 been delivered; funds to rebuild Afghanistan accounted for a mere one-quarter of that aid. "The reconstruction of Afghanistan has not begun," said Adib Farhadi, the director of economic affairs in the Afghan Ministry of Foreign Affairs. "The commitments from the Tokyo conference never became a reality."[113]

It is not that the United States, or the international peacekeeping force that came under NATO command, did not try to square the circle of "developing" Afghanistan. Plenty of civil affairs projects were launched throughout the country. Schools were built, roads were reopened. But, as in Iraq, while some local Afghan leaders were grateful, there simply was not enough money to carry through on reconstruction projects—such as by hiring teachers for the schools and completing road building—or enough soldiers to prevent warlord groups from setting up roadblocks to tax drivers.[114] Far less money and far fewer troops were committed to Afghanistan compared with Iraq, countries with comparable populations (about 28 million and 24 million respectively).[115] Moreover, disagreements periodically surfaced between international agencies and the US command over whether to emphasize security or development projects.[116] Good arguments could be made on either side; but while the arguments went on, not enough was accomplished—and there were far too many accidental civilian deaths from bombing errors—to make US soldiers welcome. Even though Afghanistan, in contrast with Iraq, had its own government, anti-US feelings two years after the supposed end of the Taliban were running high.

The appointment of Zalmay Khalilzad as US ambassador to Afghanistan in mid-2003 was another indication of the Pentagon's domination of policymaking. Khalilzad, a member of Bush's NSC staff at the time of his appointment, had all the right credentials: a Pashtun Afghani by birth; a consultant to Unocal when the company sought to build an oil pipeline from the Caspian Sea across Afghanistan; one of the signers of the PNAC's declaration of principles; and author of a RAND Corporation paper that advocated maintaining US hegemony.[117] The appointment was bound to be bad news for Afghanistan in at least three specific ways. First, it meant that little would be done to eliminate Pakistan's not-so-secret support of the Taliban. The United States evidently had long since decided that Musharraf's support in the aftermath of the Iraq war was more important than Afghanistan's stability.[118] Second, the appointment meant that Unocal's contract would finally go through. The fact that President Karzai himself had once been a Unocal board member probably didn't hurt Unocal's cause. Third, the appointment settled in favor of the military the question whether security or development—and therefore the military's prominence in development projects—should have priority.[119] (Khalilzad subsequently became the first US ambassador to postwar Iraq.)

In January 2004 the Afghan factions were able to cobble together a new constitution that in most key respects gave Karzai and the United States the strong presidency they wanted. This was followed in October by national elections, once postponed, that formalized Karzai's position. Carrying out elections was no small achievement in view of the numerous sources of division, which were out in the open throughout the constitutional convention. The real test of Afghanistan's unity depends on whether or not the constitution's provisions on a multilingual state, women's equality, and the parliament's powers will be honored. Elections for a national assembly were carried out in September 2005, but only about half the eligible population voted.

Meanwhile, the world beyond Kabul remains up for grabs. A 2003 survey of twelve provinces by Human Rights Watch not only reported on a long list of violent crimes being committed by police and warlord authorities outside Kabul. It also indicted various countries, chiefly the United States, for befriending the perpetrators of the violence.[120] As one observer said with reference to both Afghanistan and Iraq,

> Afghanistan is the place where the tension between the theoretical model [of democratic reconstruction], the will to implement it, and the new pragmatic ideas deriving from the war on terrorism is the most evident. The reality of the military situation in the country and the urgency of the task is [*sic*] leading the United States to rely on, and make deals with, some of the forces that are anathema to democracy: warlords and their militias, tribal leaders, and other powerful local figures. . . . Iraq is also likely to emerge as a country where the theory of democratic reconstruction will clash with the reality of the political situation, the scarcity of resources, and the interests of the United States and other international actors.[121]

These words were subsequently born out. On the resource side, a second Berlin conference of fifty-odd countries in March 2004 resulted in pledges of $8.2 billion in additional aid and loans over three years for Afghanistan's reconstruction. The US share was announced as $3.4 billion spread over two fiscal years. As in Iraq, the total amount was more than expected, but was well short of what the major international banks said was needed to improve security and avert rampant corruption. In coming years the average Afghan can thus expect to receive about one-sixth the foreign assistance that the average Bosnian or East Timorese is receiving.[122] On the political side, despite elections, the government in Kabul is made in America, its leader literally under US (Special Forces) protection and dependent on the support of a Northern Alliance that has an abominable record when it comes to respect for human rights and democratic processes.[123] Some Northern Alliance leaders whom an NGO human rights study has found guilty of serious violations were candidates in the October 2005 assembly election.[124]

The challenge of extending the government's reach may be judged from opium cultivation, which has leaped enormously since the Taliban were removed. Drug lords so control the trade, which accounts for nearly 90 percent of the world's opium, that various UN agencies in Afghanistan have said it is becoming a narco-state. A US embassy cable laid the failure to come close to eradicating Afghanistan's poppy fields at the door of local officials and President Karzai, who "has been unwilling to assert strong leadership."[125] According to the US State Department's own narcotics bureau, whereas in 1991 only about 4,200 acres in Afghanistan were cultivated for poppy growing, 76,000 acres were cultivated in 2002. A UN survey put the 2004 figure at over 321,000 acres.[126] With poppy growing able to earn a farmer nearly twenty times what he could earn growing wheat, the choice is obvious. So prominent had opium growing become that in 2003 an estimated 7 percent of the Afghan population was involved; the mission director for the US Agency for International Development said that opium production accounted for between 40 and 60 percent of the country's gross domestic product.[127] The best hope for reducing the supply of opium lies in the popularity of cultivating it, which has drastically reduced its price.[128] So critical to the country's political future had the drug trade become by 2005 that the US military was redeployed to counteracting it at every level, from opium production to sales.[129]

Wishful thinking grips official Washington, however, such as in Colin Powell's statement at the time of the Berlin conference that "Afghanistan has gone from being a failed state, ruled by extremists and terrorists, to a free country with a growing economy and an emerging democracy."[130] How anyone can make that claim in light of the Afghanistan economy's dependence on opium growing, its president's dependence on the US ambassador and US forces, and its security's dependence on officials, warlords, and armies that are all tied into the opium trade is hard to imagine.[131] In NATO, on the other hand, the pessimistic view prevails. There, the priority is Afghanistan's survival more so than Iraq's, as reflected in the organization's troop commitments. So far apart are the United States and NATO that the secretary general of NATO warned that the continued US unwillingness to work closely with the organization on both Iraq and Afghanistan would gravely weaken the alliance and quite possibly eventuate in having "two failed states" in the Middle East.[132]

In Conclusion: Another Vietnam?

In responding to the terrorist attack by going after Saddam, the Bush administration set itself (and the US public) up for the endless war it now has. It overthrew a dictatorship, but at great cost to civilian life and property. It eventually captured Saddam and most of his lieutenants, but it failed to catch the top leaders of Al-Qaida. It installed a more accountable leadership in Iraq, but it missed the opportunity to craft an Arab-Israeli peace or to instill confidence in the United States among Islamic peoples. Most fundamentally, the Iraq war actually increased the threat of terrorism. The invasion and occupation accomplished two things that should never have happened: They transformed Al-Qaida from a relatively small organization into an ideology with broad appeal, and they shifted the focal point of terrorist operations from Afghanistan, where Al-Qaida had been bottled up, to Iraq.[133] Iraq itself now seems to have become a training ground for terrorists.[134] Meanwhile, on a worldwide scale, the State Department's own figures—revised and reissued after gross inconsistencies were pointed out—showed that "significant" terrorist incidents worldwide and casualties from them increased in 2003 compared with 2002.[135] No wonder that Rumsfeld ruminated privately (and pessimistically) about the costs of the war on terror. "It will be a long, hard slog," he concluded in a memo.[136] In a nationwide address in June 2005, President Bush used identical language.

Iraq and Afghanistan are two different conflicts that, tragically, were perceived (or were constructed) by a doctrinaire US leadership as being one and the same. In the manner of previous US crusades, details that get in the way of doctrine are cast aside. The great struggle is now between "terrorism and democracy," conveniently bypassing the question how Saudi Arabia, Pakistan, Indonesia, and other countries hit by terrorist attacks can be considered democracies. But even more absurd is the proclamation that "democracy" is what this contest is all about. Democracy certainly had no place in the administration's original rationale for war on Iraq; the word only appeared later, when WMD could not be found there. Nor did Bush himself, much less any of his senior advisers, whether neocons or realists, favor humanitarian objectives for US foreign policy—quite the opposite. In a parody of Chairman Mao, neocons (and some liberals) have always believed that political power (pronounced "democracy") grows out of the barrel of a gun. As the Reagan administration had shown in Central America and elsewhere, if the choice was to support a right-wing rather than a left-wing dictator, the decision would always favor the right, not because it held out better prospects for democracy, but because it meant support for US interests.

Notwithstanding the supposed transfer of sovereignty to Iraq, the US occupation stares directly into the face of a humiliating defeat. The question of "another Vietnam" rears its ugly head. It is easy to dismiss the comparison: In Vietnam the United States sided with a succession of repressive governments, and its defeat came at the end of a nearly twenty-year struggle. Furthermore, the Iraqi resistance, unlike Vietnam's, does not have a unified command or ideology, or major external support. Instead, it largely reflects the dissatisfactions of the Sunni population, and thus the prospect of a widening civil war. Nor is there a significant antiwar movement in the United States, driven by high casualties and other costs. What sustains the comparison, however, goes beyond the historical details to states of mind and patterns of decisionmaking. In both wars, US forces faced intense nationalism directed at foreign occupiers. US leaders believed in the universality of US values, in the doctrine that might makes right, in the inevitable triumph of military firepower and technology, in the test of wills that resistance represented, in discounting international opinion, and in the capacity to rebuild nations in the US image. Here is the kind of self-destructive hubris that brought the Johnson and Nixon governments to their knees in Vietnam and that well might do the same to the George W. Bush administration. Common to all three administrations is the failure to recognize defeat, even when intelligence analyses available to the top leaders are highly pessimistic.[137] Instead, Bush is following form in taking every adversity as a challenge to US "credibility" as a world leader.

Perhaps most fundamentally, in both wars the United States intervened under false pretenses, was betrayed by the arrogance of its leaders, and misunderstood and was ultimately defeated by nationalism. The United States posed as a liberator in Vietnam and Iraq, and ended up being widely perceived as the oppressor in both. Notwithstanding that US power overthrew a dictator in Iraq, Washington quickly lost the mandate of legitimacy by its ambition, clear enough to ordinary Iraqis, to control Iraq's oil, its political processes, and even its destiny. The United States became, as it was in Vietnam, a colonial authority. No serious observer can mistake Iraq's government, or Afghanistan's, for an independent regime; they are creatures of the United States, and those who serve them are objects of insurgent attacks precisely for that reason.

Notes

1. David E. Sanger, "Viewing the War as a Lesson to the World," *NYT,* April 6, 2003, online ed.

2. The Iran case is discussed in Chapter 5. As for Libya, in December 2003 Muammar el-Qaddafi declared that his country would cease its fifteen-year-long effort to develop a nuclear bomb and open itself to international inspection. The declaration followed several months of secret negotiations with the US and British governments, and US interception in October 2003 of a shipment of weapon-related equipment. Qaddafi's motives were not necessarily to avoid a US invasion, however. He may have sought to reopen trade and investment opportunities that had been impeded by embargoes. UN sanctions against Libya had already been lifted in September 2003 when Libya agreed to pay $2.7 billion to the relatives of Pan American Airline passengers who were killed by a bomb placed by Libyan agents that exploded over Lockerbie, Scotland, in 1988.

3. Nationwide address, September 7, 2003; text in *NYT,* September 8, 2003, p. A10.

4. The Bush administration took some of the credit for Syria's decision to withdraw from Lebanon following mass demonstrations in Beirut, and for the

Egyptian government's decision to allow presidential elections with more than one candidate. But those developments had mainly to do with domestic circumstances in those countries, and in neither case did they result in significant advances for democracy.

5. Joseph Wilson, "Republic or Empire?" pp. 4–5.

6. The very first sentence of President George H. W. Bush's National Security Directive 54 of January 15, 1991, which was the decision to go to war against Iraq, reads: "Access to Persian Gulf oil and the security of key friendly states in the area are vital to US national security." Document obtained by the National Security Archive and available at www.gwu.edu/~nsarchiv/NSAEBB/NSAEBB21/06-01.htm.

7. *NYT,* April 1, 2003, p. A3.

8. James A. Baker III Institute for Public Policy and Council on Foreign Relations, *Strategic Energy Policy Challenges for the 21st Century.*

9. Michael Klare, "Bush-Cheney Energy Strategy: Procuring the Rest of the World's Oil."

10. Ibid., p. 5.

11. For a fuller assessment, see Michael Renner, "The Other Looting."

12. David Rieff, "Blueprint for a Mess," p. 44.

13. Greg Palast, "OPEC on the March," pp. 74–76.

14. Erik Eckholm, "White House Officials and Cheney Aide Approved Halliburton Contract in Iraq, Pentagon Says," *NYT,* June 14, 2004, p. A5.

15. Jeff Gerth and Don Van Natta Jr., "Halliburton Contracts in Iraq: The Struggle to Manage Costs," *NYT,* December 29, 2003, p. A1.

16. Don Van Natta Jr., "High Payments to Halliburton for Fuel in Iraq," *NYT,* December 10, 2003, p. A1. According to Democratic Party and *New York Times* investigators, Halliburton was "charging $2.64 for a gallon of fuel it imports from Kuwait and $1.24 per gallon for fuel from Turkey," about one-half the cost of fuel imported from Kuwait by a Pentagon agency and Iraq's own state oil company. Oil was only part of Halliburton's multibillion dollar business in Iraq; the even greater part was providing logistical support—meals, transportation, housing—to US forces there and in Kuwait. This approximately $13 billion business, like all the rest, was never competitively bid, a practice that did not stop until late in 2004. In the end, all the adverse publicity concerning KBR led it to get out of Iraq, but not before the top contracting official for the US Army Corps of Engineers called for an investigation of its possible violations of rules governing the awarding of contracts. *NYT,* October 25, 2004, p. A11.

17. Neela Banerjee, "Energy Companies Weigh Their Possible Future in Iraq," *NYT,* October 26, 2002, p. B3. In fact, under a directive authored by Paul Wolfowitz, French, German, and Russian firms were barred from competing for prime reconstruction contracts worth over $18 billion, a clear American retaliation for their unwillingness to support US policy. See *NYT,* December 10, 2003, p. A1.

18. See Sabrina Tavernise, "Oil Prize, Past and Present, Ties Russia to Iraq," *NYT,* October 17, 2002, p. A14.

19. Erin E. Arvedlund and Heather Timmons, "Conoco Wins Lukoil Bid, a Window on Iraq," *NYT,* September 30, 2004, online ed.

20. The surge in oil prices was generally attributed to increasing violence in Iraq, which caused frequent interruptions in production; the troubled future

of Yukos, Russia's main oil company; and increased demand in China, India, the United States, and other countries.

21. For example, Senator Carl Levin, chairman of the Senate Armed Services Committee, accused the Saudis of not being sufficiently cooperative in the war on terrorism and suggested that the United States might want to "find a place [for its air bases] where we are much more welcome." James Dao, "Dismay with Saudi Arabia Fuels Pullout Talk," *NYT,* January 16, 2002.

22. Clarke, *Against All Enemies,* p. 283.

23. Thom Shanker and Eric Schmitt, "Pentagon Expects Long-Term Access to Four Key Bases in Iraq," *NYT,* April 20, 2003, online ed.

24. Paul Wolfowitz, for example, testified in March 2003 before a congressional committee that Iraq's oil revenues "could bring between $50 and $100 billion over the course of the next two to three years." Cheney, on the day Baghdad fell in April, predicted that Iraq could produce 3 million barrels of oil a day by year's end. *NYT,* September 10, 2003, p. A8.

25. Jeff Gerth, "Report Offered Bleak Outlook About Iraq Oil," *NYT,* October 5, 2003, online ed. Problems such as belowground water seepage also raised questions about how much oil was ultimately recoverable. Jeff Gerth, "Oil Experts See Long-Term Risks to Iraq Reserves," *NYT,* November 30, 2003, online ed.

26. By one oil industry expert's estimate, the value of Iraq's annual oil production would not reach $15 to $20 billion until 2006 rather than, as originally anticipated, in 2004. Donald Hepburn, "Nice War; Here's the Bill," *NYT,* September 3, 2003, p. A19.

27. Palast, "OPEC on the March."

28. See Jeff Gerth, "US Fails to Curb Its Saudi Oil Habit, Experts Say," *NYT,* November 26, 2002, p. A1.

29. See Ken Silverstein, "Saudis and Americans: Friends in Need," pp. 15–20.

30. Mutual dependence may have had something to do with the special treatment accorded prominent Saudis immediately after the 9/11 attacks. Despite many months of official denials, US government records show that the FBI allowed over 160 Saudis, including relatives of Osama bin Laden as well as members of the royal family, to take charter flights out of the United States despite a nationwide shutdown of airports. Eric Lichtblau, "New Details on F.B.I. Aid for Saudis After 9/11," *NYT,* March 27, 2005, online ed.

31. Neela Banerjee, "Plan to Revive Production of Oil in Iraq Is Announced," *NYT,* July 31, 2003, p. C5.

32. Chalmers Johnson, "The War Business," p. 57.

33. Ibid., p. 58. The Lockheed executive was Bruce Jackson. Former Secretary of State George Shultz, the one-time president of Bechtel Corporation, and Senator John McCain were members of that committee.

34. Ibid., p. 56. Johnson ("The War Business," p. 53) writes: "During the first Iraq war, in 1991, one in a hundred American personnel was employed by a private contractor. In the second Iraq war, that ratio is closer to one in ten."

35. Based on a study by the Center for Public Integrity, cited in *NYT,* October 31, 2003, p. A8. These companies also gave money to Democratic candidates, but double as much to Republicans.

36. I rely here on Naomi Klein, "Baghdad Year Zero: Pillaging Iraq in Pursuit of a Neocon Utopia," pp. 43–53.

37. Iraq Revenue Watch, "Disorder, Negligence and Mismanagement: How the CPA Handled Iraq Reconstruction Funds."

38. Douglas Jehl, "Insiders' New Firm Consults on Iraq," *NYT,* September 30, 2003, p. A1.

39. *NYT,* October 31, 2003, p. A8.

40. See Unger, *House of Bush, House of Saud,* pp. 155–169.

41. Bush stated in June 2002 that a Middle East peace depended on replacing Yasir Arafat, a classic instance of hegemonic conduct. He showed no qualms about dictating the choice of Palestinian leader, in advance of elections.

42. See Richard Falk, "Gaza Illusions," *The Nation,* pp. 4-5.

43. *NYT,* April 15, 2003, p. B10.

44. See *NYT,* March 11, 2003, p. A11.

45. See Diane Sawyer's ABC-TV interview of Bush, December 16, 2003; recounted by Richard W. Stevenson, "Remember 'Weapons of Mass Destruction'? For Bush, They Are a Nonissue," *NYT,* December 18, 2003, p. A14.

46. See, for example, the *New York Times*-CBS News poll results in *NYT,* June 17, 2005, p. A14. Bush retained his popularity with respect to his handling of the war on terror generally. By the fall of 2005, polls showed a majority of Americans supporting a timetable for US withdrawal from Iraq.

47. For a number of examples, see Michael Moore, *Dude, Where's My Country?* pp. 76–81.

48. For instance, in April 2004 Sinclair directed its eight ABC affiliates to preempt a *Nightline* program that it considered "unpatriotic"—one in which longtime host Ted Koppel read aloud the names of US soldiers who had been killed in Iraq. In October 2004 all sixty-two Sinclair-owned or -managed television stations were told to carry a film about Senator John Kerry's 1971 testimony before a US Senate committee in which he related documented stories of US atrocities committed in Vietnam. See Bill Carter, "Risks Seen for TV Chain Showing Film About Kerry," *NYT,* October 18, 2004, p. C1.

49. According to the Johns Hopkins University Bloomberg School of Public Health, whose report relied on a house-to-house survey of Iraqi families in thirty-three locations. (Elisabeth Rosenthal, "Study Puts Iraqi Deaths of Civilians at 100,000," *NYT,* October 29, 2004, p. A8.) The Brookings Institution in Washington, DC, gives a variety of different (and much lower) figures as of June 2005, such as between 22,600 and 25,600. But such figures are acknowledged as being too low. (See *Iraq Index: Tracking Variables of Reconstruction & Security in Post-Saddam Iraq,* p. 8, online at http://www.brookings.org/dybdocroot/fp/saban/iraq/index.pdf.) Iraq Body Count, a London-based research group, subsequently estimated (from news accounts) that 24,865 civilians were killed in Iraq during the first two years since the US invasion. US forces accounted for 37 percent of the deaths. Hassan M. Fattah, "Civilian Toll in Iraq Is Placed at Nearly 25,000," *NYT,* July 20, 2005, p. A8.

50. A full accounting is by Howard Friel and Richard Falk, *The Record of the Paper: How the* New York Times *Misreports US Foreign Policy.*

51. The Editors, "The Times and Iraq," *NYT,* May 26, 2004, online ed. But see the much deeper criticism by the *Times*'s public editor, Daniel Okrent, "Weapons of Mass Destruction? Or Mass Distraction?" *NYT,* May 30, 2004, online ed. He argued that "the failure was not individual, it was institutional."

52. Editors of the *Washington Post* and *The New Republic* also printed limited apologies for biased coverage.

53. See Seymour M. Hersh, "The Debate Within," pp. 34–39 and "Rumsfeld, Powell at War for Control of US Foreign Policy," Knight Ridder Washington Bureau, May 4, 2003.

54. According to Bob Woodward's account (*Plan of Attack*) and an interview with Woodward by William Hamilton, "Bush Began to Plan War Three Months After 9/11," *Washington Post,* April 18, 2004, online ed.

55. Henry Kissinger, *White House Years,* pp. 663–666.

56. Thomson, "Autopsy on Vietnam," in Wittkopf and McCormick, eds., *Domestic Sources of American Foreign Policy,* pp. 259–270.

57. On Middle East policy, for instance, see Alan Sipress, "Powell vs. the Pentagon," *Washington Post National Weekly Edition,* May 6–12, 2002, p. 17.

58. See Susan V. Lawrence, "Duel Over Sanctions," *Far Eastern Economic Review,* November 6, 2003, pp. 32–33.

59. This account relies mainly on Susan V. Lawrence, "A New Threat," *Far Eastern Economic Review,* December 18, 2003, pp. 16–20.

60. "I'm sure," said Powell after leaving office, "that the Vice President's view from the very beginning was: we'll never solve this through diplomatic means." Interview with the German magazine *Stern;* http://news.channel.aol .com, March 30, 2005.

61. See, for instance, his comments after Blix and ElBaradei submitted reports to the Security Council on the first sixty days of inspections under UN Resolution 1441, in *NYT,* January 28, 2003, p. A8.

62. See, for example, *NYT,* January 28, 2003, p. A8.

63. For two lengthy analyses and rebuttals, see Hiro, *Secrets and Lies,* pp. 123–127, and Charles Hanley, "Powell's Case for Iraq War Falls Apart 6 Months Later," Associated Press, August 11, 2003; online via Common Dreams at www .commondreams.org/headlines03/0811-09.htm.

64. See Eric Alterman, "Colin Powell and the 'Power of Audacity.'"

65. Sanger, "Viewing the War as a Lesson to the World."

66. Bolton, then undersecretary of state for arms control and international security, was already well known for his tendency to exaggerate the unconventional weapons capabilities of "rogue states." CIA analyses were typically much more nuanced and qualified. See Douglas Jehl, "New Warning Was Put Off on Weapons Syria Plans," *NYT,* July 18, 2003, p. A8.

67. Bradley Graham and Peter Slevin, "Meetings with Iran-Contra Arms Dealer Confirmed," *Washington Post,* August 28, 2003, online ed.

68. This paragraph relies mainly on Peter Slevin and Dana Priest, "Wolfowitz Concedes Iraq Errors," *Washington Post,* July 24, 2003, online ed.

69. Rieff, "Blueprint for a Mess," p. 31.

70. Ibid.; Hersh, "The Debate Within," pp. 35–36.

71. This date, much earlier than the April 2002 starting time mentioned in other accounts (see the following note), further adds to the thesis here of Bush's commitment to regime change in Iraq soon after the 9/11 attacks. See the State Department documents released to the National Security Archive on August 17, 2005, at www.nsarchive.org.

72. One participant in the project reported that the plan included roles for some elements of the Iraqi military and Baath Party members. David L. Phillips, "Listening to the Wrong Iraqi," *NYT,* September 20, 2003, online ed. The defense official is quoted in Eric Schmitt and Joel Brinkley, "State Dept. Study Foresaw Trouble Now Plaguing Iraq," *NYT,* October 19, 2003, online ed.

David Rieff's article, "Blueprint for a Mess" (pp. 31–32) also contains an extended discussion of the Future of Iraq Project and the run-ins with the Pentagon.

73. Rieff, "Blueprint for a Mess," pp. 32–33; George Packer, "War After the War," p. 62.

74. Schmitt and Brinkley, "State Dept. Study Foresaw Trouble Now Plaguing Iraq."

75. Rieff, "Blueprint for a Mess," pp. 31–33.

76. On returning from a brief tour of Iraq, Wolfowitz naturally reported great progress in the occupation. But he also acknowledged three erroneous assumptions: that the Baath Party would not survive without Saddam Hussein in power; that the Iraqi military and police would quickly move to support the occupation forces; and that US forces involved in the invasion would be sufficient to keep the peace and rebuild the country. See ibid.

77. Bremer's order of May 23, 2003, to disband the Iraqi military was opposed by civilian and military leaders across the bureaucracy, not so much for eliminating a source of internal security and employment as for failing to provide quick replacements. The gap in replacement forces helped put US forces in the position of an occupying power. See Michael R. Gordon, "Debate Lingering on Decision to Dissolve the Iraqi Military," *NYT,* October 21, 2004, p. A1.

78. Cheney said: "Once you've got Baghdad, it's not clear what you do with it. It's not clear what kind of government you would put in place of the one that's currently there now. Is it going to be a Shia regime, a Sunni regime or a Kurdish regime? Or one that tilts toward the Baathists, or one that tilts toward the Islamic fundamentalists? How much credibility is that government going to have if it's set up by the United States military when it's there? How long does the United States military have to stay to protect the people that sign on for that government, and what happens to it once we leave?" Quoted by George F. Will, "What to Ask the Nominee," *Washington Post,* November 17, 2004, online ed.

79. David E. Sanger, "White House to Overhaul Iraq and Afghan Missions," *NYT,* October 6, 2003, p. A1.

80. See, for example, John Paul Lederach, *Building Peace: Sustainable Reconciliation in Divided Societies,* pp. 74–75.

81. A well-informed assessment is by a US Army Reserve major and cultural anthropologist who served in Iraq: Christopher H. Varhola, "American Challenges in Post-Conflict Iraq."

82. Remarks following the shooting down of a US helicopter in which fifteen soldiers perished. *Honolulu Star-Bulletin,* November 4, 2003.

83. See Conrad C. Crane and W. Andrew Terrill, *Reconstructing Iraq: Insight, Challenges, and Missions for Military Forces in a Post-Conflict Scenario.*

84. David E. Sanger, "Bush Cites Philippines as Model in Rebuilding Iraq," *NYT,* October 19, 2003, p. A1.

85. See, for example, Judith Miller and Lowell Bergman, "Iraq Opposition Is Pursuing Ties with Iranians," *NYT,* December 13, 2002, online ed.

86. See Patrick E. Tyler, "Leading Iraqi Shiite Cleric Emerges to Meet US Ally," *NYT,* June 6, 2003, p. A12.

87. Brookings Institution, *Iraq Index,* p. 15. A later Brookings Institution estimate puts the size of the insurgency at 18,000. See *NYT,* September 9, 2005, p. A 23.

88. Major General Charles H. Swannack Jr., commander of the 82d Airborne Division that operated along Iraq's eastern borders with Syria, Jordan, and Saudi Arabia. Joel Brinkley, "US Officers in Iraq Find Few Signs of Infiltration by Foreign Fighters," *NYT,* November 19, 2003, p. A11.

89. David Firestone and Thom Shanker, "War's Cost Brings Democratic Anger," *NYT,* July 11, 2003, p. A8.

90. *NYT,* August 21, 2003, p. 1.

91. Elisabeth Bumiller and Jodi Wilgoren, "Bremer Critique on Iraq Raises Political Furor," *NYT,* October 6, 2004, online ed.

92. As the US commander in Iraq, General John P. Abizaid, said, "You can't underestimate the public perception both within Iraq and within the Arab world about the percentage of the force being so heavily American." *NYT,* August 29, 2003, p. 1.

93. Steven R. Weisman, "US Envoy to Iraq Urges Shift of Money to Security," *NYT,* August 31, 2004, online ed.; Weisman, "US Pressures Rich Nations to Fill Gap in Iraq Reconstruction Created by Security Needs," *NYT,* October 1, 2004, p. A6.

94. For a table of troop commitments and withdrawals, see *NYT,* March 16, 2005, p. A9.

95. Prime Minister Berlusconi faces reelection and fallout from an incident at a US-guarded Iraqi checkpoint in which an Italian intelligence officer was mistakenly killed.

96. Eric Schmitt, "Commander Doesn't Expect More Foreign Troops in Iraq," *NYT,* September 26, 2003, p. A10, citing General John P. Abizaid.

97. Text in *NYT,* October 17, 2003, p. A10.

98. One positive development was the establishment in October 2003 of an independent entity under the UN and the World Bank to handle reconstruction assistance for Iraq. By design the new organization would be separate from the Pentagon-run Development Fund for Iraq, providing an alternative means of attracting European, Canadian, and Arab countries' funds.

99. Steven R. Weisman, "Rice Urges Arab States to Send Envoys to Baghdad," *NYT,* June 22, 2005, p. A9.

100. *NYT,* April 17, 2005, p. 8.

101. A top-secret CIA report in November 2003 reportedly presented a deeply pessimistic appraisal of ordinary Iraqis' anguish over the occupation and despair over the lack of an Iraqi political alternative to it. The report was said to have the support of L. Paul Bremer. Douglas Jehl, "C.I.A. Report Suggests Iraqis Are Losing Faith in US Efforts," *NYT,* November 13, 2003, p. A11.

102. Chalabi said that restoring sovereignty meant reclaiming Iraq's seat in the UN, taking immediate control of the country's finances, and keeping foreign troops other than those of the United States out of Iraq. Patrick E. Tyler and Felicity Barringer, "An Iraqi Leader Shifts to Position at Odds with US," *NYT,* September 23, 2003, p. A1.

103. "In the end, Qaeda's real interest in Iraq has been to exploit the occupation as a propaganda and recruitment tool for the global jihadist cause."

Bruce Hoffman, "Saddam Is Ours. Does Al Qaeda Care?" *NYT,* December 17, 2003, p. A35. Hoffman is a RAND Corporation staff member.

104. *NYT,* September 26, 2003, p. A10.

105. *NYT,* December 16, 2003, p. A18.

106. *NYT,* June 19, 2005, p. 1.

107. *NYT,* June 27, 2005, p. A8.

108. On Kurdish nationalism, separatist tendencies, and the crucial role of the Kurdish militia in a future bid for independence, see Nir Rosen, "In the Balance" and Edward Wong, "Kurds Vow to Retain Militia as Guardians of Autonomy," *NYT,* February 27, 2005, p. 8. Under the constitution-writing rules, Kurds have an opportunity to veto the new constitution when it comes up for a popular vote, scheduled for October 15, 2005.

109. During the occupation, criminals have sprung up everywhere, kidnapping and robbing people, counterfeiting money, and extorting funds. City streets are no longer safe. As much as any other complaint against the occupation is that it has failed to ensure the safety of ordinary people. As one Baghdad resident said: "Before [in the Saddam era] we had security but no freedom of speech. Now we have freedom to speak but no security. What's the difference?" (*The News Hour with Jim Lehrer,* PBS Television, October 29, 2003.) Crime is the second leading cause of death, far higher than the insurgency. (Fattah, "Civilian Toll in Iraq Is Placed at Nearly 25,000.") Quality of life indicators include high unemployment, high infant mortality, and lack of electricity and drinkable water. Electrical generation in mid-2005 stands at about the same level as before the war, and according to opinion polls is the number-one concern of Iraqis (with "terrorists" ranked eighth). (Brookings Institution, *Iraq Index,* June 27, 2005, p. 33.) Education is one area in which there has been improvement with the reopening of schools and number of textbooks distributed. See, for instance, Bruce Hoffman, "Plan of Attack," pp. 42–43, and Brookings Institution, *Iraq Index.*

110. A Pentagon assessment of the Iraqi security forces in mid-2005 pointed to significant gains in the number of trained personnel, but also to the limited ability of two-thirds of Iraqi army and police units to fight the insurgency on their own. See Eric Schmitt, "Iraqis Not Ready to Fight Rebels on Their Own, US Says," *NYT,* July 21, 2005, online ed.

111. Ahmed Rashid, "Safe Haven for the Taliban," *Far Eastern Economic Review,* October 16, 2003, p. 19.

112. Kirk Semple, "Afghans' Political Prognosis Is Still Hazy, U.N. Panel Says," *NYT,* November 12, 2003, p. A11.

113. The pledges made at the Tokyo conference amounted to over $4.5 billion in assistance over five years. Afghan officials said they had received only about half of the $1.8 billion in aid that they expected to receive by the fall. "Three-quarters of that money was for relief—mainly food and medicine—leaving less than $150 million for reconstructing the nation's war-ravaged water systems, power grids, schools and roads." James Dao, "Afghan Officials Say Aid Has Been Too Slow," *NYT,* July 25, 2002, online ed.

114. Amy Waldman and Dexter Filkins, "2 US Fronts: Quick Wars, But Bloody Peace," *NYT,* September 19, 2003, p. A1.

115. As of mid-2004, there were about 14,500 coalition troops in Afghanistan (including 13,000 Americans) and some 6,500 troops in a NATO security force in Kabul. The US force increased to around 17,000 in 2005.

116. Eric Schmitt, "General Urges Foreigners to Aid Afghans," *NYT,* July 9, 2003, p. A3. For a generally positive portrait of US involvement in Afghanistan's reconstruction, see Michael Ignatieff, "Nation-Building Lite."

117. Khalilzad, *From Containment to Global Leadership? America and the World After the Cold War.*

118. Rashid, "Safe Haven," pp. 20–21.

119. Kathy Gannon, "Afghanistan Unbound," pp. 35–46.

120. The report, "Killing You Is a Very Easy Thing to Do," is summarized in Carlotta Gall, "Rights Group Reports Abuses by Afghans, Some Backed by US," *NYT,* July 29, 2003, p. A3.

121. Marina Ottaway, "Promoting Democracy After Conflict: The Difficult Choices," p. 315.

122. Gannon, "Afghanistan Unbound," p. 41, based on a CARE International estimate.

123. As is well known, the deplorable behavior of Northern Alliance warlords and armies had much to do with the rise of the Taliban in the first place. After Alliance forces helped oust the Taliban, it also became evident that they had engaged in war crimes. Several hundred to perhaps a few thousand prisoners of war died while being transported from the front in closed containers. They were hastily buried in mass graves. US soldiers may have known of such treatment and said nothing. See Babek Dehghanpished, John Barry, and Roy Gutman, "The Death Convoy of Afghanistan," *Newsweek,* August 26, 2002, pp. 20–30.

124. A summary of the report by the Afghan Justice Project was carried by the *NYT,* July 18, 2005, p. A9.

125. Of course this was not the view in Washington, where optimism reigned as usual, just as it did over Iraq. David S. Cloud and Carlotta Gall, "US Memo Faults Afghan Leader on Heroin Fight," *NYT,* May 22, 2005, online ed.

126. *NYT,* August 15, 2003, p. A10, and Carlotta Gall, "Afghan Poppy Growing Reaches Record Level, U.N. Says," *NYT,* November 19, 2004, p. A3.

127. Interview of Patrick Fine on National Public Radio's *Morning Edition,* October 21, 2004.

128. David Rohde, "Poppies Flood Afghanistan; Opium Tide May Yet Turn," *NYT,* July 1, 2004, p. A10.

129. Thom Shanker, "Pentagon Sees Aggressive Antidrug Effort in Afghanistan," *NYT,* March 25, 2005, online ed.

130. Christopher Marquis, "Led by US, Nations Pledge Billions to Revive Afghanistan," *NYT,* April 1, 2004, p. A10.

131. Yet optimistic appraisals of Afghanistan's future are available. See, for instance, S. Frederick Starr, "Hamid Karzai's Key Role in Central Asia," pp. 43–46.

132. The remarks of NATO Secretary General Jaap de Hoop Scheffer were reported in *NYT,* July 3, 2004, p. A8.

133. An excellent survey and analysis of this outcome, based on extensive interviews, was written by Douglas Frantz, Josh Meyer, Sebastian Rotella, and Megan K. Stack, "Al Qaeda Seen as Wider Threat," *Los Angeles Times,* September 26, 2004, online ed.

134. A classified CIA report in 2005 concluded that many non-Iraqi insurgents were using their experience in Iraq to carry on their struggle elsewhere.

Douglas Jehl, "Iraq May Be Prime Place for Training of Militants, C.I.A. Report Concludes," *NYT,* June 22, 2005, p. A10.

135. In another embarrassing moment for the Bush administration, the revised data on terrorism showed more "significant terrorist incidents" (175) and people killed and injured from the incidents (a total of over 4,000) in 2003 than had been originally reported for that year and had been reported for 2002 (138 significant incidents and a total of about 2,700 casualties). *NYT,* June 23, 2004, p. A12.

136. In a leaked memorandum to top aides, Rumsfeld wrote that only limited progress had been made in the war on terror; that "we lack metrics to know if we are winning or losing the global war on terror"; and that the "cost-benefit ratio is against us! Our cost is billions against the terrorists' costs of millions." He expressed doubts about the Pentagon's ability to reorganize in response to terrorism. MSNBC News, October 22, 2003, online at www.msnbc.com/news/983675.asp.

137. Intelligence estimates in January 2003 and July 2004, for instance, painted gloomy pictures of the Iraq situation both before and after the entry of US forces. Powell himself acknowledged in a television interview in late September 2004 that the insurgency in Iraq was "getting worse" and that anti-US feeling in the Muslim Middle East was increasing. None of these views changed the public optimism of Bush, Cheney, and others. See, for instance, Douglas Jehl and David E. Sanger, "Prewar Assessment on Iraq Saw Chance of Strong Divisions," *NYT,* September 28, 2004, p. 1. Early in 2005 Rumsfeld refused to guess at the strength of the insurgency, leaving room for speculation that perhaps the estimates of some Iraqi sources of as many as 200,000 soldiers and supporters might be accurate.

5

Rogues and Clients:
The Long Arm of Unilateralism

THIS CHAPTER EXAMINES the relevance of the Bush Doctrine to US relations with countries that fall into five general categories: states classified as rogues by Washington because of their hostile relations with the United States (North Korea and Iran), authoritarian states that are friendly to the United States (the Central Asian "stans"), major countries that have cooperated with the United States in the war on terror but are regarded as strategic competitors (Russia and China), countries generally favorable to US policies (Japan and the ASEAN ten), and countries whose governments have been viewed with disfavor by the United States (Venezuela and Haiti). The guiding theme of this review is the distorting effects of the Bush Doctrine on policymaking—a consistent preference for strategic (including resource) priorities over potentially less costly and risky engagement options, and a willingness to use force and threat to deal with distasteful governments.

US policy toward North Korea and Iran provides the clearest examples of those misplaced priorities, lost opportunities, and consequent dangers to peace. During the Clinton administration, a peculiar semantic change occurred. The term "rogue states" was jettisoned in favor of "states of concern," perhaps because it was hard to justify calling those states "rogues" that the United States was trying to "engage." On becoming president, George W. Bush did not mince words. In his world, in which there are only enemies and friends, enemies of the United States became "rogues" again. They are to be confronted, sanctioned, contained, and if possible disarmed of their WMD. In the extreme, under the rules of "limited sovereignty," rogue states might be attacked or at least threatened with attack. Friendly rogue states, on the other hand, are treated with kid gloves, even if they are developing or exporting components of WMD and are hostile to democratization and human rights. In such cases, US respect for the principle of "self-determination" actually applies: How friendly rogues govern really is their own business. So long as they agree to support US policies and economic purposes, they will be rewarded, just like the "anticommunist" states of old, as this chapter shows.

The "Axis of Evil"

North Korea

When the Bush administration took office, it made clear in various ways that it had no taste for the Clinton approach of engaging North Korea (the Democratic People's Republic of Korea, DPRK). If anything was inevitable in the new leadership, it was that the fairly remarkable gains Clinton had made in dealing with the always unpredictable North Korean government were going to be cast aside in favor of an entirely different approach.[1] Bush's top advisers were already on record as favoring a hard line on North Korea, and the Republican-dominated Congress was fully on board. Thus, when South Korean president Kim Dae Jung, whose pathbreaking summit meeting in 2000 with North Korea's leader, Kim Jong Il, had won him the Nobel Peace Prize, visited Washington early in 2001, talks went badly. Bush told Kim of his lack of trust in the North Koreans. This amounted to a vote of no-confidence in Kim's "Sunshine" policy, which was designed to reassure North Korea that the South had no intention of absorbing it and instead wished to expand their contacts. Kim Dae Jung was reportedly "furious" with Bush.[2] Perhaps so was Powell, who was on record in favor of engaging North Korea.[3] After Kim's visit, Bush made little effort to conceal his personal distaste for Kim Jong Il. In what was reported as something of a tirade before Republican senators, Bush called Kim a "pygmy" who was in charge of "a gulag half the size of Austin."[4]

Still, the pressure was on Bush to do something inasmuch as the DPRK, unlike Iraq and Iran, was commonly assumed to have at least a few nuclear weapons and the means to deliver them as far as Japan. During 2002 North Korea's place in US strategic thinking became apparent. Bush's "axis of evil" speech was one benchmark. Another was contained in the Nuclear Posture Review, which mentioned North Korea as a potential target of US nuclear weapons. North Korea also appeared in the *National Security Strategy* paper in connection with the doctrine of preemptive attack. After the US war on Iraq began, Pentagon sources spoke of sudden air strikes on Saddam Hussein's command centers as also sending a message to Kim Jong Il.[5] Other news reports cited Pentagon plans to tighten military pressure on the DPRK, including provocative flights designed to test North Korean air defenses.[6]

Perhaps the intention of these statements and leaks was to deter Pyongyang from pursuing its nuclear weapons program. More likely, they were designed to intimidate. What Washington should have expected is that these US acts would be regarded in Pyongyang as threats, and would strengthen the hand of those in North Korea who believed that nuclear weapons were its best and only way to deter a US attack—notwithstanding that Bush and other top officials had said a number of times that the United States had no intention of attacking North Korea. When US Assistant Secretary of State James Kelly went to Pyongyang in October 2002, the North Koreans are said to have admitted that they were developing nuclear weapons along a second track, using highly enriched uranium (HEU). Washington regarded this development as a "material breach" of the Agreed Framework. From that point on, US-DPRK relations went into a tailspin.

Though it was not until February 10, 2005, that the DPRK ministry of foreign affairs officially acknowledged possession of nuclear weapons,[7] several critical aspects of its nuclear status remain ambiguous—how many nuclear weapons it has, how extensive the country's nuclear weapons production capability is, and how many of its 8,000 nuclear fuel rods have been reprocessed. The 2005 declaration should not have come as a complete surprise, however, since in the months following the meeting with Kelly, North Korea took steps that strongly suggested its preparedness to become a full-fledged nuclear weapon state. It withdrew from the Nuclear Nonproliferation Treaty, began the removal of nuclear fuel rods from their primary facility at Yongbyon, reactivated that facility, "nullified" the North-South Korea denuclearization accord of 1992, sent home IAEA inspectors and removed their monitoring devices, and declared the Agreed Framework with the United States at an end. Countering Kelly's assertions, the North Koreans declared the right to possess nuclear weapons. Thereafter, the DPRK threatened to reprocess all its spent nuclear fuel rods—and in May 2005 it announced that all the rods had indeed been removed—so that by now it may (as the head of the IAEA stated in December 2004) have four to six plutonium bombs.[8] Pyongyang may not be engaged in full-scale reprocessing; but with several nuclear weapons, it has the potential to sell plutonium.

According to one Korea expert who is now part of the administration, "hawk engagement" best characterizes the Bush strategy. This approach is "based on the idea that engagement [as practiced by Clinton and the South Korean leaders] lays the groundwork for punitive action."[9] Although advertised by the administration as a multilateral approach to dealing with North Korea, "hawk engagement" in fact is unilateralist in design and intent: It rejects genuine collaboration with other interested governments in favor of trying to line up China and South Korea, as well as Russia and Japan, behind a confrontational policy that US officials have broadly publicized.[10] The Proliferation Security Initiative (PSI), a fifteen-country group launched by the Bush administration in May 2003 to intensify searches and seizures of ships, planes, and vehicles suspected of delivering WMD, is just one of several military steps short of force that the Bush administration has undertaken against "rogue states," with North Korea foremost in mind.

But China and South Korea are not at all on the same page with Washington. They evidently see North Korea's nuclear gambits as defensive responses to the failure of diplomacy to address its security needs. The DPRK's February 2005 announcement probably reinforced their position, since the announcement linked possession of nuclear weapons to US unwillingness, in Bush's second term, to move away from talk of regime change and embrace coexistence instead. Neither China nor South Korea has therefore chosen to associate with PSI, not only because PSI raises questions of international law and has not been explicitly sanctioned by the UN, but even more so because it means confronting North Korea and risking a major blowup. Even the possibility of a North Korean nuclear test, which led Bush to threaten sanctions, has failed to budge Beijing and Seoul from their standard position that the United States and the DPRK must talk directly with one another to resolve the nuclear issue.[11] The PRC government has been emphatic in putting the onus on Washington, not only for refusing direct talks with North Korea but also for continuing its name calling ("tyrant," said Bush of Kim Jong Il; "an outpost of tyranny," said Rice of the DPRK). The South Korean government has echoed that criticism.

North Korea seeks security assurances from the United States and long-term aid from both it and Japan—in short, acceptance of its legitimacy and normalization of relations. DPRK representatives have met with US officials for informal talks and in formal Six Party Talks (6PT)[12] hosted by China. Three sessions of the 6PT accomplished little because of a complete breakdown in trust between the United States and the DPRK— a breakdown evidenced in North Korea's withdrawal from the talks as part of its February 2005 statement. Washington at that time rejected the idea of making another package deal with Pyongyang, arguing that formal security assurances and any other "rewards" to North Korea depend on its abandonment of its nuclear program. The administration's most serious proposal to North Korea on denuclearization, submitted on June 24, 2004, in Beijing, required that Pyongyang pledge to "dismantle all of its nuclear programs," after which the United States would provide "provisional" security assurances and "study" North Korea's energy requirements. Nonreciprocal proposals of that kind virtually assured rejection.[13] The United States does provide substantial amounts of food assistance to North Korea.[14] But oil deliveries stopped at the end of 2002, and the Bush administration has left other forms of humanitarian assistance to North Korea in the hands of NGOs. The essence of the US-DPRK relationship is thus a combustible mixture of provocations and occasional interaction.

What we see here are sharp differences in approach between the Clinton and Bush administrations that can be summarized as follows:

- Clinton accepted that North Korea had legitimate security concerns, whereas Bush considers North Korea an evil state.[15]
- Clinton believed it was necessary to bargain with North Korea, whereas Bush considers bargaining the equivalent of appeasement.
- Clinton believed negotiations could result in a reliable package deal, whereas Bush believes the North Koreans are completely unreliable.
- Clinton believed in the value of direct US-DPRK talks, whereas Bush believes in trying to align allies and other countries to pressure North Korea.
- Clinton believed that the use of force should be a last resort, whereas Bush believes in the utility of military threat.

Being preoccupied with Iraq and then Iran has been a key factor that has forced the administration to rely for the time being more on State Department–led diplomacy and less on the Pentagon's (and Cheney's) reportedly preferred route of sanctions and active containment of North Korea. Iraq is not the only constraint on US policy, however: The security situation on the Korean peninsula is of great importance to US allies (South Korea and Japan) and to China and Russia. Their combined weight has been enough so far to push the United States to keep the diplomatic track alive. If "hawk engagement" is the Bush strategy, however, that track will last only as long as the possibility exists that North Korea will finally cave in to US demands, or until US allies finally lose their patience with the North and accept the US argument that engagement is a bankrupt approach. The real idea is to put the spotlight on North Korea's intransigence and belligerence while avoiding mutual concessions. Such a strategy facilitates other US purposes, such as providing a rationale for theater missile defense in East Asia (in which Japan is the key ally; South Korea has rejected participation), bringing Japan into closer military coordination with the United States (such as through the PSI), and undermining the North Korean political system—that is, regime change.[16] The administration may well have exaggerated North Korea's HEU program out of a desire to "scare Japan and South Korea into reversing their policies" of conciliation toward the North.[17] Promoting missile defense and Japan-US security cooperation may relate to one other US objective: containing China.[18]

The high stakes on the Korean peninsula make a "hawk engagement" strategy a dangerous course of action. The strategy amounts to brinkmanship, much like North Korea's: It endorses multiparty talks in recognition of the anxieties of other countries and the belief that "there are no good military options" for stopping North Korea from developing nuclear weapons.[19] But the strategy makes no investment in a negotiated agreement with North Korea or a long-term solution to security issues on the Korean peninsula. To the contrary, by demonizing the North Koreans and making false charges against them,[20] the Bush administration makes a bad situation worse—and shows a serious misjudgment of North Korean nationalism. As one scholar has put it, "The fundamental difference between Clinton's near-success in resolving the issues and Bush's stalemate lies not in Bush's unwillingness to talk or in his proposal to expand the agenda for talks but in his refusal to end the enmity between the two nations."[21] In fact, US officials seem strangely complacent about the risks of doing nothing to improve the security dynamic that bedevils the US-DPRK relationship.[22] Among those risks are that North Korea will add to its nuclear weapon arsenal, export nuclear weapon ingredients, and even test a nuclear weapon; that North Korea's relations with Japan will further deteriorate and become more militarized; that the failure of diplomacy will strengthen pronuclear weapon groups in South Korea (where experimentation with elements of a nuclear weapon program has occurred) and Japan; that the NPT regime will be further weakened; and that North Korea itself will become unstable and generate many more refugees than at present.

An immediate cost of Bush's unilateralism is the damage to US relations with South Korea. In Seoul, US policies are regarded as needlessly escalating tensions with the North. Partly for that reason, anti-US sentiment is on the rise in South Korea, especially among young people, whereas public opinion is quite favorable toward China, which has become South Korea's largest economic partner. The Roh government went against public opinion in sending troops to Iraq, only to face unilateral US decisions to redeploy 3,600 troops from South Korea to Iraq and to reduce the number of US troops in South Korea by about one-third.[23] But, very much representative of a new generation of Koreans, it is seeking to reduce both political and economic dependence on the United States, and get closer to China.[24]

The alternative to the Bush strategy is twofold. First is a human security approach to North Korea, based on ultimately transforming relationships between countries and peoples in order to meet the basic needs of ordinary people and promote a positive context for improving human rights there. Second is a common security framework that supports North-South Korean engagement. The key element is *enhancing the security of North Korea* so that weapons of mass destruction no longer have value for either economic or deterrent purposes. If these approaches were undertaken, the United States would be engaging in diplomacy along two tracks: direct dialogue with North Korea and multilateral dialogue within the 6PT framework. The common purpose would be to reach a reciprocal, sequenced, and verifiable agreement with North Korea. There is no lack of proposals on the elements of a new deal; in general they entail conveying appropriate security assurances to North Korea, officially ending the Korean War, granting North Korea diplomatic recognition by Washington and Tokyo, and providing long-term economic and energy assistance to the DPRK.[25] Some proposals further suggest enhancing the role of international NGOs, not just to provide emergency relief to North Korea but also to meet its economic development needs. In return for normalized relations, the DPRK would have to refreeze its nuclear facilities, open them to regular international inspections, dismantle its nuclear weapons and ballistic missile programs, and terminate any and all exports of WMD-related equipment and materials.

North Korean spokesmen have suggested many times that the DPRK would be willing to make major concessions, including "giving up" nuclear weapons, if the United States agrees to respect its sovereignty and provide other incentives.[26] Kim Jong Il reportedly told a high-level South Korean delegation in mid-2005 that in return for US security assurances and "respect," North Korea would return to the 6PT, give up its nuclear weapons, rejoin the NPT, and reopen the country to nuclear inspectors.[27] Within a month Pyongyang announced its return to the talks, its official news agency stating that "The US side clarified its official stand to recognize the DPRK as a sovereign state, not to invade it, and hold bilateral talks within the framework of the six-party talks."[28]

When that fourth round of the 6PT adjourned in mid-September 2005, it seemed that many of the ingredients for a negotiated settlement suggested above had been accepted. In a joint statement issued by all the parties, North Korea agreed to "abandoning all nuclear weapons and existing nuclear programs," to return to the NPT, and to accept IAEA inspections. The United States agreed to join with the other countries in providing North Korea with energy assistance, including one or more light-water nuclear reactors that Washington up to the last minute had balked at including in a deal. Pyongyang and Washington further agreed "to respect each other's sovereignty, exist peacefully together and take steps to normalize their relations. " The United States reaffirmed that it "has no intention to attack or invade the DPRK with nuclear or conventional weapons."[29]

But all is not what it seems. No sooner was the ink dry on the document than DPRK and US officials offered widely different interpretations of it. The North Koreans insisted that they would not scrap their nuclear weapon program until they were assured of receiving a light-water reactor. The Americans countered that the joint statement was crystal clear in defining North Korea's commitment to verifiable disarmament first, only after which would nuclear energy assistance be "discussed." This, despite general agreement in the statement that implementation should occur "in a phased manner." Also in dispute were other critical details, such as whether or not North Korea's alleged HEU-based bomb program was part of the agreement, and which sites in the North would be open to international inspection. Consistent with the hawk engagement strategy, one high-ranking US official said Iraq's lesson "is that we can never again confront a country about its weapons unless we show that we have tried every available alternative to disarm it."[30] Thus, despite the joint statement, US policy had not actually changed: North Korea would not be "rewarded" until it had been inspected and declared free of nuclear weapons and supporting programs.

If a reciprocal agreement ever is reached, the joint statement contains the promising idea that the parties "will negotiate a permanent peace regime on the Korean pensinula" and "explore ways and means for promoting security cooperation in northeast Asia." That sets the stage for wide-ranging multilateral engagement to create a new regional (Northeast Asia) security mechanism. Its purposes might be to regularize political and military contacts among the parties, craft mutual security pledges, and regulate military transfers to both Koreas.[31] Meantime, North-South Korean economic ties and people-to-people exchanges, which have continued and even expanded despite the political tensions,[32] would extend to the military arena, where the most urgent business is troop withdrawals from within range of the demilitarized zone that divides the two countries. What is not well enough known is that North Korea's domestic policies are slowly changing, with a new openness to private markets, consumerism, and foreign investment. Once the United States and the DPRK normalize relations, the opportunity is at hand to move the North further in that direction, one that the Chinese have for years been urging on North Korea.

Perhaps the clearest sign that the United States is out of step with all other parties is that all former US ambassadors to South Korea and envoys to talks with North Korea have publicly stated their disagreement with the Bush policies and urged direct negotiations to resolve the nuclear and other issues.[33] Among them is Charles (Jack) Pritchard, who resigned as Bush's special envoy to the North Korea talks in dismay over the administration's policy. He characterized US policy as follows:

> At best it can be described only as amateurish. At worst, it is a failed attempt to lure American allies down a path that is not designed to resolve the crisis diplomatically but to lead to the failure and ultimate isolation of North Korea in hopes that its government will collapse.[34]

The DPRK dictatorship is not going to collapse, most knowledgeable observers agree; it is a reality, and its leader's view of the world needs to be taken seriously. In 1999 President Clinton sent his North Korea policy coordinator, former secretary of defense William Perry, to talk with DPRK leaders. Perry's message on returning home remains a valuable guideline for dealing with all "rogue states." "We have to deal with the North Korean government not as we wish they would be, but as in fact they are," he said. As to their missile and nuclear weapons programs, Perry said:

> I believe their primary reason is security, is deterrence. . . . We do not think of ourselves as a threat to North Korea, but I fully believe that they consider us a threat to them and, therefore, they see this missile as a means of deterrence. I think they have a very clear logic and a very clear rationale for what they are doing. We don't always understand that rationale; we don't always understand that logic, and therefore we consider it illogical.[35]

Iran

Unlike North Korea, Iran is a potential nuclear weapon state that remains a member of the NPT. Like North Korea, Iran secretly acquired the means of producing weapons-grade uranium while pretending to be interested only in nuclear energy. When that secret program, dating back to 1985, was discovered in 2003 by US intelligence, the Iranian government promised to suspend uranium enrichment efforts, though such efforts are not in themselves a violation of the NPT. Iran then reneged on its promise. How to deal with Iran in light of the experience in Iraq, the longstanding animosity between Iran and the United States, political changes inside Iran, and the challenges of multilateral cooperation to get Iran to change course all pose problems for the Bush Doctrine. If Iran's nuclear weapon capability cannot be handled through the IAEA nonproliferation regime, unilateral US action becomes a distinct possibility.

Bush's accusation that Iran was part of an "axis of evil" evidently caught many people by surprise, including some State Department officials. A "White House official's" remark at the time of Bush's speech suggested that State was out of step with Bush and his top advisers in thinking that it might be possible to work with political reformers in Iran's government.[36] To be sure, political reform in Iran has to occur within the limits set by the authoritarian clerical leadership. Mohammad Khatami, Iran's president until 2005, expressed his commitment to a theocratic state, but one marked by the rule of law, personal freedom, and democratic governance.[37] He opposed the US attacks on Afghanistan after 9/11 at the same time that he condemned terrorism. But neocons in and outside the Pentagon have for years been urging the same kind of tough policy toward Iran that they advocated against Iraq, and with the same aim: regime change. As in Saddam's Iraq, the neocons have courted Iranian exile groups devoted to overthrowing the government.[38] The involvement of thousands of Iranian agents in Iraq during the US occupation, and the close ties between the Shiite leadership in Iran and nationalistic Shiite clerics in Iraq, are sufficient to convince the neocons that the Islamic Republic of Iran needs to go.

During and especially after the war on Iraq, the Bush administration ratcheted up the pressure on Tehran. Seeming victory in Iraq led to bold statements clearly calculated to intimidate the Iranians. The United States has "no war plan right now" for Iran or Syria, said Powell. "I believe that a free Iraq can be an example of reform and progress to all the Middle East," said Bush. "We have to make it clear that we didn't just come to get rid of Saddam," said an unnamed official. "We came to get rid of the status quo."[39] The United States "will not tolerate the construction of a nuclear weapon" by Iran, Bush declared.[40] One day later, the IAEA said that Iran should "promptly and unconditionally conclude and implement" a new agreement with it that would permit additional inspections of its nuclear facilities, which by then were suspected of being engaged in enriching uranium for weapons. The Iranian government denied it was seeking to make nuclear weapons and rejected "the language of force and threat."[41] It insisted that it was only engaged in low-level uranium enrichment suitable for nuclear energy. But in August 2004 Tehran announced that it had resumed building nuclear centrifuges, which are used to enrich uranium, thus breaking an agreement reached with Britain, France, and Germany the previous October to suspend uranium enrichment. The unbroken spiral of tension sounded eerily similar to the US-UN-Iraq go-round of the year before.

Once Iran finally admitted that it was enriching uranium and had received external help (almost certainly from Pakistan) in doing so, the issue became how much it was willing to cooperate with the IAEA in opening nuclear facilities to inspection. The United States and the EU rejected Iran's claim to be interested only in nuclear energy; but they and Russia could not agree to bring the issue before the UN Security Council, where Washington wanted to put sanctions on the table. During 2004 and into 2005, the Bush administration's position remained that Iran could not be allowed to develop a nuclear weapon and that (as Bush said) "we've got to keep pressure on the [Iranian] government." In contrast with its Iraq policy in 2003, however, Bush did not thumb his nose at the UN and the inspection process. This time he said he was relying on international cooperation to "send the message for us" about Iran.[42]

But "cooperation" in the Bush lexicon has uncommon meanings. One is that the United States will not join the EU's diplomatic efforts, discussed below, to provide Iran with incentives for giving up any nuclear weapon aspirations. Another is that Israel has made threats to attack Iran—threats that recalled its strike on Iraq's Osirak nuclear reactor in June 1981. President Reagan admired that attack. It could be employed again, this time using the Bush Doctrine's rationale for preemption.[43] Reports that secret US plans concerning Iran were passed to Israel by a Pentagon intelligence analyst in the office of Douglas J. Feith gives Iran reason to be concerned about an Israeli attack.[44] If the IAEA's efforts to gain full access to Iran fail, if European initiatives do not succeed—and US nonparticipation may be designed to make that so—and if international sanctions on Iran are not imposed, Bush may again listen to the advice of neocons like Feith and Perle, whose hard-line support of Israel is of long standing.[45] Bush has plenty of other military options, such as covert warfare using anti-Iranian groups inside and outside the country, and economic pressure to destabilize the government.[46] But using Israel as a proxy may prove irresistible, and reliable reports citing the presence of Pentagon special forces units inside Iran and overflights of Iran by drone aircraft based in Iraq, all intended to survey future targets for air strikes, show how serious the Bush administration is about having a military option.[47]

Iran has provided every reason for concern about its potential to develop nuclear weapons. At the same time, unlike North Korea, it is still several years removed from actually having them, according to the latest US intelligence sources.[48] Nor does the IAEA have proof of an Iranian nuclear weapons program. Dealing effectively with Tehran will certainly test the international community's willpower. Conflicting interests among the Security Council members make it unlikely that they would favor trying to coerce Iran, however. Russia plans to continue fuel deliveries to an Iranian nuclear power reactor that it built; and construction of additional reactors is under study. China imports a good deal of oil from Iran, and Chinese companies have shipped equipment to Iran that may have been used in Iran's nuclear weapons program. France and other EU countries have strong commercial ties with Iran. Moreover, using force carries serious risks. It is generally accepted that the Iranian military is far superior to Saddam's forces and would give an invading army a much harder time. Though now surrounded by US military power in bases all over Afghanistan, Central Asia, and Iraq,[49] and faced with Israeli threats, some Iranian military leaders have turned the Bush Doctrine on its head by threatening a preventive attack on Dimona, Israel's nuclear weapons center, if Iran's nuclear facilities are struck.[50] Iran already possesses missiles of sufficient range to retaliate against an Israeli strike, and if such occurred, a quick escalation of the fighting might be unavoidable. Should a general war ensue, occupying a defeated Iran would be an even larger and more costly undertaking than occupying Iraq has been, and would probably take place amidst an enormous outpouring of anti-US vitriol throughout the Middle East. Equally daunting is the prospect of a unified Shiite resistance stretching across Iran and Iraq, with a US invasion providing the glue—and in the process putting an end to dreams of a secular democracy in either country. That possibility has been in evidence virtually from the moment the US occupation of Iraq began.[51]

A nuclear-armed Iran or an Israel-Iran war would probably engulf the entire region in conflict. To avoid such tragic consequences, the United States must take up the challenge of finding common ground with Iran's divided leadership, and in doing so, bridge the enormous gap that US support of the shah and the 1978 hostage crisis created. As one

Iran specialist has observed, the Bush administration has significantly worsened relations—first, by "the implied threat in downgrading Iran from 'rogue' to 'evil' status," then by appealing over the heads of clerics to reformists in the Iranian government, later (via Voice of America broadcasts) by suggesting to Iranians that they act against their government. Condoleezza Rice, in her first overseas trip as secretary of state, continued the pattern, saying that Iran's human rights record "is something to be loathed" and "abysmal" and telling Iranians that "America stands with you."[52] Such name-calling and pressure tactics are all too familiar to Iranians, and their real effect is probably to undermine the reformers (who risk being labeled US agents) while supporting the view of Iran's leaders that the United States is again seeking regime change in the country.[53]

Nationalism, Washington's consistent blind spot, plays on all sides in Iranian politics. "Reformers" and "conservatives" alike are committed above all to the country's independence, resistance to foreign pressure, and "union of mosque and state," just as Khatami said. Ordinary Iranians favor a nuclear energy program as a symbol of defiance of the West. For others, it means nuclear weapons as a defense against attack.[54] After all, Israel has a large arsenal of nuclear bombs that the United States has long accepted.

A more flexible US policy toward Iran, implemented collaboratively with the EU, Russia, and the UN, needs to be adopted. The new policy might include reopening commercial relations, ending US ties with Iranian exile groups, and (as in the Agreed Framework with North Korea) offering Iran energy assistance in return for the safe removal of its spent nuclear fuel and full IAEA inspection rights. An agreement reached in November 2004 between Iran and France, Britain, and Germany went partway toward resolving the nuclear issue; but it involved only a suspension of Iran's enrichment program and plutonium reprocessing. Once a new government took over in August 2005, that deal, which was to include economic incentives to Iran, was killed as the president, Mahmoud Ahmadinejad, reaffirmed Iran's right to continue uranium conversion and enrichment.

Nevertheless, the United States should also consider being part of a permanent solution with Iran, with normalization of US-Iran relations one element of it. This step might help reduce Iran's deepening involvement in Iraqi politics—the consequence of a common embrace of Shiite Islam by the leaders of the two countries—and might ultimately promote political openness in Iran. As George Perkovich has written, a final agreement requires international coordination, just as with North

Korea. It means engaging the surrounding Arab states, avoiding threatening Iran with regime change, and embracing a just Middle East peace. In short, it should contain "mutual obligations" incorporated in "a *positive agreement—without sanctions*—that would be forwarded to the UN Security Council for endorsement."[55] If the Bush administration wants Iran to follow the Libyan rather than the North Korean route to security, it is more likely to succeed by supporting a multilevel engagement policy than by making threats and provocative, ultimately dysfunctional appeals for regime change.

Friendly Rogues and Difficult Partners

The Chinese have a saying, "same bed, different dreams," that they once used to characterize relations with the former Soviet Union. The saying also has application to US policy during the Cold War, when the United States shared its bed with authoritarian regimes whose main objectives only superficially had to do with containing communism. For these regimes, the goal was about staying in power; associating with the United States in the name of anticommunism was often an indispensable means to that goal. So it is in the war on terror: Regimes of any description that profess the goal of eradicating terrorism *and* ensuring US economic and military access are virtually assured of US endorsement. Governments supported by the United States are legitimately (by Washington's definition) pursuing their ("terrorist") opponents but never practicing terrorism themselves.[56] Of course, there is nothing new in such a narrow definition: The US government often in the past turned a blind eye to state terrorism when practiced by governments it supported, from Pinochet's Chile to Iran under the shah, to mention just a few. Under George W. Bush this tradition continues, openly and without apology.

"A world order policy based on pacification, reassurance, stability, and economic interdependence expands the frontiers of insecurity for the United States," two writers asserted several years before 9/11.[57] Expanded frontiers became a fact of life after 9/11. No one in the Bush administration seemed to worry about the possibility of strategic over-extension, and even less about human rights violations by quite a few partner regimes. From Georgia, Yemen, and the Horn of Africa in the west to Indonesia and the Philippines in the east, and then across the Pacific to Colombia, the war on terrorism became global and the US military dug in.[58] Green Berets trained soldiers in Georgia, nearly 1,300 US advisers were based in the Philippines, and US military aid funded training of police, army, and border-control forces in Indonesia, Uzbek-istan, and Algeria, among others. Special Operations forces also con-ducted training in Djibouti, Mali, Mauritania, Yemen, and Colombia—in the last case, accompanying a shift from drug eradication to counter-insurgency training.[59] Military-to-military relationships were tightened with India, Pakistan, and Indonesia. About 60,000 US military person-nel moved into forward bases in the Persian Gulf area alone, with Qatar the center of operations in the anticipated war against Iraq. Besides those bases, around 4,000 US soldiers were deployed at eight other air bases in Uzbekistan, Afghanistan, Pakistan, Kyrgyzstan, and Djibouti. These deployments supplemented a large naval force in the Arabian Sea and a US Air Force base in Diego Garcia.[60] Rounding out the picture, US military installations were also set up in Romania, Poland, and Bul-garia—the "new Europe," in Rumsfeld's way of thinking. With US forces being shifted out of countries such as Germany and Turkey that did not join Washington's "coalition of the willing" in Iraq, the Eastern European governments seized the opportunity to enhance their prospects of joining the EU.[61]

All these efforts were rationalized as necessary steps to prosecute the war on terrorism; but in fact, most of them were targets of opportu-nity with no clear relationship to the pursuit of Al-Qaida or any other international terrorist network.[62] Military sales to the military-backed government in Algeria were just such a case. Despite lack of evidence of Al-Qaida activity there in support of an Islamic political party that had been banned in the early 1990s, the Bush administration went ahead with military training of Algerian officers at a cost of $200,000 in 2002 and $500,000 in 2003. Weapons sales began in 2003.[63] That US weapons would contribute to the political violence in Algeria—at least 100,000 people have been killed in the course of the regime's crackdown since the mid-1990s—and put the United States on the military's side in a civil war had no evident impact on Bush's decision.

Central Asia

By no means are all the countries that received US aid or accepted a US military presence under authoritarian rule; but many of them are, partic-ularly the former Soviet republics of Central Asia. There, Stalinism, not democracy, prevails: At the start of 2005, the presidents of Turkmenistan, Kazakhstan, Kyrgyzstan, and Uzbekistan had all been in power since 1991. Only in Kyrgyzstan did a change occur, when popular protests against fraudulent parliamentary elections led to the ouster of Askar A. Akayev, whose grip on power had been helped along by family crony-ism and repression of opposing forces.[64] Political leadership in Central Asia is firmly in the hands of despots like Akayev who are determined to cling to power for life; they have not the slightest interest in decent governance or in human security. (Any doubt about this assertion can be erased by consulting the State Department's annual reports on these coun-tries' human rights and human development conditions, which range from merely poor to abominable.)

During the Clinton administration, human rights abuses in some countries, such as Armenia and Azerbaijan, prompted sanctions on mil-itary aid. In others, such as Tajikistan, civil war constantly threatened and the emphasis was on conciliation. After 9/11, however, leaders of Central Asian countries were no doubt delighted to provide the United States with military access in return for military aid (and in some cases World Bank loans) that they could use as proof of US political support of strong-armed rule.[65] In Azerbaijan, for example, the transfer of power from father to son in October 2002 assured the continuity of dictator-ship in recognition of the country's potential oil riches. While Washing-ton congratulated the son, Ilham Aliyev, on his "strong showing" in winning a rigged election, protestors were arrested and killed, and the political opposition was kept under tight control.[66]

Following the logic of the market, the Bush administration lifted aid sanctions where they existed and substantially increased US military aid and transfers to friendly states. Besides Kazakhstan and Uzbekistan, discussed below, here are some representative military aid figures for recent fiscal years (FY):[67]

- Armenia: $94.2 million allocated in FY2002; $73.7 million re-quested by Bush in FY2003, $52.9 million in FY2004.
- Azerbaijan: $7 million allocated in FY2002; $52.9 million allo-cated in FY2003; $44.9 allocated or promised in FY2004.
- Kyrgyzstan: $83.6 million allocated in FY2002 and $41.1 million in FY2003; $47.2 million promised in FY2004.
- Tajikistan: $47.5 million allocated in FY2001 and FY2002 and $23 million in FY2003; $36 million promised in FY2004.
- Turkmenistan: $11.7 million allocated in FY2002 and $8.1 mil-lion in FY2003; $9.1 promised in FY2004.

In return for its assistance, not only did the United States gain stag-ing areas and use of air space for missions in Afghanistan and Iraq. US energy corporations had their eyes on a different prize: the Caspian Sea region's enormous untapped oil and gas reserves. Their efforts to acquire a privileged position began under Clinton; they accelerated after 9/11 as representatives of the world's major energy companies made a beeline for Kazakhstan and the rest. Under both Clinton and Bush, energy pipelines were planned that would originate in Turkmenistan and Azerbaijan; they would run through Afghanistan and Georgia but avoid Russia and Iran.[68] Just as oil politics enhanced the strategic importance of Iraq for Bush, led him to embrace Africa's major oil producers (Nigeria, Gabon, Angola, and Equatorial Guinea[69]), and prompted his support of a failed coup attempt in Venezuela (discussed below), oil drove his administration into the arms of Central Asia's authoritarian regimes. Whereas the Clinton administration had kept its distance from some of these dictators, Bush has had no such compunctions, wedded as he is to an energy policy that depends on increased supplies of imported oil.

As a result, the closer these governments get to Washington, the freer the hand their leaders believe they have to jail opponents, muzzle the press, salt away aid money and corporate bribes in personal bank accounts—and receive military aid and blessings from US officials.[70] Kazakhstan and Uzbekistan are notorious cases in point. Kazakhstan's potential oil production could make it a major player in setting prices. Bribing top Kazakh officials to get oil contracts has been a problem for years.[71] Kazakhstan's president Nursultan Nazarbayev faced indictment in the United States in a federal investigation of bribery payments made to him by US oil companies.[72] But his government allowed hundreds of US overflights in the war on Iraq, and protected private US investments. For FY2002 and 2003, Nazarbayev's government received just under $100 million in US military aid, and was promised around $36 million more in FY2004.[73] The oil contracts between Kazakhstan and the companies were in dispute for many months before an agreement was ironed out; but when the Kazakh government demanded a bigger share of the profits, some companies backed away.

The situation in Uzbekistan is different from Kazakhstan only in the details. The Uzbek leader, Islam Karimov, had been denied a visa to enter the United States in the early 1990s because of his government's human rights violations. Uzbeks, like most neighboring people, suffer under intense poverty and stifling restrictions on travel, business, and civil liberties.[74] After 9/11, though, things looked brighter, at least for the regime: Uzbekistan became the jump-off point for the initial assault on Iraq. In return, the United States provided military assistance and elevated Uzbekistan's importance. Thus fortified, Karimov rescinded a promised amnesty to hundreds of political prisoners; such a gesture was no longer necessary.[75] US military aid to Uzbekistan from then through FY2003 amounted to over $170 million, with another $53 million promised in FY2004.[76] During 2004, clashes escalated between government and antigovernment forces. Predictably, the government blamed Muslim terrorists for the violence, masking the well-known fact of its repression. According to human rights groups, there are around 7,000 political prisoners in Uzbekistan's jails; many are tortured. For reporting just that, and denouncing the use of forced confessions to fight alleged terrorism, the British ambassador was sacked in late 2004.[77]

These facts only slightly upset Uzbekistan's relationship with Washington until the middle of 2005. During an official visit in February 2004, Donald Rumsfeld said that US relations with Uzbekistan were "growing stronger every month." And Scott McClellan, the White House spokesman, responded to the increasing violence by promising "close cooperation with Uzbekistan and our other partners in the global war on terror."[78] Such statements merely reiterated the standard Cold War justification of military support to autocratic regimes, namely, that it helps their armies learn respect for human rights and the need to stay out of politics. But some direct military aid to Uzbekistan was frozen during 2004. In May 2005, however, a brief armed uprising in Uzbekistan once again upset notions of partnership and revealed anew the dangers of US association with a repressive government. The uprising, which grew out of a prison revolt, was labeled an Islamic terrorist revolution by Karimov. It was quickly quashed by Uzbek internal security forces, whose members included people trained and armed by the United States. The Pentagon's aid to the Uzbek military was just one of several "antiterrorism" programs conducted in collaboration with the regime.[79]

Washington joined with the EU in calling for an investigation of the uprising, which earned a riposte from Karimov that the United States had staged it to get rid of him. The UN did investigate. It concluded that anywhere from 200 to 700 people, mostly civilians, were killed, and that the use of force was "indiscriminate and disproportionate."[80] So much for the restraining power of US military aid. Over 400 Uzbeks fled across the border to Kyrgyzstan, where the UN agency for refugees came to their aid by airlifting them to Romania. The Uzbekistan government, which had already joined with other members of the Shanghai Cooperation Organization in calling for the closure of US bases in Central Asia (see below), formally asked the United States in late July to vacate its base. The Bush administration reacted as though it had been punished for championing human rights, when in fact its duplicity got it the outcome it deserved.

Southeast Asia

The Philippines, Indonesia, and Thailand—the pivotal members of the ten-member Association of Southeast Asian Nations (ASEAN)—find themselves on the front lines of the war on terrorism.[81] In each of these countries, however, the most serious internal enemies are weaknesses in democratic governance and the rule of law, declining economic performance, and excesses in the military. In the Philippines, corruption in the top ranks of the military is a serious problem, and the danger is ever present of a coup or mutiny. Some officers may have colluded with the very "terrorist" Muslim rebels whom the government is fighting alongside the United States. While money is thus being siphoned off by elites in these countries, personal income has declined to levels of a decade earlier. Democracy in Indonesia is the least developed of the three countries: Although Indonesians have freely elected their most recent presidents (the current one, chosen in 2004, is a former general), official corruption is widespread, the military's outrageous behavior in East Timor has largely gone unpunished, and civil society remains underdeveloped even though antigovernment sentiment is growing. As for Thailand, vote buying is a longstanding tradition, the military's influence in politics and business is substantial (just as it is in Indonesia), exploitation of children for work and prostitution is extensive, and the existence of functioning representative institutions often masks undemocratic practices by the government—such as the prime minister's campaigns against crime and drugs in 2003, which struck some observers as being politically motivated (some 50,000 people were arrested) and most certainly were extrajudicial.

Cooperation by these governments with the United States in the war on terror must be understood against this background. In the Philippines, the announced target of the antiterrorism effort is the Abu Sayyaf guerrillas. They are basically a gang that has been engaged in kidnappings for ransom for about thirty years. Wiping them out would hardly constitute a victory over global terrorism, any more than would the elimination of a Mafia operation in, say, Russia.[82] The United States dispatched a military mission to the Philippines consisting of 1,200 troops, including 160 Special Forces that "were actively involved in combat operations against Abu Sayyaf."[83] Their six-month mission ended July

31, 2002. But the bigger story was Washington's opportunism in pressing for closer military ties with Manila; Abu Sayyaf looked like a cover for an entirely different mission.

In August 2002 US and Filipino officials announced that not only would the United States increase its military aid to the Philippines, in training and equipment sales, over a five-year period; the two countries would also establish a senior civilian policymaking group, with Filipino communists now the main target.[84] "We consider [the communist rebels] a much bigger threat than the Abu Sayyaf, the Moro Islamic Liberation Front or the Jemaah Islamiyah," said a Philippines military spokesman, citing two militant Muslim groups.[85] When President Gloria Macapagal Arroyo visited Washington in May 2003, President Bush said the United States was prepared to send troops back, apparently forgetting Filipino constitutional restrictions on allowing foreign combat forces to be stationed in the country, not to mention the US War Powers Act. The dispatch of US troops consequently was delayed indefinitely.[86] But military assistance in arms sales and grants has been lavish—over $230 million since 2001.[87]

In Indonesia, prior to the disco bombing in Bali in October 2002 and a hotel bombing in August 2003, the case for a direct connection between Al-Qaida and any of the militant Islamic groups operating in that country was not persuasive.[88] Whether that has changed is a matter of opinion. Secular nationalism is the dominant political sentiment in Indonesia, and support for radical Islam and an Islamic state is confined to less than 15 percent of the population.[89] Nevertheless, even before the Bali bombing, the Bush administration had openly pressured the government of Indonesia to line up against Jemaah Islamiyah and other militant groups. Bush was clearly looking for a chance to resume a direct military relationship with the Indonesian armed forces, whose human rights abuses in East Timor (where around 200,000 people were killed) and other outlying islands—with the full knowledge and even consent of the United States starting in the Gerald Ford-Henry Kissinger years—have been well documented. Arms sales and other military ties to Indonesia were barred by Congress in 1998 and 1999; but under Bush, that has not prevented some aid (around $50 million, mostly in spare parts for the air force) from flowing, using the Pentagon's instead of the State Department's budget to evade Congress's intention.

The US approach to Indonesia once again puts security concerns ahead of democracy. "We are starting down a path to a more normal relationship with respect to military-to-military," Secretary Powell said.[90] That "normal relationship" precluded speaking out on behalf of people in the Aceh region who, like the East Timorese, have lived under the gun for many years. The US State Department intervened on the side of Exxon Mobil in a human rights case against the company's abuses that was filed by Aceh villagers in the United States.[91] But it did nothing when, in May 2003, the Indonesian army launched an offensive in Aceh against independence-minded guerrillas. Indonesian officials openly stated that attacking separatists in the name of counterterrorism without incurring international criticism was "a blessing" conferred by 9/11 and the war on Iraq.[92] The military sealed off the region from international agencies, and once again (as had happened in East Timor) organized and armed civilian groups to do its dirty work.

Yet Bush administration officials maintain that restoring ties with the Indonesian armed forces will democratize them and help the war on terror.[93] The opportunity to hasten that day came when the tsunami hit Asia in December 2004: Aceh was devastated, and the US military was allowed access to the region as part of the relief effort that won considerable goodwill. The administration wants to reinstate its international military education and training program, even though the Indonesian army has yet to demonstrate a receptivity to human rights and accountability training. In Aceh it will have another chance to redeem itself, since a peace treaty between rebels and the Indonesian government, signed in August 2005, calls for a phased, partial military withdrawal from Aceh.[94]

The Thai government, which has been a military partner of the United States since the 1950s, ardently supported the war on terror by sending military engineering troops to Afghanistan and Iraq, and by arresting people suspected of ties to Jemaah Islamiyah and thus to Al-Qaida.[95] Washington responded in 2003 by granting Thailand the status of a major non-NATO ally, which entitled Bangkok to greater access than other military aid recipients to certain US financing and technologies. Thailand also received over $30 million in various kinds of military assistance between September 2001 and 2004.

Efforts such as these were clearly part of a larger US strategy for recreating security ties across Southeast Asia, as evidenced by the August 1, 2002, treaty between ASEAN and the United States to cooperate to "prevent, disrupt and combat" international terrorism.[96] Washington gave assurances that it had no intention to base US troops on Asian soil or ignore the repression of legitimate dissent. But such assurances ring hollow: The United States has rarely remonstrated on behalf of human rights and democratic norms in countries whose governments were friendly to US interests. Among the ASEAN states, only Burma (Myanmar) has been consistently criticized for its repressive policies. Moreover, as indicated above, the United States has deepened its strategic access in the region, with potential negative consequences. Associating the United States with repressive institutions, such as the Indonesian military, making US forces and citizens targets of local opposition forces, undermining the credibility of US efforts to play the role of disinterested third party in international disputes, arousing anti-US nationalism, and becoming party to what are really long-running situations of local violence surely do not enhance the US global position or the attractiveness of its values.[97]

Propounding the notion of preemptive attack has also alienated the United States—and Australia, where the John Howard government fervently supports preemption—from regional governments. Leaders of Malaysia, Philippines, Indonesia, and Thailand, each in their own way, have distanced themselves from a concept that they believe violates principles of state sovereignty and collective security under the UN.[98] The Indonesian foreign minister, for instance, speaking in the presence of the US ambassador and a senior State Department official, had harsh words for the precedent set by the war on Iraq. Reflecting the public's generally negative view of the United States and the widespread belief that the United States has basically been engaged in a war on Islam, Foreign Minister Hassan Wirajuda said:

> An arbitrary preemptive war has been waged against a sovereign state—arbitrary because it is without sufficient justification in international law. Does that mean that any state may now individually and arbitrarily decide to use force preemptively against any other state perceived as a threat?[99]

The fact that a few Southeast Asian countries (Philippines, Thailand, and Singapore) initially joined the "coalition of the willing" did not really strengthen the US role in the region. To the contrary, a leading Singapore security specialist has written, "America's Asian alliances, always unequal entities, are more so now than they have been since the end of World War II."[100]

Bush's one-sided emphasis on terrorism has drawn its attention away from the main action in Southeast Asia, which is multilateral initiatives such as ASEAN+3 (China, South Korea, and Japan) and regional free trade agreements (FTAs). The United States persists in being an outsider to the ASEAN process: It does not have an annual summit meeting with the ASEAN leaders, is not a signatory of important ASEAN political declarations, and in general seems to view Asian regionalism as a challenge to its predominance. Just the opposite for China, which is a signatory of ASEAN's cornerstone document, the Treaty of Amity and Cooperation, is the key player in ASEAN+3, and is involved in all the other offshoots of the ASEAN process (such as the ASEAN Regional Forum). China is clearly investing in ASEAN for both long-term political as well as economic reasons.[101]

While Bush's trade strategy, like its security strategy, centers on global arrangements with the United States as the hub, Asian countries are forging ahead with FTAs to protect their interests against the WTO.[102] The principal fruit of that effort, the ASEAN-China FTA, will come into effect in stages in 2010 and 2015. Japan and the United States lag far behind, each having concluded an FTA only with Singapore.[103] Some of these agreements will promote intraregional trade while others may reinforce rivalries, such as between China and Japan. ASEAN+3, however, is a vehicle for mitigating such competition while also reducing reliance on the US market.

Japan

Japan has become the United States's most reliable ally in Asia. In a major break with tradition, after the 9/11 attacks Japan deployed both air and naval units in support of Bush's war, initially to the Indian Ocean and later to the Persian Gulf.[104] Then, in December 2003, Japanese Prime Minister Koizumi Junichiro ordered the deployment of around 600 Ground Self-Defense Force (SDF) soldiers to Iraq, the first time Japanese soldiers were sent to a war zone without UN sanction. Koizumi's decision met with overwhelming disapproval from the Japanese public. By law the soldiers were limited to rear-guard support roles for up to one year; but some Japanese critics argued that the deployment was illegal anyway inasmuch as any location in Iraq would put soldiers in the line of fire of Iraqi guerrillas, and thus to all intents, in combat situations. (Just days before the deployment, in fact, two Japanese diplomats as well as two South Korean construction workers were killed.) Koizumi decided in December 2004 to extend the deployment for another year to show support for the war on terror. Again, he defied public opinion.[105]

Japan took two other steps in support of US policy. In September 2003 it joined PSI, no doubt with North Korea's missile exports in mind. The Japanese cabinet subsequently allocated funds to deploy US-built missile defenses. Subscribing to the Bush Doctrine, Japan's foreign minister said that Japan had the right, in self-defense, to make a preemptive attack on North Korean missile sites.[106] Then, at the end of

2004, the Koizumi government announced new defense guidelines. The chief security threats to Japan are now said to be missiles and terrorists. China was specifically named a potentially threatening country. The guidelines also considerably enlarge the geographic scope of Japan's security interests, which by implication also widens the area of future SDF deployments.[107]

Taken together, what do these steps mean? From the perspective of alliance history, they can be interpreted as simply the latest indicators of Japanese followership of the United States. That is, the Japanese government is showing the same loyalty to US policy in the war on terror that it showed in the Korea and Vietnam conflicts. But it is more than that: Japan is not only being loyal, it is seeking to become a "normal nation." Given its history, that goal creates at least two problems. One is that it may conflict with Japan's best interests. Koizumi's surprise trip to Pyongyang in the fall 2002, during which he extracted an apology from Kim Jong Il for the abduction of Japanese citizens and a promise to return them to Japan, was made despite US wishes. And it produced results, so much so (as noted above) that the Bush administration may have sought deliberately to undercut such policy independence. The US strategy worked, but at the cost of setting back the normalization of Japanese–North Korean relations.

Second, Japan's responsiveness to the Bush policies, which includes new legislation to combat terrorism, may indicate significant changes in its national security policies, changes that are likely to increase tensions between Japan and its neighbors. Among those changes is a joint statement issued with the United States in February 2005 that identified Taiwan's security as a "common strategic objective." Coming at a time of renewed China-Japan tensions over historical and territorial issues, the US-Japan statement added to a growing and worrisome rivalry. Though China is now Japan's principal trade partner, Chinese nationalism, on display in anti-Japanese demonstrations during the spring of 2005, represents the other side of the relationship—reflected, for instance, in China's opposition to a permanent seat for Japan on the UN Security Council. If the United States continues to encourage more assertive Japanese security policies, it will find a ready reaction among Chinese nationalists and possibly set the stage for a new Cold War in East Asia.

"In essence," Richard Tanter has argued, "the Bush Doctrine has been welcomed [in Japan] for the cover and opportunities it affords to accelerate already existing planning preferences"—preferences, that is, for making Japan the kind of "normal country" that projects military power to protect its interests, just like the United States.[108] The first step toward "normalcy" is to remove constitutional and philosophical constraints that have kept Japan tightly under the US security umbrella. The Koizumi administration is seeking to do just that, and with the Bush Doctrine providing cover, it may well succeed.

South Asia

The war in Afghanistan led to major changes in US policy toward Pakistan and India. Sanctions (which were more symbolic than real) that had been imposed when both countries tested nuclear weapons in 1998 were removed. Despite full awareness in Washington that Pakistan's Inter-Services Intelligence, or ISI, had once been—and, some sources say, still is[109]—an important source of support of the Taliban (and the link between the CIA and Afghan rebels who fought the Soviet Union), had helped train pro-Pakistan separatist groups in Kashmir, and had stood by while ties matured between the Taliban and Al-Qaida, the Bush administration believed the need of Pakistan's cooperation exceeded its liabilities.[110] Specifically, it wanted the military dictatorship of General Pervez Musharraf to seal off the western border from fleeing Taliban and Al-Qaida soldiers. Pakistan allowed US Special Forces to roam the borderlands and use at least three of its military bases.

Besides removing sanctions on Pakistan, Washington rewarded its government, well known for corruption, human rights violations, and nuclear proliferation, with nearly $600 million in aid from 9/11 to early 2004, and an open door to IMF assistance ($135 million). Additionally, in March 2004 Colin Powell announced that Pakistan would be treated as a "major non-NATO ally," a largely symbolic upgrading of its status, but one that put it in the same category for weapons sales as Japan, Australia, and Israel. Musharraf, while cracking down on allegedly radical Islamic schools and groups in his country, used the opportunity afforded by the war to cement his rule.[111] Bypassing the parliament, he extended his presidency by five years in a national referendum in April 2002 that was widely condemned as having been rigged. His was the only name on the ballot. Four months later Musharraf gave himself a raft of new powers, including the right to amend the constitution and dissolve the parliament. The State Department politely announced that it still favored "the establishment of democratic civilian rule under constitutional means" in Pakistan.[112] Musharraf's reaction? In the fall of 2004, contrary to a previous promise, he took back leadership of the armed forces in addition to retaining the presidency.

Even the exposure in October 2002 of Pakistani assistance to North Korea's once-secret nuclear weapons program, providing the DPRK with uranium enrichment technology in exchange for missile parts, did not dampen US support of Musharraf.[113] After the overthrow of Saddam Hussein, he visited Washington in June 2003 and received a substantial new aid package: $3.5 billion, about $1 billion of which will reportedly be used to pay off part of Pakistan's $1.6 billion debt to the United States.[114] Congress also resumed grants to Pakistan that enabled it to purchase US weapons and training worth over $820 million between 2002 and 2005.[115] Bush hailed Musharraf's help in "dismantling the networks" of terrorism, his progress toward democracy, and his steps to contain Islamic fundamentalist schools—all efforts that others in and out of the administration believed were only being made halfheartedly at best.

Soon afterwards, as discussed above, the spotlight was again on Pakistan as the probable source of Iran's uranium enrichment technology.[116] Still later, following on Libya's admission that it had sought to produce nuclear weapons but had agreed with the United States and Britain to abandon the effort, Pakistan was named as the source of Libya's centrifuge design technology. North Korea also received "probably a dozen" centrifuges from Pakistan for its nuclear bomb program.[117] In fact, Pakistani shipments were made during the two years after 9/11, when Pakistan's cooperation with the United States in both the war on terror and nuclear weapon nonproliferation was supposedly rock solid.[118]

Not until January 2004, following an "internal investigation" that was almost certainly undertaken in response to US pressure, did Musharraf announce that "some individuals [meaning scientists or military officers associated with Pakistan's nuclear-weapon program] . . . were involved for personal financial gain" in nuclear exports.[119] The "individuals" turned out to be only one: Abdul Qadeer Khan, the "father" of Pakistan's atomic bomb program. In February, Khan "confessed" to being the sole source of nuclear secrets that were sold to Iraq, Iran, and North Korea—the mastermind behind a global network that stretched halfway around the world (via middlemen in Malaysia, for instance).[120] Following a televised statement, Khan was pardoned by Musharraf, who thereupon declared that neither the government nor the military had anything to do with the nuclear sales. This admission not merely strained credibility; it smelled of a political deal. For surely both the Pakistan government and elements of the military must have known about, if they did not actually authorize, such sensitive transactions. US intelligence circles are reportedly still waiting for the Pakistani government to cooperate in gaining access to A. Q. Khan's fund of information on what he provided to his customers.[121]

While Washington was thus securing Pakistan's loyalty to the larger cause, it was also improving ties with rival India. The overt US objective seemed to be to reverse years of mutual disaffection and thus accomplish at least two things: improve the US trade position in light of the expanding Indian market and India's role as a Third World leader at global trade talks; and have some leverage over Indo-Pakistani tensions in Kashmir, which by 2002 had again ratcheted up. After September 11 there was a sudden flurry of military activity between the United States and India: exchanges of official visits, joint exercises and patrols, and the resumption of military sales to India that had been suspended because of India's nuclear tests in 1998. (Most of US military assistance to India since 9/11 has taken the form of Economic Support Funds—about $32 million between FY2002 and 2004—rather than weapons sales or financing.[122])

Here again was a marriage of convenience that had little if anything to do with terrorists. For India, the United States represents access to technology and investment,[123] an upgrading of weapon systems, and a source of leverage on Musharraf for stopping "terrorist" attacks on India's portion of Kashmir. For the United States, getting closer to India is probably part of an unannounced geopolitical strategy for containing China—the joint sea patrols send just such a message—and yet another potential military staging area in the region.[124] India's positive response to US theater missile defense plans in East Asia, regarded in Beijing as directed chiefly at China, supports the containment thesis.[125] Though India's decision in mid-2003 not to send troops to assist in the US-British occupation of Iraq was a setback for Bush, the competition with China for India's friendship drives the administration's thinking.[126]

The essence of the Bush administration's approach to winning friends in South Asia—selling weapons to both—became clear in the spring of 2005. The administration decided to sell Pakistan twenty-four F-16 attack fighters, which are also capable of delivering nuclear warheads. Anticipating India's misgivings, Bush agreed to sell it as many as 126 jets. The decision was entirely in keeping with Bush's indecent conduct of international security affairs—rewarding Pakistan, an undemocratic ally that has undermined nuclear nonproliferation and is engaged in a tense relationship with its neighbor; using that deal to sustain a "strategic dialogue" (in State Department-ese) with those in Indian defense circles who emphasize a China threat and want advanced US weapons; and doing a major favor for US arms manufacturers such as Lockheed and Boeing, which need new markets to keep their fighter-jet production lines operating.[127]

Russia and China

Russia and China have also benefited from pledging to support the war on terrorism; as discussed in the next chapter, they may now count on Washington's silence while their armies and police use force to quash ethnic groups—Chechens, Uighurs, Tibetans, and other oppressed minorities—that seek either greater autonomy or independence. Following Washington's lead after 9/11, Moscow and Beijing reclassified these separatist groups as terrorists. Some analysts maintain that a common ground on terrorism will encourage more cooperative relations between the United States, China, and Russia on issues that divide them. But that is quite a long shot. They do not have a common terrorist enemy; each country defines and deals with terrorism on its own terms. The partnership is only skin deep; in fact, many younger Chinese, representing the future generation of leaders, actually gloated over the 9/11 attacks, and anti-US nationalism has become a staple of China's foreign policy outlook.[128] While US relations with China and Russia do involve shared interests—interests, in fact, that are more profound than the war on terror, such as the security of nuclear weapons–grade materials, protection of the global environment, commercial ties, and energy and resource conservation—they cannot hide the numerous sources of division.

US differences with China include China's military modernization, the political future of Taiwan,[129] political prisoners and religious persecution in China, China's huge trade surplus with the United States, China's refusal to allow Iran's suspect nuclear program to be debated in the UN Security Council, the US military buildup in Central Asia, and (as discussed earlier) Japan's security role in and beyond East Asia. Moscow and Washington disagree over strategic weapons reductions, the Russian Federation's plans for building nuclear reactors in Iran, and US bases in Russia's "near abroad"—in Georgia, Uzbekistan, and other Central Asian countries. On occasion, Putin's antidemocratic practices have also been criticized, though always politely, by the United States— for instance, during a presidential visit to Europe in early 2005. At the end of 2004, and again in the spring of 2005, US-RF relations soured over two events in Russia's backyard: a disputed presidential election in Ukraine and repression of a popular uprising in Uzbekistan. In the former instance, Washington and the EU, in support of the pro-Western opposition candidate, insisted the election was fraudulent, while Putin said the results were "absolutely clear" in favor of the candidate who stood for closer relations with Moscow. The Ukraine supreme court's unexpected decision to order a new election was a serious blow to Putin. In

Uzbekistan, Putin supported the Uzbek government's actions, which fit with his own design for dealing firmly with "Islamic terrorists." This alignment set the stage for a meeting of the Shanghai Cooperation Organization in July 2005 at which Russia, China, and the four Central Asian member states called on the United States to set a date for withdrawal from military bases in Uzbekistan and Kazakhstan.[130] Many more such conflicts over political developments around Russia's and China's periphery are likely in the years ahead.

Regime Change in the Hemisphere

Effecting regime change does not always require significant use of force. In Africa, the Bush administration embraced the concept of failed sovereignty by publicly calling for two dictators, Robert Mugabe in Zimbabwe and Charles Taylor in Liberia, to surrender their power, and in the case of Liberia by adding US soldiers to a mostly African UN peacekeeping operation.[131] And in Venezuela and Haiti, the administration attempted to achieve regime change in two other ways: by working with the incumbent government's opponents to achieve leverage in the first case; and by pressuring a democratically elected leader to leave office in the second.

The Venezuela case is worth exploring inasmuch as it had nothing to do with the war on terrorism and everything to do with traditional US power politics and economic self-interest in Latin America. During the spring of 2002, Venezuelan military and business leaders who wanted to see President Hugo Chávez removed apparently worked with US officials known to be sympathetic to their cause.[132] Chávez's populist program, dubbed "leftist" by the US press, got him into trouble with big business, leaders of the state-run oil company, and the military. His imperious leadership style contributed to the rift; but for the United States, it was his friendliness with Fidel Castro and probably above all his insistence on cutting oil production that made US leaders receptive to the idea of a coup. A general strike against the government on April 11, 2002, turned violent and, with the endorsement of several senior military officers, Chávez was arrested.

The United States has more than passing interest in Venezuelan events; its oil imports from Venezuela, around 1.5 million barrels of oil a day or 14 percent of total US oil imports, make Venezuela its third-largest provider of petroleum products. Venezuela's 1999 constitution "ban[ned] foreign investment in the oil sector, and in 2003, President Hugo Chávez fired managers of the state-owned oil company Petróleos de Venezuela S.A. who favored links with foreign firms."[133] As later events would show, when Venezuelan oil workers went on strike and brought production virtually to a halt at the end of 2003, US officials and the oil industry worried about the dependability of Venezuela's oil supplies with war looming in Iraq.[134] Rather than try to work with Chávez, however, Washington chose to help overthrow him.

The US embassy in Caracas had long been aware of discussions of a coup among military and business leaders: Two key figures on Latin America policy in the Bush administration, both former ambassadors to Venezuela, had met with anti-Chávez groups previously, and the CIA's intelligence briefs to Washington spoke knowingly of a possible coup by "disgruntled officers."[135] Furthermore, the congressionally funded National Endowment for Democracy had provided grants totaling several hundred thousand dollars to Venezuelan labor and other groups opposed to Chávez.[136] When Chávez was detained by the military and a new leader was installed, one of those US policymakers, Assistant Secretary of State Otto Reich, reportedly urged ambassadors from Latin America whom he had summoned to his office to support the new government on the basis that Chávez had resigned. An official US statement within hours of the coup expressed "our solidarity with the Venezuelan people" in support of "democratic rights." The overthrow of a constitutional government did not sit well with other Latin governments, however, and it was clearly their protests, in addition to Chávez's popularity with the poor and the incompetence of the coup regime, that led to a quick restoration of his authority.

Otto Reich and other US officials would later insist that the policy all along was to support constitutional government in Venezuela. "The United States does not support coups," he (incredibly) insisted.[137] But the facts suggest a systematic US effort to support those Venezuelan groups that were interested in undermining Chávez. In the best tradition of US Cold War diplomacy, Washington used various "assets" to attempt to replace him with a more pliant regime. The project failed that time, though by the end of 2002 Chávez again faced massive strikes and calls for his resignation. Washington, again, inserted its preference: a snap election. Neither resignation nor a snap election transpired; instead, the opposition, acting in accordance with the constitution, sought to collect enough signatures to force a recall election. But in March 2004 Venezuela's electoral council invalidated a large enough number of signatures to prevent a recall. A referendum on Chávez was held in August 2004; he won 58 percent of the vote, no doubt helped by his having put a considerable portion of oil revenues into social programs that benefited his key constituency, the poor.

The Bush administration seems resigned to having Chávez around; but into its second term, it still has him on its enemy list, an example of "creeping authoritarianism" that is somehow distinguishable from the outright authoritarianism the United States supports in friendlier countries.[138]

Haiti is Latin America's poorest and perhaps most violence-ridden country. Jean-Bertrand Aristide, a populist priest and the first democratically elected president in Haiti's history, was in the midst of his second term in office when widespread antigovernment activity erupted in February 2004. His first term had been interrupted by a military coup in 1991. Three years later, in 1994, US threats of military action and a diplomatic effort headed by former president Jimmy Carter and Colin Powell succeeded at getting rid of Haiti's military rulers and restoring Aristide to power. But on that occasion "regime change" was internationally sanctioned. A precedent-setting UN Security Council resolution (Resolution 940) authorized use of "all necessary means" to remove the junta, after the Organization of American States had imposed sanctions on the regime that had failed to work. But this was not at all like Iraq: In Haiti an elected leader was restored to power with overwhelming international approval, and a tyrannical group of generals and CIA-supported thugs who were running drugs and murdering opponents was removed.[139]

The intervening years, however, saw no fundamental change either in Haiti's corrupt and violent politics or its broken economy. Aristide never could overcome the opposition of Haiti's traditional elites nor its traditionally violent competition for political power.[140] The US-led peacekeeping force failed to completely disarm the police or the army; and Washington, along with the EU and international agencies, cut off aid to Haiti when Aristide rejected calls for new elections over a handful of disputed seats in parliament. The failure to abolish the downsized army, which Aristide had disbanded and which the great majority of Haitians wanted to see eliminated; the suspension of $500 million in international aid; and the funneling of money by US organizations to Aristide's opponents all hurt a country mired in debt and (as was probably intended) made his task of governing exceedingly difficult.[141]

Once George W. Bush took over, policymaking on Haiti passed into the same hands that had guided the attempted coup in Venezuela—the veterans of the failed contra supporters. It is entirely possible, though not yet proved, that Washington provided the rebels with arms sent in from the Dominican Republic next door. In perfect conformity with the Kirkpatrick Doctrine on support of right-wing dictators that had prevailed under Reagan, the Bush administration had no problem welcoming back to power some of the most notorious figures from Haiti's murderous past.[142]

By 2004, in the throes of a long-running political crisis, Aristide confronted demands for his resignation from both political opponents and rebel forces, the latter clearly led and backed by the very "thugs" (as Powell called them)—former army and secret police officials—who had once controlled the country. At first US officials, including the US ambassador to Haiti, correctly insisted that Aristide should be allowed to finish his term in 2006. Secretary Powell seemed believable when he said that Haiti would not be a case of regime change. Washington worked with other countries to try cobbling together a power-sharing arrangement. But as the rebels captured one town after another, and succeeded at surrounding the capital city of Port-au-Prince, Washington changed its tune (in this case, after France had called for Aristide to resign). Aristide needed to step down for the good of the country, said the president, the secretary of state, and other US officials. And so he did, on February 29.

The Bush administration may not, in the Haiti case, have engineered regime change—though Aristide told US congressional representatives, who approvingly repeated the statement, that he had been forced out by Washington, and the Jamaican prime minister (who later allowed Aristide to take up residence there) called Aristide's removal a US "coup"[143]—but it certainly facilitated it and did nothing to prevent it. Perhaps indicative of US responsibility was Colin Powell's opposition to a request from the fifteen-member Caribbean Community that the UN investigate Aristide's charge. "I don't think any purpose would be served by such an inquiry," said Powell. Aristide was in "great danger."[144] But the Caribbean Community refused to recognize the new government of Gérard Latortue, who was chosen by a US-appointed group of elders and thus joined the latest list of selected leaders.

Granting that the choices in Haiti were limited, the fact is that the United States allowed a gang of thugs, mostly consisting of disbanded army veterans and corrupt policemen who should have been disarmed and sidelined years earlier, to oust the constitutionally elected leader when a minimum show of strength by a multilateral force would surely have been sufficient to make clear the international community's preference. The US concern seems to have been that, as in past chaotic circumstances in the Caribbean, Haitian refugees would try to reach the United States. Like previous presidents, George W. Bush ordered that they be turned back—and indeed, around 600 boat people were, in contravention of international law governing flight from persecution. Once again democracy had no place in US interests; restoring order did. Why else would Bush send nearly 2,000 marines to Haiti and request endorsement from the Security Council only after Aristide was sent into exile?

What Bush's action essentially did was to reverse the restoration of Aristide to power. His action legitimized further political violence and lawlessness. In a matter of days political chaos descended on Haiti. Administration officials were forced to concede that Guy Philippe, the rebel leader who declared that he was now in charge, "is not in control of anything but a ragtag band."[145] Yet US efforts to get that "ragtag band" to disband and turn in its weapons proved difficult; the various rebel forces refused to do so until pro-Aristide forces did the same. What was painfully clear, and well known to US officials, is that Philippe and other rebel leaders had blood (and drugs) on their hands, making them unacceptable alternatives to Aristide. There was a vacuum of political authority in Haiti, a bankrupt economy, and a security vacuum. Within a matter of months, the news from Haiti was that poverty, lawlessness, and drug running were worse than before the rebellion.[146] But by then the United States, and every other country, had turned attention to other places.

Conclusion

Post-9/11 US foreign policy sacrifices a positive, peace-promoting, long-term vision to immediate interests, as happened so often during the Cold War. Whether dealing with rogue states, weak states (such as Haiti and Kazakhstan), big-power competitors (such as Russia and China), or friendly governments (such as Pakistan, India, Japan, and Indonesia), the war on terror frames and thus constrains US decisionmaking. Securing political, military, and economic gains has the highest priority; human needs, human rights, and possibilities for advancing common security get shortchanged. Creative diplomacy is AWOL. The end game, as revealed in Central and South Asia, is an old one: to create a network of international collaborators whose reliability can be purchased. The US government is thus assured of new markets for military as well as ordinary products, new jump-off points for intervention in the Middle East and elsewhere, new foreign-investment opportunities for US companies—in short, all the ingredients believed to be necessary for maintaining the empire, and all justified (for public consumption) in the name of "building democracy" and "fighting terror."

US policy toward North Korea and Iran raises a question: Why has the Bush Doctrine of regime change and preemptive attack not been immediately applied? In all probability North Korea and Iran have so far escaped the use of US power because US forces are stretched so thin in Iraq and Afghanistan, and are taking significant casualties. The administration no doubt fears—with good reason, considering its loss of credibility over the

Iraq war—that carrying out the neocon agenda will arouse a storm of opposition in Congress and the public. Not that Bush has discarded the objective of regime change; quite the opposite. More likely, he has felt compelled to give other governments time to demonstrate that diplomatic and economic engagement cannot succeed. If that happens, Bush in his second term may—depending very much on the situation in Iraq—feel free to take aim at North Korea and Iran. And that is surely the main reason why the leaderships of those countries, especially those factions that derive political strength from nuclear weapons research and development, are determined to keep the nuclear option open.

The US relationship with China now ranks among the most important in world affairs. Beijing and Washington are not at all on the same page on many issues, however, notwithstanding their strong economic ties and common commitment to fighting terrorism. But whereas differences on human rights and trade can be handled (or massaged) through ordinary diplomacy, those that strike a sensitive nationalist chord in China—Taiwan and US-Japan security relations—can make or break the relationship. US policy toward Japan risks strengthening a perception among Chinese leaders that those two countries regard China as a military and political threat, precisely at a time when the Chinese seem to be bending over backwards to demonstrate, notably in expanding economic ties with ASEAN, that they are a reliable, cooperative rising power. Chinese nationalism is the new reality in East Asia, and how the United States and Japan acknowledge it will have much to do with determining the character of that region's international politics for years to come, including China's cooperativeness with the United States on Korean peninsula issues.

Notes

1. Among these gains were the Agreed Framework, a step-by-step agreement whose main components were a nuclear freeze by North Korea in exchange for oil and nuclear energy assistance and eventual diplomatic relations; high-level diplomacy by President Clinton and Secretary of State Albright that included a US-DPRK joint communiqué (October 12, 2000) in which the parties "stated that neither government would have hostile intent toward the other" and would work "to build a new relationship free from past enmity"; Kim Jong Il's moratorium on ballistic missile testing; and, at the tail end of Clinton's tenure, meetings in North Korea that discussed trading substantial US aid for the complete termination of the DPRK's nuclear weapons and missile programs.

2. According to Lim Dong-Won, who was unification minister in Kim's government. Lim told of Kim Dae Jung's reaction on the PBS *Frontline* program, "Kim's Nuclear Gamble."

3. On the eve of Kim Dae Jung's visit to Washington, Powell said he hoped to "pick up where the Clinton administration left off" on engaging North Korea. This was clearly not the view of his boss. (See Frank S. Jannuzi, "North Korea: Back to the Brink?" in Hathaway and Lee, eds., *George W. Bush and Asia*, p. 79.) But Powell persisted, stating in a major speech on Asia policy that "we wholeheartedly support South Korea's sunshine policy." Speech to the Asia Society, June 10, 2002, ibid., p. 167.

4. Howard Fineman, "'I Sniff Some Politics,'" p. 37.

5. Thom Shanker, "Lessons from Iraq Include How to Scare Korean Leader," *NYT*, May 12, 2003, p. A17.

6. See Charles K. Armstrong, "US–North Korean Relations," pp. 13–37.

7. The foreign ministry statement, as translated by the BBC, can be found in the Northeast Asia Peace and Security Network (NAPSNet) Daily Report of February 10, 2005, online at http://napsnet@nautilus.org. This was actually not the first time North Korea's possession of nuclear weapons had been admitted. A senior DPRK official reportedly said, at the start of US-DPRK-PRC talks in Beijing in April 2003, "We already possess two nuclear bombs." Agence France-Presse, May 9, 2003; in NAPSNet Daily Report, same date.

8. David E. Sanger and William J. Broad, "North Korea Said to Expand Arms Program," *NYT*, December 6, 2004, p. A9.

9. Victor D. Cha, "Korea's Place in the Axis," pp. 79–92. Cha is now in charge of Asian affairs in Bush's National Security Council.

10. For example, a "senior [US] administration official" was quoted in 2002 as saying that "one rogue-state crisis at a time" was Bush's preferred approach, suggesting that North Korea might be next on his hit list after Iraq was subdued. (*NYT*, December 13, 2002, online ed.) That also seems to have been the view of administration hardliners in the afterglow of seeming victory in Iraq; see David E. Sanger, "Administration Divided Over North Korea," *NYT*, April 21, 2003, p. A15.

11. A top Chinese foreign ministry official took the unusual step of telling journalists that sanctions are not a workable or acceptable step, and that China would not support using food or oil deliveries to North Korea as a weapon against it. In fact, the official declared there was "no solid evidence" of a forthcoming North Korean nuclear test. Joseph Kahn, "China Says US Impeded North Korea Talks," *NYT*, May 13, 2005, p. A6.

12. The six parties are the two Koreas, the United States, China, Russia, and Japan. Three sessions of talks have been held since the summer of 2003, but a fourth session, scheduled for September 2004, was postponed and did not convene until July 2005.

13. See Selig S. Harrison, chair, *Ending the North Korean Nuclear Crisis: A Proposal by the Task Force on US Korea Policy*, p. 9.

14. Since 1995 US food and energy assistance to North Korea has been valued at around $1 billion. Food aid, delivered through the UN World Food Program, accounts for about 60 percent of the total. See Mark E. Manyin, *US Assistance to North Korea*.

15. As Vice President Cheney was quoted as saying at a policy meeting on North Korea in December 2003, "We don't negotiate with evil; we defeat it." *Philadelphia Inquirer* news report quoted in *Far Eastern Economic Review*, March 18, 2004, p. 28.

16. Chung-in Moon and Jong-Yun Bae argue (in "The Bush Doctrine and the North Korean Nuclear Crisis," in Gurtov and Van Ness, eds., *Confronting the Bush Doctrine,* pp. 39–62) that other than the military option, regime change is the most likely strategy being pursued by the Bush administration.

17. See Selig S. Harrison, "Did North Korea Cheat?" pp. 100–101. Jonathan D. Pollack's account is consistent with Harrison's assessment. Pollack writes that "the Koizumi visit [to North Korea in September 2002] in all likelihood accelerated plans for the long-deferred visit" of James Kelly to Pyongyang, where Kelly made the uranium enrichment charge. (Pollack, "Learning by Doing: the Bush Administration in East Asia," in Hathaway and Lee, eds., *George W. Bush and Asia,* p. 66.) Japan seeks to normalize relations with North Korea precisely in order to end the missile threat and obtain a full accounting of all Japanese nationals whom North Korean agents abducted years ago.

18. Beijing has long contended that theater missile defense really aims at neutralizing its own missile force, and that Japan's growing military cooperation with the United States in East Asia potentially threatens Chinese interests in reunifying with Taiwan.

19. According to senior Bush officials cited by David E. Sanger, "About-Face on North Korea: Allies Helped," *NYT,* June 24, 2004, online ed.

20. On several occasions the administration has erroneously charged North Korea with having secret bomb-making facilities and programs, preparing to conduct a nuclear weapon test, and supplying other countries with the means of making WMD. In early 2005, for instance, the administration told allied countries that North Korea had provided Libya with uranium hexafluoride, a key ingredient in nuclear bomb fuel. In fact, the supplier was Pakistan, probably via A.Q. Khan's network. See David E. Sanger and William J. Broad, "Uranium Testing Said to Indicate Libya-Korea Link," *NYT,* February 2, 2005, p. 1; Dafna Linzer, "US Misled Allies About Nuclear Export," *Washington Post,* March 20, 2005, online ed.; David E. Sanger and William J. Broad, "Using Clues from Libya to Study a Nuclear Mystery," *NYT,* March 31, 2005, p. A10.

21. Jae-Jung Suh, "Assessing the Military Balance in Korea," p. 77.

22. See, for instance, the interview of James Kelly in the *Korea Times* (Seoul, English ed.), December 13, 2004, online at http://times.hankooki.com.

23. Roh ordered around 3,000 soldiers to Iraq in mid-2004, adding to roughly 400 already there. The one US concession he did get in return, or so it seems, was an agreement to redeploy US forces based at Yongsan in central Seoul, a huge and extremely valuable piece of real estate, to less visible bases in the south of the country. As for the US troop cut of about 12,500, which South Korea protested, further talks may delay such action.

24. Gi-Wook Shin and Paul Y. Chang, "The Politics of Nationalism in US-Korean Relations," pp. 119–145. Reflecting the desire to distance South Korea from Washington, during 2005 President Roh spoke of South Korea as playing the role of a "balancer" in Northeast Asian affairs.

25. These and some other elements of a new approach to North Korea can also be found in the Council on Foreign Relations Task Force Report, *Meeting the North Korean Nuclear Challenge;* Harrison, *Ending the North Korean Nuclear Crisis;* Samuel S. Kim, "The US-DPRK Nuclear Standoff: The Case for Common-Security Engagement," pp. 41–64; Mel Gurtov, "Common Security in North Korea: Quest for a New Paradigm in Inter-Korean Relations," pp. 397–418;

Selig S. Harrison, "Time to Leave Korea?" pp. 62–78; and James Clay Moltz and C. Kenneth Quinones, "Getting Serious About a Multilateral Approach to North Korea."

26. See, for example, the statement of Li Gun, deputy director general of the DPRK Ministry for Foreign Affairs, December 16, 2003, in NAPSNet Special Report, February 6, 2004, online from http://DPRKbriefingbook@nautilus .org. Li Gun's main message was: "If the US fundamentally changes its hostile policy toward North Korea we could also give up our nuclear deterrent." The specific steps he said the United States must take were a nonaggression guarantee, diplomatic relations, and noninterference with North Korea's economic relations with other countries. See also Philip P. Pan, "N. Korea Says It Can 'Show Flexibility,'" *Washington Post*, June 26, 2004.

27. See *Korea Times* (Seoul), June 17, 2005, online ed., and Norimitsu Onishi, "North Korea's Leader Says He's Ready to Resume Talks to End Nuclear Standoff," *NYT*, June 18, 2005, p. A5. The official North Korean newspaper *Rodong Sinmun* stated in a commentary: "If the US nuclear threat to [North Korea] is removed and its hostile policy to 'bring down the system' of the latter is withdrawn, not a single nuclear weapon will be needed." Reported by the Associated Press, July 12, 2005.

28. Reuters (Beijing), in *NYT*, July 9, 2005, online ed.

29. Text in NAPSNet, September 13, 2005, available at www.nautilus.org.

30. David E. Sanger, "Yes, Parallel Tracks to North, But Parallel Tracks Don't Meet," *NYT*, September 20, 2005, p. A6.

31. See Peter Van Ness, "The North Korean Nuclear Crisis: Four-Plus-Two—An Idea Whose Time Has Come," in Gurtov and Van Ness, eds., *Confronting the Bush Doctrine*, pp. 242–259, and Jae-Jung Suh, "The Two-Wars Doctrine and the Regional Arms Race: Contradictions in US Post–Cold War Security Policy in Northeast Asia," pp. 3–32.

32. North Korea's agreement to return to the 6PT may in fact have been the result of South Korea's promise, in return for the North's scrapping of its nuclear weapons, to provide it with a substantial amount of electricity, equivalent to the amount that would have been provided under the Agreed Framework of 1994. (*Korea Times*, July 12, 2005, online ed.) That news appeared at the same time that Seoul announced a large new shipment of food to North Korea and agreement on South Korean mining of Northern mineral deposits in exchange for raw materials for the North's consumer industries. Ibid.

33. See, for example, Task Force on US Korea Policy, *Turning Point in Korea: New Dangers and New Opportunities for the United States*.

34. Jack Pritchard, "What I Saw in North Korea," *NYT*, January 21, 2003, p. A29.

35. Interview on the Public Broadcasting System, September 17, 1999; quoted in NAPSNet online, September 20, 1999.

36. The official is quoted as having said: "There are people in the State Department who want to think Iran is changing because everyone's drinking Coca Cola, but the evidence isn't there." *NYT*, January 31, 2002, p. A12.

37. See, for instance, his interview with the *New York Times*, November 9, 2001, published the following day.

38. See Robert Dreyfuss and Laura Rozen, "Still Dreaming of Tehran," pp. 16–18. Among the exile groups is the Mujahedeen Khalq. Though listed by the

State Department as a terrorist organization, it received the Pentagon's support during and after the invasion of Iraq as a means of putting pressure on Iran. The Pentagon also tried to get the State Department to remove the group from the terrorist list. Douglas Jehl, "Iranian Rebels Urge Pentagon Not to Let Iraq Expel Them," *NYT,* December 13, 2003, p. A9.

39. All quotations from *NYT,* April 16, 2003, p. B3.

40. *NYT,* June 19, 2003, p. 1.

41. Richard Bernstein, "U.N. Atom Agency Seeks Wider Scrutiny on Iran, But Is Rebuffed," *NYT,* June 20, 2003, p. A6.

42. Elisabeth Bumiller, "Bush Sees Joint World Effort to Press Iran on Nuclear Issue," *NYT,* August 10, 2004, p. A11.

43. Condoleezza Rice "declined to say whether the United States would support such action by Israel." John Damis, "Confronting the Brewing Nuclear Weapons Crisis in Iran," *The Oregonian* (Portland), August 26, 2004. Laura King reported that "Prime Minister Ariel Sharon and his top aides have been asserting for months that a nuclear-armed Iran would pose a clear threat to Israel's existence. They have repeatedly threatened, in elliptical but unmistakable terms, to use force if diplomacy and the threat of sanctions fail." "Israel May Have Iran in Its Sights," *Los Angeles Times,* October 22, 2004.

44. The information was said to have been passed via the principal pro-Israel lobbying group, the American Israel Public Affairs Committee (AIPAC). See Steven Erlanger, "Israel Denies Spying Against US," *NYT,* August 29, 2004, online ed., and Eric Schmitt, "Pentagon Office in Spying Case Was Focus of Iran Debate," *NYT,* September 2, 2004, p. A12.

45. See Hiro, *Secrets and Lies,* pp. 17–22. Cheney, in a radio interview in early 2005, also alluded to a possible Israeli preemptive strike. *NYT,* January 21, 2005, p. A6.

46. Richard L. Russell, "Iran in Iraq's Shadow: Dealing with Tehran's Nuclear Weapons Bid," pp. 31–45.

47. Seymour M. Hersh, "The Coming Wars," pp. 40–47; Dafner Linzer, "US Uses Drones to Probe Iran for Arms," *Washington Post,* February 13, 2005. While the drones' main purpose may be to gather information on Iran's nuclear program, they may also be collecting data for an invasion.

48. Steven R. Weisman and Douglas Jehl, "Estimate Revised on When Iran Could Make Nuclear Bomb," *NYT,* August 3, 2005, p. A8.

49. See Thom Shanker and Eric Schmitt, "Pentagon Expects Long-Term Access to Four Key Bases in Iraq," *NYT,* April 20, 2003, online ed.

50. See Nazila Fathi, "Iran Says It May Preempt Attack Against Its Nuclear Facilities," *NYT,* August 20, 2004, p. A4.

51. The resistance movement of the Shiite cleric Moktada al-Sadr, centered in Najaf, Iraq, which led to numerous casualties and extensive use of force by the United States, came about after the leading Shiite mullah in the Iranian holy city of Qum signed a letter that made al-Sadr his deputy. See Craig S. Smith, "Cleric in Iran Says Shiites Must Act," *NYT,* April 26, 2003, online ed.

52. *NYT,* February 4, 2005, p. 1.

53. See Jahangir Amuzegar, "Iran's Crumbling Revolution," pp. 44–57.

54. Neil MacFarquhar, "Across Iran, Nuclear Power Is a Matter of Pride," *NYT,* May 29, 2005, online ed.; George Perkovich, "Iran Is Not an Island: A Strategy to Mobilize the Neighbors," pp. 1–7.

55. Percovich, "Iran Is Not an Island," p. 6. David Kay, the one-time Bush appointee to look into Iraq's WMD, said in a television interview that the administration's case against Iran sounded eerily similar to that against Iraq before the invasion. The "challenge is to find a diplomatic basis that will keep them [Iran] from going that final mile" to actually produce a nuclear bomb. Interview on CNN with Wolf Blitzer, February 9, 2005.

56. Record, *Bounding the Global War on Terrorism*, p. 7.

57. Layne and Schwarz, "American Hegemony," p. 4.

58. For a detailed survey, see William D. Hartung, Frida Berrigan, and Michelle Ciarrocca, "Operation Endless Deployment." Most of the information that follows comes from various newspaper dispatches.

59. See Juan Forero, "Administration Shifts Focus on Colombia Aid," *NYT,* February 6, 2002, p. A6, and *NYT,* December 5, 2002, online ed. On Special Forces activities in the Horn of Africa, see Craig S. Smith, "US Training African Forces to Uproot Terrorists," *NYT,* May 11, 2004, online ed.

60. See *NYT,* January 9, 2002, p. A10, and September 23, 2002, p. A10.

61. Ian Fisher, "US Eyes a Willing Romania as a New Comrade in Arms," *NYT,* July 16, 2003, p. A1.

62. Only in Yemen is there a reasonably clear connection to Al-Qaida activities. (See Thom Shanker and Eric Schmitt, "US Moves Commandos to Base in East Africa," *New York Times,* September 18, 2002, p. A20.) Singapore has one group, Jemaah Islamiah, also active in Indonesia, that is said to have helped Al-Qaida's communications before the September 11 attacks and planned an attack in January 2002 on the US embassy in Singapore. The connection between Al-Qaida and the Bali bombing has been claimed but not yet proved, as a US Congressional Research Service has reported. See the CRS memorandum to the House Government Reform Committee, "Terrorist Attacks by Al Qaeda," March 31, 2004, p. 4, online at www/house/gov/reform/min/pdfs_108_2/pdfs_inves/pdf_admin_911_panel_crs_rep_april_6_let_rep.pdf.

63. Steven R. Weisman, "US to Sell Weapons to Algeria to Help Fight Islamic Radicals," *NYT,* December 10, 2002, p. A14.

64. See Christopher Pala, "Cries of Fraud Give Election in Kyrgyzstan Aura of Ukraine," *NYT,* March 14, 2005, p. A8; Anara Tabyshalieva, "Kyrgyzstan's Tenous Hold on Democracy," *Far Eastern Economic Review,* April 2005, pp. 26–29.

65. Figures in this paragraph are from the Center for Defense Information (CDI) web site on the global arms trade, at www.cdi.org/news/arms-trade. Also valuable is Frida Berrigan, William D. Hartung, and Leslie Heffel, *U.S. Weapons at War 2005: Promoting Freedom or Fueling Conflict?*

66. See the *New York Times* editorial, "Nepotism in Central Asia," October 27, 2003, p. A22.

67. Total military assistance typically includes some combination of military training, weapons sales, financing assistance, and counterterrorism support.

68. Lutz Kleveman, "Oil and the New 'Great Game,'" pp. 11–14. For a report that attaches less significance to the pipeline—at least as of 2002, when oil prices were low ($18 a barrel), consumption was rising rapidly, alternative routes were available, and Afghanistan was in total disarray—see Murray Hiebert, "No Big Win for Big Oil," *Far Eastern Economic Review,* January 17, 2002, pp. 24–25.

69. The small sub-Saharan nation of Equatorial Guinea is ruled by Teodoro Obiang Nguema Mbasogo, who came to power in a 1979 coup. It has a desperately poor population, but it is also the third-largest oil producer in Africa. Oil, and use of a high-powered US lobbying firm, have enabled Equatorial Guinea to avoid US sanctions over its wide-ranging human rights violations. (See Elisabeth Eaves, "Spin Doctors Without Borders," pp. 56–57.) Great Britain may also be a player here: Several months after a failed coup attempt in March 2004 that was mainly carried out by South African mercenaries, the son of former British prime minister Margaret Thatcher was arrested on the charge of having financed the conspiracy.

70. Military assistance figures for Kazakhstan and Uzbekistan are from the CDI website, www.cdi.org/news/arms-trade. Among the many reports on corruption and misrule in Central Asia that are linked to the war on terrorism and oil politics, see Edmund L. Andrews, "Spotlight on Central Asia Is Finding Repression, Too," *NYT*, April 11, 2002, p. A6; Todd S. Purdum, "Uzbekistan's Leader Doubts Chances for Afghan Peace," *NYT*, March 14, 2002, p. A18; Muhammad Salih, "America's Shady Ally Against Terror," *NYT*, March 11, 2002, p. A25; and Ahmed Rashid, "Trouble Ahead," *Far Eastern Economic Review*, May 9, 2002, pp. 14–18.

71. See *NYT*, July 28, 2000, online ed., for instance. In September 2001 the former prime minister, Akezhan Kazhegeldin, was sentenced while in exile to ten years in prison on bribery charges.

72. Jeff Gerth, "Bribery Inquiry Involves Kazakh Chief, and He's Unhappy," *NYT*, December 11, 2002, p. A14, and Lutz C. Kleveman, "The Devil's Tears," pp. 18–21.

73. www.cdi.org.

74. See, for example, Edmund L. Andrews, "New US Allies, the Uzbeks: Mired in the Past," *NYT*, May 31, 2002, online ed.

75. Muhammad Salih (exiled leader of an opposition party in Uzbekistan), "America's Shady Ally Against Terror," *NYT*, March 11, 2002, p. A25.

76. www.cdi.org.

77. Ambassador Craig Murray reportedly told his government: "Tortured dupes are forced to sign confessions showing what the Uzbek government wants the US and UK to believe—that they and we are fighting the same war against terror." *NYT*, October 15, 2004, p. A14.

78. Seth Mydans, "3rd Day of Violence Claims 23 Lives in Uzbekistan," *NYT*, March 31, 2004, p. A3.

79. See C. J. Chivers and Thom Shanker, "Uzbek Ministries in Crackdown Received US Aid," *NYT*, June 19, 2005, p. 1.

80. *NYT*, July 13, 2005, p. A11.

81. On conditions in these countries, see James Hookway, "Genuine Grievances," *Far Eastern Economic Review*, August 7, 2003, pp. 16–18; John McBeth, "The Betrayal of Indonesia," *Far Eastern Economic Review*, June 26, 2003, pp. 14-18; and Shawn W. Crispin, "Mafia Mission," *Far Eastern Economic Review*, July 3, 2003, p. 19.

82. As one writer based in the Philippines put it: "terrorists did not create the conflict in the southern Philippines and do not control any of the combatants. The troubles are rooted in specific local issues that predate the war on terror by

centuries, and neither soldiers nor money will end Mindanao's war." Steven Rogers, "Beyond the Abu Sayyaf," p. 15.

83. Amitav Acharya, "The Bush Doctrine and Asian Regional Order: The Perils and Pitfalls of Preemption," in Gurtov and Van Ness, eds., *Confronting the Bush Doctrine,* p. 208.

84. Bradley Graham, "New Defense Ties with Philippines," *Washington Post,* August 13, 2002.

85. Carlos H. Conde, "Communist Revival Worries the Philippines," *NYT,* January 4, 2004, online ed.

86. Eric Schmitt with Raymond Bonner, "Delay Seen in US-Philippine Joint Mission," *NYT,* June 7, 2003, online ed., and Acharya, "The Bush Doctrine and Asian Regional Order," p. 208.

87. Berrigan, Hartung, and Heffel, *U.S. Weapons at War 2005,* p. 20.

88. See the report in the *NYT,* January 23, 2002, p. A1, in which "several American and foreign officials said there was no hard evidence of links between Al Qaida and Laskar Jihad," the radical Indonesian organization suspected of such links.

89. R. William Liddle and Saiful Mujani, "The Real Face of Indonesian Islam," *NYT,* October 11, 2003, p. A27. As the authors write: "Survey and election results show that the number of Islamists, Muslims who want an Islamic state, is no more than 15 percent of the total Indonesian Muslim population of 200 million. The remaining 85 percent are moderately or strongly opposed to an Islamic state."

90. Todd S. Purdum, "US to Resume Aid to Train Indonesia's Military Forces," *NYT,* August 3, 2002, online ed.

91. Murray Hiebert, "The Era of Responsibility," *Far Eastern Economic Review,* July 11, 2002, pp. 14–16. The administration's letter to the judge in the case mentioned the challenge of Chinese oil companies if Exxon Mobil was forced to withdraw; but its principal—and bizarre—argument was that if Indonesia, "a focal point of US initiatives in the ongoing war against Al Qaeda," were interfered with by virtue of the lawsuit, its "cooperation in response to perceived disrespect for its sovereign interests" would be "imperiled." Jane Perlez, "US Backs Oil Giant on Lawsuit in Indonesia," *NYT,* August 8, 2002, online ed.

92. Jane Perlez, "Indonesia Says It Will Press Attacks on Separatists in Sumatra," *NYT,* May 23, 2003, p. A11.

93. Conn Hallinan, "US Underwriting Terrorism?" *Foreign Policy In Focus,* September 15, 2004, online at www.fpif.org.

94. Jane Perlez, "US Takes Steps to Mend Ties with Indonesian Military," *NYT,* February 7, 2005, p. A12. The agreement, signed in Finland, also acknowledges the right of local political parties to form. Evelyn Rusli, "Indonesia and Separatists Reach Deal to End 30 Years of Fighting," *NYT,* July 18, 2005, p. A3; Evelyn Rusli, "In Signing Accord, Indonesia and Rebels Hope for Peace, " *NYT,* August 15, 2005, online ed.

95. This paragraph is based on CDI's country report, available at www .cdi.org.

96. Associated Press dispatch, in *NYT,* August 1, 2002, online ed.

97. "The US has been criticized [in Southeast Asia] as clumsy, misguided and falling into long-standing local disputes that have festered for years and

pose little international threat." Barry Wain, "Wrong Target," *Far Eastern Economic Review,* April 18, 2002, pp. 14–18.

98. See Acharya, "The Bush Doctrine and Asian Regional Order," pp. 210–211.

99. Quoted in Raymond Bonner, "Indonesian Criticizes US Over the War in Iraq," *NYT,* December 9, 2003, p. A12.

100. Acharya, "The Bush Doctrine and Asian Regional Order," p. 221.

101. Alice D. Ba, "China-ASEAN Relations: Political Significance of an Asean Free Trade Area," in T. J. Cheng, Jacques deLisle, and Deborah Brown, eds., *China Under the Fourth Generation Leadership: Opportunities, Dangers, and Dilemmas,* forthcoming.

102. See Bernard K. Gordon, "A High-Risk Trade Policy."

103. For a comprehensive overview, see Yul Kwon, "East Asian Regionalism Focusing on ASEAN Plus Three."

104. These paragraphs on Japan rely mainly on Richard Tanter, "With Eyes Wide Shut: Japan, Heisei Militarization, and the Bush Doctrine," in Gurtov and Van Ness, eds., *Confronting the Bush Doctrine,* pp. 153–180.

105. A Kyodo news poll found that 61 percent of respondents opposed the extension and 32 percent favored it. (*Japan Times,* December 11, 2004; NAPSNet online service, December 15, 2004.) To assuage the public, the soldiers were billeted well away from populated areas, inviting the opposite criticism from some Iraqis as well as Japanese—that the soldiers were doing little good.

106. *NYT,* January 26, 2003, p. 15.

107. *Asahi Shimbun* (Tokyo, English ed.), December 13, 2004, online at www.asahi.com.

108. Tanter, "With Eyes Wide Shut," p. 156.

109. For example, Seth G. Jones, "The Danger Next Door," *NYT,* September 23, 2005, p. A19.

110. See James Risen and Judith Miller, "Pakistani Intelligence Had Links to Al Qaeda, US Officials Say," *NYT,* October 29, 2001, p. A1.

111. Amnesty International was among the international NGOs that charged that the Pakistani government had violated international human rights standards by deporting or illegally detaining numerous individuals merely on suspicion of being associated with Al-Qaida or the Taliban. Associated Press, "Amnesty Accuses Pakistan on Rights," *NYT,* June 20, 2002, online ed.

112. David Rohde, "Musharraf Redraws Constitution," *NYT,* August 22, 2002, online ed.

113. David E. Sanger, "In North Korea and Pakistan, Deep Roots of Nuclear Barter," *NYT,* November 24, 2002, online ed.

114. Carlotta Gall, "Mixed Reaction in Pakistan to US Pledge of $3 Billion in Aid," *NYT,* June 26, 2003, online ed.

115. Berrigan, Hartung, and Heffel, *U.S. Weapons at War 2005,* p. 16. The grants are under the Foreign Military Financing program.

116. Joby Warrick, "Iran Admits Foreign Help on Nuclear Facility," *NYT,* August 29, 2003, online ed. Pakistan, not having signed the Nuclear Nonproliferation Treaty, is technically not subject to its prohibition of nuclear weapon exports.

117. This admission came from Musharraf himself. See David E. Sanger, "Pakistan Leader Confirms Nuclear Exports," *NYT,* September 13, p. A8.

118. Patrick E. Tyler and David E. Sanger, "Pakistan Called Libyans' Source of Atom Design," *NYT*, January 6, 2004, online ed. US sources, which were responsible for the accusation, had no evidence that Musharraf himself was aware of the shipments.

119. Mark Landler and David E. Sanger, "Pakistan Chief Says It Appears Scientists Sold Nuclear Data," *NYT*, January 24, 2004, p. A1.

120. An excellent overview of Khan's network is by David E. Sanger and William J. Broad, "From Rogue Nuclear Programs, Web of Trails Leads to Pakistan," *NYT*, January 4, 2004, online ed.

121. William J. Broad and David E. Sanger, "As Nuclear Secrets Emerge, More Are Suspected," *NYT*, December 26, 2004, p. 1.

122. CDI section on India at www.cdi.org.

123. Such access turned out to include nuclear energy technology, which Bush agreed in July 2005 to sell to India, subject to approval from the US Congress and the other nuclear weapon states. Yet India has still not agreed to sign the NPT. *NYT*, July 19, 2005, p. 1.

124. Celia W. Dugger, "Wider Military Ties with India Offer US Diplomatic Leverage," *NYT*, June 9, 2002, p. A1; Joanna Slater and Murray Hiebert, "US and India Stage Quiet Rapprochement," *Wall Street Journal,* December 18, 2001, p. A11; Conn Hallinan, "US and India, A Dangerous Alliance," *Foreign Policy in Focus,* May 12, 2003, online at www.fpif.org/commentary/2003/0305india.html.

125. Jane Perlez, "US Ready to End Sanctions on India to Build an Alliance," *NYT*, August 27, 2001, online ed.

126. Bush's military sales pitch to India described in the next paragraph occurred just about the time of Premier Wen Jiabao's visit to New Delhi, which resulted in agreements on their disputed border and trade expansion.

127. Leslie Wayne, "Connecting to India Through Pakistan," *NYT*, April 16, 2005, p. B1.

128. Ying Ma, "China's America Problem," pp. 43–56.

129. See US Department of Defense, *Quadrennial Defense Review Report,* and US Department of Defense, *Annual Report on the Military Power of the People's Republic of China.* The latter document focuses on Taiwan as the "primary driver for China's military modernization."

130. C. J. Chivers, "Central Asians Call on US to Set a Timetable for Closing Bases," *NYT*, July 6, 2005, p. 1.

131. On Zimbabwe, see Colin L. Powell, "Robert Mugabe's Time Has Come and Gone," *International Herald Tribune,* June 25, 2003. Charles Taylor finally did step down and leave Liberia in August 2003.

132. This paragraph relies mainly on the following news reports: Larry Rohter, "Venezuela's 2 Fateful Days: Leader Is Out, and In Again," *NYT*, April 20, 2002, p. A1; Christopher Marquis, "US Bankrolling Is Under Scrutiny for Ties to Chávez Ouster," *NYT*, April 25, 2002, p. A8; Simon Romero, "Tenuous Truce in Venezuela for the State and Its Oil Company," *NYT*, April 24, 2002, p. A6; Conn Hallinan, "US Shadow Over Venezuela," online at *Foreign Policy in Focus,* www.fpif.org/commentary/2002/0204venezuela2_body.html; Christopher Marquis, "US Cautioned Leader of Plot Against Chávez," *NYT*, April 17, 2002, p. A1.

133. Klare, "Bush-Cheney Energy Strategy," p. 9.

134. See James Dao and Neela Banerjee, "Venezuela Crisis Complicates Iraq Situation, Experts Say," *NYT,* January 11, 2003, p. A3.

135. Juan Forero, "Documents Show C.I.A. Knew of a Coup Plot in Venezuela," *NYT,* December 3, 2004, p. A12.

136. The role of the NED, whose funds went to a number of anti-Chávez political groups, is examined by David Corn, "Our Gang in Venezuela."

137. "Remarks by Otto Reich, Assistant Secretary of State for Western Hemisphere Affairs, at Center for Strategic & International Studies Subject: US Relations with Brazil, Argentina and Uruguay," July 18, 2002, online at www.csis.org/americas/sa/020718reich.pdf.

138. The phrase was used by Robert B. Zoellick at hearings to confirm him as deputy secretary of state. See *NYT,* February 16, 2005, p. A6. Zoellick was never asked why his criticisms of Chávez's political practices should not be applied equally to Pakistan, Kazakhstan, or Indonesia. As for Chávez, he continues to defy the United States—for example, by ending a 35-year-old military exchange program in April 2005 and evicting thirteen US military attachés from Venezuela.

139. See Mel Gurtov and Ellen Mekjavich, "Responding to Humanitarian Crises," pp. 507–531.

140. See Chetan Kumar, "Peacebuilding in Haiti," in Elizabeth M. Cousens and Chetan Kuman, eds., *Peacebuilding as Politics: Cultivating Peace in Fragile Societies,* pp. 21–51.

141. Many international observers of Haiti's situation, such as the Nobel Laureate Oscar Arias, former president of Costa Rica, and various NGOs all documented the systematic undermining of Aristide's rule and the increasingly desperate state of Haiti's economy. See, for instance, Paul Farmer, "Haiti's Wretched of the Earth," pp. 23–26, 61.

142. Ibid., p. 61.

143. Quoted on National Public Radio, March 1, 2004.

144. *NYT,* April 6, 2004, p. A8.

145. Statement of Roger Noriega, assistant secretary of state for Latin American Affairs, in *NYT,* March 3, 2004, p. A6.

146. See, for instance, Lydia Polgreen, "Deepening Poverty Breeds Anger and Desperation in Haiti," *NYT,* May 5, 2004, p. A10; Lydia Polgreen and Tim Weiner, "Drug Traffickers Find Haiti a Hospitable Port of Call," *NYT,* May 16, 2004, p. 6.

6

The United States
as Global Citizen

GLOBAL CITIZENSHIP SHOULD mean that governments strive to act in ways that promote planetary well-being—the welfare of the vast majority of humanity, the conservation of its precious natural resources and ecology, the sanctity of its cultures, the strength of internationally accepted institutions and standards, and peaceful and equitable relations between states and peoples. When governments act as global citizens, they do so in recognition that national interests are sometimes best served by promoting the interests of the global community—for example, by setting and meeting agreed-upon standards of human rights and environmental protection, contributing to peacekeeping missions, and alleviating poverty. These are the kinds of large-scale issues that cannot be managed by one or a few countries; their scope requires transnational and global cooperation to address.

The notion of global citizenship is, unfortunately, at odds with the philosophy that informs the Bush Doctrine. Its insistence on an "American internationalism" inevitably limits support for international law and organizations except when those fall in line with US preferences. The United States has a long history of going it alone on global issues, though often that is due less to an administration's decision than to the influence of domestic forces such as lobbies, congressional committees, and large corporations. In the George W. Bush administration, however, international cooperation has been deliberately downplayed in favor of US interests and "values." This chapter provides numerous examples drawn from five areas of global concern: human rights, poverty, the environment, international law and organizations, and weapons proliferation.

Human Rights

Both in word and deed, the Bush administration has greatly set back international discourse on and state policies that might promote human rights. Putting the promotion of human rights in the context of national security strategy, using double standards to depart from widely accepted human rights practices, deciding to overlook wholesale violations of human rights by friendly governments, emphasizing human dignity but not equality or worth, ignoring international understandings and covenants on human rights—these are among the actions that have diminished the hope of the United States's founders to become a "shining example" to the rest of the world of progress in advancing human rights.[1]

To illustrate, we can begin with the contradictory effects of the war on terror, which actually undermined efforts to strengthen human rights and democratic rule. As was pointed out in the previous chapter, the war on terror is playing into the hands of authoritarian leaders around the world, who see in it opportunities to attract US aid, investments, and political support while continuing to crack down on legitimate dissent at home. This pattern is hardly new; strategic and commercial interests have always trumped democratization in US foreign policy. Nor is this a pattern only in US relations with Third World countries. The same argument long used there—that developing countries can hardly be expected to move quickly away from established traditions of strong centralized rule—applies as well to, say, Russia as it does to African countries. The real US priorities are evident in aid programs, where paltry sums are allocated to building democratic institutions in comparison with funding for commercial ventures,[2] and in military deployments, which are made for strategic and commercial advantage but not (witness Uzbekistan or Haiti) to secure democratic rule.

Ignoring repression has become a license for it in the name of fighting terrorists—a license that has been used almost worldwide.[3] As the UN High Commissioner for Human Rights, Mary Robinson, said on leaving office: "The United States could be a leader in combating terrorism while upholding human rights. Instead it has sought to put all the emphasis on combating terrorism and has not been fully upholding human rights standards. And that's having a ripple effect on other less democratic countries."[4] We have already shown this in US relations with the Central Asian countries, Indonesia, and Pakistan. Strategic partnerships are what count in Washington, greatly reducing the salience of human security issues.

US relations with three other countries further illustrate the point. Israel's escalation of attacks on city neighborhoods suspected of harboring

Palestinian suicide bombers has been rationalized as merely following the US example in Afghanistan and Iraq. (Prior to Arafat's death, the Israeli government of Ariel Sharon also spoke of "regime change" as its objective for the Palestinian Authority.) In China, crackdowns on ethnic minorities, striking workers, protesting farmers, and undesirable social groups (such as the Falungong sect and officially unrecognized religious groups) occasionally capture attention in Washington, but more often take a back seat to antiterror cooperation. When Chinese and other officials of the six-country Shanghai Cooperation Organization met in January 2002, they promised to work together against "terrorism, separatism and extremism." The many forms and goals of dissent in those countries were thus conflated into one and treated in the same brutal manner. Notwithstanding their lack of connection with one another, much less to Al-Qaida, Muslim groups are common targets.[5] Yet the Chinese government justified officially designating four Muslim organizations as "terrorist" on the basis of just such a connection.[6] The US State Department may not have agreed, but it went along; it placed a Uighur separatist group on the department's terrorist list, apparently as a reward for Beijing's announced curbs on missile exports.[7]

In Chechnya, the Russian military began a second campaign in the fall of 1999, following a series of bombings in Moscow that were attributed to Chechen separatists. Bush's declaration of war on terror gave RF President Vladimir Putin "his chance . . . Russia was transformed almost overnight into an *ally of the (Western) alliance*."[8] Russian oil, not the lives of ordinary Chechens, seemed to count most to the Bush administration.[9] The Russian military employed the "terrorist threat" to bomb not only in Chechnya itself but also ever more deeply in neighboring Georgia.[10] Instead of criticizing these Russian excesses, Washington responded to a request from Putin by designating three Chechen groups as "terrorist organizations" and freezing their assets.[11] Some Chechen groups deserve being called terrorist: The Moscow bombings in 1999 and the seizure of a school in the Caucasus in 2004 with great loss of life were terrible deeds. But the intent of such attacks is political, not psychological; and underlying their attacks is the violence committed by Russian forces in Chechnya, the systematic violations of Chechens' human rights, and the refusal of the RF government to seek a fair political settlement that would honor Chechen aspirations for greater autonomy, if not independence.

The priority of "national security" needs over human rights under Bush extends to individual dissenters as well. The US State Department is often silent on behalf of political dissenters in countries, including Russia and China, that support the antiterrorism campaign. Illustrative is the belated response to a long-term jail sentence meted out by an Egyptian court to a well-known pro-democracy advocate who clearly favored only nonviolent change.[12] It was enough to make a Sri Lankan human rights advocate lament that this inexplicably short-sighted US response opened the door to fundamentalist alternatives, in Egypt and elsewhere. More than that, she said, faith in the United States as a leader in human rights has vanished:

> None of us in the human rights community would think of appealing to the US for support for upholding a human rights case—maybe to Canada, to Norway or to Sweden—but not to the US. Before there were always three faces of America out in the world—the face of the Peace Corps, the America that helps others, the face of multinationals and the face of American military power. My sense is that the balance has gone wrong lately and that the only face of America we see now is the one of military power, and it really frightens the world.

The failure to support children's rights is another mark against the Bush administration. The reason comes down to political concerns about access to reproductive information, abortion, and the prohibition of capital punishment of minors. Instead of standing behind the 1989 Convention on the Rights of the Child, which the United States (along with only one other country, Somalia) has not ratified, Bush decided to water down the final statement issued at the conclusion of the first UN General Assembly special session on children in 2002.[13] The effects of US intransigence are twofold. First, it weakens efforts to promote safe-sex education and thereby reduce transmission of HIV and other diseases. Second, it supports capital punishment as a remedy for crime, one that is increasingly out of favor internationally.

Bush, like his predecessors, upholds the death penalty. That puts the United States in unfortunate company, such as China (where Amnesty International reports that "at least 726 people were executed" in 2003, by far the highest total in the world), Iran, and Vietnam. Capital punishment is in fact on the wane worldwide, both in law and in practice: The death penalty no longer applies in 117 countries.[14] Continued use of the death penalty in the United States is a political as well as a moral issue, since it is another source of dispute in US-EU relations.

One area of international human rights that advanced during the Bush administration was in the federal courts where, despite the best efforts of Bush's legal advisers to prevent it, noncitizens gained the right to sue for violations that occur outside the United States. The US Supreme Court decided in June 2004 that an eighteenth-century statute could be used by a Mexican doctor to sue the US government for damages after US agents kidnapped him in a drug-related case. The case took twelve years to litigate, and although the court decided against the doctor, his right to make a human rights claim was validated.[15] By implication, future victims abroad of unlawful detention, torture, and "disappearances" brought about by US policies may seek restitution in US courts.

Poverty and Globalization

Bush's approach to economic globalization follows in the footsteps of previous administrations in being attuned to the needs of the "Washington consensus." Though not keen about relying on the IMF and the World Bank to bail out troubled Third World economies, Bush's appointees have generally supported the formula those organizations usually prescribe: trade and capital liberalization, deregulation, and privatization of state-run firms. As the Bush *National Security Strategy* paper declares, "Free trade and free markets have proven their ability to lift whole societies out of poverty—so the United States will work with individual nations, entire regions, and the entire global trading community to build a world that trades in freedom and therefore grows in prosperity."[16]

The notion (to quote Bush directly) that "the best way to eradicate poverty is to encourage trade between nations"[17] blithely ignores the victims of trade liberalization and economic globalization generally: the farmers driven off their land in Mexico, Uganda, and China by cheap agricultural imports, for instance, and the assembly-line workers around the world who are unprotected and must live on substandard wages. Benjamin J. Cohen has pointed to other risks. If the privileged position of the United States in the world economy produces irresponsible behavior, it will encourage economic nationalism elsewhere:

> [Bush] Administration officials, mostly conservative and business oriented, seem inclined to emphasize gains from market liberalization to the exclusion of other considerations, discounting potential costs; and no encouragement is given to advocates of enhanced adjustment assistance, environmental and cultural protections, or limitations on capital mobility.[18]

Cohen's prediction has come true in Latin America, where rising public anger has been directed at concessions to foreign investors.[19] New trading arrangements between the United States and Latin American countries have failed to make a dent in corruption and mounting poverty. The popularity of democratization is consequently fading. Elected governments are falling as they prove unable to deliver economic progress. Economies are growing, of course, but the benefits of growth are mainly being enjoyed by employees of multinational companies. The gap between rich and poor households is wider than ever.[20] Yet the United States continues to act the role of Big Brother, determining which economies are worthy of support for rollover loans from the IMF and which are not. One word from Bush's first secretary of the treasury, Paul H. O'Neill, was sufficient to set off either a major decline or a major advance of Latin American currencies, as happened with the Brazilian *real* in the summer of 2002. O'Neill offended Latin American countries with statements about their creditworthiness and hints of corruption in government, triggering a dramatic falloff of the *real*. Then he backtracked and the *real* recovered. Of Brazil, whose international debt at the time totaled around $250 billion, he said: "I continue to favor support for Brazil and other nations [he added Uruguay] that take appropriate steps to build sound, sustainable and growing economies."[21] Within days the administration approved $1.5 billion in bridge loans to Uruguay, with World Bank and IMF assistance already en route. But for Argentina, in default with an external debt of $141 billion, no help was forthcoming until it started playing by the rules of the "Washington consensus." The extraordinary thing is that the Argentine government chose not to, with fairly remarkable results.[22]

Understandably, most Latin American leaders are highly skeptical that Bush's "free market" solutions in trade will do anything to alleviate poverty. For while the administration presses for the reduction of trade barriers, it mainly caters to domestic interests that favor protectionism. This approach, no different from that of previous administrations, has devastating consequences in the poorest countries, which typically rely on a few agricultural and textile products to earn foreign exchange, and in the so-called emerging market countries. For example, the US government, like its European and Japanese partners, provides billions of dollars in subsidies to agribusiness and textile manufacturers, thereby pricing Third World exporters out of the market. Even governments that support the war on terrorism, such as Uganda and Pakistan, have failed in their appeals to Washington to reduce if not end the subsidies, which in the end hurt farmers most of all. It took a WTO ruling to force the Bush administration to change course, though the extent of compliance remains to be seen.

Nor will ending tariffs bring relief to developing countries and peoples. A major study by the Carnegie Endowment of the impact of the

North American Free Trade Agreement (NAFTA) concluded that the biggest losers from the removal of tariff barriers were rural Mexicans, whose jobs, income, and environment were badly affected. In fact, employment in all sectors of Mexico's economy—agriculture, manufacturing, and services—was worse off after than before NAFTA. Agriculture suffered a net decline in employment between 1993 and 2002.[23] US dumping of cheap corn is one well-documented reason. Perhaps not coincidentally, on the very day the Carnegie report appeared, so did a report from Mexico City that its ambassador to the UN had been dismissed for saying in a speech what numerous Mexicans believe: that Mexico's relationship with the United States is one of "convenience and subordination" in which Mexico is seen as "a backyard."[24]

"Free trade" is never free. Some groups benefit and others lose— and these always seem to be the same ones. The Central American Free Trade Agreement (CAFTA), which the administration pushed through Congress in 2005, falls into the same category as NAFTA. While CAFTA will reduce sugar and other tariffs on Central American products, the agreement will benefit large landowners, banks, and multinational corporations long before small farmers, labor unions, or the environment. Or consider the Bush administration's decision in 2001 to slap special duties on steel imports in 2001, in violation of free-trade principles. The move pleased the US steel industry, but angered the Brazilians and other Third World steel producers, as well as US industries that depend on imported steel. However, in 2003 the WTO ruled against the administration's duties in an action initiated by the EU, forcing Bush to lift the tariff about twenty-one months after imposing it.

To this essentially neoliberal approach to Third World economic development, the Bush administration has appended the traditional conservative stance on foreign aid: If Third World countries cut corruption and choose better projects, and if bailouts of inefficient economies are limited, foreign aid can be kept to a minimum. Not too different from Clinton's approach, though just as stingy. In absolute terms, the United States ranked first in 2002 in providing official development assistance (ODA). But at about $13 billion a year, US ODA was at its lowest level as a percentage of GNP since World War II, and 700 percent below the longstanding UN aid target for all countries of 0.7 percent of GNP.[25] In 2004 US ODA ranked last among the top twenty aid-giving countries.[26]

Bush resisted calls from the EU (Britain's Tony Blair in particular[27]) that the developed economies either double foreign aid to the poorest countries or end agricultural subsidies while also providing debt relief.[28] Blair was able to persuade Bush to help eliminate the approximately $1 billion in debt owed to the World Bank by the poorest eighteen countries. But that promise is offset by the continuation of subsidies to domestic industries, which run into the hundreds of billions of dollars for industrialized countries, and by minimum ODA commitments. Even though Bush announced creation of a "Millennium Challenge Account" in 2002, which he touted as a major new commitment to alleviate global poverty, less than a half-billion dollars had been allocated to only two countries as of mid-2005. The Republican-dominated Congress decided to cut the program nearly in half for 2005.[29]

Bush's approach to global poverty may further be gauged by his dark view of family planning, which clearly caters to the Christian right's anti-abortion stance. In 2002 and again in 2003 his administration reversed previous US policy. It decided to withhold a previously approved $34 million in aid to the UN Population Fund (UNPF), which operates in over 140 countries. The administration cited a 1985 law (Kemp-Kasten) that bars funds to any international organization that the president determines "supports or participates in the management" of forced abortion or sterilization. China's family planning programs, which receive UNPF funds, were a key issue. The State Department dispatched a fact-finding team to China that found no evidence of direct UN involvement in coercive abortion or forced sterilization. Yet it recommended that the administration release the $34 million to the United Nations, but continue to withhold funds for China itself for any of its population programs.[30]

In 2004 Bush took the added step, also urged by the Christian right, of warning international organizations such as the UN Children's Fund (UNICEF) and the World Health Organization (WHO), and international NGOs that deal with population and family planning, that they might also be in danger of losing US funds. It was a case of guilt by association. What is particularly unfortunate about such a stance is that it is based on entirely wrongheaded logic. UNPF, like most other such organizations, advocates responsible family planning, not abortion, in China and everywhere else. Although China has a general one-child-per-family policy and makes widespread use of abortion, UNPF's work there is to promote female education and prenatal care, and thus to save lives. In fact, the State Department's fact-finding trip had concluded as much when it urged restoration of the funds—until Powell inexplicably reversed course.[31]

On the other hand, the Bush administration made commendable commitments to meeting two global emergencies: one of $15 billion to combat the AIDS epidemic, the other of several hundred million dollars to victims of the Asian tsunami that struck in December 2004. But both commitments turned out to be less than they seemed. The AIDS money could not be used to purchase generic drugs, on the ground that their effectiveness had yet to be proven. Eventually, the administration allowed manufacturers of generic drugs to apply to the federal Food and Drug Administration for approval. Research on these drugs determined that they worked just as well as brand-name anti-AIDS drugs, and were therefore a boon to infected people in poor countries.[32]

When the tsunami struck, the international community was called upon to undertake the single largest relief effort in history. The Bush administration, which is spending upwards of $5 billion a month for the wars in Iraq and Afghanistan, had a chance to show the world a United States prepared to conduct a war on poverty and underdevelopment, a Marshall Plan for Asia that would go beyond emergency assistance to address the 2 billion people who are living on less than $2 a day.[33] The Bush administration's initial offer of help was embarrassingly modest—$350 million, a good deal less than Japan's $500 million. To its credit the amount was later doubled, and the role of US soldiers in providing relief was exemplary. But the opportunity to offer a counterpoint to the war on terror was not taken.

Environmental Protection

The United States in 2005 is at best a country of middling attainment when it comes to protecting its air and water quality and promoting international cooperation on environmental sustainability. A recent international study that ranks countries based on their success in promoting sustainability places the United States forty-fifth of 146 countries ranked.[34] Far from being influenced by such studies, the Bush administration has gained a reputation for disputing scientific findings, even from its own ranks, and substituting political for scientific judgment. Leading US scientists have accused the administration of stacking science advisory committees with political and industry appointees, censoring scientific reports, restricting research in the name of national security, and dragging its feet in the face of urgent environmental problems.[35]

Bush's rejection of the Kyoto Protocol on global warming, by any measure a very modest step toward combating climate change,[36] secured its reputation and became the hallmark of its approach to global issues. In striking contrast with Clinton's acceptance of the need for action,[37] Bush dismissed a report written by his own Environmental Protection Agency (and other agencies) as work "put out by the bureaucracy." He ignored the views of both the EPA director and treasury secretary, instead following Cheney's lead in arguing that Kyoto's exemption of China and India from mandatory reductions of greenhouse gases, and the potential harm to the US economy of emissions standards, should guide US policy.

All evidence is that Bush caved in to the political right wing and big business, which would have pilloried him for adopting the "radical" view of the EPA report that the United States would be significantly affected by global warming.[38] Yet that "radical" view had strong support within Bush's own ranks, so strong that one leading scientist (James E. Hansen, director of the NASA Goddard Institute for Space Studies) risked his job by speaking out publicly on the administration's refusal to acknowledge the evidence of global warming.[39] In the end the United States, which accounts for about one-quarter of the world's carbon dioxide emissions, was left out in the cold when Russia's parliament—probably in return for the EU's support of its bid to join the WTO—ratified the Kyoto Protocol in 2004. It took effect in February 2005.

The flip side of abandoning Kyoto is ignoring energy efficiency and renewable energy sources. It had to be embarrassing to be a US representative at an international conference on the subject that took place in Bonn in June 2004. For at that conference the Chinese delegation, no doubt responding to a sharp increase in oil prices, pledged that China would follow the Europeans' lead and make major new investments in renewable energy. The US delegation made no such commitment, determined once again to go its own way.[40] The aim under Bush has consistently been to increase energy production, not efficiency or conservation.

Another revealing instance of global anti-environmentalism under Bush occurred when it took up the Convention on Persistent Organic Pollutants, a May 2001 treaty commonly known as the Stockholm Convention. The administration supported banning nine highly toxic chemicals and regulating three others; but it imposed obstacles to dealing swiftly with additional dangerous chemicals, thus robbing the treaty of a crucial capability.[41]

International Law and Organizations

No arena of international affairs has suffered more from the Bush Doctrine on unilateralism than international law and international regulatory regimes. The United States has always proclaimed its support of the rule of law and criticized enemy states that flouted it. But in keeping with its tilt toward private interests and its antipathy toward international agreements that might constrain its actions, the Bush administration did not seek to persuade the Senate to ratify the 1972 UN Convention on the Law of the Sea, the 1992 Biological Diversity Convention, or the 1996 Comprehensive Test Ban Treaty. The administration decided not to endorse a protocol to the 1972 Biological and Toxin Weapons Convention that would have provided for on-site verification of compliance. It also weakened other agreements, including the Framework Convention on Tobacco Control, a draft agreement to limit trafficking in small arms, and the Chemical Weapons Convention.[42] Thus, the only international agreements that Bush has supported are trade agreements, whose chief beneficiaries are multinational corporations.

Surely the most egregious example of Bush's indifference to international law is the war on Iraq. The doctrine of preemptive attack went well beyond a reasoned interpretation of international law and the "inherent right" of self-defense under article 51 of the UN Charter. The United States defied the UN Secretary-General's warning about violating the UN Charter;[43] it set itself up as the ultimate arbiter of international security, the leader of a bloc of states alternative to the UN itself.[44] As Annan said to the General Assembly, US policy "represents a fundamental challenge to the principles on which, however imperfectly, world peace and stability have rested for the last 58 years." More specifically, the policy threatened the UN system of collective security:

> Article 51 of the [UN] Charter prescribes that all states, if attacked, retain the inherent right of self-defense. But until now, it has been understood that when states go beyond that and decide to use force to deal with broader threats to international peace and security, they need the unique legitimacy provided by the United Nations. Now some say this understanding is no longer tenable, since an armed attack with weapons of mass destruction could be launched at any time without warning or by a clandestine group. Rather than wait for that to happen, they argue, states have the right and obligation to use force preemptively. . . . The Council needs to consider how it will deal with the possibility that individual states may use force preemptively against perceived threats.[45]

Preemption is a two-edged sword: It is a transparent argument for toppling undesirable governments, an act clearly contrary to international law; and it is permissive, inviting other states to do the same on the claim of self-defense. The Russian, Israeli, Chinese, and some Central Asian governments have used preemption in just that manner, as previously noted; Iran, North Korea, India, and Pakistan could do the same. Besides setting "an example that can have catastrophic consequences," as Jimmy Carter warned,[46] preventive war "would shift us away from the UN system and towards an anarchical world dominated by raw power, shifting alliances, and desperate attempts by vulnerable states to acquire the capacity to deter."[47]

It seems that only when presumably vital US interests are not at stake, such as in Liberia's civil war in 2003, will the administration—and even then, only after much dithering about how to respond—accept the need to act within the UN framework.[48] US troop contributions to international peacekeeping operations have been very small, and (as in previous administrations) have been almost exclusively to non-UN missions. In 2002, for example, the United States had 9,166 troops, 33 military observers, and 670 civilians in peacekeeping roles around the world. But with the exception of a single soldier in Eritrea, all US troops were part of non-UN (mostly NATO) missions.[49] By 2005 the United States was involved in six UN peacekeeping missions, but only ten US soldiers were serving in them. All the remaining 350 US personnel were either civilian police or military observers.[50] Neither genocide nor ethnic cleansing has affected US opposition to having its soldiers serve under the UN flag and a non-US commander.

Bush thus provides ammunition for longtime critics of US foreign policy who argue that the United States has a double standard when it comes to respect for international law and institutions. The criticism clearly applies to the US attitude toward the UN itself, for while on one hand the Bush administration has defied the UN and undermined its capacity to act as a peacemaker, on the other hand it has opposed legislation by Republican senators that would once again (as in the 1990s) withhold US dues to the UN. Bush has also favored adding two permanent members, including Japan, to the UN Security Council.[51] The likely explanation for this seeming contradiction in policy is the simplest one: pure self-interest. Bush recognizes that the United States sometimes needs the UN and will work with it when it supports US interests. At other times he will ignore it and even flout its founding principles.

The highly publicized US withdrawal from the International Criminal Court (ICC) ranks just below the war on Iraq as an indication of US disregard for international law. The 1998 Rome Treaty to establish the court "represents a great victory for the ethos of accountability," Richard Falk has written, "making those who abuse governmental power face the possibility of being held criminally accountable for their misdeeds as measured by accepted *international* standards relating to human rights, crimes against humanity, and international humanitarian law."[52] President Clinton signed the treaty on the last day of 2000, but he did not submit it to the Republican-dominated US Senate for ratification. Clinton contended that the treaty contained serious "flaws"; but he also advised that by signing it the United States would be better positioned to rectify those flaws.[53] Nevertheless, the court officially came into existence in 2002 when the sixtieth country's legislature ratified it.[54]

The Bush administration officially rejected the Rome Treaty two months before it came into effect, thus setting the awful precedent of a president unsigning a treaty that had previously been signed. With John R. Bolton, a vocal neocon and UN critic in the State Department (and Bush's choice in 2005 to be US representative at the UN), taking the lead, the administration challenged the ICC's ability to maintain independence from political pressures such as might result in prosecutions of US officials or soldiers.[55] This position was a rather transparent effort to protect US unilateral actions abroad, such as involvement in mass killings or war crimes of the kind that have been exposed in Iraq and Afghanistan.

Although it is highly unlikely that politically motivated charges against a US soldier or official would get to trial by the ICC, since there are several built-in protections of national jurisdiction and individual rights, nontreaty states may in some circumstances be subject to the ICC.[56] Bush therefore demanded a waiver that would exempt US troops from prosecution under the treaty. Europeans offered blistering criticism of the United States for undermining a major advance in the adjudication of war crimes and genocide, and for making peacekeeping missions all the more difficult to arrange. But Bush persisted, blocking arms aid to states that ratified the ICC and cutting assistance to over fifty countries that did not provide the waiver. (The one hundred or so countries that reluctantly agreed to the waiver, mostly poor countries in Latin America and Africa, were rewarded with trade privileges or aid.[57]) The administration also supported congressional legislation that would allow the president to use force to rescue US soldiers imprisoned by the court. The strong-arm tactics worked for awhile: The UN Security Council granted a one-year exemption of US troops from prosecution in July 2002, and the EU later did the same. But in June 2004, after Kofi Annan sharply criticized the US request of the Security Council for a third year of exemptions, the US delegation withdrew the request.[58]

There are several other instances of US disregard for international law on the basis of unilateralism:

• Administration officials, as mentioned in Chapter 1, sought to get around the requirements of both federal and international law in the treatment of captured soldiers, first in Afghanistan and the US naval base at Guantánamo Bay, Cuba, and then in Iraq. Instead of considering Al-Qaida and Taliban fighters prisoners of war, the administration declared them "enemy combatants" so as to deprive them of the usual treatment accorded enemy soldiers. In July 2002 Bush sought unsuccessfully to derail an optional protocol to the 1989 Convention Against Torture, which provides for greater access to member states' prisons.[59] It took objections from Colin Powell for the administration to agree that these "enemy combatants" should be protected by the Geneva Conventions though, as noted below, that promise was violated by secret detentions of high-value prisoners.[60] Here is another instance of the double standard: Under various international antiterrorism resolutions and treaties, the United States expects other countries to prosecute or extradite possible terrorists, but it is unwilling to expose its own captives to international scrutiny.[61]

When tales of abuse at the US-run Abu Ghraib prison in Iraq came to light, the Justice Department refused requests from senators to release documents that would specify the administration's policies on treatment of prisoners. But journalists were able to show that while Bush tentatively "declined to exercise" his presumed authority to ignore the Geneva Conventions, Rumsfeld in 2003 authorized a secret operation that condoned aggressive methods of interrogation.[62] Military police and military intelligence (and, for a time, the CIA, which later reportedly dropped out of the operation) interpreted the decision as license to employ various forms of torture, including sexual abuse and humiliation, to extract information from POWs. At Guantánamo, US military psychiatrists were found to have participated in various ways in coercive interrogations, another violation of international as well as domestic law.[63] These abuses occurred at a time when the US occupation was daily losing ground to insurgents and was desperate for intelligence. A Rumsfeld-appointed panel headed by former secretary of defense James R. Schlesinger later found that prison abuses had indeed occurred, and that responsibility for them stretched all the way to the "office of the secretary of defense."[64] But Rumsfeld never resigned, some senior officers at Abu Ghraib and Guantánamo were later promoted, and only a few low-ranking soldiers were convicted of any crime.[65]

Prisoner abuses are only one element of a pattern that puts the United States in violation of international law. After 9/11 the CIA maintained a global network of secret detention facilities in addition to the well-known camp at Guantánamo. Neither the locations of the CIA- or foreign-run camps, nor the names and numbers of detainees interrogated or held in them, have ever been provided. The UN's top official charged with monitoring compliance with the torture convention sharply criticized these practices, pointing out in a report to the General Assembly that the Convention on Torture contains absolute prohibitions on degrading treatment of prisoners, and that secret detentions should be considered a war crime.[66] The International Committee of the Red Cross similarly concluded after a month-long inspection of the Guantánamo base that the treatment of prisoners was "tantamount to torture."[67] The UN's acting High Commissioner for Human Rights, Bertrand Ramcharan, agreed, saying that US treatment of POWs constituted a "grave breach" of international law that "might be designated as war crimes by a competent tribunal."[68] No doubt he had in mind the ICC, which Bush had rejected precisely to evade war crimes charges. But he might also have mentioned the US War Crimes Act of 1996, under which "grave" violations of the Geneva Conventions by soldiers or civilians are prosecutable offenses.[69]

In addition to prisoner mistreatment and secret detentions, there is "rendition," the CIA's practice of transferring suspected terrorists to third countries for interrogation. The practice enables US authorities to avoid responsibility for how those suspects are subsequently treated. The program is unacknowledged and apparently lacks oversight; administration officials insist they have assurances torture is not being practiced. Yet all the countries to which suspects—between 100 and 150 cases have been documented—have been sent, including Uzbekistan, Syria, and Egypt, have been cited by the State Department for using torture to extract information. (Prisoners now under Iraqi authority run the same risks, according to the State Department, which cites "arbitrary deprivation of life, torture, impunity, poor prison conditions . . . and arbitrary arrest and detention."[70]) Renditioned former prisoners have attested to having been tortured, abused, and detained for lengthy periods without being charged.[71] Just as the *New York Times* put it in an editorial, the US practice amounts to "outsourcing torture."[72] It also violates the Convention Against Torture.

• The Bush administration continued the Clinton policy of opposing the international convention that bans landmines, which entered into force in 1999. Clinton bowed to the military in insisting on exceptions to the ban, notably landmines in South Korea. But he did commit to ceasing use of all kinds of antipersonnel mines and signing the treaty in 2006 if alternatives could be found. Bush, in company with Russia, China, Iran, North Korea, and eight other states, rejected Clinton's commitment.[73]

- In October 2002 the administration revealed that it was preparing war crimes dossiers on Iraqi leaders, civil servants, and soldiers, to be used in a tribunal that would go into business after the ouster of Saddam Hussein's regime. Originally, the plan was reportedly to convene the tribunal under US auspices; but a year later the US-appointed Iraqi Governing Council announced that it would create its own tribunal—a decision reached just prior to the capture of Saddam Hussein on December 13, 2003. In neither case was reference made to using the ICC or following the precedent of the Rwanda and Bosnia international tribunals that were convened under UN auspices. The effect of the decision to have Iraqis try Iraqis was to continue the privatization of the war and weaken international law on war crimes and crimes against humanity.[74]

- Showing that the Rwanda genocide in 1994 has had little impact on US policy, the Bush administration initially reacted with indifference to widespread killings in Sudan's civil war in 2004. The Arab-dominated government in Sudan allowed, and may have encouraged, militia known as the Janjaweed in the south of the country (the Darfur region) to go on a rampage. About a million non-Arab people were forced to flee their homes; villages were completely destroyed; around 200,000 people were killed, and many others were brutalized, raped, and abducted; and starvation became widespread. Rather than impose severe sanctions on the Khartoum government and move the issue before the ICC, the Bush administration, along with the EU, China, and other countries, debated whether or not the conditions in Darfur amounted to genocide, and therefore required sanctions within the meaning of the 1948 Genocide Convention. Though Congress passed a resolution that called the situation in Darfur genocide, Bush at first would only acknowledge that ethnic cleansing was taking place.[75] Not until September 2004, after Colin Powell returned from a visit to the region, was the "g" word finally uttered and the idea launched that the UN needed to do more than threaten action.[76]

Bush rarely spoke in public about the Darfur tragedy, or used the word "genocide" to describe it. The fact that Sudan's leaders were considered partners in the war on terror—the CIA maintained an active relationship with Sudan's intelligence director, for example—evidently was the administration's justification for associating with a government that was abetting mass murder.[77] The best the United States could do was to abstain when the UN Security Council voted in June 2005 to refer the matter to the ICC and launch an investigation of war crimes— a perfect example of exceptionalist ideology overriding human decency.

• In response to a ruling by the International Court of Justice (ICJ) in the case of fifty-one Mexicans held without hearings on death rows in Texas, Bush ordered compliance (which meant new hearings) but also withdrew the United States from an optional protocol that allows ICJ jurisdiction in such cases. The latter decision was reminiscent of Reagan's rejection of the ICJ's ruling against the United States over the CIA's mining of Nicaraguan harbors, after which he likewise withdrew the United States from ICJ jurisdiction.[78]

Weapons Proliferation

At the precise moment when as many as forty countries are believed capable of developing nuclear weapons, the Bush administration upgraded the weapons' importance. Right from the start, and very much in line with the PNAC's longstanding position,[79] Bush scrapped the Anti-Ballistic Missile (ABM) Treaty of 1972, which limited nuclear defenses, and refused to resubmit the Comprehensive Test Ban Treaty (CTBT) to the Senate for approval.[80] Instead, Bush opted for missile defense and (see below) new guidelines on strategic employment of nuclear weapons—curious choices in light of the way terrorists attacked on September 11, 2001, not to mention the huge number of US nuclear weapons (over 7,000 strategic weapons in 2002) and the unmatched ability to deliver them on target.[81] Rather than advance the process of actual strategic arms reductions begun by his father, George W. Bush significantly retarded it—and thus contributed to the global problem of nuclear weapons proliferation—by accenting the perceived advantages of possessing such weapons and resisting the strengthening of international controls on them. He thus joined a long list of US presidents who failed to meet the promise contained in article VI of the NPT to work toward the elimination of nuclear arsenals.

First, as pointed out in Chapter 2, the Bush administration's Nuclear Posture Review seemed to expand the possible uses of nuclear weapons, making them an active component of war fighting. It is not out of the question that under Bush the United States might use nuclear weapons first in an ongoing or impending conflict. Second, Bush is eroding nonproliferation norms in his policies on international arms-control agreements. An example is a previously mentioned agreement with India in 2005 to sell it technology for civilian nuclear reactors. If the sale goes through, India promises to allow international inspections and stop further nuclear testing. But it will not be obligated to sign the NPT and assume its obligations. To the contrary, the effect of the agreement will be to recognize India as a nuclear weapon state, thus giving an incentive for other states that possess or may possess nuclear weapons (starting with Pakistan) to seek the same privileged status.[82] Not only is Bush's agreement therefore a further devaluing of controls on WMD, it contradicts the US position in its nuclear dispute with North Korea and its disagreements with Russia and China over their nuclear sales.

The Moscow Treaty (officially, the Strategic Offensive Reductions Treaty, or SORT) signed by Bush and Putin in May 2002 undermines nuclear arms control in a different way.[83] The treaty commits the United States and Russia to reduce strategic warheads to between 1,700 and 2,200. But the treaty is deceptive; it will actually enable both countries to restore strategic nuclear weapons levels to those of several years earlier. Since the treaty calls for the warhead reductions to take place by 2012 but without a particular schedule, and permits withdrawal with three months' notice, actual reductions can be postponed until the last moment. Thus, the Nuclear Posture Review, while acknowledging a cap of 2,200 strategic weapons by 2012, said that the US arsenal would actually have "3,800 operationally deployed strategic nuclear warheads by 2007."[84]

Washington got its way, moreover, by insisting that "reduction" of warheads should not necessarily mean their destruction. The treaty is really a warehousing agreement: It allows deployed nuclear weapons to be put in storage, which the Bush administration has indicated is exactly what will be done with most of the "offloaded" warheads.[85] Thus the treaty does not actually require the destruction of a single strategic warhead. Nor is it verifiable. In short, from a global security point of view, the Moscow Treaty revives a tradition of sacrificing real nuclear weapons reductions and movement toward nuclear disarmament for national advantage.

Likewise, Bush's policies on the security and production of nuclear weapons materials have been incredibly shortsighted. His decision in the spring of 2002 to cut funding for the 1991 Nunn-Lugar initiative, which provides for storage or destruction of the former Soviet Union's nuclear weapons, was overturned by cooperative Senate action. Actually, extending cooperative threat-reduction programs such as Nunn-Lugar to include other states would be one way to send a different message—namely, that the security of nuclear weapons, and their ultimate destruction, is a sound investment, all the more so at a time when many experts are convinced that the most likely use of a nuclear weapon is by a terrorist group.[86]

Then, in an extraordinary reversal of previous US policy, Bush in mid-2004 refused to support conclusion of a Fissile Materials Treaty, which bans production of weapons-grade HEU and plutonium and provides for international inspection and verification. The treaty, ten years in the making, was negotiated under the auspices of the UN Conference on Disarmament. Evidently—and Bush's budgeting certainly goes along with this view,[87] as does a decision in 2005 to restart plutonium 238 production at the Idaho National Laboratory[88]—preserving the secrecy of US nuclear weapons facilities and having plenty of plutonium on hand are more urgent than bringing nuclear weapons materials under international control. Yet the latter objective would create obstacles both to the acquisition of weapons-grade materials by terrorist groups and their use by countries seeking to become nuclear weapon states.[89]

The message on nuclear weapons that the Bush administration is sending to the world is that such weapons have utility. Its support of ballistic missile defense, its seeming indifference to growing Japanese interest in nuclear weapons,[90] and its hesitancy to provide security assurances to North Korea against nuclear attack all add value to nuclear weapons and undermine prospects for a nuclear weapon–free world. So does the administration's ongoing investment in refining nuclear weapons in "virtual" (laboratory) testing and in research and development of more destructive or precise nuclear weapons.[91] An example of the latter is so-called mini-nukes or bunker busters, supposedly low-yield weapons suitable for burrowing into an enemy leadership's underground headquarters. Research and development of these weapons were approved by the US Congress in May 2003.[92]

With respect to conventional weapons, the United States, as previously noted, is by far the world leader in military spending and arms sales. As of 2005, the United States accounts for 47 percent of the roughly $1 trillion in official military spending worldwide. The Bush administration's post-9/11 arms sales and transfers to authoritarian regimes in addition to other allies ensure many years of strong customer growth. Despite all the hoopla over terrorist groups, the administration actually helps make the acquisition of arms easier for them, such as by prodding Congress to approve waiving licensing rules for military sales to Britain and Australia.[93] Bush also failed to lead efforts in Congress to extend a ban on assault weapons.

Slowly but surely, Bush, with a strong push from the US Air Force, is readying the world for a breakout into space-based weapons programs. Several such programs are already on the drawing board, and one experimental satellite is already in orbit. Although space-based weapons were banned under the ABM Treaty, abandonment of the treaty gave the green light for making space a battle station. USAF leaders are on record as arguing that space predominance is the US "destiny," and that it should be accomplished not only with defensive space-based weapons but also with weapons that can attack (in the words of the head of the US Strategic Command, General James E. Cartwright) "very quickly, with very short time lines on the planning and delivery, any place on the face of the earth."[94] Only the expense, and not the protests and probable start of a new arms race in space by Russia and China, seems to be holding up full funding of the new programs.

Conclusion

Sharing the costs, risks, and sacrifices that are necessary to combat problems of global dimensions have found the Bush administration consistently wanting. American exceptionalism has made the United States exemptionalist—too often prepared to exempt itself, that is, from the requirements of international law, standards for protecting the environment and human rights, well-established needs for improving the lives of impoverished peoples, and the logic of arms reductions. Instead of being a leader in establishing and strengthening rules and institutions that promote international peace, social justice, and environmental sustainability, the Bush Doctrine places the United States in opposition to them and hypocritically professes its adherence. Apparently, the tangible benefits of international cooperation—to the US ability to manage climate change, cope with outbreaks of new diseases, budget for nonmilitary needs, prevent terrorist attacks, protect imprisoned US military and civilian personnel, and enhance the US reputation abroad, for example—are less valuable than sustaining a stubborn nationalism.

Notes

1. For a succinct critique, see Julie Mertus, "The New US Human Rights Policy: A Radical Departure," pp. 371–384.
2. US aid to Russia is an example: see Gail W. Lapidus, "Transforming Russia: American Policy in the 1990s," in Lieber, ed., *Eagle Rules?* pp. 110–117.
3. See Serge Schmemann, "Antiterror Actions Can Be Too Harsh," *NYT*, January 12, 2002, p. A7, which includes reporting by Human Rights Watch on human rights abuses in the name of antiterrorism.
4. Julia Preston, "Departing Rights Commissioner Faults US," *NYT*, September 12, 2002, online ed. Robinson's specific objections were to the US government's racial profiling of persons of Middle East descent, civil liberties violations, and treatment of captured Taliban soldiers as "enemy combatants" rather than prisoners of war.

5. Elisabeth Rosenthal, "China, Russia and 4 Neighbors Seek Common Front on Terror," *NYT,* January 8, 2002, p. A12; Philip P. Pan, "In China's West, Ethnic Strife Becomes 'Terrorism,'" *Washington Post,* July 15, 2002, p. A12.

6. Agence France-Presse, "China Issues First Ever List of 'Terrorist' Groups, Seeks International Help," December 15, 2003; in NAPSNet online.

7. The small Uighur Muslim resistance group in Xinjiang province was placed on the US terrorist list just as a senior State Department official was visiting China to obtain assurances concerning a new export-control law on missile components that had been announced. See Erik Eckholm, "American Gives Beijing Good News: Rebels on Terror List," *NYT,* August 27, 2002, online ed.

8. Dmitri V. Trenin, "The Forgotten War: Chechnya and Russia's Future," pp. 1–7.

9. On Russian oil, see Edward L. Morse and James Richard, "The Battle for Energy Dominance," pp. 16–31.

10. The Russian minister of defense has said: "The international community has just crushed the nest of international terrorism in Afghanistan. We must not forget about Georgia nearby, where a similar nest has recently begun to emerge." The resulting crisis in Russia-Georgia relations is discussed by Steven Lee Myers, "Georgia Hearing Heavy Footsteps from Russia's War in Chechnya," *NYT,* August 15, 2002, p. A1. On September 11, 2002, President Putin warned Georgia, in language that closely followed George W. Bush's argument for invading Iraq, that unless Georgia dealt effectively with Chechnyan terrorists, Russian troops would do the job. In 2005, however, Russia agreed to withdraw from its two bases in Georgia by the end of the year.

11. *NYT,* March 1, 2003, p. A10. After the 2004 school seizure, Putin accused the United States of being two-faced about terrorism by meeting with Chechen groups. The State Department defended holding these meetings, and rightly so. What is indefensible is its failure consistently to condemn the widespread human rights violations in Chechnya.

12. This story and the following quotation are from Thomas Friedman, "Bush's Shame," *NYT,* August 4, 2002, online ed. The activist quoted is Radhika Coomaraswamy, director of the International Center for Ethnic Studies. Subsequently, the Bush administration did respond to the jailing by threatening to stop additional military aid to Egypt. The Egyptian intellectual was released late in 2002.

13. See Somini Sengupta, "Goals Set by U.N. Conference on Children Skirt Abortion," *NYT,* May 11, 2002, p. A8.

14. See the Amnesty International web site: www.amnestyusa.org/abolish.

15. The case is *Sosa v. Alvarez-Machain.* See Paul Hoffman, "Courting Justice," pp. 1 and 18.

16. *National Security Strategy of the United States,* p. 3.

17. From a speech at the Summit of the Americas, quoted in *NYT,* January 14, 2004, p. A9.

18. Cohen, "Confronting Backlash: Foreign Economic Policy in an Age of Globalization," in Lieber, ed., *Eagle Rules?* p. 322.

19. See, for example, Juan Forero, "Still Poor, Latin Americans Protest Push for Open Markets," *NYT,* July 19, 2002, online ed.

20. Juan Forero, "Latin America Graft and Poverty Trying Patience with Democracy," *NYT,* June 24, 2004, online ed. Since 2000, six presidents have

been thrown out of office, and a UN survey in April 2004 of 19,000 people in eighteen Latin American countries found that most people preferred a dictator who could bring economic benefits to their country.

21. Richard W. Stevenson, "US Says It Backs Bailouts for Brazil and Uruguay Only," *NYT*, August 2, 2002, online ed.

22. Rather than settle its debt to banks and the IMF through a structural adjustment program, which would have required considerable belt tightening and debt repayment, Argentina's economy has grown mainly by way of domestic demand and investment, and increased tax revenues. The results include reduced poverty and unemployment, and rising foreign investment. Larry Rohter, "Economic Rally for Argentines Defies Forecasts," *NYT*, December 26, 2004, p. 1.

23. Celia W. Dugger, "Report Finds Few Benefits for Mexico in Nafta," *NYT*, November 19, 2003, p. A9.

24. *NYT*, November 19, 2003, p. A5.

25. UN Development Program, *Human Development Report 2004*, table, online at http://hdr.undp.org/statistics/data/cty/cty_f_USA.html. See also Joseph Kahn, "US Rejects Bid to Double Foreign Aid to Poor Lands," *NYT*, January 29, 2002, p. A11.

26. UN Development Program, *Human Development Report 2004*, table, online at http://hdr.undp.org/statistics/data/indic/indic_152_1_1.html.

27. Blair's government has also called for canceling Africa's debt and creating a Marshall Plan for Africa. See Celia W. Dugger, "Discerning a New Course for World's Donor Nations," *NYT*, April 18, 2005, p. A10.

28. Celia W. Dugger, "Trade and Aid to Poorest Seen as Crucial on Agenda for Richest Nations," *NYT*, June 19, 2005, p. 8.

29. Celia W. Dugger, "Bush Aid Initiative for Poor Nations Faces Sharp Budget Cuts and Criticism of Slow Pace," *NYT*, June 17, 2005, p. A8. The Millennium Challenge Account was supposed to provide a total of $10 billion over three years. The actual budget, most of which has yet to be allocated, is likely to come to less than $4.5 billion.

30. Todd S. Purdum, "US Blocks Money for Family Clinics Promoted by U.N.," *NYT*, July 23, 2002, online ed.

31. Christopher Marquis, "US Is Accused of Trying to Isolate U.N. Population Unit," *NYT*, June 21, 2004, p. A3.

32. Donald G. McNeil Jr., "Study Finds Generic AIDS Drug Effective," *NYT*, July 2, 2004, p. A5.

33. On the scope of the human security crisis in East and South Asia, see my *Pacific Asia? Prospects for Security and Cooperation in East Asia*, pp. 13–14, 35–37. The estimate of poverty comes from the Asian Development Bank's report, *Asian Development Outlook 2000*, cited in those pages.

34. The study was done by researchers at Yale and Columbia Universities in cooperation with the World Economic Forum and the Joint Research Centre of the European Commission. See Daniel C. Esty et al., *2005 Environmental Sustainability Index: Benchmarking National Environmental Stewardship*.

35. See, for example, Diana Jean Schemo, "Scientists Discuss Balance of Research and Security," *NYT*, January 10, 2003, p. A12; James Glanz, "Scientists Say Administration Distorts Facts," *NYT*, February 19, 2004, online ed.; Kennedy, *Crimes Against Nature*, pp. 76–95.

36. The treaty, ratified by over 120 countries, requires thirty-six industrialized countries to cut greenhouse gas emissions such as carbon dioxide and methane to an average of 5 percent below 1990 levels by 2012. Countries may earn credits toward their treaty targets by investing abroad in cleanups of emissions-producing sites such as garbage dumps. Still, the treaty will make only a tiny dent in the global warming problem given the pace of greenhouse gas buildup in the atmosphere.

37. "With 4 percent of the world's population," said Clinton, "we enjoy 20 percent of the wealth, which helps explain why we also produce 20 percent of the world's greenhouse gases. We must be prepared to commit to realistic and binding goals on our emissions of greenhouse gases." Andrew Morse and Michael Warren, "Clinton: We're Energy Hogs," www.ABCNews.com, September 5, 1997.

38. Katharine Q. Seelye, "President Distances Himself from Global Warming Report," *NYT,* June 5, 2002, p. A19; Kennedy, *Crimes Against Nature,* pp. 50–51. The "caving in" included removing Dr. Robert Watson, head of the UN Intergovernmental Panel on Climate Change, who had consistently argued that human agency was the main culprit. (Kennedy, *Crimes Against Nature*, p. 88.) As the 2004 US general election approached, a seeming change in the administration's position occurred. Contrary to everything the administration had claimed before, an official report to the Congress from one of its top scientists, signed by the secretaries of commerce and energy, stated that climate change was mainly caused by smokestack and auto emissions of carbon dioxide. (Andrew C. Revkin, "US Report, in Shift, Turns Focus to Greenhouse Gases," *NYT,* August 26, 2004, p. A16.) However, the view of scientists this time around is no more likely than previous reports to change the president's understanding.

39. *NYT,* October 26, 2004, p. A12.

40. Mark Landler, "China Pledges to Use More Alternatives to Oil and Coal," *NYT,* June 5, 2004, p. B1.

41. Associated Press, "Senator Criticizes White House Over Limits on Pollutants Treaty," *NYT,* April 12, 2002, p. A2.

42. See P. J. Simmons, "Global Challenges: Beating the Odds," and Institute for Energy and Environmental Research and Lawyers' Committee on Nuclear Policy, "Rule of Power or Rule of Law? An Assessment of US Policies and Actions Regarding Security-Related Treaties."

43. See his comments in Patrick E. Tyler and Felicity Barringer, "Annan Says US Will Violate Charter If It Acts Without Approval," *NYT,* March 11, 2003, p. A8.

44. See ibid., the comments of White House spokesman Ari Fleischer: "If the United Nations fails to act, that means the United Nations will not be the international body that disarms Saddam Hussein. Another international body will disarm Saddam Hussein."

45. *NYT,* September 24, 2003, p. A11.

46. Speech on receiving the Nobel Peace Prize; text in *NYT,* December 11, 2002, p. A15. Carter specifically referred in the same passage to the "principle of preventive war," not to preemptive attack.

47. Michael Byers, "Jumping the Gun."

48. Largely because of Colin Powell's lobbying, the United States sent a few hundred marines to Liberia in October 2003 as part of a UN-approved

multinational force under the Economic Community of West African States (ECOWAS).

49. See the chart in *NYT,* July 3, 2002, p. A4.

50. Based on UN statistics at www.un.org/Depts/dpko/dpko/contributors/2005/june2005_3.pdf.

51. US dues to the UN amount to about $400 million a year. A bill before the House of Representatives in mid-2005, which House speaker J. Dennis Hastert supports, would withhold half of US dues unless the UN changes certain management and budget practices. See Steven R. Weisman, "White House Tries to Halt GOP Effort to Withhold UN Dues," *NYT,* June 27, 2005, online ed.

52. Falk, *The Declining World Order,* p. 30.

53. "Statement by the President on Signing the International Criminal Court Treaty," Camp David, Maryland, December 31, 2000, online at http://usembassy.state.gov/posts/pk1/wwwh01010302.html.

54. As of early 2004, ninety-four countries had ratified the Rome Treaty, including all the EU countries except Greece. China and Russia have also yet to ratify the treaty.

55. Bolton, undersecretary for arms control and international security, was once a project director at the PCNA and a vice president of the conservative think tank, the American Enterprise Institute. See his remarks in Berlin, September 16, 2002, online at www.state.gov/t/us/rm/13538.htm.

56. For example, although neither the United States nor Iraq is currently a party to the Rome Treaty, cases involving their soldiers may be referred to the court by the UN Security Council if the council determines that they are being "shielded" from prosecution by their government. And if a sovereign Iraq were to decide to join the ICC, US soldiers still in the country might be subject to prosecution. These issues were raised by Professor Pamela S. Falk in a letter to the *NYT,* June 29, 2004, p. A26.

57. See Juan Forero, "Bush's Aid Cuts on Court Issue Roil Neighbors," *NYT,* August 19, 2005, p. A7.

58. Annan said that for the Security Council to grant the request would "discredit the Council and the United Nations that stands for rule of law." *NYT,* June 18, 2004, p. A13.

59. Barbara Crossette, "US Fails in Effort to Block Vote on U.N. Convention on Torture," *NYT,* July 25, 2002, online ed.

60. The US Supreme Court in June 2004 rebuked the government's action, deciding in a case brought by fourteen of 650 Guantánamo detainees that even noncitizens held outside US territory are entitled to legal protection and therefore the right to challenge their confinement.

61. Institute for Energy and Environmental Research and Lawyers' Committee on Nuclear Policy, "Rule of Power or Rule of Law?" p. 14.

62. Besides the sources mentioned in Chapter 1, note 54, see the invaluable report by Seymour M. Hersh, "The Gray Zone."

63. "Interrogators Cite Doctors' Aid at Guantánamo," *NYT,* June 24, 2005, p. 1.

64. Douglas Jehl, "A Trail of 'Major Failures' Leads to Defense Secretary's Office," *NYT,* August 25, 2004, online ed.

65. Rumsfeld's direct responsibility for the abuses at Abu Ghraib has been charged by the prison's former commandant, Army Reserve Brigadier General Janis Karpinski. She was demoted, but makes an impressive case for higher-level

misconduct. (See her interview by Marjorie Cohn, "Abu Ghraib General Lambasts Bush Administration," August 24, 2005, at www.truthout.org/docs-2005/082405Z.shtml.) A follow-up to the Schlesinger report by Vice Admiral Albert T. Church III found seventy cases of substantiated abuse, including six deaths (the latter number subsequently raised to twenty-six), but no one was held accountable. (Eric Schmitt, "Official Declines to Pin Blame for Blunders in Interrogations," *NYT*, March 11, 2005, p. A8; Douglas Jehl and Eric Schmitt, "US Military Says 26 Inmate Deaths May Be Homicide," *NYT*, March 16, 2005, p. A1.) US military investigators considered the deaths criminal homicides, according to the last-mentioned article, and all but one occurred outside the Abu Ghraib prison in Iraq. Eleven other deaths during detention were considered justifiable homicide.

66. John H. Cushman Jr., "U.N. Condemns Harsh Methods in Campaign Against Terror," *NYT*, October 28, 2004, p. A10.

67. *NYT*, November 30, 2004, p. 1.

68. *NYT*, June 5, 2004, p. A5. Later in the same month it was revealed that at the request of the CIA and with approval from Rumsfeld, at least thirteen Iraqi prisoners were being confined in secret, without any record being kept of their whereabouts or the fact of their imprisonment.

69. See Elizabeth Holtzman, "Torture and Accountability."

70. Brian Knowlton, "US Cites Array of Abuses by the Iraqi Government in 2004," *NYT*, March 1, 2005, p. 1.

71. Douglas Jehl and David Johnston, "Rule Change Lets C.I.A. Freely Send Suspects Abroad to Jail," *NYT*, March 6, 2005, online ed.

72. Editorial, "Torture by Proxy," *NYT*, March 8, 2005, p. A22.

73. Institute for Energy and Environmental Research and Lawyers' Committee on Nuclear Policy, "Rule of Power or Rule of Law?" p. 22.

74. Robin Wright, "Iraq War Crimes Dossiers in Works," *Los Angeles Times*, October 6, 2002, online ed.; Susan Sacks, "Iraqi Governing Council Sets Up Its Own Court for War Crimes," *NYT*, December 10, 2003, p. A13.

75. Secretary Powell evidently was very conscious of the Rwanda precedent, when Clinton administration officials refused to apply "genocide" to the slaughter that was taking place. (See Marc Lacey, "White House Reconsiders Its Policy on Crisis in Sudan," *NYT*, June 12, 2004, online ed.) But Powell, who made a special trip to Sudan in June 2004, joined the word-mincing bandwagon when he said: "We see indications and elements that would start to move you to a genocidal conclusion." *NYT*, June 30, 2004, p. A3.

76. Powell made his remarks in testimony before a Senate committee. Steven R. Weisman, "Powell Says Rapes and Killings in Sudan Are Genocide," *NYT*, September 10, 2004, p. A3.

77. For example, the CIA flew Sudan's intelligence chief to Washington for consultations in April 2005, reportedly over objections by the State and Justice Departments. See Scott Shane, "C.I.A. Role in Visit of Sudan Intelligence Chief Causes Dispute Within Administration," *NYT*, June 18, 2005, p. A7.

78. Adam Liptak, "US Says It Has Withdrawn from World Judicial Body," *NYT*, March 10, 2005, p. A12.

79. Timothy L. Savage, "Letting the Genie Out of the Bottle: The Bush Nuclear Doctrine in Asia," in Gurtov and Van Ness, eds., *Confronting the Bush Doctrine*, pp. 64–66.

80. Clinton signed the CTBT in September 1996; but the treaty, needing two-thirds Senate approval for ratification, was rejected in October by a vote of 51–48. Counting heads, Clinton decided to postpone another Senate vote until the next Congress. Bush's argument for consigning the treaty to oblivion is that while the United States will continue to observe the moratorium on nuclear weapon testing, it will annually review the US nuclear stockpile to determine if testing is necessary.

81. According to the Carnegie Endowment for International Peace, in 2002 the United States possessed 7,013 strategic nuclear warheads, 1,620 tactical warheads, and about 5,000 nuclear warheads in storage. CEIP *Policy Brief,* No. 23 (February, 2003), p. 4.

82. Steven R. Weisman, "US to Broaden India's Access to Nuclear Power Technology," *NYT,* July 19, 2005, p. 1.

83. See Savage, "Letting the Genie Out of the Bottle."

84. Nuclear Posture Review Report, January 8, 2002, p. 6.

85. Michael R. Gordon, "Treaty Offers Pentagon New Flexibility for New Set of Nuclear Priorities," *NYT,* May 14, 2002, p. A8. "'What we have now agreed to do under the treaty is what we wanted to do anyway,' a senior administration official said today. 'That's our kind of treaty.'"

86. Lemann, "The War on What?" p. 43.

87. "The [Bush] administration spends one dollar on missile defenses for every quarter spent on programs to safeguard dangerous weapons and materials in the former Soviet Union. Almost five times as much is spent on programs to maintain the US stockpile of nuclear warheads and prepare for a resumption of nuclear tests than on initiatives to control 'loose nukes' and fissile material." Michael Krepon, "Dominators Rule," p. 58.

88. The decision will produce 150 kilograms at a cost of $1.5 billion over thirty years. Pentagon officials denied that the plutonium would have any weapons applications; speculation centered on its use in powering espionage devices, which could include space-based instruments. William J. Broad, "US Has Plans to Again Make Own Plutonium," *NYT,* June 27, 2005, p. 1.

89. International inspections, the State Department stated, "would have been so extensive that it could compromise key signatories' core national security interests and so costly that many countries will be hesitant to accept it." Dafna Linzer, "US Backs Out of Nuclear Inspections Treaty," *Sydney Morning Herald,* August 2, 2004.

90. See Tanter, "With Eyes Wide Shut," p. 172.

91. See William J. Broad, "Call for New Breed of Nuclear Arms Faces Hurdles," *NYT,* March 11, 2002, p. A8.

92. At a hearing on the 2005 military budget, Senator Diane Feinstein of California, quoting from a Congressional Research Service study of extended earth-penetrating nuclear weapons, pressed Secretary Rumsfeld as to whether or not the weapons were still merely in the "study" stage. Rumsfeld said that no decision to go beyond studying the feasibility of implementing the $485 million-a-year program had yet been made. ("We have only decided to find whether or not it would be plausible," he said.) But he also said that bunker busters were "worth studying," and that "many countries" (probably meaning North Korea) had dug underground bunkers that would require, in extreme cases, using such

weapons to reach hiding leaders. Feinstein reminded Rumsfeld that such weapons would release radioactive fallout at depths of 800 to 1,000 feet, where the bunkers would be located. Televised on C-Span, May 12, 2004.

93. The administration's effort to relax controls on so-called low sensitivity military items was severely criticized by Republicans and Democrats alike in the House of Representatives. They argued that stronger, not weaker, controls were needed inasmuch as such items could find their way to terrorist groups through importers fronting for them, as had happened with waivers on sales to Canada. See Christopher Marquis, "Lawmakers Oppose Plan to Ease Sales of US Arms," *NYT,* June 10, 2004, p. A10.

94. Tim Weiner, "Air Force Seeks Bush's Approval for Space Arms," *NYT,* May 18, 2005, p. 1.

7

Crusading:
Costs and Alternatives

IDEALS AND SELF-INTEREST have usually marched hand-in-hand in
the actual conduct of US foreign policy. Under George W. Bush, a crusade for "civilizational" values has justified the preeminence of the US
power position in world affairs. The sources of the crusade lie in the
beliefs of Bush's top advisers: one, faith based for some, is that the
United States is righteous and unselfish; the other (as Condoleezza Rice
has written) is that "great powers don't just mind their own business."
These are hardly unique beliefs in US administrations of modern times;
but they have been carried to excess under Bush, such that unilaterally
enforcing US interests is the norm. Law and cooperativeness are sub-
servient to order as never before: The "business" of the United States
is maintaining order in the post–Cold War system, with little regard for
legalities or the views of others.

Bush has out-Reaganed Reagan, and conservative realists have
noticed it just as have other critics. Clyde Prestowitz was on the mark
when he wrote that the Bush Doctrine, even when measured against a
long tradition of US interventions, huge military budgets, and other
abuses of "national security," is a radical agenda, one that conservatives
no less than liberals must reject. In his words:

> The imperial project of the so-called neoconservatives is not conser-
> vatism at all but radicalism, egotism, and adventurism articulated in
> the stirring rhetoric of traditional patriotism. Real conservatives have
> never been messianic or doctrinaire. The very essence of conservatism,
> which the neoconservatives constantly preach, is limited government.
> Yet the imperial project they are proposing will greatly increase the
> role of government both at home and abroad.[1]

The "imperial project" Bush leads is more than a replay of the early years of the Cold War, and the PNAC is more than a reincarnation of the Committee on the Present Danger. The September 11, 2001, attacks enabled the neocons to take over and transform the nation's political agenda, replacing a supposed lack of national purpose in the 1990s with an international crusade. Without 9/11, the balance of foreign policy thinking in Washington would not have shifted from power politics as usual to a doctrine that might makes right. By Bush's second term, there was no hiding the administration's ambitions. As one "senior aide" to Bush is quoted as telling journalists, "We're an empire now, and when we act, we create our own reality. And while you're studying that reality—judiciously, as you will—we'll act again, creating other new realities, which you can study too, and that's how things will sort out. We're history's actors . . . and you, all of you, will be left to just study what we do."[2]

Such audacious language fits comfortably with notions of American exceptionalism. Plenty of other US policymakers in the past believed they were "history's actors" and justified unilateral, sometimes illegal, and always self-interested policies on the basis of an historic, even God-given mandate. On the other hand, some distinguished analysts regard foreign policy under George W. Bush as a revolutionary departure, due either to the way his administration has exercised power or to the scope of its ambitions.[3] My analysis has tried to show that the Bush Doctrine is exceptional in degree. Philosophically, it has roots in longstanding ideas of US beneficence and innocence. Moreover, two of the doctrine's three main elements—regime change and unilateralism—were commonly practiced in past administrations. What sets the current administration apart are the theological underpinnings of ideology and policymakers' embrace not just of regime change and unilateral action but also of preventive war.

Risky Business

To its practitioners, a unilateral foreign policy is relatively cost free: Friends may be discomfited, but they depend on US largesse and have no leverage to do more than protest. Or so it is thought. But alienating close friends does carry risks and costs, just as Richard Haass said (before he joined the Bush State Department) when he urged that "unilateralism is neither wise nor sustainable" and that acting multilaterally was simply "more realistic" in most circumstances.[4] Acting alone risks being left on the sidelines—alone to pay the costs and assume the burdens that might otherwise be shared.[5] In Iraq, for instance, although thirty-two countries contributed soldiers to the war and the occupation, six times that many countries did not. This "coalition of the unwilling" included over a dozen countries (as of 2005) that later pulled troops out or announced the intention to do so, either because of the costs or public opposition back home.

The unwilling may not be able consistently to stand up to US policy out of fear of being punished. But the other side of the coin is that US leaders will also pay a price when they arrogantly disregard the views of others. As Canada's former ambassador to the UN wrote, the US image and trustworthiness were severely hurt by Iraq, and not just in the Middle East. Canadians overwhelmingly concluded that the Bush administration had lied about Iraq. For Canada, the lesson was not simply about the limits of intelligence; Canada's position in opposition to the war had been vindicated, and "we should not shrink from disagreeing with US administrations when they are wrong."[6]

Criticisms of US policy from abroad do not amount to mere carping; they challenge the legitimacy as well as the wisdom of policy.[7] Acting unlawfully as well as arrogantly affects the cooperativeness of allies and other countries on international security issues such as peacekeeping missions, trade policy, and intelligence sharing. Attacking Iraq without UN Security Council endorsement, rejecting the Kyoto Protocol, violating the Geneva Conventions, and insisting that US soldiers be exempt from prosecution when on peacekeeping missions are among the many policies that deeply angered allies in NATO and other governments, not to mention the UN leadership and many international NGOs. As a result, a number of allies, starting with Germany and France, that might have responded favorably at other times to US appeals for help in Iraq and Afghanistan—in the Persian Gulf War, it will be recalled, US allies contributed $48 billion of the war's total cost of $61 billion—preferred to stay on the sidelines or make only minimal contributions.[8]

While discouraging burden sharing, a unilateral foreign policy encourages multinational cooperation that excludes the United States, such as the numerous free-trade agreements that are being signed all over East Asia. Europeans have taken the initiative on global environmental issues, Iran's nuclear programs, and the International Criminal Court. Spanish voters showed in 2004 that it was time to reject subordination to US preferences and start thinking in terms of Europe first. One European commentator wrote that the United States is becoming the "dispensable nation": "In recent memory, nothing could be done without the US. But today, most international institution-building of any long-term importance in global diplomacy and trade occurs without American participation."[9]

Other costs to the United States arise out of a narrow focus on the war on terror. The United States is running the largest trade deficit in its history. The dollar's value, thanks to Bush's extraordinarily unconservative spending, is falling fast, prompting complaints from Europe to Asia about US fiscal irresponsibility.[10] Important partnerships are being neglected, such as with Mexico and much of the rest of Latin America, where the post-9/11 economic downturn worldwide has had profoundly destabilizing consequences.[11] In Southeast Asia, Washington has largely ignored opposition there to the war on terror as it has pressed governments to cooperate in arresting hardline Islamic leaders. That opposition, which includes senior government figures as well as the public, is based on the heavy-handed US approach to dealing with presumed terrorists and to one-sided US policy in the Middle East.[12] The war on terror also affects policy toward Russia and China in negative ways. On one hand it reduces US leverage for speaking out on behalf of human rights in Chechnya and China's western provinces. At the same time, the deployment of US forces in close proximity to areas of Russian and Chinese strategic interest detracts from the supposed partnerships with both countries, making cooperation with them on contentious issues such as Ukraine and North Korea all the more difficult.

Washington has also found that the reputation of the United States has been badly damaged by the Bush Doctrine. The administration's Middle East policies and positions on key global issues such as global warming and the Rome Treaty on the ICC are not the only reasons for rising anti-US sentiment, but they profoundly influence it. The sources of dissatisfaction vary: governments whose support Washington takes for granted; people who already think poorly of the United States, notably in the Middle East; and people whom the US government hopes will be positively moved by the "liberation" of Iraq. The indicators appeared before 9/11 and rose sharply thereafter: in surveys of global attitudes such as were conducted by the Pew Research Center;[13] in testimony by US officials in charge of public diplomacy;[14] in the findings of the 9/11 Commission, which cited US unpopularity throughout the Middle East and regardless of the size of US aid programs to countries in that region;[15] and in the voting records of US allies and friendly countries in the United Nations, where by 2001 a significant drop-off of support had occurred.[16] The war in Iraq has added immeasurably to hostility toward the United States, even among ordinarily pro-US publics such as Australians.[17] So much so that twenty-seven former senior US military officials and diplomats wrote a blistering open letter of protest of the Bush policies: "Never in the two and a quarter centuries of our history has the United States been so isolated among the nations, so broadly feared and distrusted."[18]

Failures of Leadership

The purpose of US power today seems to be to lead, not by example or by multilateral cooperation, but by unilateral action, in the achievement of both an unchallengeable power position and a predominant economic position in the world. "Multilateralism," in Bush's definition, means enlisting other countries in support of US policies, as with North Korea, and not engaging their cooperation in genuine partnership. As John Ikenberry has written: "The prevailing view [in the Bush administration] is that the United States seems prepared to use its power to go after terrorists and evil regimes, but not to use it to help build a more stable and peaceful world order. . . . To the rest of the world, neo-imperial thinking has more to do with exercising power than with exercising leadership."[19]

Being alone in *not* acting can be equally as damaging as acting alone. John Ruggie's study of US foreign policy in the 1940s and 1950s concludes that unilateralism "opened the door to isolationism" because of failures to act when an overriding human interest demanded it.[20] Particularly for an administration that wants to narrow the range of US interests it is prepared actively to defend, one would think that increased multilateral involvement would be welcome burden sharing in humanitarian crises. Under Clinton, US leadership was found wanting in Bosnia, Kosovo, and Rwanda, and hundreds of thousands of needless deaths resulted.[21] When the Bush administration did take the lead in the humanitarian crisis that deepened with the ouster of Aristide in Haiti, it proved more concerned with keeping Aristide out than with improving the lot of ordinary Haitians. France, Brazil, and a few other countries sent peacekeeping troops but precious little money for economic development or rehabilitation.

Acting after the fact is not only immoral; it costs far more than acting preventively—a lesson that should have been learned but was not when genocide reared its head again in Sudan. Instead of avoiding facing up to the responsibilities imposed by the genocide convention, the United States should line up behind the evolving UN doctrine of preventive intervention—using the collective force of the United Nations as a last resort in order to protect large numbers of endangered people.[22] The needless deaths of 200,000 people in the Darfur region should be reason enough for greatly strengthening the African Union's troops that are acting as a protective force in Sudan.

The invasion of Iraq was a leadership failure on another front, that of nuclear nonproliferation policy. Although US strategists might think that North Korea, Iran, and Syria "got the message" delivered by the invasion that seeking to acquire weapons of mass destruction invites severe US countermeasures, subsequent developments showed that what North Korea and Iran actually "got" was the importance of having a nuclear weapons option as a practical matter of self-defense. Libya did give up its quest for a nuclear weapon, but probably not mainly due to US pressure. In fact, the Libya case actually proves the opposite of the lesson drawn by the Bush administration. Besides hurting economic sanctions, Qaddafi called it quits in 2000 because of UN inspections, good intelligence, and the high cost of continuing a nuclear weapons program.[23] The same factors were working against Iraq in 2003—until Bush, sensing an easy victory, went to war.

Despite Libya, Bush's policies outlined in Chapter 6 suggest that the United States has foreclosed a precious opportunity created by the end of the Cold War to move toward a decisive reduction and eventual elimination of nuclear weapons and the means to produce and deliver them.[24] Such leadership should have started with the Moscow (SURE) Treaty and dramatic, immediate, and verifiable reductions and destruction of US and Russian strategic arsenals. Bush should also be leading the way in plugging loopholes in the NPT, strengthening the IAEA's ability to carry out inspections of nuclear facilities, reducing production of fissile materials and preventing international trafficking in them, prohibiting research, testing, and development of "mini-nukes" and other refinements, and promoting international cooperation (while spending more) to secure nuclear plants and prevent nuclear materials as well as weapons from falling into terrorists' hands. US leadership in these areas may increase pressure on unrecognized nuclear weapon states outside the NPT and the CTBT (Israel, India, and Pakistan) to place their facilities under international inspection. Lastly, the Bush administration should be giving high priority to creating security and economic incentives, in cooperation with its Asian and European partners, that will persuade North Korea and Iran to abandon the nuclear weapon option.

The prospect of more nuclear weapon states is just one of the casualties of the invasion of Iraq and the war on terror. With troops on the ground and military aid programs in countries experiencing internal conflict, the United States could become embroiled in a civil war. In Central Asia and along Russia's rim, for example, US military leaders apparently envision a long-term policing mission.[25] But taking on responsibility for these countries' internal and external security might, as in Georgia, supplant terrorism as the United States's biggest concern.[26] US exploitation of the war on terrorism to cement political and military partnerships with undemocratic governments, such as Algeria, Pakistan, Indonesia, Colombia, Uzbekistan, and Kazakhstan, undermines prospects for human rights and responsible governance in those countries, just as happened with partnerships based on anticommunism during the Cold War.[27] Libya may be the next such case of a poor tradeoff between security and democracy.[28] What these cases reveal is how much the war on terror has contributed to making US policy instrumental, unprincipled, and dangerous for human security.

A Human Development and Common Security Agenda

Toward a Humane Internationalism

Human security, as noted at the outset of this book, embraces values and norms that promote the well-being of people, communities, and their natural environments, in present and future generations, with specific attention to preserving the authentic cultures and improving the living standards and human rights of the most impoverished and oppressed peoples, at home as well as abroad. A human security–centered foreign policy would espouse and practice good global citizenship, as defined at the start of Chapter 6. The companion to a human security agenda necessarily would be a foreign policy that upholds common security as well. US policy would assign high priority to strengthening international law and global regimes, reducing and eliminating weapons of mass destruction, and drastically reducing arms spending and transfers. It would seek engagement and mutual respect even with hostile countries, and reject intervention abroad except in cases of extreme humanitarian crisis, when the United States should assume a leadership role in concert with others.

While US foreign policy has from time to time acted in accordance with these ideas, it has not consistently or systematically done so. Actual policy has markedly, and frequently, deviated from declared policy in support of humane norms, and no more so than today.[29] Nor have US leaders ever stated that human security norms are preferable to power-political norms such as the balance of power, national interest, and unilateral pursuit of advantage, or to liberal economic norms such as orderly markets, the open door, and free trade. To the contrary, the academic literature no less than official statements is replete with protestations of the United States's benevolent intentions: We are supposedly a "benign hegemon," serving the critical (and neutral) functions of "system maintenance" and "power balancing" in order to keep other states from becoming imperialistic.

None of the most prominent schools of thought in US foreign policy stands behind a human security platform—not just the realist and globalist schools, but also nonmainstream schools that favor some version of isolationism or a more selective internationalism.[30] Even radical-left critiques of US foreign policy often are inconsistent when it comes to embracing human security norms. Perhaps the reason for such neglect is that all schools employ an exclusively strategic framework that focuses on threats to (or from) the national interest. Building ethical concerns into foreign policy, so that it serves the real needs of people and planet, is of less interest. Policymakers and mavens typically dismiss as naïve the notion that foreign policy should actually aim at peace building, human rights for all (economic and social justice as well as political liberties), and preservation of the natural environment. Private ethical behavior, even if adhered to, is widely considered irrelevant to the conduct of public affairs—except, perhaps, as ritual political rhetoric.

Yet there is practicality to the ideal of bringing the US national interest into line with emerging global community interests. What I am calling a humane internationalism provides opportunities to enhance the US reputation, neutralize threats, empower people, promote good governance, and save money. It begins with conflict prevention. Responsible global engagement is one form of prevention.[31] Oddly enough, the notion of US indispensability can provide a starting point for a strategy that puts engagement back at the center of US foreign policy. For if it is true that the United States, by what it does and by what it chooses not to do, uniquely shapes international politics—in every policy sphere, from trade and environment to peacekeeping and disarmament—then the opportunity is great to influence a large-scale shift of resources to meet global community needs and provide meaningful security where it matters, in local communities and environments.

Global leadership is a precious commodity. It can be used to promote a just peace in the Middle East, Northern Ireland, and Kashmir. It can set an example of restraint in the use of force and in arms sales and transfers,[32] and in support of and adherence to international agreements on the environment, human rights, and war crimes.[33] It can reduce tensions and prevent war by regarding rogue states as weak states, and by seeking to engage them in mutually beneficial ways. The Bush administration is correct to regard weak states as the number-one strategic challenge for the United States. Strengthening their human security conditions makes more sense than trying, as Bush seems to be, to bring them to their knees or, in the case of friendly rogues, coax their leaders with aid.

Promoting human development is the companion to a foreign policy that emphasizes preventive measures to enhance security. Human immiseration is increasing. As various UN agencies have reported, more people than ever before (about 1.4 billion) earn less than $2 a day, over 850 million people do not have enough to eat, and more than half the world's children suffer from civil wars, HIV/AIDS, and the effects of poverty.[34] As a matter of human decency as much as to address the structural roots of despair and violence, the United States should direct its own and global institutions' financial, technical, and human resources to grassroots assistance programs that focus on the needs of the poor.[35] At the same time, the United States should work with other countries to promote foreign investment that creates living-wage jobs, debt forgiveness for governments that are tackling corruption, and microcredit programs that empower women to start small businesses.

New US foreign and national security priorities require far-reaching changes in mindset and practices. Decisionmakers need to be appointed whose values and norms—international cooperation, mutual respect, environmental balance, peace, minimization of violence, lawful conduct, social justice—support the notion of global citizenship. They will have to redefine the proper international role of the United States as one of "leadership without primacy" in order to deal effectively with North-South cleavages, environmental and ecological decline, and internal conflicts that create humanitarian crises.[36] To be a credible leader, however, the United States must put its own house in order, influencing the rest of the world by the example it sets at home with respect to racial and gender equality, investment in people, and environmental protection.

These three ideas—conflict prevention, human development, and shared leadership—come together around the question of what to do about terrorism.

On Terrorism

The Bush administration's understanding of terrorism fits all too neatly with the president's us-versus-them worldview. States friendly to the United States are ipso facto part of the civilized world; they stand opposed to an uncivilized world that is distinguished by its toleration, if not outright support, of terrorist organizations. The administration's National Strategy for Combating Terrorism (February 2003) draws the line still more clearly when it states that the purpose of the strategy is to build "an international order where more countries and peoples are integrated into a world consistent with the values we share with our partners—values such as human dignity, rule of law, respect for individual liberties, open and free economies, and religious tolerance."[37] Such a view—part of the "distinctly American internationalism" underlined in the Bush *National Security Strategy* paper—can only deepen mistrust of US motives. Talk of common values and "American internationalism" encourages the widespread suspicion, which terrorist groups feed on, that these are catchwords for US-style globalization and empire.

The very notion of a general war on terror, as opposed to a specific terrorist group, exposes a deep conceit and serious intellectual short-comings. Bush and his inner circle refuse to acknowledge that people join militant movements and fight on against all odds because the options open to them in a hegemonic world order are unacceptably few. The repression, corruption, and economic injustice that US foreign policies often condone and abet in the rich Arab states, and the US failure to press Israel for a just settlement with the Palestinians that can make a Palestinian state viable, weigh heavily in the terrorism equation.[38] Endorsement of that conclusion comes from none other than the Pentagon's advisory Defense Science Board, whose report in late 2004 on the ineffectiveness of US efforts to communicate to the Muslim world said: "Muslims do not 'hate our freedom' but rather they hate our policies."[39] Here, from a surprising source, was a direct slap at Bush's post-9/11 interpretation of Al-Qaida's motives.

As George Perkovich argues, moreover, Bush's emphasis on freedom slights its counterpart, justice, and thus weakens the appeal of the United States in the Middle East and elsewhere. Justice—within and between states, and in the global economy—is or should be the litmus test of any country's foreign policy.[40] In the long run, justice will determine whether or not freedom really reigns—and whether small democratic gains in Egypt, Lebanon, and Iraq really matter. Chris Hedges has put the war on terror in proper philosophical perspective:

> By accepting the facile cliché that the battle under way against terrorism is a battle against evil, by easily branding those who fight us as the barbarians, we, like them, refuse to acknowledge our own culpability. We ignore real injustices that have led many of those arrayed against us to their rage and despair.[41]

Many terrorism experts are convinced that terrorism is also a reaction to global underdevelopment—to the huge and growing gap between the industrialized North and an increasingly impoverished South comprised of many weak states—states like Sudan, Kazakhstan, and Afghanistan whose leaderships typically are corrupt, illegitimate, and incapable of or unwilling to meet citizens' basic economic and security needs.[42] Any recent UN Development Program or World Bank annual report will provide abundant statistics to demonstrate growing global impoverishment and the close relationship between human insecurity and human rights deprivations.[43] As Kofi Annan described the typical "global village" in his Millennium Report, gross inequalities based on income, gender, and opportunity translate not just into widening gaps between rich and poor but also into increased potential for violence.[44]

The obvious answer to underdevelopment as a cause of terrorism is a large-scale assault on global poverty, which would be costly but perhaps one-tenth of the $1 trillion governments are currently spending on arms.[45] Dennis Pirages, in a discussion of health care in poor countries, puts the cost in proper perspective. He asks that we consider that communicable diseases every year kill fourteen times as many people as does war, making it appropriate to think of HIV/AIDS, Ebola, SARS, and other diseases as large-scale security threats.

> If health care spending in the world's 60 poorest countries could be steadily increased from the present $13 per capita to $38 by 2015, . . . on average 8 million lives could be saved each year. This would require a total contribution from industrial countries of about $38 billion—a fraction of what the United States recently spent to unseat Saddam Hussein in Iraq.[46]

Yet, a major bipartisan report found, the Bush aid program to developing countries is not only insufficiently funded, as was pointed out in the previous chapter; it leaves out precisely those people whose economic and social development needs are greatest.[47] An index created by *Foreign Policy* magazine and the Center for Global Development to assess how well the twenty-one richest countries help the poorest ranked the United States next to last (ahead only of Japan) in six categories: official development assistance, trade, investments, immigration policies, peacekeeping contributions, and environmental policies. Only in nonagricultural trade with the Third World did the United States come out ahead of other rich countries.[48]

Trouble is, targeting unequal development requires not only domestic policy changes that would be politically hazardous, such as ending subsidies to US agricultural interests. It also requires dramatic foreign policy changes, starting in the Middle East: brokering of a just Middle East peace that would provide not only for the coexistence of Jewish and Palestinian states, but also for settlement of human security issues such as poverty and unemployment, Palestinian refugees, and Jewish settlements;[49] and elimination of support to all those despots on whom the United States depends to secure resources and sustain the empire.[50] Caught in the middle are the majority of the people who have been denied political reforms, economic opportunity, and a more tolerant Islam that would pose an alternative to Al-Qaida's message. This is no "clash of civilizations." It is more a clash of universalisms, that of terrorist organizations such as Al-Qaida and the United States.

For the United States to make progress against terrorist groups, it would have to neutralize pervasive anti-US sentiment and, through concrete acts not undercut by one-sided policies, provide hope for the future. Yet if Jeffrey Sachs is right, a human resource problem in the US government further compounds the difficulty of doing things right. He points to a woeful US government ignorance of and inattention to Third World economic conditions that give rise to political violence. Consequently, programs that address them are greatly underfunded.[51] Likewise neglected is the so-called soft power of US public diplomacy—foreign-language training, Fulbright scholar exchanges, and enlightened immigration policies—that send a message of welcome and desire for mutual understanding.[52] In fact, US public diplomacy is widely considered to be a disaster—understaffed as well as underfunded, wrongly focused on elites, and no longer in the hands of cross-culturally adept people.[53]

The United States can sometimes be its own worst enemy. The war on terror is one of those times, and this reality may be its most important long-term consequence. The extensive use of violence committed and condoned by the United States, its disdain for international law and institutions, and the tendency to regard as enemies any party that refuses to accept its rules in the "war" are precisely the beliefs of global terrorist organizations such as Al-Qaida. Thus the great danger of the Bush Doctrine goes well beyond weakening US influence in world affairs, undermining the rule of law and the principle of proportionality in responding to others' violence, and assisting the cause of terrorism as a just response to US hegemony. As an endless, boundary-less war—recall Bush's speech of September 2001 warning that the war on terror "will not end until every terrorist group of global reach has been found, stopped, and defeated"—it poses "a threat of 'global fascism'" that has awful implications for US democracy.[54]

Toward Real Homeland Security

Distorted Spending

Supporting good governance abroad requires setting a positive example of good governance at home. The United States is the leading country in many categories of hard power. But it is not the leader on the home front, in terms of access to health care, infant mortality, rates of imprisonment,[55] race relations, closing of income gaps, and equal employment opportunity. The US self-image of liberty and prosperity for all so constantly trumpeted by the Bush administration still has plenty of believers; but the on-the-ground reality tells another story, starting with spending patterns.

By the time Bush made only his second speech to the nation on Iraq policy, on September 7, 2003, paying for the war meant increasing the national debt. Bush asked Congress for $87 billion, a staggering sum. Seventy-eight percent of the money was slated for military operations; only 22 percent, or $20 billion, was to go to rebuilding efforts in Iraq and Afghanistan—money that, as we have seen, remains mostly unspent and transferred to security tasks. In all, US spending on war in those two countries for 2003 and 2004 rose to $166 billion, or twenty-five times the cost of the Gulf War in current dollars.[56] The full cost of the war remains to be calculated, of course; but early in 2005 Bush proposed adding another $80 billion to the bill, leading to a new Congressional Budget Office estimate of $285 billion in total costs for the war on terror over the next five years.[57]

These war costs, as well as the costs of US nuclear weapons programs, are not included in the Pentagon's regular budgets, which call for spending $419 billion in FY2006 (a 4.8 percent increase over FY2005) and $502 billion (a 41 percent increase) by 2011.[58] The budgetary impact of that level of spending is awesome: In 2005 the United States will run the largest deficit in its history, an estimated $427 billion that does not include continuation of tax cuts or Bush's proposed privatization of social security (which would push future budget deficits into the trillions of dollars for at least the next decade).[59] As Eisenhower famously warned in the 1950s, excessive military spending has social consequences. Health care, education, community development, clean air, and public transportation have all taken deep cuts as the Bush administration attends to the presumed needs of the war on terror. In the federal budget, military spending dominates discretionary spending, that is, funds Congress may allocate other than for mandated programs such as social security, Medicare, and Medicaid. In 2003, for example, military spending accounted for nearly one-half ($407 billion) of all discretionary spending.[60] While the war on Iraq was costing the US government about $48 billion in that year, the Bush administration was only spending $34 billion on grade and high school education, $28 billion on health research and training, $8 billion on pollution control, and $9 billion on foreign aid.[61]

By 2004 military spending exceeded all other federal spending combined. The gap between military and nonmilitary spending is bound to grow larger and faster, especially as interest costs on the federal debt are expected to crowd out social spending too. Increasingly, states, private foundations, and NGOs are being looked to for relief; but with many state budgets in serious deficit, cutbacks are commonplace there too.[62] Nothing brought home the price of military excess so much as the federal government's belated and inadequate response to Hurricane Katrina, which inundated New Orleans and other Gulf Coast areas and made tens of thousands of people refugees. Remarkably, even with such distorted national security spending, the armed forces still are short of money for basic services and equipment; veterans continue to be shortchanged; and many cities around the United States complain about insufficient federal help to cope with a possible terrorist attack.

Job creation is also a victim of military spending. The US job picture showed 2.7 million jobs lost in manufacturing between 2001 and 2003, information that was seized upon by some politicians to argue for penalizing other countries (most of all, China) whose trade surpluses with the United States were said to demonstrate that US jobs were being lost abroad rather than at home. Unemployment figures improved in 2004, but largely by massaging them: Unmentioned was the quality and wages of the jobs, the number of people who had given up finding work (and therefore do not count in official figures), and those who took part-time employment because full-time work was not available. Different ideas about national security, such as the war on drugs, help illustrate the problem: The United States has spent nearly $3 billion on counter-drug operations in Colombia, without measurable impact on either the production or street availability of cocaine.[63] Yet the Bush administration wants to spend more on these operations rather than invest it preventively at the source: the US communities that desperately need better education and training to create jobs and move people out of the drug economy.

Homeland Insecurity

So many people unemployed and underemployed mean increased poverty and declining health care coverage. From 2001 to 2003, the percentage of the US population below the poverty line (12.5 percent) and the percentage without health insurance (nearly 16 percent, or around 40 million people) grew. In 2003 the rich-poor gap also widened—the top 20 percent of households took nearly one-half of all income, a figure a good deal higher than in Latin American countries—as did the wage gap between men and women.[64] Median income in 2005 declined for a fifth consecutive year. Such figures represent a national scandal for the world's most affluent country, and a striking contrast with the Bush administration's willingness to pay for overseas adventurism. To be sure, inequality and lack of access to health insurance had been on a generally uninterrupted rise since the Reagan years (though the poverty rate had declined steadily under Clinton). But in the Bush era, with its blatant catering to the rich, income and wealth inequality is greater than at any time since the New Deal:

> The top 20 percent of households . . . commanded an astonishing 83 percent of the nation's wealth. Even more striking, the top one percent earned about 17 percent of national income and owned 38 percent of national wealth. In nearly two decades the number of millionaires had doubled, to 4.8 million, and the number of "deca-millionaires"—those worth at least $10 million—had more than tripled . . . In contrast, the bottom 40 percent of Americans earned just 10 percent of the nation's income and owned less than one percent of the nation's wealth. The bottom 60 percent did only marginally better, accounting for about 23 percent of income and less than five percent of wealth. The racial gaps are even more disheartening.[65]

Far from being a shining example of social justice, the United States has become further polarized.

The polarization extends to civil liberties, as "homeland security" provides opportunities to narrow the realm of personal freedoms. Just as happened at the outset of the Cold War under Truman, "national security" and patriotic appeals are being exploited under Bush to limit the freedoms of US citizens, especially those of Muslim faith and Middle East origins. Having pushed through Congress one Patriot Act that gave the US Department of Justice sweeping new powers for detaining and deporting citizens and immigrants, conducting secret searches of homes and property, and snooping in public libraries and businesses,[66] the administration then sought a further extension (dubbed Patriot Act II) in 2003 to limit the due process of suspected supporters of terrorism. By then a number of Congress members, including some Republicans, had become concerned about the surrender of civil liberties they had approved, so that in 2005 renewal of the act is assured, but perhaps with fewer draconian features. Mass media initially fell in line, often failing to take note that unlawful detentions, domestic spying, invasions of personal privacy, and other government practices were reminiscent of the Nixon era—except that now they were being done openly, and with little public debate. For all that, what is remarkable is how few people have actually been successfully prosecuted in the United States for terrorist acts—a mere handful, and a much smaller number than have been charged or had a clear connection to an international terrorist network.[67]

The way "homeland security" is understood makes it part of the problem. The Department of Homeland Security began business in 2002. Not since the CIA and the NSC were established under Truman had there been such an ambitious organizational response to an external threat; Bush in fact likened the proposed department to Truman's National Security Act of 1947. With a $37 billion budget, greater than the CIA's, and roughly 170,000 employees (the exact number was immediately classified) drawn from over twenty government agencies, Homeland Security exemplifies what can happen when foreign policy comes home: heavy on bureaucratization and threat dramatization, light on prevention.

Energy dependence is a good example of the warped interpretation of "homeland security." What George Kennan wrote at the time of the Soviet invasion of Afghanistan still applies today: "the greatest real threats to our security . . . [are] our self-created dependence on Arab oil and our involvement in a wholly unstable Israeli-Arab relationship," and not any military threat.[68] Around 60 percent of US oil consumption comes from abroad, and Saudi oil accounts for about one-sixth of US oil imports. This pattern is unsustainable. For one thing, a number of oil experts believe that future oil production in Saudi Arabia, the United States, and just about everywhere else is grossly overestimated, and that 2006 will probably be the peak year of worldwide oil production. Yet at the same time that US oil reserves are low and domestic production is flat to declining, oil consumption is expected to continue growing rapidly over the next twenty years.[69] Additions to oil reserves are "falling increasingly short of annual consumption," a report to the Department of Energy said in February 2005; in contrast with any other time in world history, "oil peaking will be abrupt and revolutionary."[70]

Relying for cheap oil on a Saudi government that has tolerated Islamic radicalism in its midst and has severe human rights problems is a bad long-term bet. The close financial ties of the Bush family and associates with the Saudi monarchy only strengthen that reliance. US presidents have been fond of talking about energy independence, but they have yet to seriously embrace the idea, such as by providing increased tax incentives to promote energy conservation and reliance on renewable energy sources. Solar, wind, and geothermal energy costs of production are dropping substantially, making these sources all the more economical in comparison with oil.[71]

Shrinking Accountability

Problems of governance extend to the roles of the media and Congress. As recounted in Chapter 4, the overwhelmingly pro-war sentiment in the mainstream media after 9/11 amounted to cheerleading for the USA, which often substituted for balanced, independent assessments.[72] Such followership was rarely acknowledged, much less rectified, when the truth of the Bush policies was revealed. The role of Congress in foreign policy shrunk dramatically when a majority gave the administration a virtual blank check to attack Iraq. Once again democracy gave way to executive war making, and the War Powers Resolution became almost irrelevant. As Senator Byrd eloquently put it, S.J. Resolution 46 in 2002 far exceeded the president's authority under the Constitution as well as the authorization of the Congress after 9/11 to use force. That resolution, Byrd warned, set a dangerous precedent: "justification for launching preemptive military strikes against any sovereign nations that they perceive to be a threat."[73] Byrd concurred with Kofi Annan's own warning that the US assumption of such sweeping authority would become a model for other countries that decide to attack their neighbors.

The policymaking process itself has been badly skewed by the Bush Doctrine's quest for absolute security. After 9/11, control of policymaking gravitated to the neocons in the Pentagon, with support from the top level of Rice's National Security Council. The State Department's diplomats and CIA intelligence analysts were essentially marginalized. The costs of this tilt were high: dysfunctional intelligence oversight,[74] the politicization of intelligence, a myopic view about occupying Iraq, the privatization of security, and the emasculation of public diplomacy. Yet when all the investigations were completed, the only major overhaul recommended was a reorganization of the intelligence community. Legislation was passed to appoint a new director of national intelligence (John D. Negroponte, another career diplomat with a shadowy past in the Reagan years[75]) as part of a larger effort to centralize intelligence gathering, budgeting, and analysis under a single individual responsible directly to the president. But early signs, such as Rumsfeld's resistance to the legislation and the resignations of several top CIA officials in response to the new CIA director's appointment of several House Republican aides to senior management positions, indicate just how political reorganizing intelligence will actually be. Nor is there reason to suppose that new personalities and a new bureaucratic structure will improve the effectiveness with which intelligence is handled and coordinated. Most important, experience indicates that reorganizations have no necessary connection with political accountability or transparency, much less truthfulness.

Certainly, the possibility of another terrorist act in the United States needs attention. Yet since 9/11 the principal source of terrorism has been homegrown. Anthrax and ricin found in Senate offices and at various places around the country were almost certainly the work of disgruntled US citizens, not Al-Qaida sympathizers. Airport incidents in which ordinary people managed to get through security lines with knives, or in which travelers (foreign or domestic) with the "look" of possible terrorists (in other words, dark skinned) were detained, invariably had nothing to do with the terrorist threat. But these kinds of incidents—not to mention bombings abroad—are grist for the mill, for they allow the administration at any moment to declare orange or red alerts, to claim extensive media coverage on behalf of the war on terrorism, and to make itself appear to be vigilantly serving national security.

Finding a Way Out

The Bush Doctrine draws attention to two fundamental questions about US foreign policy:

- Can a foreign policy that presumes singular responsibility for policing the world avoid the pitfalls of empire?
- Can the United States, which is officially committed to promoting human rights, spreading liberty and democracy, and upholding the self-determination of peoples, ever practice what it preaches while seeking to maintain control over world political economy?

The answer is clearly "no" to both questions: A national security doctrine founded on unilateralism and interference in others' affairs is bound to create greater insecurity abroad and at home; and endless crusading to keep the world under control invariably distorts and undermines liberal values. Just as Undersecretary of State George Ball argued before President Johnson on Vietnam, "a long, protracted war will disclose our weakness, not our strength."[76] But what if we take seriously the notion that there is another way—a more humane, equitable, conserving, even economical way—of "doing business" abroad? How will it come about?

Putting the United States on the track of human and common security requires political momentum, and that requires a convergence of forces at home and abroad to restrain US unilateralism. The "American century" of 1945–1975 initially foundered on defeat in Vietnam and its domestic consequences: stagflation, casualties, official lying, and social division. It would be tragic if it truly takes another Vietnam to forestall the neocons' project of creating a second American century. There are important restraining forces at work today, such as NGOs and other civil-society groups that are fighting at home and abroad for social justice and peace; multilateral organizations (such as the UN, the EU, and sometimes even the WTO) that reject and criticize US unilateralism and specific policies; contenders for regional power, such as China and Russia, that refuse to support or actively oppose policies of importance to Washington; members of Congress and independent media that finally decide that the costs of empire have become intolerable given domestic needs; "defectors" from within the conservatives' ranks who deplore the Bush administration's mistakes;[77] and resistance groups such as in Iraq that threaten to keep US forces bogged down for an indefinite time.

When it comes to stopping and reversing empire, however, the chief source of resistance must be the people of the United States, acting individually and collectively. The deceits that characterize US policy in Iraq and Afghanistan are a tremendous disservice to people who are serving or once served in the government. Some of them stood up with great courage to oppose the war in Iraq. They include Richard Clarke, whose memoir underscored Bush's disastrous shift of focus from pursuing Al-Qaida to pursuing Saddam; Joseph Wilson, the former chargé in Baghdad who exposed the fallacious yellow cake sale; the twenty-seven former US civilian and military officials who wrote a letter of protest cited earlier; the US Foreign Service and intelligence officers who resigned rather than support policies they believed were incompatible with US values and interests;[78] Michael Scheuer, a CIA expert on Al-Qaida, who has written at length of the administration's misguided approach to terrorism;[79] the intelligence analysts in the State Department and the CIA who told the truth about WMD in Iraq; the journalists and soldiers who broke the story of prisoner abuses; and the US military lawyers for Guantánamo detainees who, in defiance of their superior officers, criticized conditions of confinement.

In the end, however, individual heroics tend not to create a groundswell of popular antiwar feeling. Only large numbers of voters and demonstrators can compel policy changes. By the fall of 2003 public opinion did begin to shift on the war, with a majority of the public expressing the belief that the war was a mistake. That view is even stronger today. Typically, self-interest led the shift. Even though Bush's leadership in the war on terror still scores high, his approval ratings on domestic issues have fallen dramatically. Terrorism no longer counts as the number one problem for the country; the economy again occupies its customary top spot. As the occupation of Iraq goes from bad to worse—the mounting casualties, the unstoppable suicide bombings, the prisoner abuse scandal, the 9/11 Commission's findings, the absence of a withdrawal date from Iraq—Bush's voter approval ratings fall further. Whether or not these developments will lead to a changing of the guard in the 2008 presidential election cannot be known. Even if it does, there is no guarantee that a Democratic president will be able to rise above the war on terror and embrace ideas and policies significantly different from those that guide the Bush administration.

The Second Bush Administration

The most important steps President Bush ought to be taking in his second term are setting a timetable for early withdrawal from Iraq, consulting with the EU, Arab states, and the UN about a new partnership with Iraq's government to repair and secure the country, restoring a vigorous, evenhanded US diplomacy in the Israeli-Palestinian conflict, and putting relations with North Korea and Iran on a new foundation. There is no reason to expect, however, that the Bush team will take such steps. Even less likely is it that Bush will decide to work toward establishing a global coalition devoted to human and common security. The Bush administration fervently believes, as an article of faith, that it has the formula for true international security, namely that all states follow the US example and leadership. The lessons it has learned from Iraq, Afghanistan, Iran, and North Korea are that engaging enemy states is a sign of weakness, coordinating with allies dilutes authority, and recourse to the UN is a waste of time.

The failures in postinvasion Afghanistan and Iraq took some of the gloss off the neocons' image, even among some leading conservatives.[80] But the prospect that the neocons' influence would wane in Bush's second term evaporated with the departure of Colin Powell from the State Department, his replacement with Condoleezza Rice, the retention of Rumsfeld at the Pentagon, and the appointment of John Bolton to the UN. Whereas the neocons seem merely to have suffered a few nicks, the occasional voices of moderation and professional detachment, such as in the intelligence community, were told by the new Bush team to toe the line or face the consequences.[81]

Those who reject US predominance face the threat or application of US power. As Iraq shows, peace can be the nightmare scenario for Bush and company; negotiations and diplomacy automatically reduce US military options. What has been revealed so far in Pentagon planning is that there will be more, not fewer, Iraqs—Syria looms as a possible next target[82]—hence the need of still larger military budgets, more hi-tech weapons, improved information networks for warfare, more partners, and more troops. An undersecretary of defense who requested a study of US military manpower requirements wrote in January 2004:

> Our military expeditions to Afghanistan and Iraq are unlikely to be the last such excursion in the global war on terrorism. We may need to support an ally under attack by terrorists determined to replace the legitimate government; we may need to effect change in the governance of a country that is blatantly sustaining support for terrorism; or we may need to assist an ally who is unable to govern areas of their own country.[83]

Whether and how force will be used is shaped by circumstances. Iraq's costs and duration have forced the Pentagon to reconsider its traditional aim to be able to fight two major wars simultaneously. Like Vietnam, Iraq has blown apart a favored war-making model: Rumsfeld and colleagues never contemplated occupying a country and fighting an insurgency. Now, having undertaken a global war without front lines, the Pentagon finds itself with too many missions and too few soldiers.[84] But while those limitations may affect US tactics, as in North Korea, they are highly unlikely to affect US strategic ambitions. For instance, Rumsfeld reportedly lost the bureaucratic battle over running covert operations independently of the CIA and without congressional oversight; but that is unlikely to stop covert operations themselves, for instance in Iran, where Pentagon special forces are already on the ground.[85] These operations are presumably what Pentagon officials mean when they talk of "stabilization capabilities," yet another euphemism for illegal interventions abroad. Just as unnerving is that many Democrats in Congress, fearful of being left behind in the next crusade, joined Republicans in voting the funds for Pentagon warfare.[86]

A second term for a US president can be dangerous for world peace. While the conventional wisdom is that halfway through their second term, presidents become lame ducks with greatly reduced authority, we should pause to consider what previous second-termers have done abroad. Eisenhower landed troops in Lebanon; Nixon "Vietnamized" the war and secretly bombed Cambodia; Reagan pushed his covert assistance to "freedom fighters" in Central America and Afghanistan; and Clinton led NATO's bombing of Yugoslavia. These were hardly symptoms of a lame-duck presidency.

The harsh truth of the matter is that the foreign policy elite in the George W. Bush era simply doesn't get it—"get" that acting the bully in world affairs comes at a price, though often one that is not apparent until years down the road: the blowback effect that Chalmers Johnson has highlighted. September 11 is a tragic case in point, but only the most recent one. The Bush Doctrine is a reminder that while it is mainly up to nation-states to bring about human security, states are often the source of the problem and we must look elsewhere for answers to human misery and consequent violence. Refocusing resources on human needs and embracing common security also requires much more than different policies and priorities; it demands a different psychology, one that is sensitive to other cultures and histories, for example, and does not presume that the destiny of the United States is the world's destiny. The issue here goes far beyond the "image problem" that mainstream foreign policy groups cite,[87] or the marketing approach taken by the Bush administration.[88] As Robert S. McNamara learned from the bitter experience of Vietnam:

> We did not recognize that neither our people nor our leaders are omniscient. Where our own security is not directly at stake, our judgment of what is in another people's or country's best interest should be put to the test of open discussion in international forums. We do not have the God-given right to shape every nation in our own image or as we choose.[89]

The prevailing attitude on the Beltway, however, seems to be that being disliked comes with the territory, with being "history's actors." Such arrogance would be expected of imperial rulers and not leaders of a country that holds itself before the world as a model democracy.

As one appraises the costs and benefits of changing course, the objection invariably is made that the United States cannot "afford" to take the risks implied by a humane internationalism. Yet, as has recently been argued, the historically unprecedented hegemonic position of the United States today provides a very strong reason why the United States can indeed afford to wait and see: time.[90] The United States can expect to remain number one for many years. It can afford to engage China, Russia, North Korea, and Iran even as it makes principled criticisms. It can afford to rely on diplomacy, international law, and the UN system to curb the arms race and proliferation of WMD. And it can afford to adopt progressive positions on environmental protection, energy conservation, and migrant workers. Going it alone and using force are always options, but they should be the last ones, not reflexively the first.

Notes

1. Prestowitz, *Rogue Nation,* p. 277.

2. Quoted by Julian Borger, "Bush Wages War on the Enemy Within," *Guardian Weekly,* March 18–24, 2005, p. 6. I am indebted to Peter Van Ness for bringing this quotation to my attention.

3. I have in mind Hendrickson, "Toward Universal Empire," and Ikenberry, "America's Imperial Ambition." Both offer excellent critiques of the Bush policies; but in doing so, I think they neglect the excesses of US policy in previous administrations, making it seem as though until the George W. Bush era, the United States was a global benefactor that consistently acted cooperatively and lawfully. People in Third World countries, among others, would surely see that history differently.

4. Haass, "Beyond Containment," pp. 34–35.

5. See Ikenberry, "America's Imperial Ambition," and Joseph S. Nye Jr., *The Paradox of American Power: Why the World's Only Superpower Can't Go It Alone.*

6. Heinbecker, "Canada Got It Right."

7. On the importance of legitimacy, see Robert W. Tucker and David C. Hendrickson, "The Sources of American Legitimacy," pp. 18–32.

8. Germany rejected the idea that NATO should increase its military presence in Afghanistan or become involved in any way in Iraq, such as by training troops. Richard Bernstein and Mark Landler, "German Leader to Oppose Sending NATO Troops to Iraq," *NYT,* May 21, 2004, online ed.

9. Michael Lind, "How America Became the World's Dispensable Nation," *Financial Times,* January 25, 2005, online at www.newamerica.net/index.cfm?pg=article&DocID=2188.

10. David E. Sanger, "US Faces More Tensions Abroad as Dollar Slides," *NYT,* January 25, 2005, online ed.

11. On Mexico and the early disappointment of President Vicente Fox with US priorities, see the interview in *NYT,* September 13, 2002, p. A1. Three years later Mexican criticism of the United States became increasingly acerbic. Bush's failure to push for a promised guest-worker program that would legalize the presence of many of the roughly 3 million Mexicans who work in the United States pointed up a political reality: Mexico's economic need of an accepted outlet for laborers in the United States must take second place to US security concerns about illegal infiltration of the border. (James C. McKinley Jr., "At Mexican Border, Tunnels, Vile River, Rusty Fence," *NYT,* March 23, 2005, p. A8.) Mexico must also deal with local laws aimed at Mexican migrants that are not supported by the Bush administration, such as vigilante border patrols and barriers to separate US from Mexican border cities.

12. Murray Hiebert and Barry Wain, "Same Planet, Different World," *Far Eastern Economic Review,* June 17, 2004, pp. 26–27.

13. The Pew Research Center for the People and the Press, "What the World Thinks, 2002," a survey undertaken in December 2002 of 38,000 people in forty-four countries. It found that "images of the US have been tarnished in all types of nations: among longtime NATO allies, in developing countries, in Eastern Europe and, most dramatically, in Muslim countries." The study is online at www.publicdiplomacy.org/14htm.

14. For example, the top State Department official, Margaret D. Tutwiler, a former ambassador to Morocco, told a House of Representatives committee that she agreed with the findings of a bipartisan study of attitudes in the Middle East on the decline of US prestige there. She said "it will take us many years of hard, focused work" to repair the damage. Christopher Marquis, "US Image Abroad Will Take Years to Repair, Official Testifies," *NYT,* February 5, 2004, online ed.

15. *The 9/11 Report,* pp. 536–537.

16. See Samuel S. Kim, "Northeast Asia in the Local-Regional-Global Nexus: Multiple Challenges and Contending Explanations," in Kim, ed., *The International Relations of Northeast Asia,* table 1.6, p. 25.

17. A March 2005 poll found that only 58 percent of Australians had a favorable view of the United States (below France and the UN) and, even more disconcerting, that Australians were about evenly divided as to whether the United States or Islamic fundamentalism was the greatest danger in the world. *NYT,* March 29, 2005, p. A9. The poll was conducted by a major center-right research institute, the Lowy Institute for International Policy.

18. See the Middle East Policy Council web site.

19. Ikenberry, "America's Imperial Ambition," p. 60.

20. Ruggie, "The Past as Prologue?" p. 171.

21. In those cases, as Bruce W. Jentleson has argued ("Use of Force Dilemmas: Policy and Politics," in Lieber, ed., *Eagle Rules?* pp. 266–281), it was US failure to take the lead in deterring mass violence that was subject to criticism.

22. A major international study commissioned by the UN reflects a growing appreciation of the necessity to act preventively in cases of genocide and other massive threats to human life. The use of preventive force is, however, reserved for cases of state failure or a state's unwillingness or inability to protect its people from large-scale loss of life. Force can only be used as a last resort, and as the consequence of multilateral action endorsed by the UN Security Council. (International Commission on Intervention and State Sovereignty, *The Responsibility to Protect,* Report of December 2001.) Iraq in 2003 would not have qualified as a target of international intervention under these guidelines because for all the regime's human rights excesses, it was neither a failed state nor a state engaged in genocide.

23. See Patrick E. Tyler, "Libyan Stagnation a Big Factor in Qaddafi Surprise," *NYT,* January 8, 2004, online ed.

24. See the "Urgent Call" on the nuclear danger drafted by Jonathan Schell, Randall Forsberg, and others in *The Nation,* June 24, 2002, p. 12. In recent years the voices of a number of former senior US military, foreign policy, and intelligence officials have been raised in support of these changes in nuclear weapons policies. See, for example, the statements of US Air Force General Lee Butler and Army General Andrew Goodpaster, brought together in a NAPSNet Special Report, December 6, 1996, online, and the comments of

Admiral Stansfield Turner, former CIA director: "Post–Cold War World Demands New Ways to Deal with Warheads," *Los Angeles Times,* January 11, 1999.

25. For instance, General Tommy Franks, head of the US Central Command, has said: "The relationships that we have with surrounding states around Afghanistan will permit us over time to do the work that . . . all of us recognize needs to be done. It won't be finished until it's all done." Reuters, "General Suggests Extending US Campaign Against Afghan Neighbors," *NYT,* August 25, 2002, online ed.

26. US and British soldiers are currently training the army in Georgia, which has had to deal with secessionist movements in three regions since the 1990s. In two of them—South Ossetia and Abkhazia—tensions are at the boiling point. US closeness to the Georgia government, owing as much to the country's oil wealth (a major BP-led consortium heads the list of foreign investors) as to counterterrorism, could bring the United States into confrontation with Russia.

27. In Indonesia, for example, a longtime expert who has resided there has written that instead of pushing the government to embrace stronger internal security measures, the United States would do better to support good governance, since the very forces that people would ordinarily look to for security— the army and police in Indonesia, for instance—have the most abominable record when it comes to respect for human rights. Sidney Jones, "Terror's Aftermath in Indonesia," *NYT,* October 16, 2002, p. A27.

28. On human rights and internal political conditions in Libya, see Michele Dunne, "Libya: Security Is Not Enough," pp. 1–7. Libya's potential security value to the United States was hinted at by Marine General James L. Jones, who said that Libya "could certainly become an important player . . . in view of its geostrategic location. Ultimately, it certainly could have the same relationships that we have with other countries" in the war on terror. (*NYT,* March 27, 2004, p. A7.) Prior to Qaddafi's seizure of power in 1969, the United States based air force and other troops at Wheelus Air Base in Libya.

29. See, for example, Robert C. Johansen, *The National Interest and the Human Interest: An Analysis of US Foreign Policy,* and Julie A. Mertus, *Bait and Switch: Human Rights and US Foreign Policy.*

30. These other schools go by many names, such as neo- (or semi-) isolationism, post–Cold War internationalism, and selective engagement. In US historical perspective, Walter Russell Means has identified four prominent schools: Hamiltonian, Jeffersonian, Jacksonian, and Wilsonian. Means, *Special Providence: American Foreign Policy and How It Changed the World.*

31. For further comment on the policy changes advocated below, see the concluding remarks in Johnson, *Blowback,* and my own recent works: *Global Politics in the Human Interest,* 4th ed., and, with specific respect to East Asia, *Pacific Asia? Prospects for Security and Cooperation in East Asia.*

32. US arms manufacturers, with all-out support from the government, have used 9/11 as a springboard for pushing sales all across East Asia, with major fighter aircraft sales to South Korea, Australia, and Taiwan topping the list. European arms dealers seem to have no chance. David Lague, "Gripes Over US Grip on Arms Trade," *Far Eastern Economic Review,* September 26, 2002, pp. 14–18.

33. For more detailed assessment, see the joint publication of the Institute for Energy and Environmental Research and the Lawyers' Committee on Nuclear Policy, *Rule of Power or Rule of Law?*

34. See *NYT,* December 8, 2004, p. A5, and December 10, 2004, p. A18.

35. See, in this connection, Ahmed Rashid, "New Wars to Fight," *Far Eastern Economic Review,* September 12, 2002, pp. 14–22.

36. Jessica Tuchman Mathews, "Redefining Security," p. 175.

37. Quoted by Record, *Bounding the Global War on Terrorism,* p. 13.

38. See Fareed Zakaria, "Why Do They Hate Us?" pp. 22–40.

39. Thom Shanker, "US Fails to Explain Policies to Muslim World, Panel Says," *NYT,* November 24, 2004, p. A12.

40. George Perkovich, "Giving Justice Its Due," pp. 79–93.

41. Hedges, *War Is a Force That Gives Us Meaning,* p. 180.

42. In Afghanistan and elsewhere in South Asia, the story is of "political ineptitude and corruption, and of a postcolonial class struggle between the disenfranchised poor and these countries' elites." Waleed Ziad, "How the Holy Warriors Learned to Hate," *NYT,* June 18, 2004, p. A27.

43. See, for example, the UN Development Program's *Human Development Report 2000.*

44. "'We the Peoples': The Role of the United Nations in the 21st Century," The Millennium Report of the UN Secretary-General Kofi Annan, online at www.un.org/millennium/sg/report.

45. A worldwide program to meet basic needs in developing countries is likely to cost well below $100 billion. See Dick Bell and Michael Renner, "A New Marshall Plan? Advancing Human Security and Controlling Terrorism."

46. Pirages, "Containing Infectious Diseases," in Michael Renner et al., eds., *State of the World 2005: A Worldwatch Institute Report on Progress Toward a Sustainable Society,* pp. 43–44.

47. Jeremy M. Weinstein, John Edward Porter, and Stuart E. Eizenstat, *On the Brink: Weak States and US National Security.*

48. "Ranking the Rich," *Foreign Policy,* May–June 2003, pp. 56–66.

49. That such an agreement can be constructed may be seen in the Geneva Initiative, an unofficial accord that was put together in meetings between Israeli and Palestinian ministers and presented to the world on December 1, 2003. Text in *Tikkun,* vol. 19, No. 1 (January–February, 2004), pp. 33–45 and at www.tikkun .org. Poverty is extreme and increasing among Palestinians, according to the World Bank. It estimates that 47 percent of Palestinians are living below the poverty line, that unemployment in the West Bank and Gaza Strip is 26 percent, and that the economy has shrunk by 23 percent since 1999. Poverty is also increasing in Israel. Greg Myre, "Poverty Worsening in Israel and Palestinian Areas, 2 Studies Find," *NYT,* November 24, 2004, p. A5.

50. As the report cited above (in Shanker, "US Fails to Explain Policies") of the Defense Science Board put it: "Today we reflexively compare Muslim 'masses' to those oppressed under Soviet rule. This is a strategic mistake. There is no yearning-to-be-liberated-by-the-US groundswell among Muslim societies—except to be liberated perhaps from what they see as apostate tyrannies that the US so determinedly promotes and defends."

51. Jeffrey D. Sachs, "Don't Know, Should Care," *NYT,* June 5, 2004, p. A25.

52. See Joseph S. Nye Jr., "The Decline of America's Soft Power: Why Washington Should Worry," pp. 16–20, as well as Nye's book, *The Paradox of American Power.*

53. See Christopher Marquis, "Effort to Promote US Falls Short, Critics Say," *NYT,* December 29, 2003, p. A6.

54. See Richard A. Falk, *The Declining World Order: America's Imperial Geopolitics,* especially Chapter 12.

55. The total number of inmates in US federal and state prisons was 1.3 million in 2000, the highest by far in the world and more than three times the number in 1980. The total number of prisons was 1,023, about twice that of 1980. Prison construction has become an economic way of life for many poor US counties. See Fox Butterfield, "Study Tracks Boom in Prisons and Notes Impact on Counties," *NYT,* April 30, 2004, p. A15.

56. Richard W. Stevenson, "78% of Bush's Planned War Costs Is to Go to Military," *NYT,* September 9, 2003, p. A6. In personal terms, US military spending is averaging over $1,400 for every citizen, a figure topped only by Israel and one far higher than Japan ($367 a year), Britain ($627), or China ($25). SIPRI, "The Major Spenders in 2003," online at www.sipri.se.

57. Edmund L. Andrews, "Bush Aides Say Budget Deficit Will Rise Again," *NYT,* January 26, 2005, p. A1.

58. Thom Shanker and Eric Schmitt, "Pentagon Budget Up; War Cost Is Excluded," *NYT,* February 8, 2005, online ed.

59. Ibid.

60. Total discretionary spending in 2003 was $825.9 billion. Graphic on "Government Growth" in *Washington Post,* November 12, 2003, online ed.

61. David Firestone and Thom Shanker, "War's Cost Brings Democratic Anger," *NYT,* July 11, 2003, p. A8.

62. Although state budgets rebounded in the 2005 fiscal year, the improvement may only be temporary. Medical insurance, education, and pension plan costs pose very large obstacles to keeping budgets in balance. Robert Pear, "After Bleak Period, States' Revenues Rise, Governors Report," *NYT,* July 8, 2005, p. A20.

63. Joel Brinkley, "Anti-Drug Gains in Colombia Don't Reduce Flow to US," *NYT,* April 28, 2005, p. 3.

64. Based on US Census Bureau figures. See David Leonhardt, "More Americans Were Uninsured and Poor in 2003, Census Finds," *NYT,* August 27, 2004, p. A1.

65. Ray Boshara, "The $6,000 Solution," p. 94.

66. See Ronald Dworkin, "The Threat to Patriotism."

67. See Kevin Sack, "Chasing Terrorists or Fears?" *Los Angeles Times,* October 24, 2004. The article cites, questioningly, the Justice Department's figures of 364 terrorism suspects charged and 193 convicted since September 11, 2001.

68. George F. Kennan, "US 'Lack of Balance' in the Afghan Crisis," *San Francisco Chronicle,* February 8, 1980, p. 8.

69. See *NYT,* January 3, 2005, p. C4, and Jad Mouawad and Matthew L. Wald, "The Oil Uproar That Isn't," *NYT,* July 12, 2005, p. C1. These trends are quite different from those at the time of the 1970s oil crisis, which was driven by supply limitations and when imported oil accounted for only a third of US consumption.

70. Quoted in Peter Maass, "The Breaking Point," *New York Times Magazine,* August 21, 2005, p. 33.

71. See Barnaby J. Feder, "A Different Era for the Alternative Energy Business," *NYT,* May 29, 2004, online ed.

72. Even after all the wrong intelligence on Iraq and the alleged Al-Qaida connection had been brought to light, only a few journalists dared to call the administration's story what it was: a lie. An exception is Paul Waldman, "Why the Media Don't Call It as They See It," *Washington Post,* September 28, 2003.

73. Excerpts of the speech in *NYT,* October 4, 2002, p. A13.

74. See the blistering critique by David Kay of Condoleezza Rice's NSC, which he called "the dog that did not bark" because of NSC's failure to tell Bush the full story of what the intelligence on Iraq really showed. Kay also said that "Iraq was an overwhelming system failure of the Central Intelligence Agency." Philip Shenon, "Former Iraq Arms Inspector Faults Prewar Intelligence," *NYT,* August 19, 2004, p. A14.

75. While ambassador to Honduras, Negroponte was surely aware of a CIA-trained Honduran army intelligence unit that kidnapped and tortured suspected subversives. The findings on human rights abuses during his tenure are cited in David Corn, "Bush's New Iraq Viceroy," *The Nation,* May 10, 2004, pp. 6 and 24. Negroponte was never asked about these events during his Senate confirmation hearings.

76. See Hunt, ed., *Crises in US Foreign Policy,* p. 353.

77. One such is Frances Fukuyama, a leading neocon intellectual and PNAC adherent, who in 2004 publicly broke with the administration's nation-building strategy in Iraq.

78. The officers who resigned were stationed in Athens, Greece, Washington, D.C., and Australia; see *NYT,* February 27, 2003, online ed., and March 12, 2003, p. A8.

79. Scheuer is the anonymous author of *Imperial Hubris: Why the West Is Losing the War on Terror.* The book makes the same case made here, that the main reason for the terrorist threat to the United States is its Middle East policies and not the terrorists' dislike of Western culture or democracy. Subsequently, Scheuer went public to charge that the Bush administration was operating on the false assumption that capturing some Al-Qaida leaders would defeat the organization, when in fact Al-Qaida had become a global insurgency whose leadership was being easily replenished. See *NYT,* November 8, 2004, p. A18.

80. See David D. Kirkpatrick, "Lack of Resolution in Iraq Finds Conservatives Divided," *NYT,* April 19, 2004, p. A17; Jim Lobe, "Is the Neo-con Reign Over?" *Foreign Policy in Focus,* June 17, 2004, online ed.

81. The Bush administration's displeasure with the CIA was widely reported during November 2004, and the new director of central intelligence, Porter J. Goss, let his staff know it. See Douglas Jehl, "Chief of C.I.A. Tells His Staff to Back Bush," *NYT,* November 17, 2004, p. A1.

82. Zalmay Khalilzad, the US ambassador to Iraq, was the latest official to warn Syria that US patience was wearing thin due to its belief that Syria was allowing terrorists to be trained there and sent on to Iraq. US policy, said another (unnamed) official, was to "keep the heat on Syria, keep the criticism up." Joel Brinkley, "American Envoy Says Syria Assists Training of Terrorists," *NYT,* September 13, 2005, p. A6.

83. Quoted by Thom Shanker, "Panel Calls US Troop Size Insufficient for Demands," *NYT,* September 24, 2004, p. A12.

84. See Thom Shanker and Eric Schmitt, "Pentagon Weighs Strategy Change to Deter Terror," *NYT,* July 5, 2005, p. 1.

85. Hersh, "The Coming Wars." See also Eric Schmitt, "Pentagon Sends Its Spies to Join Fight on Terror," *NYT,* January 24, 2005, online ed. The latter article notes that Pentagon special operations teams "have been operating in Iraq, Afghanistan *and other countries* [emphasis added] for about two years."

86. Douglas Jehl and Eric Schmitt, "Law Gives Spending Power to Special Operations Forces," *NYT,* February 1, 2005, p. A11.

87. For example, the Council on Foreign Relations, in a report in 2002 on foreign criticisms and resentment of the United States, cited the widespread perception of the United States as being "arrogant, self-indulgent, hypocritical, inattentive," culturally insensitive, and out of touch with Third World underdevelopment. But its recommendations, instead of proposing changes in US policies, consisted mainly of ways to improve US overseas propaganda. See an adaptation of the report by Peter Peterson, "Public Diplomacy and the War on Terrorism," pp. 74–94.

88. After September 11 a former Madison Avenue advertising executive, Charlotte Beers, was appointed undersecretary of state for public diplomacy to improve the selling of US values in Islamic countries. She retired in March 2003 after a less-than-effective tenure.

89. McNamara and DeMark, *In Retrospect: The Tragedy and Lessons of Vietnam,* p. 323.

90. Stephen G. Brooks and William C. Wohlforth, "American Primacy in Perspective," pp. 20–33.

Bibliography

Ackerman, Spencer and John B. Judis, "The First Casualty," *The New Republic,* June 30, 2003, at www.tnr.com/docprint.mhtml?i=20030630&c=ackerman judis063003.

Alterman, Eric, "Colin Powell and the 'Power of Audacity,'" *The Nation,* September 22, 2003, p. 10.

Amnesty International, www.amnestyusa.org.

Amuzegar, Jahangir, "Iran's Crumbling Revolution," *Foreign Affairs,* vol. 82, No. 1 (January–February, 2003), pp. 44–57.

Anonymous (Michael Scheuer), *Imperial Hubris: Why the West Is Losing the War on Terror* (New York: Brassey's, 2004).

Armstrong, Charles K., "U.S.–North Korean Relations," *Asian Perspective,* vol. 28, No. 4 (2004), pp. 13–37.

Armstrong, David, "Dick Cheney's Song of America," *Harper's,* October 2002, pp. 76–83.

Bacevich, Andrew J., *American Empire: The Realities and Consequences of U.S. Diplomacy* (Cambridge , Mass.: Harvard University Press, 2002).

James A. Baker III Institute for Public Policy and Council on Foreign Relations, *Strategic Energy Policy Challenges for the 21st Century* (2001), online at http://bakerinstitute.org/pubs/workingpapers/cfrbipp_energy/energy cfr.pdf.

Barnet, Richard J., *Intervention and Revolution: The United States in the Third World* (Cleveland: World Publishing, 1968).

Bell, Dick and Michael Renner, "A New Marshall Plan? Advancing Human Security and Controlling Terrorism," Worldwatch Institute paper, October 9, 2001, at www.worldwatch.org.

Berrigan, Frida, William D. Hartung, and Leslie Heffel, *U.S. Weapons at War 2005: Promoting Freedom or Fueling Conflict?* (New York: World Policy Institute, June 2005).

"The Big Book of Bush," *Sierra,* vol. 87, No. 5 (September–October, 2002), pp. 39, 41.

Blight, James G. and Peter Kornbluh, *Politics of Illusion: The Bay of Pigs Invasion Reexamined* (Boulder, Colo.: Lynne Rienner, 1998).

Blix, Hans, *Disarming Iraq: The Search for Weapons of Mass Destruction* (New York: Pantheon, 2004).

Boot, Max, "The New American Way of War," *Foreign Affairs,* vol. 82, No. 4 (July–August, 2003), pp. 41–58.

———, *The Savage Wars of Peace: Small Wars and the Rise of American Power* (New York: Basic Books, 2003).

Boshara, Ray, "The $6,000 Solution," *The Atlantic,* January–February 2003, pp. 91–95.

Brodie, Fawn M., *Jefferson: An Intimate History* (New York: W. W. Norton, 1974).

Brookings Institution, *Tracking Variables of Reconstruction & Security in Post-Saddam Iraq,* online at www.brookings.org/dybdocroot/fp/saban/iraq/index .pdf.

Brooks, Stephen G. and William C. Wohlforth, "American Primacy in Perspective," *Foreign Affairs,* vol. 81, No. 4 (July–August, 2002), pp. 20–33.

Brown, Michael et al., eds., *America's Strategic Choices* (Cambridge, Mass.: MIT Press, 1997).

Byers, Michael, "Jumping the Gun," *London Review of Books,* vol. 24, No. 14 (July 25, 2002), at www.lrb.co.uk/v24/n14/byer2414.htm.

Campbell, Kurt M. and Celeste Johnson Ward, "New Battle Stations?" *Foreign Affairs,* vol. 82, No. 5 (September–October, 2003), pp. 95–103.

Carter, Ashton B., William J. Perry, and John D. Steinbruner, *A New Concept of Cooperative Security* (Washington, D.C.: Brookings Institution, 1992).

Cha, Victor D., "Korea's Place in the Axis," *Foreign Affairs,* vol. 81, No. 3 (May–June, 2002), pp. 79–92.

Chace, James, "Imperial America and the Common Interest," *World Policy Journal,* vol. 19, No. 1 (Spring 2002), pp. 1–9.

Cheng, T. J., Jacques deLisle, and Deborah Brown, eds., *China Under the Fourth Generation Leadership: Opportunities, Dangers, and Dilemmas* (Singapore: World Scientific Publishing, 2005), forthcoming.

Cirincione, Joseph and Jessica T. Mathews, *Iraq: A New Approach* (New York: Carnegie Endowment for International Peace, August 2002).

Clark, Wesley K., *Winning Modern Wars: Iraq, Terrorism, and the American Empire* (New York: Public Affairs, 2003).

Clarke, Richard A., *Against All Enemies: Inside America's War on Terror* (New York: Free Press, 2004).

Clinton, Bill, *My Life* (New York: Knopf, 2004).

Cohen, William S., *Report of the Quadrennial Defense Review* (May, 1997) at www.dtic.mil/defenselink/pubs/qdr/sec2.html.

Cohn, Marjorie, "Abu Ghraib General Lambasts Bush Administration," August 24, 2005, at www.truthout.org/docs_2005/082405z.shtml.

Commission on Integrated Long-Term Strategy, "Discriminate Deterrence" (Washington, D.C.: G.P.O., January 1988).

Corn, David, "Our Gang in Venezuela," *The Nation,* August 5–12, 2002, pp. 24–28.

Council on Foreign Relations, *Meeting the North Korean Nuclear Challenge: Report of an Independent Task Force Sponsored by the Council on Foreign Relations* (New York: CFR, 2003).

Cousens, Elizabeth M. and Chetan Kumar, eds., *Peacebuilding as Politics: Cultivating Peace in Fragile Societies* (Boulder, Colo.: Lynne Rienner, 2001).

Crane, Conrad C. and W. Andrew Terrill, *Reconstructing Iraq: Insights, Challenges, and Missions for Military Forces in a Post-Conflict Scenario* (Carlisle, Pa.: Strategic Studies Institute, U.S. Army War College, February 2003).

Crocker, Chester A. and Fen Osler Hampson, eds., *Managing Global Chaos: Sources of and Responses to International Conflict* (Washington, D.C.: United States Institute of Peace Press, 1996).

Daalder, Ivo H. and James M. Lindsay, *America Unbound: The Bush Revolution in Foreign Policy* (Washington, D.C.: Brookings Institution Press, 2003).

Dehghanpished, Babek, John Barry, and Roy Gutman, "The Death Convoy of Afghanistan," *Newsweek,* August 26, 2002, pp. 20–30.

DeMott, Benjamin, "Whitewash as Public Service: How *The 9/11 Commission Report* Defrauds the Nation," *Harper's,* October 2004, pp. 35–45.

Doran, Michael Scott, "Somebody Else's Civil War," *Foreign Affairs,* vol. 81, No. 1 (January–February, 2002), pp. 22–42.

Dreyfuss, Robert and Laura Rozen, "Still Dreaming of Tehran," *The Nation,* April 12, 2004, pp. 16–18.

Dunne, Michele, "Libya: Security Is Not Enough," *Policy Brief* (Carnegie Endowment for International Peace), No. 32 (October, 2004), pp. 1–7.

Dworkin, Ronald, "The Threat to Patriotism," *The New York Review of Books,* February 28, 2002, at www.nybooks.com/articles/15145.

Eaves, Elizabeth, "Spin Doctors Without Borders," *Harper's,* March 2004, pp. 56–57.

Esty, Daniel C. et al., *2005 Environmental Sustainability Index: Benchmarking National Environmental Stewardship* (New Haven, Conn.: Yale Center for Environmental Law and Policy, 2005).

Falk, Richard A., *The Declining World Order: America's Imperial Geopolitics* (London: Routledge, 2004).

———, "Gaza Illusions," *The Nation,* September 12, 2005, pp. 4-5.

———, "The New Bush Doctrine," *The Nation,* July 15, 2002, pp. 9–11.

Farmer, Paul, "Haiti's Wretched of the Earth," *Tikkun,* vol. 19, No. 3 (May–June, 2004), pp. 23–26, 61.

Feffer, John, ed., *Power Trip: U.S. Unilateralism and Global Strategy After September 11* (New York: Seven Stories Press, 2003).

Ferguson, Niall, "A World Without Power," *Foreign Policy,* No. 143 (July–August, 2004), pp. 32–39.

———, *Colossus: The Rise and Fall of the American Empire* (New York: Penguin, 2004).

———, "Hegemony or Empire?" *Foreign Affairs,* vol. 82, No. 5 (September–October, 2003), pp. 154–161.

Fineman, Howard, "I Sniff Some Politics," *Newsweek,* May 27, 2002, pp. 37–38.

Friel, Howard and Richard Falk, *The Record of the Paper: How the* New York Times *Misreports US Foreign Policy* (London: Verso, 2004).

Gannon, Kathy, "Afghanistan Unbound," *Foreign Affairs,* vol. 83, No. 3 (May–June, 2004), pp. 35–46.

Glass, Charles, "The First Lies Club," *Harper's,* January 2003, pp. 71–77.

Gleason, S., ed., *Foreign Relations of the United States 1950,* vol. 1 (Washington, D.C.: U.S. Government Printing Office, 1977).

Gordon, Bernard K., "A High-Risk Trade Policy," *Foreign Affairs,* vol. 82, No. 4 (July–August, 2003), pp. 105–118.

Gordon, Joy, "Cool War," *Harper's,* November 2002, pp. 43–49.

Greenberg, Karen J., Joshua L. Dratel, eds., and Anthony Lewis, *The Torture Papers: The Road to Abu Ghraib* (Cambridge: Cambridge University Press, 2005).

Gurtov, Mel, "Common Security in North Korea: Quest for a New Paradigm," *Asian Survey,* vol. 42, No. 3 (May–June 2002), pp. 397–418.

———, *Global Politics in the Human Interest,* 4th ed. (Boulder, Colo.: Lynne Rienner, 2000).

———, *Pacific Asia? Prospects for Security and Cooperation in East Asia* (Lanham, Md.: Rowman & Littlefield, 2002).

———, *The United States Against the Third World: Anti-nationalism and Intervention* (New York: Praeger, 1971).

Gurtov, Mel and Ellen Mekjavich, "Responding to Humanitarian Crises," *Notre Dame Journal of Law, Ethics & Public Policy,* vol. 15, No. 2 (2001), pp. 507–531.

Gurtov, Mel and Peter Van Ness, eds., *Confronting the Bush Doctrine: Critical Views from the Asia-Pacific* (London: Routledge, 2005).

Hardt, Michael and Antonio Negri, *Empire* (Cambridge, Mass.: Harvard University Press, 2003).

Harries, Owen, *Benign or Imperial? Reflections on American Hegemony* (Sydney: ABC Books, 2004).

Harrison, Selig S., "Did North Korea Cheat?" *Foreign Affairs,* vol. 84, No. 1 (January–February, 2005), pp. 99–110.

———, chair, *Ending the North Korean Nuclear Crisis: A Proposal by the Task Force on U.S. Korea Policy* (Chicago, Ill.: Center for International Policy and Center for East Asian Studies, University of Chicago, 2004).

———, "Time to Leave Korea?" *Foreign Affairs,* vol. 80, No. 2 (March–April, 2001), pp. 62–78.

Hartung, William D., Frida Berrigan, and Michelle Ciarrocca, "Operation Endless Deployment," *The Nation,* October 21, 2002, pp. 21–24.

Hathaway, Robert M. and Wilson Lee, eds., *George W. Bush and Asia: A Midterm Assessment* (Washington, D.C.: Woodrow Wilson International Center for Scholars, 2003).

Hedges, Chris, *War Is a Force That Gives Us Meaning* (New York: Public Affairs, 2002).

Hendrickson, David C., "Toward Universal Empire: The Dangerous Quest for Absolute Security," *World Policy Journal,* vol. 19, No. 3 (Fall, 2002), pp. 1–10.

Hersh, Seymour M., "The Coming Wars," *The New Yorker,* January 24–31, 2005, pp. 40–47.

———, "The Debate Within," *The New Yorker,* March 11, 2002, pp. 34–39.

———, "The Gray Zone," *The New Yorker,* May 24, 2004, at www.newyorker .com/printable/?fact/040524fa_fact.

Hiro, Dilip, *Secrets and Lies: Operation "Iraqi Freedom" and After* (New York: Nation Books, 2004).

Hoffman, Bruce, "Plan of Attack" *The Atlantic,* July–August 2004, pp. 42–43.

Hoffman, Paul, "Courting Justice," *Amnesty Now,* Fall 2004, pp. 1 and 18.

Holtzman, Elizabeth, "Torture and Accountability," *The Nation,* July 18–25, 2005, pp. 20–24.

Huisken, Ron, "We Don't Want the Smoking Gun to be a Mushroom Cloud: Intelligence on Iraq's WMD," Working Paper No. 390, Australian National University, Strategic & Defence Studies Centre (June, 2004).

Hunt, Michael H., ed., *Crises in U.S. Foreign Policy: An International History Reader* (New Haven, Conn.: Yale University Press, 1996).

Huntington, Samuel, "The Erosion of American National Interests," *Foreign Affairs,* vol. 76, No. 5 (September–October, 1997), pp. 28–49.

Ignatieff, Michael, "Nation-Building Lite," *The New York Times Magazine,* July 28, 2002, online edition.

Ikenberry, G. John, "America's Imperial Ambition," *Foreign Affairs,* vol. 81, No. 5 (September–October, 2002), pp. 44–60.

Institute for Energy and Environmental Research and Lawyers' Committee on Nuclear Policy, "Rule of Power or Rule of Law? An Assessment of U.S. Policies and Actions Regarding Security-Related Treaties" (April, 2002) at www.ieer.org/reports/treaties/index.html.

International Commission on Intervention and State Sovereignty, *The Responsibility to Protect* (Ottawa: International Development Research Centre, 2001).

Iraq Revenue Watch, "Disorder, Negligence and Mismanagement: How the CPA Handled Iraq Reconstruction Funds," September 2004, at www.iraqrevenue watch.org/reports/092404.shtml.

Johansen, Robert C., *The National Interest and the Human Interest: An Analysis of U.S. Foreign Policy* (Princeton, N.J.: Princeton University Press, 1980).

Johnson, Chalmers, *Blowback: The Costs and Consequences of American Empire* (New York: Metropolitan Books, 2000).

———, "The War Business," *Harper's,* November 2003, pp. 53–58.

Junt, Tony, "Dreams of Empire," *United States Military Review,* vol. 51, No. 17 (November 4, 2004), online at www.wam.edu/~dcrocker/courses/Docs/PUAF698J-Judt-Dreams%20of%20Empire.pdf.

Kegley, Charles W. Jr. and Eugene R. Wittkopf, eds., *The Domestic Sources of American Foreign Policy: Insights and Evidence* (New York: St. Martin's Press, 1988).

Kegley, Charles W. Jr. and Gregory A. Raymond, "Preventive War and Permissive Normative Order," *International Studies Perspectives,* vol. 4, No. 4 (November, 2003), pp. 385–394.

Keller, Bill, "Reagan's Son," *The New York Times Magazine,* January 26, 2003, pp. 26–31, 42.

Kennedy, Robert F. Jr. *Crimes Against Nature: How George W. Bush and His Corporate Pals Are Plundering the Country and Hijacking Our Democracy* (New York: HarperCollins, 2004).

———, "Dick Cheney's Energy Crisis: The Secret Process That Plundered a Nation," *Sierra,* vol. 89, No. 5 (September–October, 2004), pp. 44–47, 63–65.

Khalilzad, Zalmay M., *From Containment to Global Leadership? America and the World After the Cold War* (Santa Monica, Calif.: RAND Corporation, 1995).

Kim, Samuel S., ed., *The International Relations of Northeast Asia* (Lanham, Md.: Rowman & Littlefield, 2004).

———, "The U.S.–DPRK Nuclear Standoff: The Case for Common-Security Engagement," *Joint U.S.-Korea Academic Studies,* vol. 14 (2004), pp. 41–64.

Kissinger, Henry, *White House Years* (Boston: Little, Brown, 1979).

Klare, Michael, "Bush-Cheney Energy Strategy: Procuring the Rest of the World's Oil," *Foreign Policy in Focus,* January 2004, at www.fpif.org/papers/03petropol/politics_body.html.

———, "Endless Military Superiority," *The Nation,* July 15, 2002, pp. 12–16.

Klein, Naomi, "Baghdad Year Zero: Pillaging Iraq in Pursuit of a Neocon Utopia," *Harper's,* September 2004, pp. 43–53.

Kleveman, Lutz C., "The Devil's Tears," *Amnesty Now* (Spring, 2004), pp. 18–21.

———, "Oil and the New 'Great Game,'" *The Nation,* February 16, 2004, pp. 11–14.

Komisar, Lucy, "Big-Time Embarrassment," Institute for Global Communications, March 1, 1999, at http://igcf.igc.org:8082.

Kornbluh, Peter, *Bay of Pigs Declassified: The Secret CIA Report on the Invasion of Cuba* (New York: National Security Archive, 1998).

———, "Chile Declassified," *The Nation,* August 9–16, 1999, pp. 21–24.

Krauthammer, Charles, "The Unipolar Moment," *Foreign Affairs,* vol. 70, No. 1 (1990/91), pp. 23–33.

Krepon, Michael, "Dominators Rule," *The Bulletin of the Atomic Scientists* (January–February, 2003), p. 58.

Kristol, William and Robert Kagan, "Reject the Global Buddy System," October 26, 1999, at www.newamericancentury.org/def_natl_sec_pdf_012.pdf.

———, "Toward a Neo-Reaganite Foreign Policy," *Foreign Affairs,* vol. 75, No. 4 (July–August, 1996), pp. 18–32.

Kwon, Yul, "East Asian Regionalism Focusing on ASEAN Plus Three," *Journal of East Asian Affairs,* vol. 18, No. 1 (Spring–Summer, 2004), pp. 98–130.

LaFeber, Walter, ed., *Origins of the Cold War, 1941–1947: A Historical Problem with Interpretations and Documents* (New York: John Wiley, 1971).

Lapham, Lewis H., "Notebook: Deus Lo Volt," *Harper's,* May 2002, pp. 7–9.

Layne, Christopher and Benjamin Schwarz, "American Hegemony—Without an Enemy," *Foreign Policy,* No. 92 (Fall, 1993), pp. 1–8.

Lederach, John Paul, *Building Peace: Sustainable Reconciliation in Divided Societies* (Washington, D.C.: United States Institute of Peace Press, 1997).

Lemann, Nicholas, "The Next World Order," *The New Yorker,* April 1, 2002, pp. 42–48.

———, "The War on What?" *The New Yorker,* September 16, 2002, pp. 36–44.

Lieber, Robert J., ed., *Eagle Rules? Foreign Policy and American Primacy in the Twenty-First Century* (Upper Saddle River, N.J.: Prentice Hall, 2002).

Lobe, Jim, "Is the Neo-con Reign Over?" *Foreign Policy in Focus,* June 17, 2004, at www.fpif.org/commentary/2004/0406reignover.html.

Lopez, George A. and David Cortright, "Containing Iraq: Sanctions Worked," *Foreign Affairs*, vol. 83, No. 4 (July–August, 2004), pp. 90–103.

Ma, Ying, "China's America Problem," *Policy Review*, No. 111 (February–March, 2002), pp. 43–56.

Maass, Peter, "The Breaking Point," *New York Times Magazine*, August 21, 2005, pp. 30–35, 50–59.

Manyin, Mark E., *U.S. Assistance to North Korea* (Washington, D.C.: Congressional Research Service, April 26, 2005).

Mathews, Jessica Tuchman, "Redefining Security," *Foreign Affairs*, vol. 68, No. 2 (Spring, 1989), pp. 162–177.

McNamara, Robert S. and Brian DeMark, *In Retrospect: The Tragedy and Lessons of Vietnam* (New York: Times Books, 1995).

Means, Walter Russell, *Special Providence: American Foreign Policy and How It Changed the World* (New York: Knopf, 2003).

Mertus, Julie A., *Bait and Switch: Human Rights and U.S. Foreign Policy* (New York: Routledge, 2004).

———, "The New U.S. Human Rights Policy: A Radical Departure," *International Studies Perspectives*, vol. 4, No. 4 (November, 2003), pp. 371–384.

Middle East Policy Council at www.mepc.org/public_asp/whats/dmccstatement.asp.

Mills, James, "The Serious Implications of a 1971 Conversation with Ronald Reagan," *San Diego Magazine*, August 1985, pp. 140–141, 258.

Moltz, James Clay and C. Kenneth Quinones, "Getting Serious About a Multilateral Approach to North Korea," *The Nonproliferation Review* (Spring, 2004), online at http://cns.miis.edu/pubs/npr/vol11/111/111moltz.pdf.

Moore, James and Wayne Slater, *Bush's Brain: How Karl Rove Made George W. Bush Presidential* (Hoboken, N.J.: John Wiley & Sons, 2003).

Moore, Michael, *Dude, Where's My Country?* (New York: Warner Books, 2003).

Morse, Edward L. and James Richard, "The Battle for Energy Dominance," *Foreign Affairs*, vol. 81, No. 2 (March–April, 2002), pp. 16–31.

Muravchik, Joshua, "The Bush Manifesto," *Commentary*, December, 2002, pp. 23–30.

A National Security Strategy of Engagement and Enlargement (Washington, D.C.: White House publication, February, 1996).

The National Security Strategy of the United States of America, September 20, 2002, at www.whitehouse.gov/nsc/nss.html.

New York Times, *The 9/11 Report: The National Commission on Terrorist Attacks Upon the United States* (New York: St. Martin's Press, 2004).

Nuclear Posture Review Report, www.globalsecurity.org/wmd/library/policy/dod/npr/htm.

Nye, Joseph S. Jr., "The Decline of America's Soft Power: Why Washington Should Worry," *Foreign Affairs*, vol. 83, No. 3 (May–June, 2004), pp. 16–20.

———, *The Paradox of American Power: Why the World's Only Superpower Can't Go It Alone* (New York: Oxford University Press, 2002).

O'Hanlon, Michael E., "A Flawed Masterpiece," *Foreign Affairs*, vol. 81, No. 3 (May–June, 2002), pp. 47–63.

Ottaway, Marina, "Promoting Democracy After Conflict: The Difficult Choices," *International Studies Perspectives*, vol. 4, No. 3 (August, 2003), pp. 314–322.

Packer, George, "War After the War," *The New Yorker,* November 24, 2003, pp. 58–85.

Palast, Greg, "OPEC on the March," *Harper's,* April 2005, pp. 74–76.

Pei, Minxin, "The Paradoxes of American Nationalism," *Foreign Policy* (May–June, 2003), pp. 31–37.

Perkovich, George, "Giving Justice Its Due," *Foreign Affairs,* vol. 84, No. 4 (July–August, 2005), pp. 79–93.

———, "Iran Is Not an Island: A Strategy to Mobilize the Neighbors," Carnegie Endowment for International Peace *Policy Brief,* No. 34 (February, 2005), pp. 1–7.

Perle, Richard and David Frum, *An End to Evil: How to Win the War on Terror* (New York: Random House, 2003).

Peterson, Peter, "Public Diplomacy and the War on Terrorism," *Foreign Affairs,* vol. 81, No. 5 (September–October, 2002), pp. 74–94.

Petras, James and Morris Morley, *The United States and Chile: Imperialism and the Overthrow of the Allende Government* (New York: Monthly Review Press, 1975).

Pollack, Kenneth M., "Next Stop Baghdad?" *Foreign Affairs,* vol. 81, No. 2 (March–April, 2002), pp. 32–47.

———, "Spies, Lies, and Weapons: What Went Wrong," *The Atlantic Monthly,* January–February 2004, pp. 79–92.

Powell, Colin, "A Strategy of Partnerships," *Foreign Affairs,* vol. 83, No. 1 (January–February, 2004), pp. 22–34.

Prestowitz, Clyde, *Rogue Nation: American Unilateralism and the Failure of Good Intentions* (New York: Basic Books, 2003).

Project for the New American Century (PNAC), www.newamericancentury.org.

Public Broadcasting System (PBS), *Frontline* program, "The Jesus Factor," April 28, 2004, Portland, Oregon.

———, *Frontline* program, "Kim's Nuclear Gamble," December 2, 2004, at www.pbs.org/wgbh/pages/frontline/shows/kim/etc/script.html.

Record, Jeffrey, *Bounding the Global War on Terrorism* (Carlisle, Pa.: Strategic Studies Institute, U.S. Army War College, December 2003).

Renner, Michael, "The Other Looting," *Foreign Policy in Focus Special Report,* July 2003, at www.fpif.org/papers/looting2003_body.html.

Renner, Michael et al., eds., *State of the World 2005: A Worldwatch Institute Report on Progress Toward a Sustainable Society* (New York: W. W. Norton, 2005).

Rice, Condoleezza, "Promoting the National Interest," *Foreign Affairs,* vol. 79, No. 1 (January–February, 2000), pp. 45–62.

Rieff, David, "Blueprint for a Mess," *New York Times Magazine,* November 2, 2003, pp. 28–33, 44–78.

Ritter, Scott, *Endgame: Solving the Iraq Problem—Once and For All* (New York: Simon and Schuster, 1999).

Rogers, Steven, "Beyond the Abu Sayyaf," *Foreign Affairs,* vol. 83, No. 1 (January–February, 2004), pp. 15–20.

Rosati, Jerel A., *The Politics of United States Foreign Policy,* 2d ed. (Ft. Worth, Tex.: Harcourt Brace, 1999).

———, ed., *Readings in the Politics of United States Foreign Policy* (Ft. Worth, Tex.: Harcourt Brace, 1998).

Rosen, Nir, "In the Balance," *New York Times Magazine,* February 20, 2005, pp. 30–37, 50, 56–58.

Rubin, James P., "Stumbling into War," *Foreign Affairs,* vol. 82, No. 5 (September–October, 2003), pp. 46–66.

Ruggie, John G., "The Past as Prologue?" *International Security,* vol. 21, No. 4 (Spring, 1997), pp. 166–182.

Rumsfeld, Donald, "Transforming the Military," *Foreign Affairs,* vol. 81, No. 3 (May–June, 2002), p. 31.

Russell, Richard L., "Iran in Iraq's Shadow: Dealing with Tehran's Nuclear Weapons Bid," *Parameters* (Autumn, 2004), pp. 31–45.

Schilling, Warner R., Paul Y. Hammond, and Glenn H. Snyder, *Strategy, Politics and Defense Budgets* (New York: Columbia University Press, 1962).

Schlesinger, Arthur M. Jr., *A Thousand Days* (New York: Random House, 1976).

Schmitt, Gary J., "American Primacy and the Defense Spending Crisis," *Joint Forces Quarterly* (Spring, 1998), online at www.newamericancentury.org/def_natl_sec_pdf_014.pdf.

Schwarz, Benjamin, "Why America Thinks It Has to Run the World," *The Atlantic Monthly,* June 1996, pp. 92–102.

Segal, Leon V. *Disarming Strangers: Nuclear Diplomacy with North Korea* (Princeton, N.J.: Princeton University Press, 1998).

Sheehan, Neil et al., eds., *The Pentagon Papers* (New York: Bantam Books, 1971).

Shin, Gi-Wook and Paul Y. Chang, "The Politics of Nationalism in U.S.-Korean Relations," *Asian Perspective,* vol. 28, No. 4 (2004), pp.119–145.

Shultz, George P., "New Realities and New Ways of Thinking," *Foreign Affairs,* vol. 63, No. 4 (Spring, 1985), pp. 705–721.

Silverstein, Ken, "Saudis and Americans: Friends in Need," *The Nation,* December 3, 2001, pp. 15–20.

Simes, Dimitri K., "America's Imperial Dilemma," *Foreign Affairs,* vol. 82, No. 6 (November–December, 2003), pp. 91–102.

Simmons, P. J., "Global Challenges: Beating the Odds," Carnegie Endowment *Policy Brief,* No.17 (August, 2002), pp. 1–7.

Singer, P. W., *Corporate Warriors: The Rise of the Privatized Military Industry* (Ithaca, N.Y.: Cornell University Press, 2003).

Slouka, Mark, "A Year Later: Notes on America's Intimations of Mortality," *Harper's Magazine,* September 2002, pp. 35–41.

Stockholm International Peace Research Institute, http://projects.sipri.se.

Stuart, Douglas T., "Ministry of Fear: The 1947 National Security Act in Historical and Institutional Context," *International Studies Perspectives,* vol. 4, No. 3 (August, 2003), pp. 293–313.

Suh, Jae-Jung, "Assessing the Military Balance in Korea," *Asian Perspective,* vol. 28, No. 4 (2004), pp. 63–88.

———, "The Two-Wars Doctrine and the Regional Arms Race: Contradictions in U.S. Post–Cold War Security Policy in Northeast Asia," *Critical Asian Studies,* vol. 35, No. 1 (2003), pp. 3–32.

Sullivan, Michael J. III, *American Adventurism Abroad: 30 Invasions, Interventions, and Regime Changes Since World War II* (Westport, Conn: Greenwood, 2004).

Suskind, Ron, "Without a Doubt," *New York Times Magazine,* October 17, 2004, pp. 46–51, 64, 102–106.

Swaine, Michael, "Reverse Course? The Fragile Turnaround in U.S.-China Relations," *Policy Brief* (Carnegie Endowment for International Peace), No. 22 (February, 2003), pp. 1–7.

Task Force on US Korea Policy, *Turning Point in Korea: New Dangers and New Opportunities for the United States* (Chicago: Center for International Policy and Center for East Asian Studies, University of Chicago, February 2003).

Trenin, Dmitri V., "The Forgotten War: Chechnya and Russia's Future," Carnegie Endowment *Policy Brief,* No. 28 (November, 2003), pp. 1–7.

Tucker, Robert W., *The Just War: A Study in Contemporary American Doctrine* (Baltimore, Md.: Johns Hopkins University Press, 1960).

Tucker, Robert W. and David C. Hendrickson, "The Sources of American Legitimacy," *Foreign Affairs,* vol. 83, No. 6 (November–December, 2004), pp. 18–32.

Unger, Craig, *House of Bush, House of Saud: The Secret Relationship Between the World's Two Most Powerful Dynasties* (New York: Scribner, 2004).

United Nations Development Program (UNDP), *Human Development Report 2000* (New York: Oxford University Press, 2000).

———, *Human Development Report 2004,* at http://hdr.undp.org/statistics.

United Nations, *The Millennium Report,* www.un.org/millennium/sg/report.

———, Commission on Human Security (CHS), *Human Security Now* (New York: UNCHS, 2003).

US Central Intelligence Agency, "Regime Strategic Intent: Key Findings," at www.cia.gov/cia/reports/iraq_wmd_2004/Comp_Report_Key_Findings.pdf (Duelfer Report).

US Department of Defense, *Annual Report on the Military Power of the People's Republic of China,* online at www.nautilus.org/pub/ftp/napsact/special _reports/d20020712chiná.pdf.

US Department of Defense, *Quadrennial Defense Review Report,* September 30, 2001, online at www.defenselink.mil/pubs/qdr2001.pdf.

US Senate, Select Committee on Intelligence, *Report on the U.S. Intelligence Community's Prewar Intelligence Assessments on Iraq,* 108th Cong., July 7, 2004 (Washington, D.C.: U.S. Government Printing Office, 2004).

Varhola, Christopher H., "American Challenges in Post-Conflict Iraq," Foreign Policy Research Institute, May 27, 2004, via e-mail from www.fpri.org.

Weinstein, Jeremy M., John Edward Porter, and Stuart E. Eizenstat, *On the Brink: Weak States and US National Security* (Washington, D.C.: Report of the Commission on Weak States and US National Security, Center for Global Development, June, 2004), at www.cgdev.org.

"What the World Thinks," at www.publicdiplomacy.org/14htm.

Williams, William A., "Empire as a Way of Life," *The Nation,* August 2–9, 1980, pp. 104–119.

Wilson, Joseph, *The Politics of Truth: Inside the Lies That Led to War and Betrayed My Wife's CIA Identity* (New York: Carroll & Graf, 2004).

———, "Republic or Empire?" *The Nation,* March 3, 2003, pp. 4–5.

Wittkopf, Eugene R. and Christopher M. Jones, eds., *The Future of American Foreign Policy,* 3d ed. (New York: St. Martin's/Worth, 1999).

Wittkopf, Eugene R. and James M. McCormick, eds., *The Domestic Sources of American Foreign Policy: Insights and Evidence,* 4th ed. (Lanham, Md.: Rowman & Littlefield, 2004).

Woodward, Bob, *Bush at War* (New York: Simon & Schuster, 2002).

————, *Plan of Attack* (New York: Simon & Schuster, 2004).

Zakaria, Fareed, "Why Do They Hate Us?" *Newsweek,* October 15, 2001, pp. 22–40.

Index

Abizaid, John, 133*n92*
Abraham, Spencer, 101
Abrams, Elliot, 29; administration appointment, 29; indictment against, 51*n45*
Abu Ghraib prison scandal, 47, 114, 194
Abu Sayyaf, 155
Acheson, Dean, 3
Adelman, Kenneth, 34
Afghanistan: Al-Qaida in, 121–125; anti-Americanism in, 123; bin Laden in, 58; Bush Doctrine and, 2; contracts for rebuilding given to political contributors, 48; doubt concerning democratization of, 99; intervention by Soviet Union, 30; new constitution in, 123; occupation of, 2; postwar processes in, 112–125; punitive raids on, 40; radical regime in, 31; rebuilding, 121–125; reconstruction errors in, 112–125; reemergence of Taliban in, 99, 114, 121–125; support for Al-Qaida in, 32; United States intervention in, 151; US intervention in, 31, 61
Ahmadinejad, Mahmoud, 149
Akayev, Askar, 152
Albright, Madeleine, 18, 24*n63*
Algeria: United States military in, 151
Aliyev, Ilham, 152
Allbaugh, Joe, 105

Allende, Salvador, 16, 23*n53;* attempts to overthrow, 22n*36*
Alliances: avoidance of, 60; based on self-interest, 9; cohesion of, 3; enlargement and maintenance of, 11; entangling, 60; exclusively with those supporting US objectives, 13; military, 3; multilateral, 3; strategic usefulness of, 13
Al-Qaida: in Afghanistan, 121–125; American membership in, 88*n9;* belief that attack from was imminent, 58; decentralization of, 60; effect of United States policy on recruitment for, 39; hatred of US-led globalization, 15; as lesser priority in Iraq war, 59; motives for WTC attack, 15; Saudi connections to, 89*n12*
American Enterprise Institute, 112
Angola: radical regime in, 31; US intervention in, 31
al-Ani, Ahmad Khalil Ibrahim Samir, 93*n82*
Annan, Kofi, 42, 193; Millennium Report by, 219; proposal for Security Council authorization for Iraq war, 59, 60
Anti-Americanism: in Afghanistan, 123; in Iran, 146, 149; in Jordan, 91*n49, 95n102;* in Middle East, 79; over Iraq war, 79; in South Korea, 142, 143

Anti-Ballistic Missile Treaty, 197
Appeasement, 4
Arbenz, Jacobo: attempts to overthrow, 22n36
Argentina: authoritarian regime in, 16, 17; "dirty" war in, 16, 23n55; international debt in, 186
Aristide, Jean-Bertrand, 167, 168, 169
Armenia, 152
Arroyo, Gloria Macapagal, 156
Ashcroft, John, 37
Association of South East Asian Nations (ASEAN), 155, 157, 159
Australia, 158
"Axis of evil," 40, 138–150
Azerbaijan, 152

Ball, George, 10, 21n28, 21n30
Ballistic missile defense, 35, 197–200; Project for the New American Century support for, 29
Bauer, Gary, 29
Bechtel Corporation, 68, 114, 129n30
Bennett, William, 29
Berlusconi, Silvio, 133n95
bin Laden, Osama, 4; abandonment of effort to capture, 61; pursuit of, 57–61
Biological Diversity Convention (1992), 191
Blair, Tony, 69, 82, 97n118, 97n119, 187
Blix, Hans, 84, 93n84
Boeing Corporation, 45
Bolton, John, 111, 131n66, 193
Bosch, Juan, 9
Bosnia, 10; private soldiers in, 46
Brazil: international debt in, 186; overthrow of leftist leaders in, 22n36
Bremer, L. Paul III, 61, 114; criticism of administration by, 61, 62; structural adjustment strategy of, 104
Brinkmanship, 43, 44
Brzezinski, Zbigniew: on Commission on Integrated Long-Term Strategy, 50n30
Bulgaria: United States military in, 151
Bush, George H.W., 19, 25n69; failure to eliminate Saddam Hussein, 28; foreign policy lies from, 66; military interventions by, 40; protection of

Israel and, 11; "pseudo-realism" of, 28
Bush, George W. and administration of, 4; as born-again Christian, 35, 36; confrontational approach to international politics, 86; conventional foreign policy goals of, 35; decisions on use of torture methods, 194, 195; delegation of authority by, 30; disregard for international law, 190–197; disregard of United States Congress in promotion of Iraq war, 76–80; divisions in foreign policy ranks over Iraq war, 109–112; downplay of international cooperation by, 181; efforts to deceive public concerning Iraq, 67; environmental protection and, 189–190; exaggerations of threat posed by Iraq, 78; expansion of possible use of nuclear weapons, 197–200; faith-based opinions of, 30; goal of regime change in Iraq, 61–63; internationalism of, 35; interpretation of Al-Qaida motivations for attack, 15; lack of planning for post-war Iraq, 99, 115–121; military spending by, 45; 'Millennium Challenge Account' and, 188; neoconservatism and, 33–36; neoimperial views, 42; neoliberal economic development approach, 187; no recall of briefings on Al-Qaida, 88n9; preparation for Iraq war, 63–66; priority of national security over human rights in, 182–185; as realist hegemonist, 34; rejection of arms control treaties, 35; rejection of convention on landmines, 195, 196; relation to Spectrum 7 and Harken Energy, 51n44; request to intelligence staff to locate connection between Iraq and Al-Qaida, 62, 63; revelation of false intelligence concerning Iraq war by, 80–85; "roadmap" peace plan for Middle East, 51n38, 105–106; secretive administration of, 47–48; selling Iraq war to United States Congress and public, 69–80; statements on bin Laden, 57–61; support for Israel, 35; unilateralism

and, 19; view on Southeast Asian regionalism, 158

Bush, Jeb, 29

Bush Doctrine: Afghanistan and, 2; agenda, 39–48; avoidance of alliances in, 60; in Central Asia, 151–155; in China, 164–165; costs/alternatives to, 209–231; criticisms of, 211–213; defining, 27–48; disinterest in nation building, 46, 115–121; distorting effects of on policymaking, 137; effect of World Trade Center attacks on, 36–39; environmental protection and, 189–190; evangelical crusade in, 36–39; expanding capabilities and, 43–47; failures of leadership through, 213–215; global citizenship and, 181–200; global issues and, 2, 185–189; groundwork in Reagan presidency, 10, 30–33; in Haiti, 167–169; of 'hawk engagement' in North Korea, 139, 140, 141; human rights and, 182–185; importance of weapons in, 45; international law and, 190–197; in Iran, 145–150; Iraq and, 2; in Japan, 159–161; limited-sovereignty thesis in, 41, 42; neoconservatism and, 2, 33–36; neoimperial tilt in, 42; in North Korea, 2, 138–145; origins of, 2; preemptive attack, 2, 4, 32, 39–42, 138, 139, 158, 191–192, 210; preventive war and, 5; radical right and, 28–30; regime change and, 4, 32, 42–43, 165–169; in Russia, 164–165; secrecy and, 47–48; in South Asia, 161–163; in Southeast Asia, 155–159; in states cooperating with war on terror, 150–165; in states with authoritarian regimes, 150–165; support of empire in, 5; unilateralism and, 2, 4, 10, 32, 33, 42–43; in Venezuela, 165, 166; view on terrorism, 217–220; war on terror and, 36–39; World Trade Center attacks and, 4

Cambodia: overthrow of leftist leaders in, 22n36; radical regime in, 31; US intervention in, 31

Canada, 102

Capital punishment, 184

Card, Andrew, 51n44

Caribbean Community, 168

Carlyle Group, 105

Carroll, Philip, 101

Carter, Jimmy: effort in Haiti by, 167; foreign policy lies from, 66; opposition to US hegemony, 28; on preventive war, 191–192; priority given to human rights by, 30

Castro, Fidel, 4, 9, 41, 165; attempts to overthrow, 22n36

Center for Public Integrity, 48

Center for Security Policy, 29

Center for Strategic and International Studies, 29

Central America: conflicts in, 3

Central Asia: Bush Doctrine in, 151–155; troop deployment to, 46; United States foreign policy in, 151–155

Central Intelligence Agency (CIA): establishment of, 7; in reconstruction planning, 113

Chalabi, Ahmad, 73, 92n61, 112, 113

Chávez, Hugo, 165, 166, 167

Chechnya: human rights and, 183

Cheney, Dick, 109; change of opinion on Saddam Hussein, 49n9; "Defense Planning Guidance" paper by, 32; energy policy meetings and, 47–48, 101; exceptionalism of, 38; hardline defense policy of, 28; membership in Project for the New American Century, 28; offers evidence in support of war, 70, 71; opposition to early action on Iraq, 89n23; position on state sponsorship of terrorism, 63; re-emergence in Bush administration, 34; relation to Halliburton, 51n44; revelation of false intelligence concerning Iraq war by, 80–85; secretive dealings of, 47–48; testimony on Iraqi oil, 129n24; understanding of problems in 'ownership' of Iraq, 114; on United States role in war on terror, 52n57; on winning war on terrorism, 38

Chen Shui-bian, 110, 111

Chile, 150; military coup in, 16; overthrow of leftist leaders in, 22n36;

United States support for authoritarian regime in, 16, 17
China, 7; Bush Doctrine in, 164–165; containment of, 43; human rights in, 183; relations with Association of South East Asian Nations (ASEAN), 159; rivalry with, 33, 35; technology trade and, 43; World Trade Organization and, 43
Chirac, Jacques, 79
Christian Zionist movement, 51n38
Clark, Wesley, 94n87
Clarke, Richard, 70, 88n9, 90n31, 227; criticisms of administration by, 61; informs Bush of no connection between Iraq and Al-Qaida, 63; support for report from, 89n21; testifies that warnings were disregarded, 62
Clinton, Bill, 19, 25n69, 94n87; advice to Bush administration on bin Laden, 88n7; Agreed Framework with North Korea and, 60, 89n16; authorization of *Desert Fox,* 29; coalition-building under, 11; engagement and enlargement doctrine of, 11; faith in international conventions, 35; military spending by, 45; multilateralism and, 35; North Korean policy of, 138; opposition to US hegemony, 28; protection of Israel and, 11; realism of, 27; signing of Iraq Liberation Act, 29
Cohen, Eliot, 34
Cold War: core values of, 8; intensification of, 7; legacies of, 8–12; patterns of behavior of, 8
Colombia: private soldiers in, 46; United States military in, 151
Colonialism, 7
Commission on Integrated Long-Term Strategy, 50n30
Committee for the Liberation of Iraq, 104
Committee on the Present Danger, 30, 31, 210
Comprehensive Test Ban Treaty (1996), 35, 191
Congo: overthrow of leftist leaders in, 22n36
Convention on the Law of the Sea (1972), 191

Convention on the Rights of the Child (1989), 184
Cook, Robin, 97n118
Council for National Policy, 47–48
Council on Foreign Relations, 52n50, 101
Crest Investment, 105
Cuba, 4, 22n36; accused of fostering terrorism, 32; overthrow of leftist leaders in, 22n36; US intervention in, 40
Cyprus: overthrow of leftist leaders in, 22n36
Czechoslovakia: communist coup in, 7

"Defense Planning Guidance" (Cheny, Wolfowitz), 32
Defense Policy Board, 29, 34, 64, 95n103
DeLay, Tom, 51n38
Democracy: intervention abroad and, 16; "saving," 16
Democratization: global, 35; in Latin America, 186
Department of Defense: acknowledgment of disinformation from exiles, 92n61; call for United States to maintain capacity to act unilaterally, 25n67; capabilities-based approach in, 43; establishment of, 7; rivalry with Department of State, 37, 109–112; role in national security, 12
Department of State: accused of obstructionism, 109; displacement in policymaking system, 7, 109–112; rivalry with Department of Defense, 37
Diplomacy, 3; Middle East, 35; preference for military policies over, 7; Track II, 60; traditional, 37
Djibouti: United States military in, 151
Dole, Robert, 10, 27
Dominican Republic: removal of no longer useful leaders in, 22n36; United States intervention in, 9, 40
Downing Street Memo, 69, 82
Duelfer Report, 74, 85
Dulles, John Foster, 43, 44
Duvalier, François, 22n36, 31
DynCorp, 104

Earth Summit, 10
East Asia: foreign investment in, 11
Egypt: multi-candidate elections in, 127n4
Eisenhower, Dwight, 18, 23n46; anti-American feelings and, 15; authorization of CIA operation to overthrow Iran, 15; foreign policy lies from, 66; military interventions by, 40
ElBaradei, Mohamed, 75
Empire: favoring, 20n12; perils/profits of, 99–127; reversing, 226–228; seeking, 20n12
Energy resources: growth in consumption, 224; Iraq and, 100–105; secretive administration meetings concerning, 47–48; security import of, 34; views of neoconservatives on, 34
Engagement, selective, 11
Environmental protection: Bush Doctrine and, 189–190; ignored by neoconservatives, 34; security import of, 34
European Union: agreement with Iran, 149; call for investigation of uprising in Uzbekistan, 154
Evans, Don, 51n44
Exceptionalism: belief in, 14, 15, 22n43; of Reagan, 28
Expansionism: open-door, 13

Farhadi, Adib, 122
Feith, Douglas, 73, 102, 113, 147
Forbes, Steve, 29
Foreign policy: belief system emphasizing global responsibility in, 14; bipartisan consensus breakdown in, 30; Bush moralism and, 36; call for refocus of on human security issues, 10; in Central Asia, 151–155; with China, 164–165; commercialism and, 27; containment strategies, 3; continuity and, 1; deceit and cover-up in, 66–69; disregard for sovereignty/rights of others in, 16; ethnic politics in, 27; expansionism and, 22n43; fear of diminished American leadership, 24n66; inconsistencies between preaching and practice in, 17; in India, 163; internationalist, 1; interventions in other countries' affairs, 3; involvement/disengagement from global issues and, 1; in Iran, 145–150; isolationist, 1; in Japan, 159–161; in Latin America, 165–169; limited-sovereignty thesis, 41, 42; multilateral, 42; neoimperial, 42–43; in North Korea, 138–150; in Pakistan, 161–163; particularistic interests in, 27; priority of interests over principles in, 16; with Russia, 164–165; terrorism as priority of, 31; unilateralist, 1
Freedom of Information Act, 32, 47–48
Fukuyama, Frances, 12, 29

Gaffney, Frank, 29
Galbraith, John Kenneth, 10, 21n30
Garner, Jay, 112, 113, 114
Geneva Conventions, 17
Geoeconomics, 17
Geopolitics, 17
Georgia, 150
Germany: containment of, 3, 33; fear of greater voice in international affairs from, 24n65; redeployment of troops from, 45, 46, 54n94
Globalism, 185–189; Bush Doctrine and, 185–189; effect of World Trade Center attacks on, 37; geoeconomics and, 17; realism and, 18; Washington consensus and, 185
Gonzales, Alberto, 24n57; relation to Enron, 51n44
Goulart, Joao, 22n36
Graham, Bob, 93n78
Grenada: radical regime in, 31; US intervention in, 31, 32, 40, 54n100
Guatemala: overthrow of leftist leaders in, 22n36
Gun, Katherine, 95n97
Gutierrez, Lino, 51n45

Haass, Richard, 41, 210, 211; on goals of foreign policy, 53n76
Haig, Alexander, 32
Haiti: abandonment of, 31; Bush Doctrine in, 167–169; removal of no longer useful leaders in, 22n36
Halliburton Corporation, 101, 102, 104, 114, 128n16

"Hawk engagement," 139, 140, 141
Hegemony, 2–8; as policy, 5; seeking, 20n12; United States exertion of, 5
Helms, Jesse, 10, 27
Ho Chi Minh, 4
Howard, John, 158
Human rights, 19n1, 23n54; in Bush administration, 182–185; in Central Asia, 151, 152; in Indonesia, 41, 156; prioritized by Carter, 30; priority of national security over, 183, 184; in Thailand, 157; war on terror and, 182–185
Human Rights Watch, 123
Huntington, Samuel, 27, 37

Ikenberry, John, 42
Iklé, Fred: on Commission on Integrated Long-Term Strategy, 50n30; hardline defense policy of, 29; membership in Project for the New American Century, 29
India: United States foreign policy in, 163; United States military in, 151
Indochina, 7
Indonesia: Bush Doctrine in, 155–159; human rights in, 156; overthrow of leftist leaders in, 22n36; secular nationalism in, 156; tsunami in, 157; United States foreign policy in, 155–159; United States military in, 150, 151
Institutions: global, 1
Intelligence community: does not find evidence for weapons of mass destruction, 90n28; efforts to correct disputed intelligence statements, 73; offers evidence in support of war, 72–75; pressure from administration to find evidence, 73
International Atomic Energy Agency (IAEA), 74, 75, 82, 147
International community: criticism of Bush administration for disinterest in coalition-building, 91n45; distancing from United States by, 79; lack of interest in rebuilding Iraq, 99, 119–121; lack of support for United States in Iraq war, 65, 66, 79; objections to unilateralism, 33; omitted from contracts for rebuilding Iraq,

102; view of United States priorities in attack on Iraq, 57–61
International Criminal Court, 59; disregard by United States, 192, 193
Internationalism: Bush Doctrine and, 35; conservative, 30; "hard-headed," 28; humane, 215–217; liberal, 17, 30
International Monetary Fund (IMF), 105, 185; call for United States disengagement from, 10
Interventionism: call for end to policy of, 10; liberal, 41; preemptive, 8; strategic, 41; time-limited, 40
Iran: accused of fostering terrorism, 32; agreement with European Union, 149; anti-Americanism in, 146, 149; in 'axis of evil,' 40, 145–150; Bush Doctrine in, 145–150; clerical leadership in, 146; hopes that Iraq war would cause changes in, 60; labeled "rogue" state, 44; national-ism in, 149; nuclear weapons pro-gram in, 145–150; political reform in, 146; preemptive attack and, 39; relations with Israel, 147, 148; United States foreign policy in, 145–150; United States support for authoritarian regime in, 17
Iran-Contra affair, 31
Iraq: in 'axis of evil,' 40; Bush Doctrine and, 2; claims of nuclear weapons program in, 27; compari-sons to Vietnam, 125–127; contracts for rebuilding given to political contributors, 48, 101, 102; doubt concerning democratization of, 99; inspection teams in, 83–85; insur-gency in, 99; labeled "rogue" state, 44; lack of evidence for Al-Qaida connection with, 75, 83–85; lifting sanctions on, 101; nationalist up-rising in, 99; nation-building in, 115–121; occupation of, 2; oil-for-food program, 74; policymaking and, 2; possible negotiated outcome in, 86, 87; post-war oil production, 100–105; post-war political mis-judgments in, 112–125; post-war processes in, 112–125; preemptive attack and, 39; private contractors in, 129n34; reconstruction errors in,

112–125; sanctions on, 74; secret US aid to, 92*n53;* as target in war against terrorism, 62; underestimation of post-war resistance in, 116, 117; US intervention in, 57–88; weapons of mass destruction capability of, 70
Iraq Business Forum, 104
Iraqi National Congress, 73
Iraq Liberation Act (1998), 29, 112
Iraq Survey Group, 82, 83, 84, 85
Iraq war: Bush refusal to request UN authorization for, 59, 76–80; disruption in foreign policy process from, 109–112; Downing Street Memo and, 69; as failure in United States leadership, 214; false pretenses concerning, 2, 57–88; groupthink in weighing evidence for war, 71; Iraqi exiles offer evidence in support of war, 70; lack of international support for, 59, 65, 66; massaging evidence for, 67, 69–80; media admission of shortcomings in reportage, 108, 109; media issues in, 106–109; neglect of alternative conflict-resolution formats, 60; oil factor, 100–105; planning for post-war oil control, 62; policy agenda in99-105; preparation for, 63–66; profiteering in, 104; public opinion of, 74, 99; regime change as primary objective, 57, 62, 63; revelation of false intelligence concerning, 80–85; selling to United States Congress and public, 67, 69–80; United States willingness to act alone, 64
Isolationism, 15, 18
Israel: attack on Iraqi nuclear reactor, 64; peace talks with Palestinians, 105–106; protection of, 11; relations with Iran, 147, 148; support for, 35; support from Project for the New American Century, 29; United States failure to press for Palestinian settlement, 218

Jackson, Jesse, 89*n17*
James Baker III, 105
Japan: Bush Doctrine in, 159–161; containment of, 3, 33; defense of, 7;

fear of greater voice in international affairs from, 24*n65;* security policies in, 160; United States foreign relations with, 159–161
Jefferson, Thomas, 2
Jemaah Islamiyah, 156, 157
Johnson, Louis, 6
Johnson, Lyndon, 21*n30, 23n47;* concern about revolutionaries and communism, 15; decision to continue in Vietnam, 9; Dominican Republic and, 9; fear of impeachment, 9; foreign policy lies from, 66; military interventions by, 40
Jordan: anti-Americanism in, 79, 91*n49,* 95*n102*
Justice: social, 1, 9, 223

Kagan, Robert, 28, 29
Kamel, Hussein, 72
Karimov, Islam, 153
Karzai, Hamid, 123, 124
Kay, David, 83, 84, 85, 88, 98*n130*
Kazakhstan, 151–155, 153; United States forces in, 46; United States military in, 153; United States support for authoritarian regime in, 46
Kelly, James, 139
Kennan, George, 6, 96*n107,* 224
Kennedy, John F., 3, 18, 21*n30;* Bay of Pigs invasion and, 40; Dominican Republic and, 9; foreign policy lies from, 66; intentions of regime change by, 40; quarantine of Cuba by, 40
Khadaffi, Omar: attempts to overthrow, 22*n36;* disruption of rule of, 54*n100*
Khalilzad, Zalmay, 29, 123; appointment to administration post, 29
Khatami, Mohammad, 146, 149
Khomeini, Ayatollah, 41
Khrushchev, Nikita, 40
Kim Dae Jung, 138, 170*n2, 171n3*
Kim Il Sung, 41, 42
Kim Jong Il, 41, 138, 139, 143, 160, 170*n2*
Kirkpatrick, Jeanne, 29, 31
Kissinger, Henry, 15, 23*n53,* 68, 109; assurance of support to Pinochet, 16,

23*n54;* on Commission on Integrated Long-Term Strategy, 50*n30;* in Iraq Business Forum, 104; statements on human rights, 23*n54*

Koizumi, Junichiro, 159, 160, 161, 172*n17*

Korean War, 3, 6, 7, 24*n65*

Kosovo, 10

Krauthammer, Charles, 27, 28, 48*n1*

Kristol, William: membership in Project for the New American Century, 29

Kyoto Protocol, 189, 190

Kyrgyzstan, 151, 152; United States military in, 151

Latin America: assassinations and torture in, 16; democratization in, 186; interventions in, 4; regime change in, 165–169; skepticism over Bush policies in, 186, 187; trade issues with, 185, 186; United States foreign relations with, 165–169

Latortue, Gérard, 168

Law, international: Bush Doctrine and, 190–197; disregard of in Iraq war, 57; ignored by neoconservatives, 34; narrowing of United States obligations under, 17; redefining in war on terror, 17; selective adherence to, 3

Lebanon, 32; US intervention in, 40, 66

Levin, Carl, 129*n21*

Libby, Lewis "Scooter": re-emergence in Bush administration, 34

Libya: accused of fostering terrorism, 32; cessation of nuclear program, 127*n2;* disruption of rule of Qaddafi in, 54*n100;* labeled "rogue" state, 44; overthrow of leftist leaders in, 22*n36;* punitive raids on, 40

Lieberman, Joseph, 38

Lockheed Martin Corporation, 45

Lodge, Henry Cabot, 21*n24*

Luce, Henry, 2, 19*n4*, 28

Lumumba, Patrice, 22*n36*, 41

MacArthur, Douglas, 6, 7

Mali: United States military in, 151

Mao Zedong, 4

Marcos, Ferdinand, 22*n36*, 31

Market(s): access to, 13; expansion, 13; free, 17, 186

Mauritania: United States military in, 151

McCain, John, 129*n30*

McClellan, Scott, 154

McKee, Rob, 101

McNamara, Robert, 21*n24*, 230

Mexico: economic assistance to, 11; losses due to North American Free Trade Agreement (NAFTA), 187; trade with, 53*n77*

Middle East: road map peace plan, 105–106; troop deployment to, 46

Military: alliances, 3; budgets, 6, 12, 28, 33; contractors, 46, 47; dominance, 3; forces, 33; immunization from war crimes charges, 17; maintenance of, 11; private forces, 46; reportes "embedded" with, 48, 107; selective engagement of, 11; spending, 30, 34, 35, 45; troop deployment to Eastern Europe, Middle East and Central Asia, 46; troop redeployment in Germany and South Korea, 45, 46

Mobutu Sese Seko, 22n36

Moore, Michael, 107

Moro Islamic Liberation Front, 156

Mossadegh, Mohammed: attempts to overthrow, 22*n36*

Mugabe, Robert, 165

Multilateralism, 18, 213; binding authority of, 18; Clinton and, 35; self-interest and, 19

Murdoch, Rupert, 107

Musharraf, Pervez, 79, 123

National Endowment for Democracy, 29, 166

National Energy Policy report, 101

National Intelligence Estimate, 71, 74

Nationalism, 2–8; American, 27; assertive, 50*n32;* secular, 156; United States intolerance of others', 9

National Security Act (1947), 7

National Security Council, 20*n18*, 64; assessment of Soviet threat by, 5; Cold War and, 7; containment of Soviet Union and, 6; empire-building and, 7

National Security Strategy of the United States, The, 40, 60, 63, 138, 185
National Strategy for Combating Terrorism, 218
Nazarbayev, Nursultan, 153
Negroponte, John: indictment against, 51*n45*
Neoconservatism: anti-multilateral feelings in, 27; beliefs of, 34; Bush Doctrine and, 2, 33–36; effect of World Trade Center attacks on, 37; opportunity presented by election of Bush, 30; radicalism of, 209, 210; in Reagan administration, 32; rise of, 2
Netanyahu, Benjamin, 64
Nicaragua: accused of fostering terrorism, 32; radical regime in, 31; removal of no longer useful leaders in, 22n*36;* US intervention in, 31
Niger, 85
9/11 Commission: Al-Qaida findings, 88*n1;* concludes no connection between Iraq and Al-Qaida, 63; Rice appearance before, 88*n9;* on Saudi connections to Al-Qaida, 89*n12*
Nitze, Paul, 6
Nixon , Richard: foreign policy lies from, 66; national commitments and, 12
Noriega, Manuel, 22n*36*
North American Free Trade Agreement (NAFTA), 10, 187; negative impacts of, 187
North Atlantic Treaty Organization (NATO): expansion of, 35
Northern Alliance, 58, 135*n123*
North Korea: accused of fostering terrorism, 32; Agreed Framework with, 60; alternatives to Bush Doctrine in, 143–145; in 'axis of evil,' 40, 138–145; Bush Doctrine in, 138–145; changes in domestic policies in, 145; defensive strategies of, 140–145; differences in Clinton/ Bush approaches to, 141; doctrine of preemptive attack and, 138, 139; foreign policy toward, 138–150; humanitarian assistance to, 141; labeled "rogue" state, 44; Nuclear Proliferation Treaty an d, 143, 144;

nuclear weapons program in, 10, 27, 139–145, 171*n7;* preemptive attack and, 39; regime change in policy toward, 140; unilateralism in policy toward, 138–145
Northrop Grumman Corporation, 45
Nuclear Nonproliferation Treaty (1968), 74
Nuclear Posture Review (NPR), 44, 138

Office of Special Plans, 73
O'Neill, Paul, 70, 90*n26,* 186; relation to Alcoa, 51*n44*
Operation *Condor,* 16, 23*n55*
Operation Mongoose, 66
Organization of American States, 23*n54*

Pahlevi, Reza, 17
Pakistan, 60; anti-Americanism in, 79; Inter-Services Intelligence in, 161– 163; United States foreign relations with, 161–163; United States military in, 151; United States support for authoritarian regime in, 17
Panama: removal of no longer useful leaders in, 22n*36;* US intervention in, 40
Perle, Richard, 31, 67, 90*n31,* 95*n103,* 109, 112; advocate for preemptive action, 64; appointment to administration post, 29; on Defense Policy Board, 34; favors unilateral action in Iraq war, 64; hardline defense policy of, 29; membership in Project for the New American Century, 29; speaks against coalitions, 91*n43;* in Vulcan group, 34
Perricos, Demetriu, 84
Perry, William, 145
Philippe, Guy, 169
Philippines: abandonment of, 31; Bush Doctrine in, 155–159; military assistance to, 156; removal of no longer useful leaders in, 22n*36;* United States foreign policy in, 155–159; United States military in, 150
Pinochet, Augusto, 16, 150
Podhoretz, Norman, 29
Poindexter, John: indictment against, 51*n45*

Poland: United States military in, 151
Policies: bipartisan security, 50n30;
   of limited sovereignty, 137; multilateral, 1; preference for military
   over diplomatic, 7
Political: assassinations, 16;
   independence, 9; stability, 9; will, 18
Politics: ethnic, 27; international, 5;
   oil, 103
Pollack, Kenneth, 64; criticism of
   administration by, 90n31
Poverty, 34; Bush Doctrine and, 185–
   189; ignored by neoconservatives,
   34; as security threat, 219; in United
   States, 222, 223
Powell, Colin, 8, 11, 23n51, 52n47, 84,
   112, 156; on benefits of coalitions,
   91n43; cabilities-based approach in
   military affairs and, 43; China policy
   and, 110; concern for expansion of
   war policy to Syria, Iran and North
   Korea, 111; concerns over Bush
   Doctrine, 33; contention over, 109;
   effort in Haiti by, 167; engagement
   with North Korea and, 138; on multilateral foreign policy, 42; offers
   evidence in support of war, 70;
   opposition to early action on Iraq,
   89n23; position on Iraq policy, 111;
   on preemptive attack, 40; resignation
   of, 115; role in road map settlement
   plan, 110; speech to Security
   Council, 111; statement on Geneva
   Conventions, 24n57; understanding
   of problems in 'ownership' of Iraq,
   114; warnings concerning loss of
   coalition support in Iraq war, 62
Preemptive attack, 39–42, 191–192;
   Bush Doctrine and, 2, 4, 32, 158; as
   'deterrence,' 39; in initiation of full-
   scale war, 40; justification for,
   53n67; precedent for, 40; in regard
   to North Korea, 138, 139
Preventive war, 5; Bush Doctrine and,
   5; defining, 41
Pritchard, Charles, 145
Privatization, 185
Project for the New American Century
   (PNAC), 28, 34, 110, 210; ballistic
   missile defense and, 29; call for
   American presence in Persian Gulf,
   30; calls for removal of Saddam
   Hussein, 29; members appointed to
   key administration posts, 29; military
   spending increases and, 28; neoconservative agenda, 35; policy
   agenda of, 29; support for Israel, 29
Proliferation Security Initiative (PSI),
   140
Putin, Vladimir, 164, 165

Quayle, Dan, 29

Reagan, Ronald, 2; antiterrorism efforts
   of, 32; appeal to national pride, 31;
   approval from radical right, 28;
   approval of Israeli attack on Iraqi
   nuclear reactor, 64; authorization of
   illegal means of fighting terrorism,
   39; containment strategy of, 31;
   delegation of authority by, 30;
   endorsement of preemptive attack
   policy, 31; exceptionalism and, 28;
   foreign policy lies from, 66; groundwork for Bush Doctrine in presidency of, 10; Iran-Contra affair and,
   31; military interventions by, 40;
   neoconservatives in administration
   of, 32; policy of regime change, 31;
   reinvention of, 30–33; relations with
   Iraq 67,68; restoration of exceptionalism by, 31; support for Israel, 31
Realism: effect of World Trade Center
   attacks on, 37; geopolitics and, 17;
   globalism and, 18; offensive, 28;
   "pseudo," 28; radical version of, 27
Rearmament, 7
Regime change. See also Bush
   Doctrine: by assassination, 22n36;
   Bush Doctrine and, 2, 4, 32, 42–43;
   as constant option, 13; by coup,
   22n36; by covert action to influence
   election s, 22n36; in policy toward
   North Korea, 140
Reich, Otto, 166; indictment against,
   51n45
Republican Party: attacks on Clinton,
   28
Revolution in military affairs (RMA),
   43, 45
Rice, Condoleezza, 18, 34, 85, 109;
   appearance before 9/11 Commission,

88*n9;* foreign policy priorities of, 34, 50*n33;* in "Iraq Stabilization Group," 114; media appearances in support of war, 73; national commitments and, 12; offers evidence in support of war, 71; position on state sponsorship of terrorism, 63; relation to Chevron Oil, 51*n44;* on terrorism, 38

Robinson, Mary, 182

Rodman, Peter, 29

Romania: United States military in, 151

Roosevelt, Franklin, 3, 4

Roosevelt, Theodore, 18

Rostow, Walt, 9

Rove, Karl, 91*n50*

Rowen, Henry, 29

Rumsfeld, Donald, 62, 109; appointment to administration post, 29; authorization of secret operation on methods of interrogation, 194; on deterrence, 44; domination of Iraq policy, 112, 113; hardline defense policy of, 28; intelligence evaluation of threat from Iraq, 73; membership in Project for the New American Century, 28; military build-up goals, 44; neoimperial views, 42; offers evidence in support of war, 70; preference for confrontational methods, 110; pro-war stance by, 89*n21;* re-emergence in Bush administration, 34; on relations with Uzbekistan, 154; statements on weapons of mass destruction, 82

Russell, David, 108

Russia: Bush Doctrine in, 164–165; rivalry with, 33; United States foreign policy with, 164–165

Rwanda, 196

Sachs, Jeffrey, 220

Saddam Hussein, 4; arguments for containment of, 29; legitimization of attack on, 41; proponents of overthrow of, 29

Saudi Arabia: anti-Americanism in, 79; arms purchases from United States, 103; bin Laden in, 58; connections to Al-Qaida, 89*n12;* extremism in, 15; redeployment of troops from, 46;

relations with United States government, 129*n30*

Sayyaf Abu, 156

Scheuer, Michael, 227

Schlesinger, James, 23*n52*

Schmitt, Gary, 34, 50*n34*

Schröder, Gerard, 79

Security: collective, 3, 19*n2;* common, 1, 19*n2,* 215–220; cooperative, 18, 19*n2;* environmental sabotage and, 12; global, 4, 13, 19*n2;* homeland, 221–226; human, 1, 10, 19*n1,* 143, 215; interventions in affairs of other countries and, 3; national, 4, 5, 7, 10, 12–14, 31, 32, 33, 34, 35, 37, 39; preparedness, 12; terrorist tactics and, 31; through exercise of power, 35

Serbia, 11

Shalikashvili, John, 94*n87*

Shanghai Cooperation Organization, 154, 183

Sharon, Ariel, 51*n38,* 105, 183

Short, Claire, 95*n97*

Shultz, George, 129*n33*

Sihanou, Norodom, 22n36

Six Party Talks (6PT), 140, 143, 144, 171*n12*

Social: equity, 3; justice, 1, 9, 223

Somalia, 10

Somoza, Anastacio, 22n36

Sorensen, Theodore, 41

South Asia: Bush Doctrine in, 161–163

Southeast Asia: Bush Doctrine in, 155–159; in 'coalition of the willing,' 158; regional free trade agreements in, 158

South Korea: anti-Americanism in, 142, 143; defense of, 7; redeployment of troops from, 45, 46, 54*n94;* 'sunshine policy' in, 138; trade with, 53*n77;* United States support for authoritarian regime in, 17

South Vietnam: removal of no longer useful leaders in, 22n36

Soviet Union. *See also* Russia: accused of fostering terrorism, 32; containment of, 3; intervention in Afghanistan, 30; move to control Middle East, 30; policy of containment of, 6; pretensions to empire of, 2

Spain, 211, 212
Spanish-American War, 4, 5
Stalin, Josef, 2, 4
State(s): authoritarian, 137, 150–
165; in 'axis of evil,' 40, 138–150;
competitor, 137; in disfavor, 137;
friendly rogue, 137, 150–165;
national-security, 13; realignment
of, 8; rogue, 2, 29, 37, 44, 60, 137;
sovereignty, 9, 41; terrorism, 46;
weak, 219
Sudan, 196; punitive raids on, 40; US
intervention in, 40
Syria: hopes that Iraq war would
cause changes in, 60; labeled
"rogue" state, 44; withdrawal
from Lebanon, 127*n4*

Taiwan, 11; clarification of status,
110; security issues in, 160; trade
with, 53*n77;* upgrading of ties with,
36
Tajikistan, 152
Taliban, 58; elimination of, 60;
reemergence of, 99, 114, 121–125;
United States support of, 60
Taylor, Charles, 165
Taylor, Maxwell, 21*n23*
Tenet, George, 73, 74, 81, 84, 93*n78,*
93*n80,* 109
Terrorism. *See also* War on terror:
arming governments directly
supporting, 46; environmental
sabotage and, 12; as foreign policy
priority, 31; as reaction to global
underdevelopment, 219
Thailand: Bush Doctrine in, 155–159;
human rights in, 157; United States
foreign policy in, 155–159
Thomson, James, 109
Trade: expansion, 52*n50;* free, 35, 187;
liberalization, 185; promotion of, 11,
53*n77;* sanctions, 103; technology,
43
Trujillo, Rafael, 9, 22*n36*
Truman, Harry, 3, 4, 5, 7, 20*n9,* 24*n65;*
foreign policy lies from, 66
Truman Doctrine, 3
Turkey, 79, 80, 96*n106*
Turkmenistan, 151, 152, 153
Tutwiller, Margaret, 114

Unilateralism. *See also* Bush Doctrine:
appropriateness of, 1; Bush Doctrine
and, 2, 10, 32, 33, 42–43; criticisms
of, 211–213; effects of World Trade
Center attacks on, 37; interference in
other countries' affairs and, 2; international community objections to,
33; lack of domestic opposition to, 1;
in policy toward North Korea, 138–
145; precedent for, 1; as preference
for invasion over persuasion, 41;
presumption of, 33; sustainability
of, 210
United Nations: calls for United States
disengagement from peacekeeping
missions in, 10; Convention on
Torture, 17; Development Program,
19*n1,* 219; Monitoring, Verification
and Inspection Commission
(UNMOVIC), 75; Security Council,
59, 70, 147
United States: in Afghanistan, 61;
alliances with only those who
support US objectives, 13; arbitrary
use of rule of law, 5; arms sales by,
45; arms sales to Saudi Arabia, 103;
belief in exceptionalism of, 14, 15;
belief in superiority of, 3; belief that
God is on the side of, 14; capability
to eliminate threats to, 13; compelled
to use force in defense of liberty, 4;
cooperation with authoritarian
regimes by, 16, 46; as 'dispensable
nation,' 211; in Dominican Republic,
9; economic superiority of, 2;
exceptionalism of, 65; expectation
of privatization of Iraq oil industry,
101; failures of leadership by, 213–
215; foreign policy (*See* Foreign
policy); former support for Al-Qaida,
32; freeworld dependence on leadership of, 13; frequent use of coercion
and sanctions, 5; as global citizen,
181–200; hegemony of, 5; humanitarian assistance to North Korea,
141; human rights and, 182–185;
inattention to Third World economic
conditions, 220; as "indispensable
nation," 18, 24*n63;* ineffectiveness
of communication with Muslim
world, 218; institutionalization of

global ambitions by, 13; international cooperation and, 182–185; in Iraq, 57–88; justification of use of violence by, 5; knowledge of assassinations and torture in Latin America, 16; in Korea, 7; in Latin America, 4; moral purity of, 14; national debt in, 221; need for access to resources, 13; non-ratification of cooperative conventions, 184, 190–197; policy-making objectives of, 5; poverty in, 222, 223; projection of values of, 11; as "reluctant" superpower, 5, 6, 20*n9;* resistance to independent authority of multilateral organizations, 18, 24*n64;* responsibility for maintenance of order in anarchic world, 12; role in regime changes, 22*n36;* secret aid to Iraq, 92*n53;* seeking empire, 5; self-serving alliances of, 9; sovereignty preservation, 10; support for Iraq, 67–69; underestimation of post-war resistance in Iraq, 116, 117; universal values of, 2; in Vietnam, 8, 9

United States Congress: activism and, 10; evangelical Christians in, 51*n38;* lessening accountability in, 225–226; passage of War Powers Resolution by, 10; presidential disregard for in promotion of Iraq war, 76–80; role in Vietnam War, 10

US Information Agency, 54*n100*

Uzbekistan, 153; United States forces in, 46; United States military in, 151, 153, 154; United States support for authoritarian regime in, 46; uprising in, 154, 164, 165

Venezuela: Bush Doctrine in, 165, 166; oil politics in, 103, 165, 166

Viet Cong: ability to recruit, 8, 21*n23;* nationalist credentials of, 8

Vietnam: United States support for authoritarian regime in, 17; US intervention in, 40

Vietnam War: as antigovernment movement, 8; corruption of Saigon officials and, 8; decisionmaking in, 8; decision to continue, 9, 10; reasons for lack of disengagement in, 9;

referred to as "noble cause," 31; United States advisors in, 9; United States fear of humiliation in, 9, 21*n29*

Vinnell Corporation, 104

Vulcans, The (foreign policy group), 34, 50*n32*

War, just, 8

War Crimes Act (1996), 17

War on terror, 4; in Bush Doctrine, 10; cost of, 212; distorted spending on, 221–222; expansion of intelligence gathering rules, 17; groundwork in Reagan presidency, 10; human rights and, 182–185; immunization from war crimes charges on soldiers in, 17; intellectual shortcomings in, 218; legal responsibilities toward captured soldiers and civilians redefined, 16, 17; maximization of presidential authority in, 17; suspension of legal principles in, 17; truthtelling about, 226–228

War Powers Act, 156

War Powers Resolution, 10, 76, 94*n89*

Washington consensus, 105, 185

Weapons: high-tech, 12; nuclear, 197–200

Weapons of mass destruction: actual use of, 3; alleged sale of uranium from Niger and, 70; cooperative security and, 19*n2;* failure of Iraq Survey Group to find evidence of, 83–85; as false front in Iraq war, 57; mistakes in analysis of Iraq's programs in, 69–80; policy determination of facts in finding, 69; preemptive attacks on countries possessing, 33; proliferation of, 11, 33; threats of, 3

Weber, Vin, 29

Wen Jiabao, 110

White, Thomas, 51*n44*

Wilson, Joseph, 81, 227

Wilson, Sir Richard, 69

Wilson, Woodrow, 3, 4, 18

Wohlstetter, Albert, 50*n30*

Wolfowitz, Paul, 62, 63, 85, 90*n31,* 109, 113; appointment to administration post, 29; bars non-participants in Iraq war from rebuilding contracts, 128*n17;* cabilities-based approach in military affairs and, 43; "Defense Planning Guidance" paper by, 32; hardline defense policy of, 29; intelligence evaluation of threat from Iraq, 73; membership in Project for the New American Century, 29; position on state sponsorship of terrorism, 63; pro-war stance by, 89*n21;* re-emergence in Bush administration, 34; testimony on Iraqi oil, 129*n24;* in Vulcan group, 34

Woodward, Bob, 62, 89*n21,* 89*n23,* 112

Woolsey, James, 34

World Bank (WB), 185, 219

World Trade Center attacks: advance warning of, 58; arms sales and, 45; Bush Doctrine and, 4; disappearance of constraints on policy after, 38; effect on Bush agenda, 36–39; effect on traditional realism and globalism, 37; effect on unilateralism, 37; elevation of neoconservative thinking after, 37; erosion of deterrence as military strategy and, 43; as opportunity for national security players to expand authority, 44–45; undermining rogue states and, 37

World Trade Organization: China and, 43; ruling on subsidies, 186

Yemen, 150; United States military in, 151

Zaire: removal of no longer useful leaders in, 22n*36*

About the Book

WITH ITS EMPHASIS on unilateralism, preemptive attack, and regime change, US foreign policy under George W. Bush continues the long-standing US quest for primacy—but with some radical departures from previous approaches.

Superpower on Crusade offers a critical exploration of the origins and implementation of the Bush Doctrine.

Gurtov first traces the sources of US missionary and expansionist tendencies and highlights their particular manifestations in the Bush administration. Then turning to the war on Iraq, he focuses on real vs. stated objectives, the Pentagon's primacy in shaping security policy, and the roles of Congress, the UN, and US allies. Subsequent chapters examine US policy with regard to such issues as nuclear proliferation, international law, development assistance, the environment, and human rights.

Assessing the costs of the Bush Doctrine at home and abroad, *Superpower on Crusade* presents a concise critique of US foreign policy intended to stimulate debate in the classroom, as well as among scholars.

Mel Gurtov is professor of political science and international studies at Portland State University. His numerous publications include *Global Politics in the Human Interest* (translated into Chinese, Japanese, and Spanish) and, most recently, *Pacific Asia? Prospects for Security and Cooperation in East Asia.*